P9-CQH-722

INSIGHT GUIDE

NORWAY

DISCOVERY
CHANNEL

APA PUBLICATIONS   **L**

Part of the Langenscheidt Publishing Group

ABOUT THIS BOOK

Editorial

Project Editor
Simon Ryder
Managing Editor
Cameron Duff
Editorial Director
Brian Bell

Distribution

UK & Ireland
GeoCenter International Ltd
The Viables Centre , Harrow Way
Basingstoke, Hants RG22 4BJ
Fax: (44) 1256-817988

United States
Langenscheidt Publishers, Inc.
46–35 54th Road, Maspeth, NY 11378
Fax: (718) 784-0640

Canada
Prologue Inc.
1650 Lionel Bertrand Blvd., Boisbriand
Québec, Canada J7H 1N7
Tel: (450) 434-0306. Fax: (450) 434-2627

Worldwide
Apa Publications GmbH & Co.
Verlag KG (Singapore branch)
38 Joo Koon Road, Singapore 628990
Tel: (65) 865-1600. Fax: (65) 861-6438

Printing

Insight Print Services (Pte) Ltd
38 Joo Koon Road, Singapore 628990
Tel: (65) 865-1600. Fax: (65) 861-6438

© 2000 Apa Publications GmbH & Co.
Verlag KG (Singapore branch)
All Rights Reserved

First Edition 1991
Third Edition 1999 (Reprinted 2000)

This guidebook combines the interests and enthusiasms of two of the world's best known information providers: Insight Guides, whose titles have set the standard for visual travel guides since 1970, and Discovery Channel, the world's premier source of nonfiction television programming.

The editors of Insight Guides provide practical advice and general understanding about a destination's history, culture, institutions and people.

Discovery Channel and its Web site, www.discovery.com, help millions of viewers explore their world from the comfort of their own home and also encourage them to explore it firsthand.

Fjords, midnight sun and Vikings are the aspects most often identified with Norway – apart, that is, from the high cost of beer. But to see what else Norway has to offer there is no better place to start than Snorri Sturluson's chronicle of the lives of the Vikings.

How to use this book

This book is carefully structured to convey an understanding of the country and its culture, and to guide readers through its sights and activities:

EXPLORE YOUR WORLD'

Discovery CHANNEL

The contributors

Edited by **Simon Ryder**, this fully updated guide builds on earlier editions produced by the late **Doreen Taylor-Wilkie**. A Scottish broadcaster and travel writer, she leapt at the chance to edit the original edition because Norway had first inspired her to write about travel. She also wrote the chapters on the fjord country.

The history section was the work of **Rowlinson Carter**, who became obsessed during his researches with the tales recounted by Snorri Sturlusson. **Michael Brady** arrived in Norway in 1958 from the United States. As an active outdoor man and specialist on skiing and fitness, he was well suited to writing the chapters on customs, sport and the outdoor life.

Other contributors included one of Sweden's most eminent journalists, **Inga Wallerius**, who has a deep interest in ethnic cultures and wrote on the Sami people. **Bobby Tulloch**'s chapter on Svalbard was the result of an expedition there, while **Jim Hardy** contributed his knowledge on Scandinavian arts.

Karen Fossli wrote about the oil industry, film and Norway's neighbours, and **Anita Peltonen** provided the chapters on Oslo and its environs. **Robert Spark** contributed the Places chapters outside of the capital and the fjord country.

This edition has been extensively updated by the Oslo-based travel writer **John Harley**, who has described Norway as "one of God's best kept secrets".

◆ To understand Norway today, you need to know something of its past. The first section, with a yellow colour bar, covers the country's history and culture in lively **features** written by specialists.

◆ The main **Places** section, with a blue bar, provides a full rundown of all the attractions worth seeing.

◆ The **Travel Tips** section is a convenient point of reference for information on travel, hotels, restaurants, shops and festivals. Information may be located quickly on the index printed on the back cover flap – and the flaps are designed to serve as bookmarks.

Map Legend

— ‥ —	International Boundary
— — —	County Boundary
⊖	Border Crossing
—•—	National Park/Reserve
— — —	Ferry Route
Ⓣ	Metro
✈ ✈	Airport: International/Regional
🚌	Bus Station
🅿	Parking
❶	Tourist Information
✉	Post Office
† † †	Church / Ruins
†	Monastery
☾	Mosque
✡	Synagogue
⚔	Castle / Ruins
∴	Archaeological Site
∩	Cave
⚑	Statue/Monument
★	Place of Interest

The main places of interest in the Places section are co-ordinated by number with a full-colour map (e.g. ❶), and a symbol at the top of every right-hand page tells you where to find the map.

CONTENTS

A map of the whole country showing the extent of the area maps listed above is in the inside front cover.

A map of Oslo is in the inside back cover.

Norwegian
patriotism
runs strong

Information panels

Insight on ...

Travel Tips

Places

NORTHERN CONTRASTS

Norway offers the visitor a beguiling mix of tradition and modern convenience, spectacular nature and city delights

The most accurate observation made about Norway is that it is a land of contrasts: the landscape is both beautiful and brutal, hospitable and hostile; barren rock submits to soft fertile plains, majestic mountains tower above mysterious fjords; harsh winters are relieved by glorious summers; and long polar nights give way to the radiant midnight sun. One of the oldest civilisations in Europe has become one of its youngest nations. The Norwegians themselves have adapted rather quickly. The lusty Vikings have turned into global peacemakers. It is a country where Grieg and Ibsen compete with Aqua and Disney; where environmental concern challenges overconsumption. Norway has urban excitement and rural tranquillity; shopping malls and Mercedes rub shoulders with compass and rucksack; hi-technology parallels steadfast tradition.

A thriving offshore oil industry has brought prosperity, and as a consequence, social habits are changing rapidly, though, in a society where the divorce rate is high and co-habitation the norm, the home and family still remain important. Politically, democracy and debate pervade all levels of society, and a blend of national pride and an engaged electorate continue to ensure political independence. Murray's *Handbook for Travellers in Norway* described the Norwegians in 1874 thus: "Great patriotism and hospitality are two of the leading characteristics of the Norwegians; they are often cold and reserved, and combine great simplicity of manner with firmness and kindness. 'Deeds, not words' is their motto." – 125 years later, little has changed!

But where does all this place the visitor?

Most people are pleasantly surprised when they visit Norway. For a start, the people are friendlier and far more open than the stereotype Scandinavian image would have us believe, and secondly, the scenery is even more breathtaking in reality than any guidebook can ever hope to inspire. Although the country is vast – stick a pin in Kristiansand and rotate the country through 180° and the people in Kirkenes would be eating pasta! – the main town centres are more than manageable with good public transport and everywhere within walking distance anyway. Add to this the fact that things work, communications and services are efficient, and that it is safe to go out at night, and you have all the ingredients for a pleasant stay.

As for prices, it all depends on the reason for your visit and how you spend your money. Surveys persistently place Oslo among the top ten most expensive cities in the world, but the statistics tend rather to reflect the spending habits of businessmen with expense accounts than those of the selective tourist. ❑

PRECEDING PAGES: winter on the fjord; snow on the fishing fleet; wooden houses in the old copper-mining town of Røros; waiting for confirmation in Kautokeino.
LEFT: Norwegian fjords provide breathtaking views.

Decisive Dates

ICE AGE TO BRONZE AGE

10,000 years ago The first people appear in the territory of what is now Norway, following the retreat of the great inland ice sheets. They hunted reindeer and other prey on their trek northwards.

5,000 to 6,000 years ago First agricultural settlements appear around Oslofjord.

1500–500 BC Agricultural settlements develop in southern Norway, while people in the north continue hunting.

ROMAN AGE

AD 0–400 Burial sites indicate links with the civilised countries to the south. Utensils of bronze and glass have been discovered. Latin-based runic letters appear for the first time.

(The migrations of AD 400–550, including to coastal areas in the west, herald a restless period. Farmers pushed into marginal areas. Forts have been found on Lake Mjøsa.)

AD 793 Norwegian Vikings loot the English monastery of Lindisfarne. They raid (or trade with) and colonise parts of west and south-west Europe. Vikings settle in the Orkneys, the Shetlands, the Hebrides, and on the Isle of Man (remaining there until 1405).

VIKING AGE

AD 800–1030 Our knowledge of this period is largely based on archaeological remains. Although written down some time later, the Norse sagas reveal that the Viking Age was the richest of all the early periods in Norway.

840 Vikings found Dublin, which remains under Nordic rule until 1171.

844 Dublin's Norwegian king exchanges envoys with Emir Abderrhaman II, the Moorish king in Spain.

861 Vikings sack Paris.

866 Vikings control most of England.

872 Battle at Hafrsfjord near Stavanger. King Harald Fairhair strengthens his position as ruler of large areas of the country.

1001 The sagas relate that it was Leiv Eiriksson who discovered Vinland (America).

1028 King Canute of Denmark invades Norway. King Olav flees, but later regains control.

1030 Battle of Stiklestad. Christianity arrives through trading contacts with the rest of Europe. This culminates with three missionary kings, Håkon the Good, Olaf Trygvasson and Olaf the Stout, who becomes St Olav following his death at the Battle of Stiklestad.

1050 Harald Hardråde founds Oslo.

1066 King Harald Hardråde is defeated at the Battle of Stamford Bridge, in England, bringing the Viking Age to an end.

MIDDLE AGES

1100 The first bishoprics appear, among them the see of Nidaros (Trondheim) in 1152.

1130 Beginning of civil wars which last to 1227. But this period was also the start of the so-called High Middle Ages. It was a period of population growth, consolidation within the Church and the development of towns. The monarchy dominates both Church and nobility. Farmers change from being freeholders to tenants.

1241 Saga writer Snorri Sturluson is put to death by the King of Norway's men.

1299–1319 Oslo becomes the capital during the reign of King Håkon V.

1349 Onslaught of the Black Death. Population Oslo: 3,000; Bergen: 7,000; Trondheim: 4,000 reduced to a half or even possibly a third. (Towards the end of the High Middle Ages state revenues were inadequate to finance the desired expansion of the Crown and state. This prompted the king and the nobility to seek revenues from neighbouring lands, leading to the growth of the political unions.)

1319–43 Inter-Scandinavian royal marriages produce joint Norwegian-Swedish monarchy, later to include Denmark.

1380 Olav, son of Håkon VI (1340–80) becomes king of Denmark and Norway.

Trinity Sunday 1397 The union of the three crowns is formalised at a coronation in the Swedish town of Kalmar.

1450 Union with Denmark set up by treaty.

UNION WITH DENMARK

1536 Norway ceases to be an independent kingdom. Norway's Council of the Realm is disbanded. Danish noblemen start to take over control of the running of Norway.

1537 The Reformation of the Norwegian church is enforced by royal (Danish) decree. From the early 1600s the Lutheran creed was the sole creed of Norway.

1624 Oslo burns to the ground.

1645 The Danish king surrenders Jemtland and Herjedalen to Sweden. The fief of Trondheim is surrendered in 1658 (but is then regained in 1660).

1660 Fredrik III is acclaimed heir to the throne by an assembly of the States General in Copenhagen and assigned the task of giving the kingdoms a new constitution. (In this way the two kingdoms were subject to an absolute monarchy. However, real power lay in the hands of the state officials and Denmark and Norway were treated as one.)

1662 Town privileges are introduced to concentrate wealth from the timber trade in the hands of urban, middle-class merchants.

1807–14 Napoleonic Wars. Denmark/Norway ally with France, and the resulting blockade isolates Norway both from Denmark and from the market. Shipping and timber exports collapse, and famine and hunger spread.

INDEPENDENCE AND NEW UNION

January 1814 Secession from Denmark.

17 May 1814 The new Norwegian constitution is formally adopted at Eidsvoll.

PRECEDING PAGES: Viking gold.
LEFT: the Stiklestad open-air play.
RIGHT: 1905, Danish Prince Carl arrives in Norway, carrying his son, to become King Håkon VII.

10 October 1814 Norway unites with its neighbour, Sweden.

1825 The great exodus to the United States begins.

1854 The first railway line is laid.

1872 The first trade union is formed.

1884 Norway's first political parties are set up.

August 1905 National referendum leads to the end of the union with Sweden.

NORWEGIAN INDEPENDENCE

18 November 1905 The Storting chooses a Danish prince as King (Håkon VII) of Norway.

1913 Universal suffrage is granted to women.

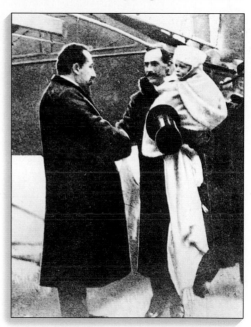

1920 Norway joins the League of Nations. Following WWI, Norway retains Spitsbergen.

1939 At the outbreak of WWII, Norway proclaims neutrality.

9 April 1940 German forces attack Norway.

7 June 1945 King Håkon returns from exile.

1957 King Håkon VII dies. King Olav V takes over the throne.

1960s Exploration in the North Sea begins.

1972 Norway votes against EU membership (and again in 1994).

1991 King Olav V dies. King Harald V assumes the throne.

1993 Norway manages to broker peace between Israel and the Palestinians. ❑

BEGINNINGS

For two centuries the Vikings terrorised large parts of Europe, travelling far and wide in search of land, wealth and, when it suited them, trade

Life in Norway has been influenced to an extraordinary degree by the terrain and the weather. The original inhabitants hugged the coastal areas which, warmed by the Gulf Stream, made life more bearable. With the gradual recession of the last Ice Age about 12,000 years ago, the hunters and fishers inched northwards but again only along the coast because the interior remained inhospitable.

The thaw was followed by mild weather, unknown before or since. Around 500 BC, however, just as iron was beginning to replace bronze and the Athenians were getting ready to build the Parthenon, the climate inexplicably deteriorated. The impact of suddenly colder, wetter weather was dramatic.

Taking a step back

During the preceding Bronze Age considerable progress had been made in weapons, ornaments and utensils made out of metal imported from Britain and Continental Europe. Contemporary rock drawings show boats that were capable of carrying 30 men (although not yet with sails), warriors on horseback and either two- or four-wheeled carts drawn by horses or oxen. These developments were thrown into reverse by the climate change and a large part of the population perished.

Survival in the new Ice Age demanded cultural adjustments. Men, who until then had usually worn a kind of belted cloak, pulled on underwear and trousers. Instead of a semi-nomadic existence, all had to settle on farms in order to secure winter fodder and shelter for livestock which had previously grazed outside all year round. People and animals occupied either end of the same house, an unhygienic but necessary form of early central heating.

In common with most of Europe, Norway was again struck by the weather in the 14th century. The economic decline that followed was exacerbated terribly by the Black Death. The resulting acute shortage of labour led to the collapse of the aristocratic estates, demoting the owners to peasantry. The number of knights in Norway dropped from 270 to 60.

But who were these people? The recorded history of Norway begins remarkably late, only

in about AD 800, and the archaeological pointers towards specific events in earlier times are comparatively scanty. The ancient world had curious opinions about the ancient northerners: one, advanced by Pomponius Mela, was that, living on birds' eggs, the people had hoofed feet, and ears so large that they covered their bodies, thereby dispensing with the need for any clothing.

Another, Greek in origin and containing an element of truth, had the territory populated by Hyperboreans, a jolly race who lived in forests and sang and danced their way to incredible longevity. When eventually tired of life, they feasted, bedecked themselves with flowers and

LEFT: discovered in 1880, the Gokstad ship is now in the *Vikingskipshuset* (Viking Ship Museum), Oslo.
RIGHT: Odin, king of the Norse gods.

threw themselves off cliffs. Norwegians continue to live longer than practically anyone else in Europe. Furthermore, they remain energetic to the end. It is one thing for a foreigner struggling on skis to be overtaken by a blasé six-year-old, quite another if the speed demon turns out to be a venerable grandmother.

Lieutenant W. H. Breton, a 19th-century tourist, was amazed by reports of a man who married at 113 and lasted until he was 146. Another visitor commented on four peasants who were the principal dancers at an entertainment laid on for King Christian VI. All of them were well over 100. One Derwent Conway, in

about 1820, asked a fit 74-year-old in Telemark for the secret of his robust health. Pouring himself a fifth glass of home-made corn brandy, he replied that it was due to this excellent drink.

New blood

That the original inhabitants of Norway received infusions of new blood, probably from the east, is indicated by artefacts which have given their name to their respective cultures: Funnel-Beaker, Battle-Axe and Boat-Axe peoples. Changing burial practices are another reliable sign of influential immigration.

It was once thought that the Sami (Lapps of Finnmark) were the original inhabitants. Being Mongoloid and short of stature, they are very different from the familiar Scandinavian stereotype. However, it seems theirs was a relatively recent migration from Siberia, long after European types had moved in. The great majority of Norwegians are directly descended from the people who were occupying their territory long before 3000 BC, the date customarily taken as the beginning of Western civilisation.

Like a Nordic Rip van Winkle, Norway slept through the millennium in which Greece and then Rome flourished, although the runic alphabet did appear around the 3rd century AD. It was Latin in origin but dispensed with the curved Latin letters because, perhaps, straight lines were easier to cut into wood, stone and metal, as runic inscriptions invariably were.

Norway was ignored by the civilised world until the late 8th century, by which time the Muslim tide had been turned back and Charlemagne was building his empire. Nowhere in Pliny the Elder, Tacitus, Ptolemy or any of the celebrated descriptions of the then known world are the Norwegian people mentioned by name. Even the term 'Scandinavia' is a misreading of a text by Pliny, who referred to the unknown land beyond Jutland as *Scatinavia*.

Development in secret

Foreign ignorance, however, did not mean that nothing was happening locally. The evolution of ship design was the most potent of these hidden developments. Although the Phoenicians had undertaken stupendous voyages very much earlier, they routinely stayed within sight of land. The Norwegians were working on vessels capable of crossing oceans.

The Gokstad ship, found in a burial mound near Sandefjord in 1880, was a masterpiece. Made out of oak planks, it was 25 metres (82 ft) long and five metres (16 ft) wide. It had a mast and 16 pairs of oars. The crew handled one oar each which left enough room for an equal number of marines. The *styrbord* or rudder, which hung on the right (hence, starboard) side, could be raised for fast beaching. A modern replica crossed the Atlantic in just four weeks. These ships represented a menacing mobility, and once the Norwegians had cause to take their unsuspecting neighbours to the south by surprise, they were able to do so with stunning efficiency.

The Norwegians introduced themselves to

the rest of the world with deceptive tranquillity. The *Anglo-Saxon Chronicle* for the year 787 contains the laconic entry: "In this year King Breohtric married King Offa's daughter Eadburge. And in his days came the first three ships of the Northmen from Hercoalande" (known today as Hordaland, on Norway's west coast).

The Vikings appear

In 793 the Vikings opened their account in earnest by plundering the monastery of Lindis-

> ### BAD NEIGHBOURS
> In Arthurian romances the Vikings were described as being "wild and savage and had not in them the love of God nor their neighbours."

among their victims in the 9th and 10th centuries that it was synonymous with the term "pirate" or "sea robber". This is further confused by the tendency in English chronicles to call all Vikings "Danes", while many were actually "Northmen", "Norsemen" or, in present terminology, Norwegians. In contrast, in Continental records Norwegians take all the credit (or blame) for what was usually the work of Danes. Swedish Vikings were busy too, but they tended to direct their attentions overland via Russia.

farne, one of the great sanctuaries of the Western Christian church. The next year they attacked the monastery of Jarrow in Northumbria, and the year after that they arrived in South Wales with more than 100 ships. They were driven off by King Maredudd and that, together with the resistance they had encountered in England, persuaded them, for a period of 40 years, to turn their attention to softer targets in Ireland.

Various opinions prevail about the origin of the name "Viking", but there was no doubt

LEFT: early sailing equipment.
ABOVE: a set of Viking keys.

Proper outside investigation into the geography and demography of Norway began with Alfred the Great of England, who had every reason to wonder about people who had become painful tormentors. He was enlightened by Ottar, a Norwegian chieftain from Hålogaland, at the same time as Alfred was waging war with other Viking chieftains. He told the king that Norway was a very long and narrow country, full of rocks and mountains. The only places which could be pastured or ploughed were those close to the sea, the inhabitants kept sheep and swine and bred tame deer, which they called reindeer.

In reality, the Vikings were land-hungry

adventurers for whom rich and undefended coastal abbeys were irresistible business opportunities. They had no scruples about violating their supposed sacrosanctity; on the contrary, they saw Christianity as a heretical threat to their heathen beliefs.

Truculent population

While Christians put their faith in the sign of the Cross, the Vikings trusted the hammer of Thor the Thunderer, defender of heaven against giants, men against monsters, and themselves from the "followers of the White Cross", as they called Christians. Small Viking raiding

parties faced with a large and truculent population found that a reputation for uncompromising destruction and cruelty served their purposes well, encouraging the enemy to flee rather than put up a fight. Viking victory celebrations – "wild outburst of triumphant rejoicing" – included the proven intimidatory tactic of transfixing captured children with spears and drinking out of the skulls of fallen enemies.

The Vikings also have apologists who prefer to concentrate on their apparent managerial talents in occupied territory and an artistic streak manifested in the finely worked ornaments recovered from excavated ships. In the early 18th century, Baron de Montesquieu praised them as an army of free men in an age when armies were usually press-ganged.

The historian Snorri Sturluson is disarmingly indifferent to matters which others might consider to be grave flaws in their heroes. The royal pretender Harald Gille is summarised as "friendly, jovial, playful, unassuming, generous, accommodating and easily led". All this glosses over the fact, which Sturluson himself recounts, that he blinded and castrated a rival, hanged a bishop and died drunk in the arms of his mistress with his wife standing by.

The reason sometimes given for the sudden explosion of Viking activity abroad is that it was the result of another explosion, that of population because of uniform polygamy. Overpopulation was certainly the case in Western Norway where agricultural land was so scarce, but the problem was less acute elsewhere.

Nevertheless, all sons, legitimate and otherwise, were entitled to equal shares of their father's inheritance, and as political power and social standing were invested in property, the aristocracy especially were reluctant to carve land up into smaller and smaller parcels. The surfeit of sons was thus encouraged to seek a fortune abroad.

The profits of piracy

Women and children often accompanied the men but they were usually parked in fortified camps while the men "harried". Occasionally they did join in and one of them, an Amazon who rose to command her own army in Ireland, was acclaimed as the fearsome Red Maiden.

When the Vikings came across unoccupied land or, as in the Orkneys, rendered it so by annihilating the natives, they were keen to settle it. If that proved to be impractical, a raid might at least produce some slaves who could either be sold or, increasingly, put to good use at home. When piracy could not be made to pay, however, the Vikings were willing to engage in conventional trade.

Profits from piracy and trade generated in Norway the nucleus of a merchant class which complemented the traditional structure of aristocratic earls, free men and thralls (or slaves). The pecking order was reflected in Western Norway by *wergild*, a system which stipulated the compensation due in the event of murder. A slave was worth half the value of an ordinary peasant and a quarter of that of a land owner, who in turn was worth only a quarter of a chieftain and one-eighth of a king.

Slaves must have been worked hard because there was a provision in law which absolved owners of guilt if a slave died through exhaustion or ill-treatment. Owners were permitted, when slaves died, to throw their children into an open grave to die from exposure. They were obliged, however, to step in and rescue the last one left alive.

Some slaves, such as captured craftsmen, were prized, as were young women with whom

VIKINGS ABROAD

The Viking kingdom on the Isle of Man lasted until 1263, when it was sold to Alexander III of Scotland along with the Western Isles.

the Moorish leader in Spain. Alghazal, a poet, was appointed to the court of the King of the Pagans and became enchanted by the queen. While keen to further their acquaintance, he was alarmed at the prospect of the king finding out. The queen reassured him that "it is not customary with us to be jealous. Our women stay with their husbands only as long as they please, and leave them whenever they choose." She seems not to have added that Viking husbands reciprocated in kind. Viking men traded wives, or even gave

masters could replenish or increase the labour pool. Unlike the custom in nearby Sweden, the child of the union between a Norwegian master and slave woman remained a slave.

Viking women made an impression abroad in a way which hints at the liberated attitudes ascribed to them in the 20th century, albeit a reputation bestowed less frequently on Norwegian women than on the other Scandinavians. In 844 a Norwegian king ruling in Dublin exchanged envoys with Emir Abderrhaman II,

LEFT: a confrontation from the *Frithiof Saga* by E. Tégnér, illustrated by Knut Ekwall.
ABOVE: runic script at Skjeberg, south of Oslo.

them away to friends, if they bored or displeased them.

Protection money

The renewed Viking campaigns were launched from the west coast of Norway, from strongholds on the Scottish islands or from the Norwegian kingdom in Ireland, centred on a castle built in Dublin in 841 by Torgisl. The Vikings were overlords rather than settlers in Ireland, although some intermarried. Norway might still have overseas territories today if a Danish king, as we shall see, had not mortgaged the Orkney and Shetland Isles to raise money for his daughter's dowry.

The Viking raids into Europe were conducted like annual summer holidays, and year after year the fleets grew larger. An alarmed Charlemagne threw up military posts along his northern borders to guard against them. The defence of Paris against the Vikings was led by another King Charles, known as Charles the Bald. The city was attacked in 857 and sacked in 861. Charles offered one lot of Vikings 1,360 kg (3,000 lb) of silver to go and fight some of their compatriots instead of him. In 885, however, both were back and it cost a further 318 kg (700 lb) of silver to get rid of them.

The most enduring Viking presence in France was in Normandy which, of course, was named after them. Over the years the Viking armies on the continent grew to massive proportions and were not finally driven off until 891, by the German emperor Arnulf.

Although geographical proximity recommended the British Isles, Vikings were active wherever the pickings looked good. At one point they laid siege to Lisbon and they penetrated the Mediterranean as far as Constantinople. Nor did they restrict their territorial ambitions to Continental Europe. Vikings sailed west to Iceland, Greenland and eventually to the American continent. As many as 20,000

THE VIKINGS IN BRITAIN

The Vikings attacked the British Isles in earnest from 834. The most spectacular effort was in 851 when they took 350 ships up the Thames, stopping off to capture Canterbury before storming London, only to be finally turned back by Ethelwulf at the battle of Aclea. By 866 most of England was under their control with only Wessex, ruled by Alfred the Great, staying independent. After the initial success of a winter campaign in 878, they were defeated by Alfred, but continued to rule large parts of England and a kingdom based in York. All further territorial ambitions were curtailed with the arrival of William the Conqueror in 1066.

Norwegians emigrated to Iceland; by the latter half of the 10th century there were no fewer than 39 petty kingdoms established there.

This surging mixture of colonialism, plunder, trade and adventurism lasted for two centuries between the fall of the western Roman Empire and the First Crusade, and it nearly brought about the overthrow of Christianity in Europe (as the Muslims had been close to doing earlier). The benefits to those left at home were considerable. The period produced unprecedented wealth. ❑

ABOVE: a detail from a drawing by Halvfdan Egedins in Snorri Sturluson's *Sagas of the Norse Kings*.

A Viking Burial

In the year AD 921, a peripatetic Arab named Ahmad bin Fudlan came across Vikings who had settled on the banks of the Volga river. They were trading with Constantinople: furs and slaves for gold, silver ornaments and silks. A chieftain died while he was with them, and his account of the funeral is an antidote to some of the romantic nonsense that has been written about the Vikings.

When the chieftain died, Ahmad reported, his maidservants were asked: "Who will die with him?" The first to volunteer was immediately put under guard in case she changed her mind, not that she gave any indication of wishing to do so.

The elaborate formalities began with the division of the chieftain's estate into three equal parts. One went to his family, the second to cover the cost of the funeral, and the last on drink. The boat in which the chieftain was to be despatched was drawn out of the water and decorated with quilts and cushions. Ahmad then met "the angel of death"; he described her as "dusky, hale, strongly built and austere". Austere she might well have been, for it was her function eventually to kill the carousing maidservant.

The chieftain's body was removed from the temporary grave where it had lain for 10 days. Ahmad had a good look at it. "I saw that he had gone black, because of the cold", he said; but otherwise "the corpse had in no way altered." The body was dressed in finery and propped up on cushions in a tent erected on the boat.

"They now brought liquor, fruit, and herbs and put them by him, then they brought bread, meat, and onions, and threw them down in front of him. They brought a dog, cut it in half, and threw it into the boat, then brought all his weapons, and put them by his side. After that they took two beasts of burden, drove them along until they sweated, then cut them up with swords and threw their flesh into the boat. The girl who was to be killed, meanwhile, was going up and down, entering one tent after another, and one man after another had intercourse with her. Each one said to her, 'Tell your master that I only do this for love of him'." The girl was later taken to the boat, where she handed over her bracelets and anklets to the "angel of death" and the two girls who had been guarding her. They were joined by men carrying shields and pieces of wood.

RIGHT: a romantic view of a Viking (1828).

Farewell drinks and songs followed until, Ahmad wrote, "I saw that she had become bewildered and wished to enter the tent."

The old woman followed her into the tent, whereupon "the men began beating the shields with the pieces of wood so that the sound of her screams should not be heard. Six men then entered the tent, and all of them had intercourse with her. They then made her lie down by the side of her dead master, and two took hold of her hands and two her feet. The 'angel of death' put a rope done into a noose round her neck, and gave it to two men to pull. She came forward with a large, broad-bladed knife and began thrusting it in and

out between the girl's ribs in place after place, while the two men strangled her until she died."

Walking backwards, the next of kin then naked to the boat and lit kindling which had been placed beneath it. "At this moment, an awe-inspiring gale got up, so that the flames of the fire grew stronger. One of the Vikings chose to compare the funeral arrangements with what he had heard about Islamic rites. 'You Arabs are stupid,' he remarked to Ahmad, 'because you take your dearest and most honourable men and cast them into the dust, so that creeping things and worms eat them. We burn them with fire in a twinkling and they enter Paradise the very same hour'." Then, according to Ahmad bin Fudlan, "he laughed heartily." ❑

KINGS AND CHRISTIANITY

Constant battles for the throne and the arrival of Christianity in a stubbornly pagan land were the unlikely precursors to Norway's "Period of Greatness"

With Snorri Sturluson, Norwegian history begins to speak for itself instead of relying on outsiders who observed or passed on fantastic tales about the land and its people. Sturluson's epic *Heimskringla* (*Sagas of the Norse Kings*) is a work of genius.

He visited Norway only twice, but working on his remote saga island of Iceland he compiled an almost inconceivable mass of information beginning in prehistory and continuing until 1177 (two years before he was born), by which time the Vikings had been tamed, Christianity had taken hold in Norway and the country had endured a century of civil war.

Amusing tale

Although Sturluson was himself a foreigner, he drew on the oral history of the skalds at the courts of the Norwegian kings. He was obviously a discriminating historian, although never one to exclude an amusing tale because he did not believe it: "It is the way of skalds, of course, to give most praise to him for whom they composed, but no one would dare tell the king himself such deeds of his as all listeners and the king himself knew to be lies and loose talk; that would be mockery, but not praise."

There are no fewer than 2,000 names of persons and places in his saga and he gives his readers a vivid sense of what was happening, as it were, at home. But Sturluson's unlucky recompense was to be put to death by the King of Norway's men in 1241.

Sturluson introduces the Norwegian royal line in the person of Halvdan the Black, a king troubled by his inability to dream. He consulted Torleiv the Wise, who said he had suffered from the same complaint and had cured it by sleeping in a pigsty. The king followed his example "and then it always happened that he dreamed".

More prosaically, Halvdan was descended from the Swedish Ynglinger family who ruled in Uppsala. His branch had moved to Norway

about a century before the Viking period, when the concept of Norway as an entity existed only in the term *Norovegr*, or North Way, the coastal stretch from Vestfold to Hålogaland.

A king dreaming in a pigsty might seem to belong to mythology rather than history, but he was real enough. The Oseberg ship unearthed in

Vestfold in 1904 proved to be that in which his mother, a Danish princess, was buried. When Halvdan died, his body was chopped up so that the pieces could be more widely distributed to bring good luck to the recipients.

Female demands

Halvdan's son, known as Harald Hårfagre (Fair Hair), was to become the first ruler of a united Norway. It was said of this subsequent unification that he was put up to it by a woman whom he wished to take to bed. Her reply to his proposition, conveyed by messengers, was that she could not possibly "waste her maidenhood" on a man who ruled over a kingdom which

LEFT: one of the oldest stave churches, Borgund.
RIGHT: Harald Hårfagre (*circa* 1200).

compared so unfavourably in size with those in Denmark and Sweden. His messengers nervously reported her comment but were relieved by the philosophical way in which he took it: "She has reminded me of those things", he said, "which it now seems strange I have not thought of before."

Harald advanced north from Vestfold to improve his conjugal prospects. He made contact with the powerful Earl Håkon, whose interests extended south from Trøndelag, the region surrounding what was eventually to become Trondheim. The cold facts, never as interesting as Sturluson's version, are that Harald and

Håkon saw the mutual benefits of trade but first had to suppress unruly Viking bands along the coast who would have disrupted it.

Harald needed assistance and set the precedent for cooperation between the Norwegian and English thrones by turning to Athelstan, King of England. As a pledge of friendship, accompanied by some mutual chicanery, he initiated what was to become another quite common practice: he sent his infant son Håkon to be fostered at Athelstan's court.

Harald's campaigns sent many of his dispossessed opponents into exile in Iceland, Shetland, the Orkney Islands and the Hebrides. The decisive battle was at Hafrsfjord, near present-

day Stavanger, in southwestern Norway about AD 900. The victory made him, Sturluson says, the first king of the Norwegians, and also won him the postponed hand of the "large-minded maid", who proceeded to bear him five children. As a love story, however, the conclusion is not completely satisfactory. Sturluson writes: "They say that when he took Ragnhild the Mighty…, he had divorced himself from nine other women."

Too many children

The awesome number of royal progeny was to prove a constant source of havoc in the matter of choosing a successor. The English chronicler Roger of Hoveden wrote: "it is the custom of the kingdom of Norway… that everyone who is recognised to be the son of any King of Norway, even though he be a bastard and born of a serving wench, can claim for himself as great a right to the kingdom of Norway as the son of a wedded king and one born of a free woman. And so fighting goes on incessantly between them…"

Harald Hårfagre's umpteenth son, but the only one by Ragnhild, was the wretched Erik Bloodaxe, who advanced his succession by murdering all but one of his legitimate half-brothers. The exception was Håkon, the boy who had been fostered by King Athelstan. Erik had none of his father's authority and the united kingdom quickly degenerated into squabbling petty kingdoms ruled by various of Harald's bastard sons. On Håkon's return from England, Erik was forced to flee in the opposite direction, ending up as King of Northumberland.

First Christian

Håkon den Gode (the Good) was more successful than Erik at holding hostile factions together. Before he died, he was acknowledged as king over the whole coastal area from Oslo to Hålogaland. He was a notable reformer of law and defence; he was also the first Norwegian Christian king, having been baptised while in England. He imported an English bishop and missionaries with a view to converting his countrymen; but that wasn't easy.

Nowhere was resistance to Christianity more forcibly expressed than in Trondheim, which was then against any form of imposed authority whether by Håkon or, as they had just convincingly demonstrated, by the rival King

Øystein of Oppland. Øystein, to some "the Mighty" and to others "the Evil", had offered them as king a choice between one of his thralls, known as Tore the Hairy, or his dog, Saur. They chose the dog. "Then they bewitched the dog with the wit of three men", sufficient to enable the hound to communicate through a mixture of barking and speech. It was into this unorthodox regal set-up that Håkon tried to introduce Christianity. He urged people to "believe in one God, Christ, the son of Mary,

SAUR, THE DOG KING

According to *the Sagas of the Norse Kings*: "The king lived in a palatial kennel and was carried 'when it was muddy' on the shoulders of its subjects."

parishioners would drink themselves into extinction and, by instructing them in the cultivation of fruit and vegetables, hoped to persuade them to consume at least some solids. In the end the missionaries realised that pious sobriety was unattainable. The best they could hope for was to have the toasting converted to Christian saints rather than pagan gods. They provided a long list of saints' names and it seems that some of their parishioners were content to drink to them with undiminished frequency and pleasure.

and give up all blood offerings... and fast every seventh day". From the typical audience "there was straightaway a mighty uproar", followed by devious ploys to trick Håkon into eating a morsel of horse flesh on a day when he was self-righteously fasting or make him participate in a toast to one of their pagan gods.

Håkon's imported missionaries despaired. Their targets would not deviate from toasting their pagan gods morning, noon and night. They were concerned, too, that their potential

Left: the monument at Hafrsfjord, where Harald Hårfagre first united Norway.
Above: traditional Norwegian houses with turf roofs.

Missionaries' fate

The missionaries had less luck in suppressing traditions like blood sacrifices (usually animals but occasionally humans). In Trondheim the obdurate response to the message they preached was to send out four ships looking for tiresome missionaries: they "slew three priests and burned three churches; they then went home".

Even when Christianity was finally adopted in Norway, much of the old religion lingered until the Reformation and beyond. The early Christian clergy, for instance, ignored papal injunctions about celibacy. The medieval stave churches are another case in point. Their intricate construction resembles nothing if not the keel of a Viking ship, and they are festooned with dragon heads and scenes from heathen mythology. Many of these churches lasted into the 19th century, when they finally succumbed beneath a torrent of Pietism.

On the military front, Håkon was under constant threat from Erik Bloodaxe's avenging sons coming over from Northumberland. In defeat they turned to their uncle, the Danish King, Harald Bluetooth, who wanted to regain old Danish territories at the mouth of Oslofjord. At a decisive battle in 960 Håkon was defeated and killed. With him, for the time being, went Christianity's immediate prospects in Norway.

Unlikely convert

Christianity had to wait for its next champion until Olav Tryggvason, later King Olav I and a monument in Norwegian history. Sturluson says he was a great sportsman who could walk on the oars along the outside of a ship, "smote equally well with both hands" and could hurl two spears at a time. By the age of 12 he was a full-blooded Viking, cruising the Baltic in command of five longships and later moving west to terrorise the English coast. His personality changed through a chance meeting in the Scilly Isles, where he was resting after some strenuous atrocities. A wise old man took him aside and explained the True Path. Transformed

overnight, Olav returned to England "and now went about peacefully, for England was a Christian country and he was also a Christian".

He was not so peaceful when converting his compatriots at home. Those who opposed him "he dealt with hard; some he slew, some he maimed and some he drove away from the land". In the circumstances, it is understandable that a man who was elected to argue theological niceties with the king stood up only to develop "such a cough and choking in the chest that he could not bring forth one word and he sat himself down".

Olav Tryggvason was unlucky in love. In proposing marriage to the wealthy Queen Sigrid of Sweden, he insisted she would first have to be baptised. She demurred: "King Olav was very wroth and answered hastily, 'Why should I wed thee, thou heathen bitch?'" reinforcing his point with a smack in the face. "That may well be thy death", she observed: so it proved.

She was a crafty enemy. Her wealth attracted a procession of proposals from minor kings, which she found irksome. King Swein Forkbeard of Denmark, son of Harald Bluetooth, was the type she preferred, and as soon as they were married she talked her husband into an alliance with the Swedish King Olav the Tax Gatherer against Norway. A great sea battle ensued, at the climax of which Olav, who was being assisted by King Boleslav of Poland, was forced to jump overboard. He was never seen again and the victors, including the gratified queen, divided the spoils among themselves.

First saint

The man who would soon restore Norway's integrity had, like Olav Tryggvason, embarked on a naval career at 12. Olav Haraldson, later St Olav, was in England when the same Swein Forkbeard landed his forces and was responsible for the then King of England, Ethelred, being castigated ever more as "the Unready".

Olav allied himself with Ethelred in an anti-Danish war which came to a head at London Bridge across the Thames. The Danish forces looked, and probably felt, impregnable on their fortified bridge, but they reckoned without Olav's well-built Vikings. Having fastened ropes to the piles under the bridge, they heaved at the oars and brought the whole thing down. Several churches in England are still dedicated to St Olav for this remarkable feat.

Olav managed to lay the foundations of the Church, even in petulant Trøndelag, but in so doing antagonised many potential rivals. He faced a greater threat from the expansionist King Canute of Denmark, who invaded in 1028 with overwhelming forces. Olav fled to Kiev until he learned that the earl whom Canute had appointed to rule Norway was dead. He returned to regain his kingdom but miscalculated his level of support in Trøndelag and was killed.

Olav was elevated to sainthood and his body placed in the church of St Clement in Trondheim (later to be moved). In spite of his insensitive missionary zeal, the memory of Olav kept

for the Byzantine emperor in Constantinople and saw service in Syria, Armenia, Palestine, Sicily and Africa. He was an enterprising warrior. During one siege he faked his own funeral and, emulating the Trojan Horse, his men persuaded the townspeople to open the gates to admit his coffin which, they promised, would work powerful magic to their benefit.

All of this was immensely profitable because the mercenaries were entitled to keep as much treasure from captured palaces as they could grab with both hands. An oblique memorial to Norwegians like Harald who served with the Varangians exists on the great Piraeus marble

alive the notion of a united and independent Norway through the troubled centuries ahead.

King Canute's kingdom fell apart after his death, the Scandinavian component reforming into three distinct and generally hostile kingdoms. Norway was ruled first by Magnus I and then by Harald Hårdråda.

Noble mercenary

Harald was typical of the young nobles who were forced to look abroad to enrich themselves. He signed up as a Varangian mercenary

LEFT: detail of the carving on Borgund stave church.
ABOVE: runic inscription on a Viking monument.

lion which the Venetians carried away after their conquest of Athens in 1687 and which now stands at the entrance to the Arsenal in Venice. Very faded, but still visible, is an example of Varangian graffiti: a runic inscription etched into its flanks.

Harald consolidated the kingdom of Norway. Troubled as Norwegian kings invariably were by the people of Trøndelag and its capital, Trondheim, he founded Oslo in 1048 as a counterbalance. He provided the town with a patron saint, Hallvard, whose main claim to sainthood seems to have been the refusal of his body to sink after being thrown into a fjord with a stone around the neck.

Defeat in England

As King Canute's sovereignty over England was still within living memory, it was possibly inevitable that a confident Harald would develop similar ambitions. In any case, there had been so much toing and froing between the west coast of Norway and Britain that the affinities between them were as close, or closer, than those between scattered settlements in Norway. Harald therefore probably felt he was exercising a natural right in his invasion of England.

His approach was from the north but his army was stopped at Stamford Bridge, in York-

taneously acclaimed kings who were all minors. One died young, Sigurd went off to the Holy Land to earn his title, "the Crusader", and Øystein mixed Viking raids with improvements to fisheries, harbours and roads and the establishment of monasteries. Sigurd had the throne to himself after Øystein's death, though he continued to be confronted by the complicated rules of succession throughout his reign.

These battles to occupy the Norwegian throne went on and on. There were brilliant interludes under a king like Sverre, but more often than not the succession was a squabble between the powers behind official contestants

shire. Some historians argue that the English army's rush north to meet Harald weakened its ability to resist William the Conqueror when he materialised in the south.

After Harald's death in this abortive conquest of England, he was succeeded by his sons Magnus and Olav the Peaceful, the latter founding the towns of Bergen and Stavanger before being succeeded by his son, yet another Magnus, but in this instance unforgettably "the Bareleg" because, after visiting Scotland (which he dearly wanted to annex), he took to wearing a kilt.

Magnus's death produced the familiar pattern of multiple heirs, in this case three simul-

who might be children not yet six years old. With the stability of Håkon IV's 46-year reign and that of his son, Magnus the Lawmender, however, Norway achieved its 13th-century "Period of Greatness".

Cultural awakening

Money was spent on cathedrals and churches, the arts flourished and Norwegians assiduously studied and followed European fashions. This cultural awakening was to some extent through the creation of a wealthy upper class and the consolidation of state and Church. It was not so beneficial for the peasants; riches were not evenly spread, and the number of independent farmers dropped significantly as they defaulted on mortgages, leaving the Church and big landowners free to repossess their land.

Norway's overseas empire contributed to a sense of greatness. Jämtland in Sweden was Norwegian, as were the Orkney and Shetland Islands. In 1262 Iceland accepted Norwegian sovereignty, as did Greenland. It was the period, too, which saw the growth of towns like Bergen with a rich trade in dried fish from the north. Foreign trade, to begin with, was mainly with Britain but it then tilted towards the Baltic coast, especially Lübeck and the merchants of the Hanseatic League. The Germans had plenty of corn but a shortage of fish; a perfect trade balance with Norway.

The Lübeck merchants grew ever more powerful because of Norway's almost total reliance on them. They were allowed to buy property in Bergen and settle there. If their demands were not met, they simply threatened to cut off corn supplies. Reliance on imported food was effectively costing the country a degree of independence, an unsettling vulnerability which persists in the current national obsession about subsidising agriculture wherever it is remotely possible (and refusing to join the European Union in order to continue to be able to do so).

The Black Death

A galley arriving in Sicily from the Far East in October 1347 brought the Black Death to Europe. Within a couple of years, a third of the European population was dead. The plague was carried north to Bergen in 1349 in the hold of an English ship. The effect on isolated Norwegian farming communities, especially, was catastrophic: farms which had been painfully created in conditions difficult at the best of times were reduced to waste, in some cases to this day.

The estates generating the wealth which was the necessary platform for general economic development could not be maintained while labourers dropped dead. The nobles who survived were reduced to scratching a living out of the land like everyone else. The effect of force

COURTLY BEHAVIOUR

The court of King Magnus the Lawmender was a polite affair, with a prescibed set of rules relating to court etiquette.

majeure acting as a social leveller assumed a pattern in Norwegian history which cannot be discounted in explaining the easy-going classlessness which pertains today.

The decimation of the nobility removed the impetus behind the normally turbulent activity around the Norwegian throne. Unchallenged, two successive kings sat out long peaceful reigns, a foretaste of the comparative stability about to be foisted on all Scandinavia in the late 14th century through the cunning manipulation of Margareta, widow of King Håkon.

A Danish princess, Margareta was married to Håkon at the age of 10 and was thus steeped in the machinery of monarchy. She has been credited with "the greatest personal position ever achieved in Scandinavia" and was sometimes addressed as "Lady King". She first persuaded the Danes to accept as king her son Olav, then aged five.

With mother active behind the scenes, Olav also took over the crown of Norway at 10, and not long afterwards inherited the claim of the dispossessed Folkung dynasty in Sweden. He died suddenly at 17 and Margareta found a suitable substitute to don the united crowns in Erik of Pomerania, her five-year-old nephew. ❑

LEFT: the Ring of Brodgar, Viking remains on the Isles of Orkney off the northeastern tip of Scotland.
RIGHT: runic inscription in Orkney.

THE 400-YEAR SLEEP

A long spell under the control of its more powerful neighbours brought Norway
mixed fortunes and, ultimately, something to celebrate – a constitution

The union of the three crowns was formalised at a coronation in the Swedish town of Kalmar, close to the then border with Denmark. The date, appropriately, was Trinity Sunday, 1397. The coronation was performed by the Danish and Swedish archbishops; Norway was represented by the Bishop of Orkney. Although

Whilst taking steps to undermine the authority of the nobility, Erik also tried to squeeze the Hanseatic merchants for money. Their response included an attack on Copenhagen, where they were seen off by 200 examples of a new invention, the cannon. He was less successful when the merchants retaliated with a blockade. Those

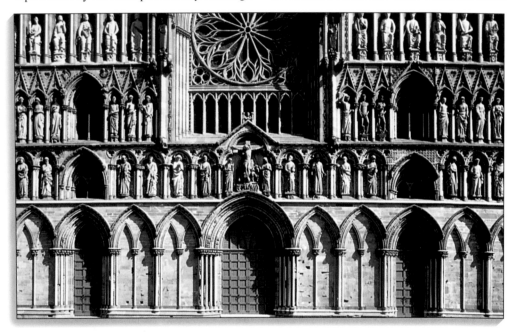

there may have been an attempt to draft a constitution which would have united the three realms forever under a single king, the rules of succession adopted left a gaping loophole. Erik of Pomerania was given full rights to dispose of the crown as he saw fit, a recipe for reversion to the old royal uncertainties after his death.

End of the union

In the event, the union collapsed in his lifetime. His greatest difficulty was paying for the court and administration in Copenhagen. The united crown had no significant estates of its own; the nobility did and was comparatively well off, but it was not inclined to surrender its wealth.

hardest hit were the nobility and wealthy merchants who, holding Erik responsible for their misfortune, conspired to dethrone him.

Erik retreated to the island of Gotland in the hope that they would change their minds. Norway would have done so, but the Danish nobles wanted to make a fresh start. The invitation went to Christian of Oldenburg, who thereupon rose from the title of count in an obscure part of German to found a dynasty which was to last for more than four centuries. Sweden resisted the choice, but Norway went along with it.

Christian I was almost as short of money as Erik had been. His attempts to make up shortfalls were notoriously at the expense of Norway, the weaker partner. Expected to hand over 60,000 guilders as a dowry for his daughter Margaret's marriage to the heir to the Scottish throne, he mortgaged the Orkney Islands to Scotland for 50,000. When the time came for the wedding, he was still 8,000 guilders short, and so mortgaged Shetland as well. To put 8,000 guilders into perspective, he spent three times that on a trip to Rome a few years later (which he had to borrow from the Hanseatics). The Scots gloated over the deal; not merely the trifling price but that Margaret "deemed it a greater thing to be queen in Scotland than daughter of a king who wears three crowns".

Treacherous murder

Norway's resentment at such exploitation eventually boiled over. On the turn of the 16th century, Knut Alvsson, a Swedish-Norwegian nobleman, led an uprising which created a potentially independent state stretching from Oslo to Bergen. Danish troops were sent to put a stop to it. The outcome, however, was thoroughly dishonourable. Alvsson had established himself in Akershus Castle in Oslo. He was invited to negotiate under a flag of truce and promptly murdered. In the poem *At Akershus*, Ibsen called his death a blow to Norway's heart.

Norwegian resentment at the treatment meted out to Alvsson was exacerbated by punitive taxes to pay for Christian II of Denmark's wars with the restless Swedes. Norwegians were not altogether sorry to see him toppled and bundled off into exile, but they were not ready to extend a welcome to his successor, Frederik I.

Norway was nominally Roman Catholic and there was little interest in the forces of the Reformation which lay behind the tussle for the Danish throne. The country did not have the urban bourgeoisie who elsewhere were the first to adopt Lutheranism. Norway's peasant culture was deeply conservative, not to say backward, so much so that many scholars classify Norway as "medieval" until the early 16th century.

It could be said that the Reformation, when it reached Norway, was the first of the great European cultural swathes that had any real impact on the country. Feudalism passed it by (never a Norwegian knight in armour rescuing damsels in distress) as did the Renaissance. Most of rural Norway remained doggedly in its past, Christianity providing only a veneer on what were fundamentally old heathen ways.

A new leader

It was at this point that a new Norwegian leader emerged. He was Olav Engelbrektsson, the Archbishop of Trondheim (or Nidaros, as it was then known). Olav raised an army with a view to getting Christian II back. The exiled king was able to muster a fleet with Dutch help and in 1531 set sail for Oslo. A storm scattered the fleet so that only a small part of it went into

action against Akershus Castle. The attack was futile. Christian was captured and imprisoned, and the Norwegians were forced to acclaim Frederik I as their king.

Christian II was still in prison when Frederik died and was replaced by Christian III, a Protestant. He rounded up the Danish bishops and then ordered the Archbishopric of Trondheim to be abolished, if necessary by force. Olav thought of resisting but, having weighed up the likely repercussions, fled to the Netherlands.

Any further hope of Norwegian independence was squashed by Christian III's 1536 edict demoting the country to the status of a Danish province: "and it shall henceforth neither be nor

---

LEFT: the main entrance to Nidaros Domkirke (Cathedral), Trondheim.
RIGHT: Akershus Festning (Fortress), Oslo.

be called a kingdom in itself." The humbled status was intended to last in perpetuity; in the event it lasted for less than 300 years, culminating not in independence but in an 1814 takeover by Sweden after Norway had become a coveted prize bobbing between its more powerful neighbours.

The loss of political sovereignty under Denmark could not obliterate Norway's separate identity at once. People went on speaking the same language as before and local administration retained many traditional features, but the creeping effects of the Reformation, and Christian III's determination to Danicise Norway, could not be postponed forever.

The Danish influence

Most of the new Protestant clergy were Danes. The revised version of the Bible was in Danish and so were the hymns. Official jobs were invariably given to Danes, who conducted them in the Danish language and reported back to the administration in Copenhagen.

With the spread of schooling and therefore literacy in books imported, naturally, from Denmark (the first printing press was late in arriving in Norway), the anomaly arose of people speaking one language among themselves but reading, albeit with characteristic Norwegian pronunciation, writing and conducting all official business in another. The result was a hybrid Dano-Norwegian and the genesis of a language dispute which has not been settled to this day.

Norway won a measure of Danish respect in the latter's frequent wars with Sweden, in which the Norwegian contingents acquitted themselves well. Denmark began to realise that Norway could only be governed in its own way. Sweden was forever peering enviously over Denmark's shoulder at Norway. Too much antagonism could result in Norway accepting a more attractive offer of union with Sweden.

A valuable asset

The Norwegian economy began to recover from its long decline, partly as the result of vast shoals of herring which materialised off the coast and partly because of the invention of the water-driven saw, which made exploitation of the timber forests lucrative. Christian IV was far more positive about Norway than his predecessors. He visited the country at least 30 times, making a special trip on learning of the discovery of silver at what is now Kongsberg. He supervised the founding of the town, hence the name, which translates as "King's Mountain". He founded and attached his name to Kristiansand, as he did "Christiania" to the new city built on the site where the former Oslo had burned down in 1624.

Nevertheless, Christian ran the country as if it were a private company. He cracked down on the Hanseatic traders, making them take out Norwegian citizenship, if they had not already done so of their own accord, or leave. Foreigners from other parts were encouraged to bring to Norway their skills, enterprise and, best of all, their money. Under his encouragement, former trading posts became towns in places like Drammen, Moss, Larvik, Mandal and Arendal.

The Norwegians did not always receive these foreigners with uncritical joy. In 1700, for example, a simple fight between two men in Arendal escalated into a brawl which pitched all 900 resident foreigners against everyone else. It lasted a week. Nevertheless, a population which had been reduced by the Black Death to something like 180,000 picked up under Christian's energetic policies, reaching 440,000 in 1665 and nearly 900,000 by 1801.

Not all of Christian IV's successors shared his delicate touch with regard to Norwegian sensibilities. There were periods when the Danish crown was autocratically absolute, and respite depended on having an independently-minded Stattholder, the crown agent with responsibility for Norway.

Ulrik Frederik Gyldenløve, the illegitimate son of Frederik III, conscientiously protected his Norwegian charges. He intervened to save peasants from the more rapacious taxes sought by Copenhagen, and he built up the Norwegian armed forces so that at Kvistrum in 1677 they were able to humiliate a far larger force of Swedes. Peter Wessel Tordenskiold became a great

THE DEVIL'S DRINK

The legacy of the zealous Pietism that arrived in Norway in the 18th century can still be felt today, especially when it comes to alcohol.

lous. Gripped by a kind of manic fundamentalism, they despised their folk culture and, particularly in the 19th century when Pietism was still going strong, were encouraged to tear down the ornately carved, wooden stave churches. Confirmation and attendance at church on Sunday were made compulsory.

Looking around them, the Pietists were appalled by the realisation that in their midst, or anyway within the national boundaries, there were still heathens. Thomas von Weston, a superb linguist,

naval hero for many daring feats, the best of which was sailing a small squadron up a fjord (Dynekilen) and destroying a Swedish fleet.

Hellfire and brimstone

As Norway belatedly shed the mantle of medievalism and got to grips with Protestantism, it adopted the faith as zealously as it had once defended paganism. The rural areas, especially, embraced Pietism, real hellfire-and-brimstone stuff which persuaded peasants that their austere existence was actually abominably frivo-

took it on himself to remedy the situation among the Sami (Lapps). Hans Egede went further afield to save souls in Greenland and, although he worked tirelessly, it took him eight years to win his first Innuit convert.

On the other hand, when a liberal wind blew in Copenhagen, it was also felt in Norway. For example, when Christian VII went mad the affairs of state fell into the hands of his physician, a German named Johann Friedrich Struensee. He believed in unrestricted trade, freedom of the press and so on.

Norway was gratified to see the abolition of a trading system which placed a fixed and artificially low value on Norwegian iron imported

---

LEFT: an old rose-painted *stuene* (living room).
ABOVE: a traditional, rural Norwegian Sunday.

into Denmark, whereas Danish corn exports to Norway were sold at whatever the market would bear. Correcting the imbalance helped, but prospects of additional economic reforms ended abruptly when it was discovered that Struensee had been having an affair with Caroline Mathilde, the wife of his deranged patient, and was executed.

One-man Enlightenment

Against a backdrop of Pietism and the death penalty for sexual irregularity, one of the first rays of the Enlightenment shone through in the person of Ludvig Holberg. He was born in

Nelson attacks

Co-existence between Denmark and Norway was traumatised from the unlikely quarter of Napoleon Bonaparte. Britain had fallen out with Denmark (and hence Norway) over the Danish alliance with Prussia and Russia. A total of 149 Danish and Norwegian vessels were seized in British ports; in response, a Danish force marched into Hamburg and appropriated British property worth £15 million.

Nelson moved on Copenhagen with a powerful fleet. Danish and Norwegian crews manning a line of blockships put up a spirited defence, and after a six-hour battle Nelson

Bergen but later became a resident of Copenhagen, a playwright, historian and satirist (in Latin) who, according to the distinguished historian T.K. Derry, "in his own generation had no obvious superior in range of intellect except Voltaire". Holberg's impressive output included 26 plays for the newly founded Copenhagen theatre between 1722 and 1727.

Holberg never returned to his home town of Bergen after leaving at the age of 21, and it is a pithy comment on the difficulty of drawing a clear line between specifically Norwegian and Danish history during the four centuries when the two countries were so closely tied that both countries now claim Holberg as their own.

urged the Danish Crown Prince Regent to capitulate, failing which he would have to destroy the blockships "without having the power to save the brave Danes who have defended them". The Prince agreed.

A few years later Napoleon insisted that Denmark-Norway join his continental system and close their ports to British ships. A large British fleet demanded the handing-over of the Danish navy, which Napoleon sorely needed after losing his at Trafalgar, and when this met with refusal, Copenhagen was bombarded with at least 14,000 rounds over three days.

British troops occupied the capital for six weeks, after which they went home with the

Danish fleet and vast quantities of naval stores. The enormity of such an attack on what was a neutral country put Denmark and Norway firmly into Napoleon's camp, a position which required them to join him in attacking Sweden.

The division thus rendered between Sweden and Denmark was bound to have serious consequences. The impotent "pig in the middle" was Norway. The inevitable was set rolling in 1810 when Sweden's King Karl XIII appointed as his heir (of all people, considering the events which had just passed) Jean-Baptiste Bernadotte, one of Napoleon's marshals. Bernadotte improved his Swedish credentials by changing his name to Karl Johan and succeeded to the throne in 1818.

Karl Johan conceived a plan whereby Russia and Britain would support Swedish claims on Norway. They agreed, with the result that Norwegian ports were blockaded to secure a "voluntary" union with Sweden. The Danish Crown Prince Christian Frederik tried to rally Norwegian loyalty, among other things by agreeing to

EIDSVOLL CONSTITUTION

On 17 May 1814 Norway became a "free, independent and an indivisible realm" according to the new constitution, but it would take a further 91 years for these words to become a reality.

let Norway have the national bank it had long craved. In the end, the decision did not rest in either Norwegian or Danish hands. Union between Sweden and Norway was imposed by the Peace of Kiel (following Napoleon's defeat at Leipzig) in 1814.

Battle for the throne

Christian Frederik was not going to surrender Norway without a struggle. He entertained the idea of getting himself popularly acclaimed as king (he thought his chances best in Trondheim) but the feeling among the population at large was that the Danish line had renounced its sovereignty and the Norwegians were now entitled to choose their own king.

In April 1814, an assembly of 37 farmers, 16 businessmen and 59 bureaucrats met in Eidsvoll to decide what that future should be. The constitution they prepared was signed on 17 May, still the biggest day of the year in Norway. On the same day a new king was elected; it was the tenacious Christian Frederik. Sweden would have none of it. The Norwegians fought well in a one-sided contest but Christian Frederik soon had to sue for peace. Karl Johan stepped forward to occupy his double throne. ❑

LEFT: the old mining town of Røros, Sør-Trøndelag.
ABOVE: a northern graveyard on Andøya, Vesterålen.

UNION WITH SWEDEN

Through such artists as Ibsen, Grieg and Munch, the voice of an increasingly
restless and independent-minded Norway could be heard beyond its own borders

Divorce from Denmark was followed by a quarrel over the division of joint assets and liabilities. The assets were Iceland, Greenland and the Faroes which, Norway claimed, were Norwegian colonies long before marriage with Denmark. The liabilities were the Danish-Norwegian national debt.

Who owed what? The Norwegian position was not only that Denmark alone should shoulder the burden but that compensation was due to Norway for centuries of exploitation. Assuming powers granted under the Treaty of Kiel which had brought about the new union, Karl Johan declared that Norway would pay off some of the debt. The matter of the colonies was not finally resolved until 1931, when the International Court at The Hague found in favour of Denmark.

Two kingdoms

Friction between Karl Johan and the Norwegian half of his kingdom was present right from the start: he envisaged a gradual merging of the two kingdoms, while Norway was determined to consolidate the independence ratified by the 1814 constitution.

A constitutional battle took place over a bill to abolish all noble titles and privileges. Again and again the Storting presented the bill – and the king refused to sanction it. The constitution said he could refuse a bill only twice; the third time it automatically became law. Karl Johan objected strongly to this limitation on his authority which did not exist in Sweden.

A fundamental principle was at stake and the dispute was not to be resolved easily. Indeed, it remained the biggest bone of contention for the life of the union and, as much as anything else, was the author of its eventual dissolution. Norwegian pride was prickly. Merchant ships could fly the Norwegian flag close to home but not in waters notoriously under the sway of North

LEFT: Eidsvoll, where the Norwegian constitution was signed on 17 May 1814.
RIGHT: King Karl Johan XIV.

African pirates. Sweden had bought off the pirates but the immunity extended only to the Swedish flag; if Norwegian ships wanted to take advantage of it, they had to switch flags.

Sweden's dogged refusal to allow Norway its own diplomatic and consular representation abroad was not only an insult but a practical

handicap because the Norwegian merchant fleet was well on its way to becoming, by 1880, the third largest in the world. Its far-flung crews wanted and needed a purely Norwegian diplomatic service.

Oslo once again

Karl Johan was adept at making a timely concession to court popularity, and the welcome he received on visiting Christiania in 1838 was probably sincere, as was the public grief when he died six years later. Although changing Christiania's name back to Oslo obliterated a Danish memory, the capital was, and is, content to leave its main street named after Karl Johan.

The Great Exodus

One thousand years after the first Norwegian Vikings turned their longships towards the west, pushing out as far as North America, a second wave of Norwegians began to cast their eyes in the same direction.

The motives of these new emigrants were similar – lack of opportunity and poverty – but they had none of the warlike excitement of the earlier exodus. These new "Vikings" sought a place where they could work and prosper in peace rather than a place for exploration and conquest.

Yet the first emigrant boat, the 16-metre (54-ft) sloop *Restauration*, crammed full with 52 crew and passengers, must have been scarcely more seaworthy than the superbly built longships. But these early "sloopers", who sailed from Stavanger in July 1825, were idealistic and highly motivated. The leader, Lars Larsen Geilane, was a Quaker and there were members of the religious Haugeans sect among the crew. Their intention to found a classless society where they could follow their own religion had been further encouraged when the previous year another Norwegian pioneer, Cleng Peerson, returned with reports of the promised land.

The *Restauration* reached New York in October of the same year and these farming people, mostly from Rogaland, lost no time in settling on land bought for them by Cleng Peerson at Kendall on the shores of Lake Ontario. This settlement became a staging post on the road to Illinois, where many Norwegians made their homes.

When the *Restauration* left in 1825, Norway's population was only one million, yet the next three generations sent 750,000 Norwegians to North America, reflecting a population increase at home rather than an emptying of the Norwegian countryside, though early industrialists began to campaign against such a dribbling away of potential labour.

The early "sloopers" had more in common with the Pilgrim Fathers who left Plymouth in the *Mayflower* two centuries earlier than with those emigrants who came after them. The main motive among the second and later waves of country people was good land and good farming prospects rather than religious or political repression. To be an *odelsbonde*, who owned his own land, was to be a free man and the goal of every Norwegian peasant. The American merchant fleets were also eager to make use of skilful Norwegian seamen.

The newcomers prospered and regular letters home, reports, and Norwegian visitors from the New World increased the fever. The letters were printed in newspapers all over the country and one or two mid-Western American states began to use agents to encourage emigration.

By the middle of the 1830s new emigrants and some of the original "sloopers" had moved on to Illinois. Forty years later, their numbers had increased to more than 12,500. The 1862 Homestead Law, which granted land to immigrants, turned the early trickle into a steady flow, and Cleng Peerson founded Norwegian settlements in Iowa.

For many patriotic Norwegians it became *de rigueur* to help the expansion. The great violinist Ole Bull had a well-intentioned but crashing failure with a planned settlement, "Oleana", in Pennsylvania. He was too far from his Norwegian farming roots. The soil was ungrateful, communications impossible, and Bull lost more than $40,000.

Later, Norwegians also settled in Canada; but by the 1930s emigration had dwindled to a trickle. Yet the Norwegian influence was strong in the places where they settled. Today, the overt "Norwegian-ness" may have gone, but anyone who doubts it still exists need only read Garrison Keillor's winsome tales of life around Lake Wobegon. ❏

LEFT: this boy, aged eight, crossed the Atlantic alone in 1907 after his mother died.

His successor, Oskar I, immediately tried to placate Norway through gestures such as his title which, locally, became King of Norway and Sweden, rather than vice versa. He also agreed to a new flag which gave equal prominence to the Swedish and Norwegian colours.

Norwegian politics in the 19th century were dominated at first by the Venstre party which carried the banner of separatism and rallied against the royal veto. Its leader, Johan Sverdrup, was a lawyer who worked at creating an alliance between urban radicals and wealthy farmers. Their interests were too divergent, however, and the party split, leaving room for

The farmers' grip on the national heart-strings, and purse, has never been relinquished.

Putting peasants on a pedestal, however, did not ameliorate the hard facts of life. Emigration to the United States began in 1825, although statistics reveal the irony that emigration was highest when the economic conditions at home were good, and lowest when they were bad. Perhaps it was a case of being too poor in the lean times to pay the fare. In 1882 a record 29,000 Norwegians left, and by 1910 there were more than 400,000 people of Norwegian birth in the United States, their numbers growing right the way through to World War I.

the strong labour movement which has characterised most of the 20th century.

It dawned on poorer farmers and peasants who had previously let the land-owning and merchant classes get on with government, that their special interests, especially a reduction in taxes, could be advanced only if they too became involved in the political process. They were assisted by a general mood in the country of national romanticism, a Nordic adaptation of the French philosopher Rousseau's belief in the nobility of savages. The Norwegian peasant farmer was portrayed as the salt of the earth.

ABOVE: emigrants leave Stavanger for the New World.

The arts flourish

The rise of nationalism throughout Europe produced in Norway an unprecedented, and subsequently unequalled flowering of the arts. Henrik Ibsen (1828–1906) and Alexander Kielland (1849–1906), giants among an extraordinarily talented assortment of writers – not forgetting composers, such as Edvard Grieg (1843–1907), and the painter Edvard Munch (1863–1944) – presented the world with a clearer insight into Norway than was available from the best-selling romantic writers.

It may be worth summarising, for strong stomachs, the plot of one such work, *Thelma: A Norwegian Princess*, by Miss Marie Corelli, which ran to no fewer than 47 editions. Sir Philip Bruce-Errington encounters a crazy dwarf who lives in a cavern illuminated by antique Etruscan lamps. Sir Philip and the dwarf converse comfortably in English but that does not prevent Sir Philip from being amazed by the dwarf's intellect, when he correctly guesses his nationality.

Sir Philip then makes the acquaintance of old Olaf Guldmar, Princess Thelma's father. He is a wretched peasant farmer who is also fluent in English. Sir Philip is understandably full of admiration and respect when he discovers Olaf's library. It contains, for example, the

which appeared in the *Spectator* magazine in 1872 about a previously unheard of Norwegian poet named Ibsen who had written "short songs of irregular measure after the manner of Heine". The poet wrote a note of thanks to the writer, Edmund Gosse, adding "I shall consider myself most fortunate if you decide to translate one or more of my books", a modest hint that he may have written more than poems.

Poet and playwright

At home Ibsen and others like Bjørnstjerne Bjørnson (1832–1910) were leading lights in agitation against Danish domination in the arts.

works of Shakespeare, Byron, Keats, Plutarch and Chapman's translation of Homer. It turns out that he is an accomplished Latin scholar, although in religious belief still a devout pagan, "by Valhalla!" being his favourite oath.

Not a moment too soon, Olaf feels death coming on and, following custom, is carried aboard his vessel which is set on fire and pushed out to sea. "He raised his arms as though in ecstasy: 'Glory! – joy! – victory!' And, like a noble tree struck down by lightning, he fell – dead."

That the reality of Norway might be different from the picture conveyed above was first mooted, at least in England, by a short article

The campaign included, for example, that Danish actors should no longer be employed on the Norwegian stage.

Henrik Johan Ibsen was born in the small town of Skien in Telemark. His father's financial indiscretions plunged the family into poverty, and Ibsen was apprenticed at an early age to a chemist in the even smaller town of Grimstad. His first poems, with titles like *Resignation*, *Doubt* and *The Corpse's Ball*, give a clue to the majestic gloom – punctuated, nevertheless by delicious wit – of his later work.

After working in the theatre in Bergen, he joined the Christiania Norske Theater (in Oslo), which had been founded to promote specifically Norwegian theatre. He fared miserably with one failure after another, poor health and no money. In the depths of depression he began to question the deplorable position of the creative artist in Norwegain society and that, ironically, put him on the road to better things. *The Pretenders*, first performed in 1864, was a great success and helped him to a travelling scholarship. He went abroad, first to Italy, and did not live in Norway again for another 27 years.

The plays for which he is best remembered were produced from about 1877 onwards. The first of these, *Pillars of Society*, broke new ground in dealing with the untruth and humbug of a small provincial town. In creating any number of great female roles, Ibsen touched on subjects that audiences and critics were not ready for. If his work was controversial at home, it was considered outrageous when eventually it travelled abroad. According to *The Daily Telegraph* in London the first overseas production of *Ghosts* was "positively abominable... a dirty act done publicly, a (lavatory) with all its doors and windows open ... gross, almost putrid indecorum ... crapulous stuff".

There were other points of view, however, like that of the essayist Havelock Ellis and of George Bernard Shaw who summarised Ibsen's importance to the English theatre with: "The Norman conquest was a mere nothing compared with the Norwegian Conquest."

While the Norwegian element in the work of the great playwright Ludvig Holberg in the previous century could hardly be told apart from the Danish, there was no ambiguity about Ibsen. As a curious footnote, however, Ibsen once wrote to a friend in England saying that "there are very strong traces in me of Scotch descent. But this is only a feeling – perhaps only a wish that it were so."

Battle of wills

Ibsen's strong sense of national identity was mirrored in the political events swirling around him. Problems within the union with Sweden came to a head in 1905 over the long-running dispute about diplomatic representation. The government wanted its own consular service; King Oskar II refused. The government then argued that, if it resigned and the king was unable to obtain an alternative government, his royal power would effectively have lapsed. It would then revert to the Storting, which would choose a new king. The Storting agreed to this plan.

Oskar was hurt and the Swedish government outraged. Neither would have been placated

by a plebiscite which showed 368,208 in favour of breaking away from Sweden and only 184 against. The "compromise" reached in 1905 was in truth a surrender to Norwegian demands: Oskar's abdication and Norwegian independence. The king's parting shot was that no member of his house would be allowed to accept the vacated throne even if it were offered. This was only in part petulance. Oskar was privately convinced that an independent Norway was bound to collapse and whoever was then king would thus be discredited. When that happened, an unsullied member of his house would, of course, be standing by to answer the call. That call was never heard. ❏

LEFT: an early picture of Oslo's Stortinget (Parliament).
RIGHT: King Oskar II.

AN INDEPENDENT MODERN COUNTRY

Invaded by Germany, then caught up in the Cold War, Norway has passed through difficult times to emerge as an international peace-broker

The Prime Minister who led Norway to independence was Christian Michelsen, a Bergen solicitor who founded one of the biggest shipping companies in Norway and was by 1903 a member of the government. In the meantime, he had formed a breakaway group in Bergen of "liberals" from the Radical Left.

Michelsen's initial modest aim was to settle the issue of whether Norway should have its own consuls abroad, which finally destroyed the union with Sweden; but by 1904 he was warning the Swedes not to assume that if negotiations failed this time, they could be resumed.

Michelsen had recognised the way Norwegian public opinion was running and the support the cause was getting from such famous Norwegians as the explorer Fridtjof Nansen (who later became Norwegian Ambassador in London) and the writer Bjørnstjerne Bjørnson. Soon Michelsen was heading a cabinet that included ministers from a wide range of parties and of many shades of opinion.

With independence established in 1905 and King Håkon VII on the throne, Michelsen quickly left the stormy waters of politics for a calmer and more profitable life in his shipping business, though he remained an active elder statesman until his death in 1925.

No foreign policy

In the long years of struggle, Bjørnson had claimed that "the foreign policy of Norway should be to have no foreign policy", and immediately after independence, the aim of all parties was to avoid entanglement in the affairs of the Great Powers. But, despite its determined neutrality, World War I had the ironic effect of throwing Norway and Sweden back into one another's arms. "A new union, not of the old sort, but a union of heartfelt understanding", was the Swedish king's description, "to maintain the neutrality of the respective kingdoms in relation to all the belligerent powers."

Norway did well out of its neutrality, at least for the first two years of the war. Germany was willing to pay top prices for all the fish Norway could supply, which attracted British attention and led to a secret agreement, backed by the threat to cut off supplies of British oil and coal, under which Britain would buy most of the fish itself. Norway, in return, would not export vital copper pyrites to Germany, but otherwise it was free to trade with both sides.

Those lucky enough to get a share of this trade, and of the domestic black market, flaunted their overnight fortunes in such a way that workers on fixed wages, which were forever falling behind rampant inflation, became rebellious. Employers retaliated with lockouts, and the government was forced to introduce compulsory arbitration.

German submarine warfare put a damper on profiteering. Most of the Norwegian merchant fleet was under charter to Britain and by the end of the war half of it, together with 2,000 crew members, was lost. In absolute terms only Britain lost more of its shipping. The intervention of the United States also made matters worse. The Americans demanded big cuts in trade with Germany before agreeing to make supplies available to Norway.

At the end of the war the neutral countries had little say in deciding the terms of peace. Despite its heavy losses the Norwegian merchant navy received no compensation in the shape of ships from the confiscated German navy, and it was 10 years before injured seamen and the families of those killed received any compensation from the German government.

THE NANSEN PASSPORT

Devised by Fridtjof Nansen, this "passport" offered those people made stateless by World War I a means of official identification.

tral countries just two months after the League was founded to seek membership.

Norway, temperamentally against alliances, was fiercely divided and it was not until 1920 that the Storting finally voted for membership of the League, Norway's first real move into internationalism. Nansen, who had been so influential in the struggle for Norwegian independence, now had international links to America, the Soviet Union and elsewhere, and became active in the League, particularly in the slow repatriation of nearly

Nansen and the League

During the war the Scandinavian monarchs had met to discuss and set up committees to review the position of neutral countries when hostilities ceased. Under Nansen, Norway formed an Association for the League of Nations and drafted a potential constitution. But, as the war ended, the great powers were not inclined to take much notice of mere neutrals. They themselves laid down the rules and allowed the neu-

PRECEDING PAGES: a factory in Christiania (Oslo) producing iron stairs (*circa* 1895).
LEFT: King Håkon VII.
ABOVE: the Royal Family with their ski instructor.

half a million prisoners-of-war from Russia. He later donated his own Nobel Peace Prize money for similar work for Russian and Armenian refugees. He was still working on this at the time of his death in 1930.

But in 1920, of the Storting's 20 votes against membership of the League of Nations, 16 came from the steadily growing Labour Party which, at the time, took most of its principles and goals from the ideas behind the Russian Revolution.

Briefly in credit

Although Norway was one of the creditor nations when the war ended, the cavalier business atmosphere of the war years carried over as financial recklessness, if not ignorance. In very short order the country was further into debt than it had so recently been in credit.

By 1921 conditions had deteriorated into a full-blown economic depression with more than a million tons of shipping laid up, free-spending local authorities in difficulty and, unthinkably to Norwegians, one of the biggest banks going bankrupt in spite of secret state support.

The rise of Labour

Storms and controversies over prohibition caused the downfall of three different cabinets. The steadily growing Labour Party became

A lock-out at Norsk Hydro produced not only the most notorious incident in the history of Norwegian industrial relations (police and troops fighting demonstrators) but also the rise to public prominence of a figure as shameful in Norwegian memory as anyone since, say, Erik Bloodaxe.

The defence minister who ordered the troops in was Vidkun Quisling, and he was soon accusing Labour of plotting an armed revolution. Quisling was largely discredited in his own country by 1939. At that time he was in Berlin for reasons that were soon to become very clear.

more revolutionary in its beliefs, and passed a resolution reserving the right to use "revolutionary action in the struggle for the economic liberation of the working classes". The point having been made, militancy declined and by the end of the decade the Party had turned its attention back to parliamentary rule. In the 1927 elections, in spite of fragmentation, it became the biggest party in the Storting.

The Wall Street crash of 1929 compounded the ecominic misery. A third of all trade unionists were already out of work when employers tried to reduce wages which, in spite of nearly a decade of economic turmoil, were still very high compared to most European countries.

By 1933, the economic crisis was so bad that the unlikely alliance of the Labour Party with the Agrarian (Farmers') Party put a Labour Prime Minister into power. He was Johan Nygaardsvold, with lengthy experience in the Storting. He was Prime Minister from 1935 with a direct responsibility for creating employment and, by 1939, the average day's wage had risen by 15 percent.

Precarious neutrality

When World War II broke out in September 1939 Norway immediately proclaimed neutrality, but had taken almost no precautions to defend itself. (Perhaps Nygaardsvold was too immersed in his economic renaissance. He remained Prime Minister until 1945 but in the recriminations and resultant inquiry that followed the end of the war, he was deemed partly to blame for not making adequate preparations for Norway's defence.)

The first warning signs came from the Allied side, with Britain complaining that its ships were being sunk by Germany in Norwegian territorial waters. Furthermore, German ships were being given free access to strategic iron-ore from the northern port of Narvik. The

UNPREPARED

When World War II broke out, Norway called up just 7,000 men and its coastal defences were only half-manned.

the men while two small Norwegian vessels looked on, making vain protests. The Norwegian government complained to Britain about violation of its neutrality. The British government asked why Norway had been unable to prevent German abuse of its neutral waters, and Germany posed the same question, but the other way round.

Invasion by sea

Britain unilaterally began laying its own mines along the Norwegian coastline and, on the very

ancient Norwegian fleet was in no position to keep territorial waters neutral, so the British suggested mining them.

The dilemma was highlighted by the well-known *Altmark* affair. The *Altmark*, an auxiliary to the battleship *Graf Spee*, was on its way to Germany with 300 captured British seamen when it sought refuge in Norwegian waters near Egersund. The Royal Navy was alerted to its presence and charged into the fjord to rescue

---

LEFT: the meeting between Vidkun Quisling and Adolf Hitler prior to World War II.

ABOVE LEFT: strategic map from World War II.

ABOVE RIGHT: the struggle for Narvik, 1941.

day Norway lodged a protest – 8 April 1940 –German forces were on the high seas bound for Norway. Once the invasion was under way, the German minister in Oslo sent a note to say that Germany was only occupying a few strategic points to keep the British out.

At last the Norwegian government woke up to what was going on. The German heavy cruiser *Blücher* was sunk by the Oscarsborg fortress in the Oslo fjord near Drøbak, and two creaking Norwegian destroyers boldly took on a much larger German force at Narvik.

The Storting granted the government full powers "to take whatever decisions might be necessary to ensure the best interests of the

The Heroes of Telemark

The most celebrated act of resistance in Norway during World War II was the sabotage of the Vemork heavy water plant at Rjukan, in Telemark, in February 1943. No visitor to Rjukan, dwarfed and darkened by mountains all round, could fail to be awed by the audacity of the saboteurs. More importantly, the production of heavy water in the plant, if it had not been stopped, could conceivably have given Hitler the atomic bomb.

The operation was originally planned for a joint force of Norwegian volunteers and British commandos in two towed gliders. It ended disastrously when both gliders and one of the aircraft towing them crashed 160 km (100 miles) from Rjukan.

The second attempt was an all-Norwegian affair. "Gunnerside", the code name for six men who had been trained in Scotland, parachuted on to a frozen lake where they were supposed to join up with "Swallow", an advance party on the ground. The first person they bumped into was a reindeer hunter. He was later released with food and money on the promise that he would reveal nothing.

Once the parties had linked up, they skied to the ridge above Rjukan for the perilous descent on

foot. They slithered down, up to their waists in snow. Just after midnight, the covering party took up positions while the six-man demolition team cut a chain on the gates and crept forward to the basement of the concrete building where the most vital equipment and the heavy water storage tanks were located. All wore British uniforms and were agreed that no lights would be carried; weapons would be unloaded to avoid the accidental discharge of arms and anyone captured would take his own life.

As the basement was locked, the best way in appeared to be a funnel carrying cables and piping. Two went through it. The solitary Norwegian guard was astonished but agreed to lead them to vital components. "I had placed half the charges in position when there was a crash of broken glass behind me", one of the pair wrote later. The other members of the team, not realising that their leaders had managed to get in, had decided to smash in through a window. With the rest of the charges laid, the six began a rapid withdrawal. They were nonplussed by the co-operative guard who, understandably getting out as well while the going was good, implored to be let in again. He had forgotten his glasses! The request was granted, but the delay meant that the party had only gone a few yards when there was what members later variously described as "a cataclysmic explosion" and "a tiny, insignificant pop".

Five members of the parachute team reached Sweden after a 400-km (250-mile) journey on skis in indescribably difficult conditions; the sixth stayed on for another year. Of the Swallow party, an irrepressible character named Claus Helberg had the liveliest time. He was chased through the mountains by a German soldier who was evidently an expert skier but, luckily for Helberg, a poor shot. Having killed the German, he almost immediately fell over a cliff and broke an arm. The next morning he walked Into a German patrol but had a good enough story to be taken to a hotel to await treatment. Most of the hotel guests (but not the injured Norwegian) were turned out of their rooms to make way for Reichskommissar Terboven (the Nazi who ruled Norway) and his entourage. Later, and through no fault of his own, he was bundled along with the remaining guests "into a bus and sent off to the Grini concentration camp". Helberg jumped from the bus and escaped. In due course he turned up in Britain, reporting for further duties. ❑

LEFT: Kirk Douglas in the film *The Heroes of Telemark*.

country", the point on which many a debate would later hinge. On 10 April the Germans showed their hand. Quisling, whose National Unity party commanded all of 1.8 percent of the electorate, was their choice as new prime minister. The government, which had moved itself from Oslo to Trysil, repeatedly refused to comply, and its defiance was repaid with a German bombing attack on the meeting place.

Norway's only hope against such lopsided odds lay in the Allies. From Britain's point of view, Narvik was the key because of the iron-ore traffic. The Royal Navy went into action against German naval units in the area and destroyed them. A combined force of Norwegians, British, French and Poles fought to regain control of the city itself and on 28 May succeeded in doing so.

Earlier, on 14 and 15 April, other Allied troops had landed near Trondheim. They were joined by small Norwegian units. They put up a plucky fight but, practically without any air cover against the Luftwaffe, took a pasting from above. Towns where there was a British presence were bombed to ruin: Åndalsnes, Namsos, Steinkjer and Mosjøen. The fight for Norway was overshadowed, however, by the German steamroller in western Europe and, with what were seen to be greater needs there, the Allied forces withdrew, leaving Norway alone.

The king and government, evacuated to the north and ready to fight on, decided that the best course of action was to decamp to Britain. On 7 June 1940 they boarded a British cruiser.

Reprisals begin

A Nazi, Josef Terboven, was despatched to Norway as Reichskommissar. Quisling was appalled; he had expected to be appointed Führer, in which capacity he would then conclude peace with Germany and mobilise Norwegian forces on its side. Terboven had little time for Quisling, but the latter had friends in Berlin who arranged to have him appointed "Minister President". As such, Quisling ordered all children between the ages of 10 and 18 to join his version of the Hitler Youth. His plans

> ### THE "SHETLAND BUS"
>
> The old Viking character was alive in the small boats that regularly made the crossing between Shetland and Norway, keeping links open with the exiled king and government in Britain.

for the Nazification of the civil service, courts, all professional bodies and trade unions were in every instance fiercely rejected.

Resistance met with grim reprisals. Two trade union leaders, Viggo Hansteen and Rolf Wickstrøm, were shot; the rector of Oslo University was arrested. A steady flow of prisoners, including 1,300 uncooperative teachers, arrived at Grini, the concentration camp established outside Oslo. The most summary reprisals were meted out to members of the

military underground, Milorg, a nucleus of survivors of the 1940 fighting augmented by volunteers and armed by clandestine shipments from Britain.

Telavåg, a village near Bergen, was razed to the ground when the German's discovered it to be an assembly point for a clandestine ferry service, the "Shetland Bus", between Norway and Britain. The men of the village were deported to Germany, the women and children interned. A group of 18 men waiting in Ålesund for the trip to Britain were found and shot.

The most famous of the resistance operations was conducted against the heavy water factory at Rjukan in Telemark.

RIGHT: Vidkun Quisling inspecting German troops in Berlin.

Celebration party

The final chapter of the Occupation was played out by German troops retreating from Finland through Finnmark in northern Norway. They adopted a scorched-earth policy which utterly destroyed many towns and villages. The inhabitants were herded into fishing boats to find their own way to the south.

The Germans were still very strong in Norway while their forces elsewhere capitulated – the army alone numbered 350,000. Fears that the whole country might be put to the torch were laid to rest only when they surrendered on 7 May 1945. The gates of Grini were thrown

destroyed during the war, and to modernise and expand industry and the economy. The whole of northern Norway had been so heavily devastated that in some cases traces of hasty rebuilding are only now being replaced, and many of the small northern towns still have an austere anonymity.

Rising standards

Fast economic expansion and many crash programmes led to large investment and overemployment, but it provided a rising standard of living that climbed faster and farther than most countries in Europe. By the early 1960s

open and thousands streamed out to join what was undoubtedly the biggest street party ever held in Oslo. It was still going strong a week later when Crown Prince Olav returned, five years to the day of his reluctant departure.

Cleaning up after the war concentrated on Quisling's prosecution. Charges were brought against 50,000, many for petty crimes rather than full-scale collaboration. The courts were not unduly harsh, perhaps sensing that participation in Quisling's so-called "NS" would remain a stigma. Only 25 were executed, including Quisling and two of his ministers.

After that necessary purging, Norway's greatest needs were to replace what had been

Norway used more electricity per head than any other country in the world and only three people in every thousand in remote areas had no supply. The mercantile marine had made good its wartime shipping losses by 1949 and tonnage tripled within 15 years. By the 1970s Norway was almost overwhelmed by the riches it was receiving from the oil industry.

All this went along with 20 years of Socialist government, which introduced comprehensive social welfare services, Scandinavian style, and much state control of industry. But this was no far-left Labour Party in the style of its post-World War I predecessors, and many shared its belief in an equal society and care for all.

In keeping with similar parties in Sweden and Denmark, post-war Norwegian socialism has been middle-of-the-road, led first by Einar Gerhardsen, who had been a prominent Resistance worker, then Oscar Torp, and Trygve Brattel. In recent years, the best known Norwegian prime minister, ranking high in international esteem, has been Gro Harlem Brundtland. She was appointed Prime Minister for the time in 1981. At 41, she was the youngest person ever to hold the office, and the first woman. In total, she held the post for

BRUNTLAND REPORT

Norway's Gro Harlem Brundtland was responsible for "Our Common Future", the United Nations' report on world environmental issues.

International links

In 1945 Norway was one of the founding signatories of the United Nations, and a former Norwegian Foreign Minister, Trygve Lie, became its first secretary-general. Lie held the office during the first hopeful years and continued to do so into the Korean War, in which United Nation troops took an active fighting role for the first and last time. Norway provided and staffed a field hospital in Korea. Since then some 32,000 Norwegians have worn a UN blue beret.

more than 10 years before finally deciding to step down in 1996. In 1998 she became Director-General of the World Health Organization.

The attitude of King Olav V, who reigned between 1957 and 1991, also helped to keep Norway tranquil. King Olav took his father's motto of "All for Norway". When he died in 1991 his son Harald V succeeded him to the throne. Like his father, he is interested in sports and equally liked by his people.

LEFT: Crown Prince Olav (later King Olav V) returns to Norway at the end of the war.
ABOVE: for years Lenin's likeness looked across the border from Russia.

Norway has continued its commitment to internationalism and peace, notably as broker in the 1993 Israeli-Palestinian peace proposals. Like the other Scandinavian nations, it has concentrated very much on human rights, humanitarian help and environmental issues.

Joining NATO, however, was more problematic. Norway saw its role as bridging the Cold War divide, and the country had no particular reason to fear its Russian neighbour. Unlike neighbouring Sweden, Norway had never been at war with Russia. The Russians had recently acted as liberators in Finnmark, and the two countries were, in fact, negotiating joint occupation of Spitsbergen.

Nevertheless, for most of the war years Trygve Lie had been advocating an alliance with the great Atlantic Powers for his "seafaring people", rather than with any power in Europe. The fate of Czechoslovakia, a country which also saw itself as a bridge-builder until the Iron Curtain came down behind it, convinced the doubters that Norway's security depended on more tangible Western links than would be afforded by Swedish-style neutrality.

As NATO's most northeasterly outpost, with a short 196-km (122-mile) border with Russia, Norway inevitably walked a tightrope between the super powers. Soviet "merchant ships" vis-

ited the northern sea coast and unaccountably needed lengthy, unspecified repairs which kept them in harbour for months. Ships of the Soviet Northern Fleet, based on the Kola peninsula, were a common sight in the North Atlantic when crossing to Iceland. But there was never any major incidents, and, long before *glasnost*, Norway turned a philosophical face to its massive neighbour. Since the break-up of the Soviet Union, Norway has been more concerned about the environmental threat presented by out-dated nickel works, unsafe nuclear power stations, and nuclear waste from decommissioned submarines and other vessels of the former Soviet Northern Fleet.

Maintaining independence

The debate over whether to join the European Community aroused great passions, especially among farmers and fishermen who were convinced that membership would terminate their subsidies. The Storting was generally in favour of applying for membership along with Denmark and Britain, partners in the European Free Trade Association (EFTA), but the first approaches were rebuffed by an imperious General Charles de Gaulle.

A referendum was organised in 1972 to gauge public opinion on whether another attempt ought to be made. There was never any doubting where the farmers and rural Norway as a whole would stand. In the event, the country opposed joining by a vote of 52.5 percent.

In 1993 the anti-European Centre Party of farmers gained ground but not enough to stop Gro Harlem Brundtland taking the Labour Party back to power. Sweden and Finland having voted to join Denmark in the European Union, she felt confident enough to hold another referendum on membership in 1994, warning that, with oil and gas revenues rapidly declining, Norway could no longer afford to stay out in the cold. But again the country voted no, by almost the same margin as in 1972. Having been ruled by Denmark, Sweden and the Nazis, Norwegians seemed determined to hang on to every shred of their hard-won independence.

Although the opposite sides of the 1994 EU debate were very unyielding, the situation normalised fairly quickly once the vote was over. The Centre Party continued to fight after the vote against "continuous EU accommodation", but this did not prevent the party from suffering considerable setbacks in local elections in 1995 and in the general election in 1997. A reassuring factor for many has certainly been Gro Harlem Brundtland's statement to the effect that Norway will not be likely to attempt new EU membership negotiations before the start of the new millennium.

Another important factor is that the Agreement on the European Economic Area (EEA), signed by the EU and EFTA countries in 1992, ensures Norwegian participation in the future of the EEA, gives it access to the EU market and opens the door to further co-operation. ❏

LEFT: Mother Teresa receiving the Nobel Peace Prize in 1979.

Norway and its Neighbours

I f you walked into a room and met three Scandinavians, it would be hard to tell which was the Norwegian, which the Dane and which the Swede. They look alike, have similar interests, and seem to speak the same language, even if the accent is somewhat different.

The written languages, all based on Old Norse, are so similar they are easily understood by all, and Scandinavian Air Service, the airline shared by the three countries, solves communication problems by allowing its crews to use their own language. This works well when a crew is Norwegian, but less well with Danes and Swedes who sometimes find each other incomprehensible.

This Scandinavian family is often taken to include Finland, though the Finns are of a different race with a language related to Hungarian – and that only marginally. In any event, all four countries are part of the Nordic group, which includes Iceland, the autonomous territories of the Faroes, Greenland and the Åland Islands in the Gulf of Bothnia.

Like all families, Scandinavians have the usual squabbles, jealousies, misunderstandings and false images of one another that come out of close proximity. To other Scandinavians, Norwegians are "blue-eyed" or naive, often the butt of innocuous jokes, yet both Swedes and Danes are astonished to learn that similar jokes are told by Norwegians against them. The family analogy continues in that the Danes tend to look on Norway as a younger brother, with all that that implies.

Sweden, with which Norway shares a 1,700-km (1,000-mile) border, is often looked on by Norway (and to a lesser extent by Denmark) as an elder brother, with allegations of arrogance and insensitivity from the smaller countries and a tendency for the larger to think it "knows best". But since Norway discovered oil in 1969, the big-brother attitude has taken a knock, and left Sweden looking at Norway with a degree of wonder and envy. The image of Norway as the junior partner is partly due to the fact that, after 500 years ruled first by Denmark then Sweden, the present Norwegian state is less than a century old, though Norway has been a nation for as long as any Scandinavian country.

RIGHT: conscripts undergoing winter training in the far north of the country.

Norway's only non-Nordic neighbour is Russia. The two countries co-exist without much friction on Spitsbergen (Svalbard), the remote northern islands, best known for coal, bird and plant life, and the sealers and whalers of former days.

In the days of the Soviet Union they were at odds over their joint border in the far northern Barents Sea, where the two countries are face to face on a dividing line more than 1,700 km (1,000 miles) long. Norway favours a border on the median line equidistant between the two countries, but their Russian neighbours have wanted to adopt a sector principle. The area under dispute is as big as Belgium, Switzerland and Austria combined, and the

Russian proposals would give Russia control of larger fish stocks and oil reserves.

During World War II, when only Sweden was neutral, the Scandinavian countries did their best to help one another, although neither Norway nor Sweden has yet managed to forget that Sweden allowed German troops to pass through its country on their way to attack Norway. Many Finnish children left for homes in Sweden, and that country also became an escape route from Norway. At the end of the war, Norway, Denmark and Iceland became members of NATO, Sweden continued to be non-aligned, and Finland (stuck in an uneasy position between the eastern and western blocs) declared itself neutral. ❑

WHO ARE THE NORWEGIANS?

Ask a visitor what defines a Norwegian and you might get a general description of a Scandinavian. While some of the stereotypes ring true, differences abound

One character in a Hans Christian Andersen story proclaims: "I'm a Norwegian. And when I say I'm Norwegian, I think I've said enough. I'm as firm in my foundations as the ancient mountains of old Norway... It thrills me to the marrow to think what I am, and let my thoughts ring out in words of granite."

Andersen was, of course, a Dane, and he was teasing the Norwegians, as their Scandinavian neighbours are apt to do. In much the same way as Italians are satirically reduced to being tearful opera and ice cream fiends, and Frenchmen become obtuse philosophers in onion necklaces, so the typical Norwegian is portrayed as a simple, stubborn peasant who from time to time needs a comforting pat on the head. The country's refusal, in 1972 and again in 1994, to join other Scandinavian countries in the European Union confirmed this view to many.

Naturally enough, Norwegians see themselves rather differently. A Gallup poll once asked 200 people from each of 12 countries to rank themselves in terms of culture, food, living standards, beauty, *joie de vivre*, and national pride. The Norwegians gave themselves top marks in virtually every category. This sweeping victory for the home side was surpassed only by the conceit of the American entry.

Generous hospitality

The Norwegian character is of course far more complex than Andersen would allow or Gallup could measure. It is sometimes said that Norwegians are xenophobic. While this may be an exaggeration, it is certainly the case that they do not accept outside criticism. Yet the hospitality shown towards foreign visitors far exceeds the demands of mere good manners. An English visitor arriving late was whisked off spontaneously to a wedding party in Oslo. As the only foreigner among 200 guests, he was dis-

armed when the bride's father, advised of his surprise presence, gave away his daughter in English. Although the younger Norwegian guests were, as usual, fluent in English, some older ones were left in the dark, but they thoroughly approved of the gesture.

The same English visitor, immobilised by

skis around his neck after capsizing on a narrow cross-country ski trail, brought down a party of local skiers who descended on him too fast and too late to stop. The victims of this pile-up were disgruntled until they made sense of his choked apologies, in English of course, at which point they tried to make him feel that, in the circumstances, the violent introduction was an unexpected pleasure, not to say privilege.

Other signs of welcome are given without thinking. A visitor in the house is the signal for lighting candles, probably a throwback to the days when, compounded by the long hours of winter darkness, houses shuttered against the cold were rather gloomy. Until quite recently,

---

PRECEDING PAGES: 17 May, National Day; fishermen at Verdens Ende; Royal Palace guards.
LEFT: a passion for sport.
ABOVE RIGHT: shopping on Karl Johans gate, Oslo.

most of Norway's population was thinly scattered across a vast landscape in a patchwork of tiny communities, so visitors invariably arrived after a long and exhausting journey, sometimes on skis. The assumption was that they arrived hungry, and restorative food and drink still appear as if by magic. A planned meal for guests requires elaborate place-settings, and includes food that bears little resemblance to the normal low-calorie diet of everyday life.

Visitors will not be allowed to leave without a tour of the house and a look at the family album. The Norwegians are attentive hosts who

the experience. One of the themes running through Ibsen's work is the double-edged nature of life in such a community: mutual support in adversity weighed against a suffocating lack of privacy at other times.

The lesser-known Aksel Sandemose wrote Ten Commandments for village life, the essence being humility bordering on self-abasement. They included: "You must not think that you are worth anything; you must not think that you are better than anyone else; you must not think yourself capable of anything worthwhile; and you must not think that you are in any way exceptional."

expect very little in return – common courtesy, and some appreciative comments about their warm welcome as well as the tasteful interior decoration of the house. Norway's vaunted standard of living is a relatively recent phenomenon, thanks mainly to a prosperous offshore oil industry.

Critical eye

The more enigmatic aspects of the Norwegian psyche – including the Nordic gloom which descends after a drink too many – have been famously scrutinised by a native, Henrik Ibsen. He was brought up in small communities and, during a long exile, turned his critical eye on

Jingoistic chest pounding of the sort noted by Hans Christian Andersen is derived to some extent from Norway's peculiar position as both one of the oldest, if not the oldest, nation in Europe and at the same time one of the youngest. It is the oldest in the sense that the Norwegians can trace an unbroken line of descent from people who inhabited their territory in prehistoric times, a homogeneity whose origins antedate the beginnings of Western civilisation in the Aegean.

Yet the present state of Norway was reconstituted only in 1905, which makes it younger than many of the junior members in the United Nations, themselves pasted together by the imperial powers in the 19th century. Having been relegated to a back seat in Scandinavian affairs for hundreds of years, these distant descendants of the illustrious Vikings need to pinch themselves – or blow a trumpet – as if they nervously expect to wake up and discover that their independence was a cruel dream.

Norwegians enjoy amazing longevity. They manage to look remarkably healthy all their lives, and the octogenarian grandmother whizzing by on skis is not a myth.

FLAG HAPPY

Many houses have flagpoles and every household possesses a flag which is hoisted on the slightest pretext, if only to indicate that the owner is in residence.

eign waters, relegating it to no more than a patch on a much larger Swedish flag. The flag flown on Norwegian shipping was, like separate consular representation and the establishment of a national bank, a perennial bone of contention before independence.

Norwegians would be distressed at the thought of their revered flag being desecrated as a pair of underpants or on shopping bags. Their dignity as a sovereign state is not to be trivialised. The Swedish king who reluctantly oversaw Norway's independence

In any case, there are Norwegians alive who can remember, or have had drummed into them, the euphoria of liberation from their domineering Scandinavian partners.

Free to show the flag

Well-deserved national pride makes Norwegians ardent flag-wavers. This could be construed as a rude gesture to the Swedes who, under the union, decided when, where and how the Norwegian colours were to be shown in for-

---

FAR LEFT: still cutting the grass by hand at 89.
LEFT: a great-grandmother with her 19th grandchild.
ABOVE: enjoying the September sun.

predicted that bureaucratic incompetence would soon have Norwegians begging to be returned to the fold. The response, even now, is a reluctance to admit (to outsiders) that they are capable of making a mistake, as if to do so would vindicate the Swedish king.

As long as authority was vested in foreigners, Norwegians did not regard it too highly. On assuming it themselves, however, authority was allowed to assume the aura of divine right, before which loyal citizens should willingly prostrate themselves.

Norwegian history is full of swings from one extreme to another. Pagans who held out against Christianity until a surprisingly late date became, and in some cases remain, doggedly fundamentalist after seeing the light. A nation which was once thought to be in danger of drinking itself to death has by no means buried the bottle. Drinking alcohol is now restricted mainly to the weekend and Alcoholics Anonymous are not the only ones to welcome austere state measures.

Visitors sampling the state television service might wonder, too, at the litany of self-congratulation in almost daily items about the excellence of the health and welfare services. Programmes about children – for example, choirs singing carols at Christmas – are bound

If proved, the evidence would be difficult to swallow, as it was when statistics revealed that suicides had overtaken the number of traffic deaths in a certain period. Was that not, an apologist ventured, excellent proof of road safety standards?

The Norwegian language(s)

In contrast with these examples of mild paranoia, Norwegians can be remarkably robust where they might be expected to be most sensitive. There is no alarm about the predatory impact of, say, satellite television on a language which hardly exists outside Norway. Far from

to include an unrealistic proportion of Third World immigrants. The way the camera seeks out and locks on to black, brown or yellow faces, possibly in difficulty with unfamiliar tunes and words, seems a rather contrived message to the effect that Norway can show the world a thing or two about liberal decency. This is a role which many are pleased to play; appeals for money by international relief agencies are always met with astonishing generosity, and the country spends more per capita on foreign aid than any other in the West.

Such open-handedness has inevitably attracted abuse, and questions are increasingly asked about the real credentials of political "refugees".

resenting visitors who presume to address them in a foreign language, Norwegians positively relish the challenge, and usually respond with considerable fluency.

Confidence in the hardiness of their language is curiously at odds with the historical background. Language was a burning issue in Norwegian politics until the 1950s, having forced a prime minister to resign in 1912. The long-running controversy started as a form of agitation against Danish rule, throughout which Danish was the language of the civil service, schools and the Church. For a long time after the Reformation the revised Bible was available only in Danish, as were all the new hymns. Denmark got its first printing press in 1480 but Norway had to wait until 1643. Until then books were imported and in Danish.

When reading aloud, Norwegians modified standard Danish through the use of their own pronunciation and intonation. This mixture eventually produced a hybrid known as *bokmål* (book language).

The search for a native language

The 19th-century nationalists still saw it as fundamentally Danish, however, and wanted a national language which was authentically Norwegian. Unfortunately, there was no single

the theatre, and if Norwegian had to be spoken, a Danicised pronunciation was fashionable. These tendencies eroded as intellectuals like Ibsen lent respectability to the campaign for the revivification of a purely Norwegian language.

In 1929 *bokmål* and *nynorsk* were recognised as dual official languages, the hope being that they would drift towards a blend which would be known as *samnorsk*. The names of cities and towns lost their Danish connotations. Christiania, for example, reverted to a good old Norwegian name, Oslo. The reformers also tackled the habit of referring to the number 25 as "five-and-twenty". It became "twenty five".

Norwegian substitute, because the language had developed many distinct dialects. Rather than choose one dialect at the expense of the others, the language reformers concentrated on developing a composite.

The early language reformers included Ivar Aasen and Knut Knudsen, the latter a schoolmaster driven by his pupils' frustration in trying to work out Danish spelling. They worked on what became known as *landsmål* or *nynorsk*, but their efforts were not unreservedly welcomed. Danish was the language of society and

LEFT: winter skiing in the Nordmarka.
ABOVE: summer on a Telemark beach.

Progress towards *samnorsk* was given a nudge in the 1950s with a proposal to have school textbooks converted into it. There was such an outcry, however, that the government backed down. Subsequent policy has been to treat the two languages even-handedly, still hoping that they will one day converge. In spite of attempts to shore up *nynorsk* through radio and television, it looks as if it is losing ground.

Individualistic tongue

Educated speech is distinctly that of the southeast, although that does not prevent country dwellers on a visit to the capital, say, from laying on their regional accents thick for effect.

The Bergensere (people from Bergen), at the heart of the *nynorsk* area, are certainly proud of their individualistic tongue.

The regional fragmentation at the heart of the language debate extends to most facets of cultural and economic life. While Norway has since Viking times been a single nation, it has been a confederation of many parts. Norway can be divided north–south, east–west or a dozen different ways. Like the Renaissance, the Industrial Revolution hardly intruded, so there was not the rapid urbanisation which occurred elsewhere. Trondheim, Bergen and Oslo were towns rather than cities. A later creation like

Stavanger owed its existence to the arrival of vast shoals of herring, which were the basis of jobs, trade and other prerequisites of a cash economy. Most of Norway remained rooted in subsistence agriculture.

Preserving old necessities

Rural families tended to be isolated and self-sufficient. Their lives depended on agriculture, and the land was not good enough to support more than a family or two in a single valley. Separated from their neighbours by mountains which were ironically easier to cross in winter (on skis) than in summer, they effectively lived in worlds apart. There were hardly any villages

where tradesmen could be found and paid in cash. The versatile family managed on its own, a resourcefulness which still runs in the blood. It is not unknown for young couples living in Oslo today to solicit the help of friends to build their first home with their own hands.

The modern Norwegian makes a virtue out of what used to be necessity. The ideal *hytte*, as a country cabin is known, is isolated. It will probably have electricity, but running water may be considered effete. Visitors who decide, sensibly, to rent a *hytte* will almost certainly come round to the view that water drawn from a stream is not merely an exercise in rural nostalgia but also doubly delicious. In winter there is the added joy of first having to drill a hole through the ice to reach it.

Messing about in boats

The old necessities carry over to the passion for owning a boat. On summer evenings, Oslo fjord is alive with boats, a pattern repeated everywhere. Although Norwegians are said to grow up on skis, messing about in boats is equally ingrained. Both used to represent basic transport in a land where road and rail construction costs billions because of the mountainous terrain and deep fjords. Although the country is now well served in both departments, the boat was once both a tool of daily life as well as a source of recreation.

Modern Norway has the reputation of being an enlightened, progressive state on the Scandinavian model, but it does Norwegians no disservice to recognise the Viking beneath. A man found sitting in a hole on the snowbound Oslo golf course said with a twinkle that his ancestors had devised a system of digging holes which, taking into account the direction of the wind, provided an emergency – and actually quite comfortable – refuge in the event of snowstorms. He felt he was doing his bit, preserving some of his heritage for posterity. He put his palms to his temples and waggled his outstretched fingers.

That the Vikings wore horns is doubtful, if not an outright fallacy, but only the most churlish observer would wish to deny someone who saw sport in sitting in a hole in the snow a certain degree of historical licence. ❑

LEFT: at the end of a day on the fjord.
RIGHT: traditional *bunads* worn for church on Sunday.

EPIC EXPLORERS

Whether because of exile, scientific exploration, or wanting to be the first,
Norwegian explorers have travelled the world from North to South Pole

Although exploration is most often associated in modern times with rocket journeys into space, the names of at least two Norwegian explorers are as evocative now as at the time of their epic achievements: Roald Amundsen (1861–1930) is forever remembered as the man who beat Captain Scott to the South Pole; and Thor Heyerdahl (born 1914) for the *Kon-Tiki* expedition.

Their fame steals some of the limelight which ought to be apportioned to a much larger cast of intrepid Norwegians, beginning with Bjarni Herjulfsson who, in 986, lost his way while sailing from Iceland to Greenland and ended up, according to an ancient saga, as the first European to sight the American continent. On Bjarni's return, Leiv Eiriksson borrowed his boat to investigate the mysterious sighting and became the first European to set foot on the American continent.

Early migrations

A 19th-century Norwegian explorer, Fridtjof Nansen (1861–1930), set the pattern for the investigation of human migration. He established his reputation in 1888 with a hazardous crossing of Greenland from east to west. A few years later he was excited by the discovery near the southern tip of Greenland of some wreckage whose origins were traced to the New Siberian Islands. How had it got there?

Nansen determined to find out. His vessel, *Fram*, was designed to lift herself under the crushing pressure of the drift ice in the Arctic Ocean. She was set adrift off the New Siberian Islands in September 1893 and, two years later, emerged near Spitsbergen – but without Nansen. He had left the ship in charge of his second-in-command in a heroic but vain attempt to reach the North Pole with dog-drawn sledges. He and his companion survived a win-

ter in Franz Josef Land, living in an ice hut and eating whatever they could shoot. They reached safety on practically the same day as *Fram*, and Nansen's six volumes of findings are the basis of the science of oceanography.

Such was Nansen's fame that, when war threatened between Norway and Sweden over

the dissolution of their union, he was sent to London and Copenhagen to win support for the Norwegian cause.

The purpose of the 1947 *Kon-Tiki* expedition was to test a theory about the origins of the Polynesian people and culture. Heyerdahl demonstrated that a balsawood raft set adrift off the coast of Peru could eventually – it took him about four months – reach the Tuamotu archipelago 8,000 km (5,000 miles) to the west. In the 1960s he successfully conducted a similar experiment – the *Ra* expedition – in this instance to discover whether West African voyagers using their traditional rafts might have reached the West Indies before Columbus.

PRECEDING PAGES: the *Fram* stuck fast in the Arctic ice.
LEFT: Hanssen, one of Amundsen's expedition members to the South Pole, next to the flag.
RIGHT: Roald Amundsen.

Viking explorers

The father of Norwegian exploration, or at least the earliest recorded explorer, is Erik the Red, a man who seems to have had a liking for slaughter. In the 10th century he was banished from Norway to Iceland for murder, and then from Iceland as well for several more killings. Unwelcome anywhere, he sailed west with a shipload of livestock and discovered the world's largest island – a lump of ice, more than three kilometres (two miles) thick in places.

Obviously a keen angler, Erik was so engrossed by the excellent catches to be had in summer that he neglected to collect enough ani-

and in every respect a temperate, fair-dealing man", which would seem to set him apart from his father. His 35-man expedition left Greenland about the year 1000. They landed first at "Markland", a wooded region on the coast of Labrador, and then continued south to "Vinland".

An inscription on a map probably drawn by a monk in Basel in 1440 – about half a century before Columbus sailed to the New World – describes Leiv Eiriksson's discovery of "a new land, extremely fertile, and even having vines… a truly vast and very rich land". Attempts to settle the land were defeated by the hostile natives.

mal fodder for the winter. His livestock starved to death. He resolved to risk violation of his ostracism to collect replacements from Iceland and to persuade others to join his return. Erik trumpeted his new-found land with the zeal of an unprincipled estate agent. It was so wonderful, he told his audiences, that he had decided to call it Greenland. By 985 he had acquired animals and enticed enough colonisers to fill 25 ships, of which 14 reached the destination.

It was in one of the settlements founded by Erik the Red that his son, Leiv, having heard Bjarni Herjulfsson's strange tale, prepared to find out for himself what it was all about. He was "big and strong, of striking appearance,

American proof

Certainly the existence of "Vinland" was known to Adam of Bremen, a chronicler in the 1070s, and to writers of the sagas, but it was through a typically bizarre quirk of archaeology that Eiriksson's discovery of America is put virtually beyond doubt. Excavations on the site of a Greenland farm which belonged to a member of the "Vinland" expedition produced a lump of coal which proved to be anthracite, a material unobtainable in Greenland but plentiful on the surface in Rhode Island.

The case was strengthened in 1960 by Helge Ingstad, who thought about the likely landing place on the American continent of an expedition from Greenland. Working like a detective, he backed a hunch and at L'anse aux Meadows, on the northern tip of Newfoundland, discovered that six buildings had once stood on the site. Carbon dating proved they were medieval, and the archaeological remains left no doubt that the occupants had been Norsemen.

Race for the Pole

Roald Amundsen had served a rigorous apprenticeship for his famous assault on the South Pole, which came about as a last-minute change

NORTH TO SOUTH

Børge Ousland was the fist man to reach both the North (1994) and South (1995) Poles alone on skis without the help of man or beast.

pipped him to the post, he secretly went south instead in Nansen's old ship, *Fram*. But not until he reached Madeira did he let anyone know what his intentions were.

Amundsen decided to dispense with all scientific work in his sprint to the South Pole. Scott had a head start but discovered too late that his Siberian ponies were useless in the conditions. He and his team had to pull their sledges. Amundsen took a shorter, rougher route and had the benefit of dog teams. In the event, he beat Scott by a month.

of plans. Although he had taken part in a Belgian expedition to Antarctica his first interest was the Arctic. He was stuck for two years off King William Island in a seal-hunting boat, *Gjøa*, and applied his time to studying the Innuit inhabitants and making reckonings on the magnetic pole.

Amundsen knew about Captain Scott's ambitions to reach the South Pole but he himself was more concerned in reaching the North. Nevertheless, faced with the shattering disappointment of the news that Robert Peary had

The dispirited English team perished on their return, and this unlucky fate took some of the lustre off Amundsen's feat. At last, though, the director of London's Royal Geographical Society, which had backed Scott, paid tribute to Amundsen's effort as "the most successful polar journey on record".

To the overwhelmingly male-dominated ranks of Norwegian "explorers" it is refreshing to add the names of Liv Arnesen (born 1953), who, in 1994, was the first woman to reach the South Pole alone, and Monika Kristensen (born 1950) who led a South Pole expedition in 1986–87, following the footsteps of Roald Amundsen. ❑

LEFT: Thor Heyerdahl's *Ra* under construction in Egypt.
ABOVE: Monika Kristensen.

FOLKLORE: SAGAS AND FOLKTALES

Among the treasures of Norwegian heritage are its legends and sagas. This form of popular story-telling is an important part of the national psyche

The Norwegian word for folktale, "*eventyr*", crops us as early as the 12th century in the form "*ævintyr*", borrowed from the Latin word "*adventura*", meaning event or strange occurrence. These folktales were imaginative stories passed from storyteller to storyteller, and depicted relationships expressed in fantastic and symbolic terms. Narrators were often clergymen who used folklore as a moralistic vehicle. The folktale style was, above all, objective: however fantastic the subject, the narrative was always realistic and believable.

COUNTRY LEGENDS

A constant topic in Norwegian legend is its landscape. Many of the stories connected with the sea involved mythical creatures, the best known of which are the Lake Mjøsa monster and Draugen, the personification of all who have died at sea. In lakes and rivers lives the sprite Nøkken (*Nixie*). Many mythical creatures inhabit the mountains and forests, and tales about landmarks created by trolls exist all over the country. Marks left by trolls show their size, such as the Giant Cut (Jutul-hogget) in Østerdal.

▽ **PAGAN RELIGION**
Lom stave church in Gudbrandsdal, dating from around 1200, is decorated with carved dragons and fantasy creatures entwined with tendrils of vine.

◁ **TROLLS**
The immoral troll's ambition is to wield power over mortals, but they are stupid and easily duped.

△ **THE GOLDEN BIRD**
Theodor Kittelsen's illustration of a Norwegian folktale, *The Golden Bird*, is from the collection of legends and sagas by Asbjørnsen and Moe.

◁ **CHRISTMAS CHARACTER**
The Norwegian version of Santa Claus, *Julenissen*, is a mixture of the Nordic *nisse* (the mischievous gnome) and St Nicholas.

▽ **MYTHS AND MONSTERS**
Stories about fantastical beasts form the largest group of Norwegian folktales. They often lurk in bottomless lakes and terrorise the forest.

◁ **BRONZE AGE TOTEMS**
The Bronze Age rock carvings at Leirfall (Lerfald), near Hegra include totemic figures depicting pagan rituals linked to hunting seasons.

▷ **ANCIENT GRAFFITI**
The prehistoric rock carvings (*c.* 4500 BC) on the Lista peninsula indicate early ship building skills and a sea-faring culture.

THE GOLDEN AGE OF LITERATURE

On 17 May 1814, after almost 300 years of Danish rule, Norway signed the constitution at Eidsvoll. This event heralded a revival of the Norwegian language that spanned the remainder of the century. Per Christen Asbjørnsen (1812–55) and Jørgen Moe (1818–82) were part of this "golden age". Inspired by the German Brothers Grimm and Norwegian Andreas Faye, who published *Norske Sagn* (Norwegian Legends) in 1833, Asbjørnsen and Moe set about compiling the first collection of Norwegian folktales as *Norske Huldre-Eventyr og Folkesagn* (Norwegian Ghost Stories and Folk Legends). Their first volume appeared in 1845, the second edition in 1852. Asbjørnsen went on to publish an illustrated version, commissioning some of the best Norwegian painters of the time, including Erik Werenskiold (above) and Theodor Kittelsen. Asbjørnsen and Moe's collections have become classic Norwegian folktales; Kittelsen and Werenskiold's illustrations have given the troll its visual image.

OFF-THE-SHELF MONARCHY

Imported from Sweden in 1905, Norway's popular monarchy has passed through various trials on its way to the very heart of the nation

For the chronically under-employed off-shoots of European royalty, the rash of new states in the 19th and early 20th century brought blessed job opportunities. Their prospects were reduced by republican tendencies and other disappointments: Albania offered its throne to the England cricket captain, who

declined, but in 1905 Norway's criteria were less capricious. The new state had a long royal pedigree, but it had died out during 400 years under Danish and Swedish rule. While Norwegians saw some advantages in a Scandinavian as king, there was the feeling that a Danish or Swedish monarch would amount to the despised *status ante quo*. In the event, the former considerations outweighed the latter, and an invitation went to Prince Carl, second son of the future King Christian IX of Denmark and grandson of Sweden's King Karl XV.

Prince Carl, then 33, was married to Maud, Princess of Wales and daughter of England's Edward VII. He insisted first on a plebiscite.

The result was favourable, so on 25 November 1905, having assumed the title Håkon VII, he stepped ashore in Norway sheltering his young son, born Alexander Edward Christian Frederick but quickly renamed Olav, from driving snow. Håkon himself continued to sign letters to friends and relatives in England as "Charles".

Republicanism survived in Norway. Politicians complained that the cost of the monarchy was too high. The royal apartments in the palace were scarcely habitable to begin with and the government would pay only half the repair costs. Frugality was paramount. By watching expenses as carefully as he observed constitutional niceties, Håkon gradually won over the sceptics. Left-wing doubts ceased in 1926 when he called on the Labour Party to form a government.

The king worked hard at not being a foreigner. He travelled widely and impressed his subjects with a dignified modesty. The crown prince needed no encouragement to make up the perceived deficiency in the family tree. Although born in England, he felt at home and proved it by winning prizes on the Holmenkollen ski jump, as daunting a test of Norwegian authenticity as there could be. He also represented Norway as an Olympic sailor, another huge plus to his sea-minded subjects.

Resistance in exile

World War II was the supreme challenge. Implacably opposed to Hitler, King Håkon had to contend with the local clamour for neutrality. "I must be careful… not to say too much", he wrote to Queen Mary, his sister-in-law in London, "so that my ministers cannot say I am more English than Norwegian." He would abdicate rather than bow to German demands for recognition of the Quisling government. Running the gauntlet of the Luftwaffe, he escaped to England. His work, and that of the crown prince, with the Norwegian exile movement inspired dogged resistance at home and cemented a bond which gave the king a tumultuous reception on his eventual return to Oslo.

Håkon died in 1957 at the age of 85, and became known as Håkon the Good. His only child, who succeeded as Olav V, inherited the same unassuming manner, evident in his endearing discomfort while delivering the traditional New Year's Eve television broadcast, and the affection in which his father was held.

When he died in 1991, the people's grief was genuine. It was not just the passing of an old man, but personal sorrow at the loss of one so dear to many.

> ### PERSONAL PROTECTION
>
> When an American reporter found King Olav V travelling alone on the train and asked whether it wasn't a security risk, the king replied "not with four million bodyguards!".

Changing with the times

King Olav V was succeeded by his 44-year-old son, who assumed the title of Harald V. Harald had been raised to carry out his royal duties, while maintaining strong personal ties with the people and his own time. King Olav's announcement in 1968 that Crown Prince Harald wished to marry a commoner triggered a heated debate on the future of the monarchy. The decision was made by King Olav himself after consultations with the government. The response was favourable and the majority of the population immediately accepted Sonja Haraldsen as queen. She quickly became inseparably linked with the national unity symbolised by the royal family.

King Harald has made a name for himself as a competitive sailor. In 1987 he won the world championship with his new yacht *Fram X*, which was a gift from the Norwegian business community on his 50th birthday. Both King Harald and Queen Sonja are involved in various outdoor sports, as is their daughter, Princess Martha Louise, who is heading for Olympic fame in the equestrian field.

Public face, private lives

The king was less than amused when, in 1994, Princess Martha Louise's interest in equestrian sports extended to being cited as co-respondent in a British divorce case as a result of an alleged affair with a married show jumper. He ruled that she should not give evidence in court. Not that it caused much of a stir in the Norwegian press (which has tacitly agreed not to encroach on the private lives of the members of the

Royal household). This privacy was certainly respected when the successor to the throne, Crown Prince Haakon Magnus, donned his overalls and tasselled cap and went off on a week's binge with his school mates to celebrate graduation from high school.

Untraditional heir

Crown Prince Haakon looks certain to be every bit as popular a monarch as his father. Willing to leave the sporting traditions to his sister, he has followed a somewhat untraditional academic career by

studying political science in the United States. While his father remains king, Haakon is expected to assume a common role, possibly in the public administration, and like his father will "marry the girl he loves rather than love the girl he marries"

All this, of course, fits in perfectly with the egalitarian outlook that pervades Norwegian society. But like the flag and the 17th of May celebrations, the monarchy symbolises independence from the almost 400-year rule under first Denmark and then Sweden. What often appears to be fervent nationalism is in fact no more than national pride and a desire to hold on to a hard-earned self-determination. ❏

LEFT: King Harald, Queen Sonja and their children.
RIGHT: King Harald at a skiing event.

THE SAMI: PEOPLE OF FOUR NATIONS

Behind the popular image of the Sami with their colourful costumes and large herds

of reindeer lies a rich complex culture that is an important part of modern Norway

The Sami (or Lapps, as they are often called) have lived in Norway from time immemorial. Traces of their presence stretch back more than 8,000 years. The name Sami comes from the Sami *sápmi*, denoting both the people themselves and their traditional territory. Samiland extends from Idre in Sweden and adjacent areas in Norway south to Engerdal in Hedmark; to the north and east it stretches to Utsjoki in Finland, Varanger in Norway and on to the Kola peninsula in Russia. It covers a larger area than Norway and Denmark put together, and the population is cautiously estimated at about 70,000, of which around 40,000 live in Norway, mainly in Finnmark.

Norwegian Sami divide roughly into three groups. The Mountain Sami are the most widespread, ranging from Varanger to Femunden. They live mainly by breeding reindeer. The River Sami live around the waterways in the interior of Finnmark and have turned increasingly to agriculture and animal husbandry, though hunting, fishing and berry-picking still add to their income. The third group, the Sea Sami, is the largest, making a living from fishing and farming in a lifestyle that differs little today from that of other northern Norwegians.

Ancient culture

The Sami people have been very successful in conserving their rich cultural heritage and many unique traditions. Not the least important is the Sami language, which derives from the Finno-Ugric branch of the Uralic family and is closely related to the Baltic Sea-Finnish languages.

From ancient times, the sea has been of great importance as an abundant source of fish, and of seal to provide them with valuable hides and skins. Walruses, with their precious tusks, were also highly prized, particularly by the Sami craftspeople who produced all sorts of tools and

utensils including needles, buttons, spoons, cups, and a variety of musical instruments.

Samiland is a mighty land, rich in lakes, rivers, small streams, grandiose mountains and boundless hills, which in some places reach as far as the Atlantic coast. Besides fishing, hunting also used to be important and there was

much game, big and small. Squirrels, martens, foxes, even bears were all hunted but the most important animal was – and to a certain extent still is – the reindeer. About 10 percent of Norway's land mass is used for reindeer grazing (mostly in Finnmark). While the economic value of this industry is minor on a national scale, it is important both financially and culturally to the Sami, with about 40 percent of the population living from herding reindeer.

Very few of the truly nomadic Sami people are left. Most Sami have settled down in the sense that they have a permanent address but move with their herds to the high ground in the summer. During late summer and in the autumn

PRECEDING PAGES: children in Kautokeino, Finnmark, ready for confirmation.
LEFT: traditionally Sami women love smoking pipes.
RIGHT: a Sami boy.

the reindeer are driven down to the woods near the foot of the summer mountain pastures where there is plenty of lichen. There they stay during winter, roaming in freedom until the spring when it is time once more to move up the mountain to the high slopes, now covered with succulent, nourishing vegetation.

Brilliant colours

Many visitors to Norway come north to Sami-land and to the beautiful *fjell* (mountains) in search of untouched Nature. Mosses and lichens give a gentle splash of colour to the vast land, and grasses, especially the sedges are abundant here as in few other areas. At the beginning of summer the rare, pale Pasque flower (*Pulsatilla vernalis*) is in bloom and the rosy cinnamon rose (*Rosa majalis*) gives colour to the rocky hillside and the edges of the bog. Carpets of mountain avons (*Dryas octopetala*) are characteristic of soil that is rich in calcium, as are many other species, often with names that begin with *fjell*.

It could be that the colours all around them have been a source of inspiration for the tradi-tional Sami costume. In days gone by, this dress was for daily use; now it is kept for festivals, weddings, funerals and other important occa-

SINFUL SINGING

Of great importance when trying to get inside the world of the Sami people is to understand the importance of the yoik, a kind of primitive singing comparable with unaccompanied humming or melodic scanning. To outsiders, it is particularly difficult to grasp since the words can be isolated or subordinated to melody and rhythm, followed by long sentences of meaningless syllables, such as *voia-voia, ala ala, or lu-lu-lu.*

The yoik probably originated as a way of keeping reindeer quiet and at the same time frightened wild animals away. But it is also used as entertainment, when people are gathered together or alone. In Finnmark, "yoiking" has grown strong

and each Sami has his own personal melody. Traditionally, a young Sami boy will compose his own yoik for the girl he is courting. However, today a suitable yoik can be composed to order for almost any occasion.

Like many other Sami traditions, the yoik was forbidden by the missionary Christians. At a time when the only decent song was a hymn, the yoik was seen as sinful. But a yoik could not be burnt like a troll-drum. Many of the old melodies are still alive, handed on from one generation to the next. With the current spread of world music, the Sami singer Mari Boine is known all over Europe, and her success has brought new life to Sami music and culture.

sions. Easter is *the* big feast, particularly in Kautokeino, with traditional reindeer racing and other events. Then the richly ribboned skirts and frocks, with red their most outstanding colour, are fetched from drawers and chests. These generous ribbons are used as wristbands or cuffs and as "stockings".

There are no bounds to this richness and colour, which makes a magnificent sight. With these lavish dresses go jewellery in silver, exquisitely worked into neck chains and elegant pendants. Another speciality is pewter embroidery, in which very thin threads of pewter are sewn in ingenious patterns on fine bracelets or on bags made of reindeer hide.

The old religion

Like many other people living in close contact with nature, the Sami had, and still have, a religion related to shamanism, in which nature and its forces are of the greatest importance. Beaive (the Sun) and Mannu (the Moon) were the supreme gods; next came Horagalles, the god of thunderstorms. Under these main gods there were many lesser gods and spirit beings, who ruled over fertility and over wild animals and the hunt, as well as over lakes and their fishes and other inhabitants. There were evil spirits as well. One was Rota or Ruta, the demon of illness and death; another was the Devil himself, Fuadno. In many areas Sami religion was related to Norse mythology: Horagalles corresponding to the Norse god of Thunder, Thor.

Christianity did its best to combat and extinguish this popular belief and Swedish Laestadianism did much to destroy the Sami religion. Many of the ceremonial "troll-drums", of great importance in Sami culture but an anathema to the would-be missionaries, were burned.

The most effective Christian missionary was King Christian IV. He travelled to Finnmark around the turn of the 17th century and in 1609 introduced the death penalty for Sami who refused to give up their traditional faith. He followed this with an order to build the first Christian church in Varanger.

To go to church regularly was, nevertheless, impossible for many of the nomadic Sami, who had to travel over mountains and vast lakes. It was the great festivals which gathered the Sami

together and so it is today: New Year, Easter, Lady Day, and the spring and autumn equinoxes. In addition, the Sami people count eight seasons, all of them related to their reindeer and these too must be celebrated.

Language revival

Traditionally, Sami culture possessed an extensive oral "literature", including an enormous number and variety of legends and fairytales, many of which were written down earlier this century by J.K. Ovigstad in his *Sami Fairytales and Legends*. This literature also includes a distinctive form of poetry designed to accompany

the traditional Sami "song" or *yoik*. The oldest written *yoik* poem is found in Johannes Schefferus' *Lapponia*, published in 1673, which contains two of these poems.

In the first half of this century, it was government policy to encourage the Norwegianisation of the Sami people and its language. This led to the irony that one of the greatest writers of Sami descent, Mario Aikio from Karasjok, wrote only in Norwegian, though today a number of younger writers are once again using the Sami language.

As happened with many minority languages in recent times, Norway now pursues a policy of encouraging the Sami language. It is taught

LEFT: a Sami woman at the reindeer round-up.
RIGHT: a character from the Sami theatre.

from the start of schooling and Sami people can pursue higher education in their own language in various establishments such as the Universities of Oslo and Tromsø and their own Teachers' Training College in Alta. Karasjok also has the modern De Samiske Samlinger (Sami Museum) while in Kautokeino, where the great Easter celebrations take place, there is the Kautokeino Kulturhuset (Culture Centre).

When the Norwegian Broadcasting Corporation (NRK) planned a second radio channel in

> ### FALLOUT
>
> In 1986, radioactive pollution from the Chernobyl nuclear disaster hit the Sami hard, both culturally and economically, through contamination of their reindeer which had eaten polluted lichen.

pensation for reindeer grazing areas and recognition of the right to hunt and fish. Sami have in some cases also succeeded in curtailing electricity development projects which would have flooded whole districts and jeopardised the local reindeer economy.

Today, the Sami people have their own Sametinget (parliament), based in Karasjok, which was opened by King Olav in October 1989 with great ceremony and many festivities as the king met adults and children. The parliament is an elected body and to vote you must have a grandparent speaking the Sami language or, with typical Norwegian pragmatism, "feel that you are a Sami". Further progress was made in 1990 when Norway ratified the ILO Convention, which dealt with the rights of indigenous and tribal peoples.

The Sametinget deals with all matters pertinent to the Sami people and is gradually being given more autonomy, but so far its power is fairly limited, mainly advisory. It has developed a plan of action for Sami coastal and fjord areas, an agricultural plan, and has participated in a Sami fisheries committee. In addition it has conducted its own studies aimed at boosting local employment (in which tourism is playing an increasingly important role).

Nordic co-operation is also a central part of its activities. The Sami parliaments in Norway, Sweden and Finland decided in 1996 to collaborate through a special parliamentary council. There is now a political adviser for Sami issues at the Ministry of Local Government.

The most contentious issue currently being debated is Sami land rights, and in particular mineral rights. The Sami recognise the enormous wealth that lies beneath the frozen tracts of the Finnmarksvidda (the great Finnmark plain). Major international mining companies are continuously charting the area for mineral deposits and there is even talk of Klondyke-like gold deposits. Similarly, international oil companies are continuing to explore the Barents Sea, where major gas fields have already been discovered.   ❑

the early 1980s, it had the unusual idea of placing the first station in the remote north of Norway and starting broadcasts with the first Sami service, then gradually working its way south.

Towards home rule

The Norwegian Sami have also fought for political control over their own affairs and for the preservation of their way of life which has continued to be eroded by the opening up of the northern areas through improved roads and other forms of communication.

The establishment of national parks, for example, can lead to the protection of wild animals that prey on the reindeer herds and Sami people have been successful in gaining com-

LEFT: the Sami singer Mari Boine is now known internationally.
RIGHT: an old Sami woman fixing her traditional *lavvu* (skin tent).

BOAT BUILDERS AND ENGINEERS

Travelling around Norway has never been easy. However, Norwegian engineers have come up with some spectacular solutions to speed you on your way

Norway is 1,600 km (1,000 miles) long and has a coastline that resembles a set of jagged teeth, a myriad of islands and more than its fair share of mountains. Added to such geographical difficulties are a harsh winter climate and a population of only 4.5 million people scattered the length and breadth of the country. In short, a nightmare for those whose job it is to plan and build a transport network.

In the 1980s offshore oil came to the rescue, generating wealth that was used partly to upgrade roads and improve the mountain and undersea tunnels that are so vital in this fierce terrain. Such spending produced some spectacular feats of engineering, but the North Sea bonanza is reaching its peak and so new solutions will have to be found.

In the wake of the Vikings

It is not surprising that Norway has traditionally relied on the sea (which had for so long concealed those oil riches) as its basic means of transport, or that most towns and villages lie along the coast and fjords and have harbours. When roads were still primitive tracks and railways in the early stages of construction, shipping routes for passengers and cargo were already well established. This was the main reason that early tours of Norway seldom penetrated inland but kept to the coast and fjords.

The backbone of the domestic sea transport system was, and still is, the famous Hurtigrute, the coastal express steamers which have linked the numerous communities along the coast for many years. These ships followed the route of the Vikings and were originally a series of unconnected independent services. Many operated only during the summer, anchored at dusk, and did not sail through the night.

It was the Vesteraalens Dampskibsselskab (Steamship Company) that established the first year-round express service in 1893, which

sailed between Trondheim and Hammerfest – without overnight stops. Later, other lines joined in and the Hurtigrute assumed a major role, carrying mail, cargo and passengers, including tourists, from Bergen in the southwest to Kirkenes in the northeast. Today, in spite of the development of other forms of

transport, coastal shipping continues to play an important part in the Norwegian communications network.

From *stolkjaerre* to the car

As new roads and bridges have been built and new tunnels bored, the number of smaller ferry services has steadily declined; but the ferries in the west and north of Norway will continue to play an important role well into the next millennium. The National Route 1 in west Norway, for example, crosses no fewer than eight fjords between Stavanger and Ålesund.

Until a couple of decades ago, many quite important roads were still unsurfaced. Road

LEFT: Tjeldsund Bridge connecting the island of Hinnøya to the mainland.
RIGHT: landing on an Arctic airstrip.

building has never been an easy option in Norway and a lot of highways were narrow and rough, while those which crossed the mountains and *fjells* were closed in winter and regularly damaged by the harsh weather.

Before the car, the principal form of transport was the *stolk-jaerre*, a two-wheeled horse-drawn cart without springs which seated two persons. An alternative, a *kalesjevogn*, seated a maximum of six passengers. When the car made its first appearance there was little to

engineers have risen to the challenge and created new highways with good surfaces, built superb bridges, and blasted numerous and lengthy tunnels.

The Norwegian skill at tunnelling through the solid rock that forms their mountains creates one of the biggest impressions on visitors. Norwegian tunnels are rarely flat or straight, but wind up and down the mountains with gradients, curves and spirals to make for adventurous underground driving. The more dramatic exam-

encourage it; gradually roads improved, although it was not until after World War II that the Norwegians made major progress.

The Norwegian art of tunnelling

Since the 1980s a surge in road building has gained increasing momentum. But even today there are only a few short sections of motorway, and Norway has its own types of hazard, ranging from reindeer on the road to narrow bridges, blind corners and steep gradients.

Minor roads, particularly in the mountains, are frequently unsurfaced while some of those covered with asphalt – especially in the north – suffer from frost heave. But Norway's civil

ples can gain 300 metres (1,000 ft) in a few minutes replacing roads that once clung to the mountainside in a succession of hairpin bends and steep gradients and which were closed by snow all winter long.

Nothing has deterred Norwegian engineers from tackling the incredibly difficult to the near impossible – such as the tunnel on the road between Skei and Fjærland which lies beneath an arm of the mighty Jostedal glacier. Previously Fjærland was isolated, reached only by ferry. The only hazards now are sheep, which have learned to appreciate the comfort of lying in tunnel entrances where it is cool in summer and warm in winter.

Underwater motoring

Having mastered the skill of tunnelling on land, the Norwegian engineers have now turned their attention to the seabed and undersea tunnels. One of the most spectacular burrows out from the mainland to Vardø, which lies on a small island off the north Finnmark coast. It is nearly three kilometres (two miles) long and descends 88 metres (288 ft) below the cold waters of the Arctic Ocean.

At Ålesund on the west coast two undersea tunnels, totalling nearly eight kilometres (five miles) now link the main town to the island of Vigra, where the airport is, and have cut out a

Airport travels 14 kilometres (9 miles) underground from Oslo S to Lillestrøm: the original budget was doubled when engineers struck a fault through which several lakes in Østmarka began to drain. The initial decision to build the tunnel was based on environmental considerations: the resulting ecological damage is still not fully understood.

Public transport

Public transport makes good use of Norway's road system to reach outlying towns and villages. The bus station in the centre of any town is busy from morning to night – a revelation to

ferry crossing. With an economical turn of mind, the Norwegians used the rock drilled out of the tunnels to extend the airport's runway.

The cost of these projects is enormous and the pace of the work has made it impossible for the government to contain them within its budget limits. So more and more of these improvements are now paid for by tolls. Some complain that tunnel development has got out of hand, and, to a certain extent, this is true. The high-speed rail link to the new Oslo Gardermoen

those for whom a bus is almost an extinct species. What is more, Norwegian public transport has done a marvellous job of integrating road, rail, ferry and even airline schedules. The ferry waits for the train, and the smaller planes owned by Braathens and others, which carry most of the internal passengers, hop neatly from small airfield to small airfield.

There are also long-distance buses, the most outstanding being Express 2000 which runs between Oslo in the south and Hammerfest in the far north. It takes 25 hours, travelling through Sweden and Finland on the way, and claims to be the longest service of its kind in the whole of Europe.

LEFT: a steam train at Voss on what was to become the Oslo-Bergen railway line.
RIGHT: island-hopping in the Lofotens Islands.

The slow train

A technical article published in 1850 came to the conclusion that because of the difficult terrain and inhospitable climate "the use of the locomotive is impossible or impracticable". But the engineers proved the writer wrong, although building a railway was slow going. The first line from Christiania (now Oslo) to Eidsvoll opened in 1854, principally for the transport of timber from the Lake Mjøsa region to the harbour at Christiania from which it was exported.

This was typical of how the railways developed piecemeal, with unconnected segments serving a particular industry. The tracks were

not even the same width and, although the question of the gauge was resolved in 1894, it was 1949 before the last line of importance converted to European standard gauge.

The most important rail route in Norway, from Oslo to Bergen, was also one of the most difficult to build and its 470 kilometres (295 miles) did not open until 1909. Now electrified, the Oslo-Bergen line is regarded as one of the great railway journeys of the world. It climbs over the massif of the Hardangervidda, which was conquered by engineering audacity, sheer sweat and a state budget. To protect the line against snowdrifts, the engineers built snow fences, tunnels and snow sheds along the most

exposed stretches: from Utstaoset 100 kilometres (60 miles) of track lies above the tree-line. It includes 178 tunnels, and for many years the Gravhal tunnel was Norway's longest at 5,310 metres (5,800 yds).

At Myrdal there is a spectacular branch line to Flåm, on the Aurland fjord, which descends from 870 metres (2,845 ft) to just two metres (six feet) above sea level in 20 kilometres (12 miles). It is now one of the major tourist attractions of Western Norway. The trains pause midway on the journey so that passengers can see and photograph the spectacular Kjosfossen waterfall. For safety reasons the engine has five independent braking systems!

All over Norway the many gradients and curves on virtually every line, plus the fact that much of the system is single track, mean that train speeds, even today, are not high. A limit on the volume of traffic, because the railways link comparatively small centres of population, also mean infrequent services.

Taking to the air

Just as Norway's natural conditions encouraged the development of coastal shipping, so the same conditions have proved to be made-to-measure for air transport. The thin spread of the population has not inhibited the development of an extensive domestic air network with 50 airports scattered all over the country.

These services are used by five million passengers a year – a ratio of passengers to population which is claimed to be a world record. The domestic and international network is long established and the spur of daunting distances has meant that the Norwegians have brought to aviation much of the same spirit that they brought to the development of shipping.

The major international airline is Scandinavian Airlines System (SAS), a joint operation of Norway, Sweden and Denmark, but the dominant domestic airline is Braathens. Widerøe is the main operator on the "thinner" routes serving many small communities, especially in the north of the country. Short-runway aircraft provide a regular service, even during the harsh winters, and most of the airports are tiny and carved out of what would appear to be, except to a Norwegian engineer, quite unsuitable terrain. ❑

LEFT: satellite communications in the Arctic.

Black Gold

It became clear in the 1970s that vast oil and gas riches lay beneath the ocean floor off the Norwegian coast, and yet the full extent of these resources is still being determined today. Current estimates predict that without major new oil discoveries oil production will gradually decline in the next century, but as a major gas exporter Norway can count on a longer perspective.

It all started in 1962 when, prompted by a gas find off Holland, the American Phillips oil company acquired the right to explore in Norwegian waters. Other companies soon followed. After clarification of legal problems and territorial rights with Denmark and Britain, drilling started in earnest in 1966. Four years later, Phillips announced the discovery of a giant oil field, Ekofisk. The 1970s saw a series of major discoveries: French Elf found Frigg; American Mobil found the world's largest offshore oil field, Statfjord; Shell confirmed the giant Troll gas field off Bergen. The wily Norwegians learned quickly and two Norwegian oil companies joined the fray. The state-owned Statoil discovered Gullfaks, and the semi-nationalised Norsk Hydro became the operator at Oseberg.

Oil production at the Ekofisk field started modestly from a floating rig in 1971. Permanent installations and a pipeline to Teesside in England were commissioned in 1975. By the end of the 1970s Norway had built a gas processing plant at Kårstø, near Stavanger, and was exporting dry gas to the rest of continental Europe, and the Norwegian shipbuilding industry was entering a golden age as far as contracts were concerned. The rest, as they say, is history.

Activities were for some time restricted to areas south of the 62nd parallel, on the basis of wanting to maintain a moderate tempo. Exploration off mid- and north Norway was not permitted until 1980, and even then it was strictly regulated. New finds were soon made at Haltenbanken off Trøndelag. Shell brought the Draugen oil reserves on stream in 1993. Further north, the Heidrun field started production in 1995. After several years of discussing production levels, the offshore industry was finally forced (by low oil prices and an inexperienced centre coalition government) into a three percent production cut, with the hope that this would help oil prices rise again.

RIGHT: at work on an offshore oil platform.

To the far north in the Barents Sea, some 50 wells have been sunk. So far no oil has been found, but plenty of gas, though as yet these fields are too far from Europe to be commercially viable. Nor is there any agreement with Russia over the demarcation line in the Barents Sea.

The Norwegian state has three sources of revenue from its offshore industry: taxes and duties levied on the oil companies; the state's direct economic involvement; and share dividends from its 100 percent ownership in Statoil and 50 percent ownership in Norsk Hydro. In 1997, the Labour government established an Oil Investment Fund, created from surplus oil revenues. The plan is to

invest half of the fund with a view to *inter alia* financing future pension demands.

With copious quantities of natural gas, not to mention all the country's existing hydroelectric schemes, you would think that Norway would have plenty of energy: but you'd be wrong. With demand already outstripping supply by 10 percent, and bound by the 1998 Kyoto conference on climate change to reduce carbon dioxide emissions into the atmosphere, Norway is having to look elsewhere to regain self-sufficiency in electricity production. Whilst looking into clean ways of burning natural gas, attention is now focusing on such renewable sources as bio-energy (burning wood), heat pumps and solar sources. ❑

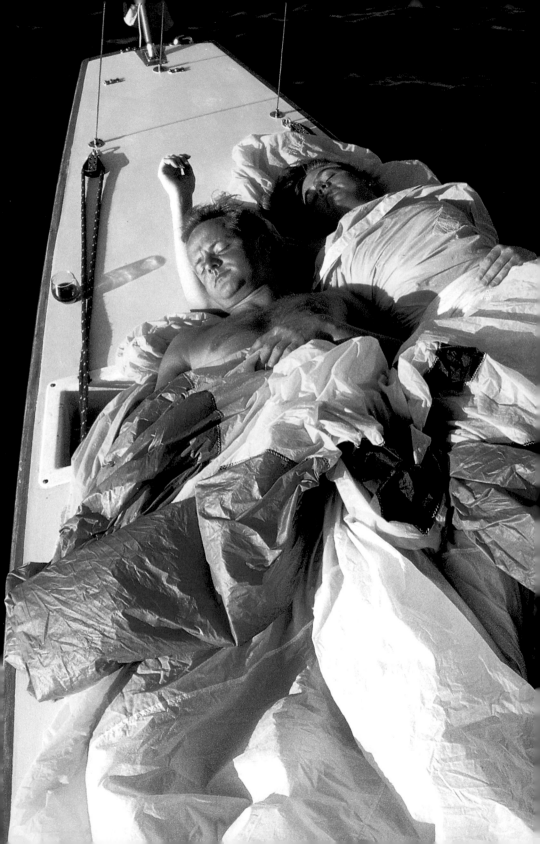

AN OUTDOOR LIFE

In Norway you are free to roam, through forest or over mountain; but wherever you end up, however remote, you can rely on the homely comforts of a hytte

As a race, Norwegians are quite at home in their wild, unspoilt country, and have a great feeling for its mountains. Composer Edvard Grieg, who did much to capture the Norwegian landscape in his music, wrote with passion of the Jotunheimen range in central Norway: "When I contemplate the possibility of a future visit to the mountains, I shudder with joy and expectation, as if it were a matter of hearing Beethoven's Tenth Symphony." There are higher, more remote, more exotically named countries with more photographically stunning landscapes, yet few can claim a population so attuned to its great outdoors.

One Norwegian in four counts outdoor recreation as a first pastime, and Norwegians excel at sports evolved from outdoor pursuits such as cross-country running or skiing, orienteering and cycling. Everyone, from all walks of life, takes part: urbanite and ruralist, commoner and king tramp the terrain, year round. Foreign visitors, unaware of this, often find the mass migration to the open air unnerving, especially if they arrive on business at Easter or during July, the prime times of the year for moor and mountain, sea and shore.

Free to roam

Centuries of that view evolved into one of the country's shortest laws – the 1957 *Lov om friluftslivet* (Outdoor Recreations Act) – which states succinctly that: "At any time of the year, outlying property may be crossed on foot, with consideration and due caution." The few restraints imposed are for environmental or safety reasons. Camping isn't permitted in the immediate watersheds of drinking-water reservoirs, and bonfires are forbidden during summer dry spells that can turn the taiga to tinder.

This liking for untethered roaming seems an integral part of the national character. Among the country's real-life heroes are Fridtjof

---

PRECEDING PAGES: walking along a forest trail.
LEFT: at the end of a day's sailing.
RIGHT: climbing a glacier in the Jotunheimen.

Nansen and Roald Amundsen, towering figures of polar exploration around the turn of the 20th century, and Thor Heyerdahl, probably the most widely known Norwegian abroad.

Though on a smaller scale, encounters with nature thread the fabric of everyday life. A family returning from an autumn hike to collect

wild mushrooms for the table will drop into a public mushroom check station to verify the edibility of their harvest. In the winter, city dwellers heading for a ski tour in a nearby forest dial the same snow report number as they dialled the previous summer for the water temperatures at local bathing areas.

Norwegian kindergartens and day-care centres are usually small buildings attached to extensive outdoor playgrounds, designed for day-long activity. Only in extreme weather, defined in most places as below –10°C (–5° F), do the kids stay indoors or at home. Coddling in Norway does not include separation from the wrath of the elements.

Yet Norwegians see no valour in doing battle with nature. As the British polar exploration chronicler Roland Huntford points out, that's more the British psyche: Norwegians are much likelier to meet nature on its own terms and seek or make their own comfort wherever they go.

The *hytte*, a home from home

In a country where winter days are short and nasty weather can crop up any time of the year, comfort translates to secure shelter, often your own. Fully a quarter of the country's households also own a holiday home, or *hytte*. By an accident of etymology, *hytte* translates to "hut",

Following the red "T"

Supreme on that scale are the *hytter* run by Den Norske Turistforeningen (DNT), literally "The Norwegian Tourist Association", with Tourist implying "on foot". Now well into its second century of housing and otherwise providing for walkers, skiers and climbers, DNT and its sibling local tourist associations own *hytter* throughout the Norwegian wilderness. Even the simplest put to rest any thought of a "hut", while the larger make the title ludicrous.

Well-marked walking trails connect the lodges or cabins (two better translations of *hytter*) which stand at crossroads on networks so

but there the similarity stops. A *hytte* is by no means a rough structure; most are well-appointed small wooden houses, and many are larger than their owners' permanent homes.

Those without a *hytte* of their own are frequently related to, or are close friends of, *hytte* owners. Otherwise, there are many paths to the comforts of a *hytte*. Clubs and associations often own one, and one of the standard business "perks" is liberal use of the company *hytte*. Even though holiday flats and time-share apartments are on the increase, the *hytte* still reigns supreme in fulfilling its original intent: to supply comfort in remoter places where it is otherwise unavailable.

extensive that DNT's trail marker, a red painted letter "T" on cairns, has become synonymous with serious walking. When winter snows cover the cairns, poles in the snow serve the same purpose.

The bulk of the trails and lodges are conveniently in the middle of the triangle bounded by the cities of Oslo, Bergen and Trondheim. A central entry point is Finse, situated above the timber line at 1,200 metres (4,000 ft). Finse's main street is the station platform; there are no cars because there are no roads. When a train has gone and the last passengers have left, Finse returns to normal, a speck in a seemingly infinite expanse of rock, ice and snow.

A few hundred metres from Finse railway station is the DNT *hytte*, with its 114 bunk beds in two and four-person rooms, hot showers, a staffed dining room serving three meals a day, a snack bar and three lounges. Other DNT lodges are still larger: Gjendesheim in Jotunheimen has 129 bunks. The DNT also has unstaffed self-service accommodation. Here you can prepare your own food or purchase from a pantry. You pay upon leaving, by putting money in a box on the wall. The honour system works well.

> **FARAWAY SO NEAR**
>
> So ethereal yet so accessible is Finse that it was chosen as a location for the space adventure film *The Empire Strikes Back*, the sequel to *Star Wars*.

tains where sheer altitude, not challenge, is the main criterion. Though this fact has led to relative anonymity – few Norwegian peaks appear in the classic mountaineering literature – it does mean that you can ascend the equivalent of the Matterhorn or Mont Blanc without having to cope with the problems of altitude. Most Jotunheimen trails meander from around 900–1,200 metres (3,000–4,000 ft) above sea level and there are few or no acclimatisation problems at that height.

Accessible mountaineering

To the north of Finse lie the Jotunheimen mountains, the range that took its name from Norse mythology, literally "Home of the Giants". The name is appropriate: peaks jut a kilometre and more skywards from lake-studded, moraine-strewn flats, all above the timber line. Nonetheless, even the loftiest of the Jotunheimen peaks, Galdhøpiggen and Glittertind, which are the highest in Northern Europe with summits over 2,400 metres (7,900 ft), rank low on the international scale of note-worthy moun-

Some of the glaciers that hewed the Norwegian landscape left offspring. One, Jostedalsbreen (the Jostedal Glacier), is the largest on the mainland of Europe. Jostedalsbreen and its siblings throughout the country are the places to see crampon-shod parties wielding ice axes from spring until autumn. Contact with the ice that shaped their land is currently the Norwegians' fastest growing wilderness recreation and many centres now organise specialist courses.

Skiing

Skis have been a source of benefit and pleasure to Norwegians for thousands of years. Until about 1,000 years ago, much of local commu-

LEFT: a typical *hytte*, in Ottadalen.
ABOVE: going for a quick dip in the fjord.

nity life in winter was dependent on skis. Then skiing evolved into a mass sport, urged on by the Morgedal pioneer Sondre Norheim. The first skiing competitions were arranged in the mid 1880s – the term "slalom" originated in Morgedal from the Norwegian words *sla*, meaning slope or hill, and *låm*, depicting the track down it.

STONE AGE SKIER

The Rodøy Man, a 4,000-year-old rock carving in Nordland, is evidence that skiing in Norway dates back to the Stone Age.

Norwegians have practically unlimited access to skiing and skating facilities. About 30,000 kilometres (18,600 miles) – three times the distance between Norway and Australia – of

jumping has decreased somewhat in popularity in recent years. Nevertherless there are some 600 ski-jumps in Norway. In the total absence of snow, there is always skating or ice hockey. In winter, municipalities up and down the country convert sports fields and playgrounds into ice rinks by getting the local fire brigade to spray them with water. These are then used for ice hockey and speed skating. When the fjords freeze over, whole families take Sunday "walks" on skates among the rocks and islets.

marked ski trails wind their way through unspoiled scenery. Cross-country skiing in the mountains may be enjoyed until well into the month of May. The winter darkness is no obstacle with some 2,500 illuminated tracks providing for a bit of serious exercise after work.

Alpine skiing has gradually increased in popularity in Norway. Though by no means as universal as cross-country skiing, most communities have a locally prepared piste. Major ski resorts include Trysil in Hedmark, Hemsedal and Geilo in Buskerud, Voss in Hordeland (which is an all-year-round resort), and, of course, Lillehammer in Oppland, the location of the 1994 Winter Olympics. Ski-

Outdoors in reach

In travelling time, even the remote wilderness areas are close to the bulk of the population: the wilderness itself is still closer. Oslo is bounded on its landward side by Øslomarka, a vast area of forests (larger than greater London) set aside for outdoor recreation. Likewise, Bergen has its Vidden, Trondheim its Bymarka, Tromsø its Tromsdalen. No Norwegian city is without nearby natural surprises. But to Norwegians, who are as likely to shoulder rucksacks as to carry a briefcase, that's no surprise. ❏

ABOVE: one of the many small harbours along Norway's long coastline.

The Great Ski-Jump

The Holmenkollen Ski Festival is the oldest in the world and one million people leave the centre of Oslo for Holmenkollen during the 11 days of the festival in March each year. At the climax on Holmenkollen Sunday, more than 50,000 people gather at this famous ski-jump hill to watch ski-jumping in the country that invented it. But though the Nordic skiing competitions (cross-country and ski-jumping) and the newer events attract top competitors eager for World Cup points, Holmenkollen is much more than yet another international winter competition. This is very much a citizens' festival, a chance for ordinary Norwegians and visitors to take part in the events.

The idea of sitting or strolling as a spectator all day in the middle of a Norwegian winter might sound like the best way of catching a cold but the excitement is high. Wrapped in boots, anoraks, gloves and hat, with the necessary extra of a warm cushion to sit on, everything is happening and you need no more than a regular quick coffee, best laced with aquavit, to keep out the cold.

Norway was the first country to introduce ski competitions when Norwegian soldiers began to compete as early as 1767 and the first civilian event took place in 1843 at Tromsø. By the 1880s, the Norwegian Society for the Promotion of Skiing already held a winter competition and in 1892, this transferred to Holmenkollen. That year, the longest ski-jump was 22 metres (72 ft). Today, it is more than 126 metres (413 ft).

In the very first days the competitors were all Norwegian but even by 1903 Swedes had arrived, and were soon joined by French and German skiers. Since World War II, foreigners from most skiing countries have taken part – and won. Women first competed in 1947, when Alpine skiing events were introduced, but they weren't admitted to the cross-country race until 1954.

Norway's King Olav V, a first-class sportsman, made his debut on the Holmenkollen jump in 1922, and was a faithful spectator for nearly 70 years. His son seems to have inherited this keen interest in the sport. As long as there is a jump at Holmenkollen, the Royal Family will watch the events from the Royal box.

The fortnight begins with the Handicap Ski Race; next comes the Guards' Race, followed by the Nor-

wegian Members of Parliament – fitter perhaps than their counterparts elsewhere – and local politicians, and cross-country skiing at all levels. On Children's Day more than 5,000 children swarm into the arena, for events to mark the end of the season at the children's ski school, and on Holmenkollen Sunday itself, the Holmenkollen March attracts around 7,000 to 8,000, many just ordinary skiers, to ski either 21 or 42 kilometres (13 or 26 miles) through the Nordmarka forest finishing right under the jump.

The atmosphere of Holmenkollen Sunday is electric. They call it Norway's second national day, after Constitution Day on 17 May, and most spectators

arrive early for a large breakfast-cum-brunch at one of the local hotels to keep out the minus-zero cold, before making their way to their seats. First come the children's events and demonstrations of skills such as Telemark skiing and parachute jumping. Next is the finish of the Holmenkollen March which leads up to the climax, the great ski-jump.

The huge crowd packed into the arena hushes as the first skier appears. Up there on the top platform, he looks like a being from another world. The silence lasts until the tiny, bright figure takes off and, in a second, is flying through space with an ease that makes it look simple. Then as skier follows skier in graceful arcs, a roar loud enough to cause an avalanche fills Holmenkollen. ❑

RIGHT: Holmenkollen Sunday.

SPORTING PASSIONS

To Norwegians, sport is almost a religion, permeating every aspect of life, and there is room for everyone, from Olympic champions to Sunday goalkeepers

Put the question "Are you a skier?" at almost any social gathering anywhere in Europe, and you could expect a few positive responses and perhaps a lecture or two on the virtues of the sport. Put the same question to someone you meet of a Sunday afternoon at one of the ski trail lodges in Norway, which you can only reach on skis, and the answers will be quite different: "No, I'm a bank clerk"; "Who me? Never dream of it!".

Why the disparity? The answer lies in a tradition that has woven sport deeply into the fabric of Norwegian life. It is even reflected in the language. While English has just one word, "sport", Norwegian has two: *sport* and *idrett*. The Norwegian *sport* is the umbrella word that covers all sporting events, so that a sports journalist in Norway plies exactly the same trade as his or her foreign counterpart. The word *idrett* is reserved for events in which the limits in performance are determined by the capabilities of the human body. Horse riding is not *idrett*, while scuba diving is. There is a further nuance: *aktiv* (active) means a person currently competing in a sport classified as *idrett*.

This explains why, when you ask skiing Norwegians "are you a skier?", you have asked if they currently compete in the sport. Ask often enough, and you unearth the astonishing fact that one Norwegian in three is *aktiv*.

Mad about sport

This amazing statistic reflects the high priority Norwegians give to sport. Oslo has numerous statues of living Norwegians in sporting poses: a statue of King Olav V skiing, near the Holmenkollen ski jump, one of marathon runner Grete Waitz running, of course, at the marathon gate of Bislett Stadium, and statues of speed skater Oscar Mathisen and figure skater Sonja Henie near the Frogner Park Stadium. All new high-rise flats are obliged by law to include "sports gear storage rooms". Within the Ministry of Church and Education there is a department for "Youth and *Idrett*". City newspapers vie with each other for sales on the strengths of their sports sections, and almost 14 percent of the Norwegian Broadcasting Corporation's output is devoted to sports.

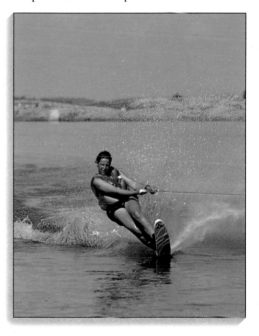

So pervasive is sport that visitors sometimes ask "Where is the flash, the excitement?" The answer is that the pinnacles are there, as high and sometimes higher than elsewhere, but the surrounding plateau of sporting achievement is so high that it makes the peaks less prominent.

Norges Idrettsforbund (NIF), the Norwegian Confederation of Sports, is the umbrella organisation for 53 separate sports federations with, in total, more than 1.7 million members. It spotlights this fact in its motto "Sport for All", and the pinnacles are grouped and designated "elite". So, for the Confederation and its member associations, competitive sport is both egalitarian and elitist.

LEFT: on the cross-country trail.
RIGHT: Prince Haakon Magnus shows his skill as a water-skier.

Morgedal and Telemark Revival

For jazz fans, New Orleans is the ultimate magnet, just as Wimbledon is for tennis players. For skiers, the start of it all is Morgedal, in the southern county of Telemark, a hamlet that long remained an entry only found in history books pored over by scholars of the sport of skiing. Today, that has all changed because of a reawakening of interest in the style of skiing called Telemark, which evolved in Morgedal.

In the mid 19th century, there were even fewer people than the 200,000 who live in Telemark today – a hardy breed of woodsmen, small farmers, hunters and traders, who fashioned their own implements including the skis they needed to get about on winter snows. Morgedal is in the mountains, so the ski makers there sought designs that would perform well in the surrounding rugged terrain, both in everyday winter skiing and for impromptu sporting meetings. Among the best in the mid -1800s was Sondre Norheim, a young tenant farmer. He excelled not only in village ski meetings but also in ski-making skills.

Norheim devised bindings (devices that hold ski boots to skis) that were firm and were the first to give the feet control over the skis. He also gave the skis what is known as "sidecut", the slight hourglass profile of a ski seen from above. Sidecut is what enables skis to run true and turn easily, even to this day.

Norheim and his fellow Morgedal skiers used the new designs to perfect new skiing manoeuvres, including ways of turning and stopping on snow, and ways of landing from airborne flights off snow-covered rooftops and natural outcrops. Their fame spread and, by 1868, Norheim and his farmers from Telemark were ready to show off their new skills. He led them on skis for the 180-kilometre (112-mile) journey from Morgedal to Christiania (now Oslo), where the city crowds turned out to greet and applaud the peasant skiers and their miraculous new techniques. This led to the start of the big ski-jumping contest at Husaby near Oslo in 1879, where 10,000 spectators led by the king cheered the skiing pioneers from Telemark. Around the same time, the Telemark skiers established the world's first ski school in Oslo.

In 1902, the first ski-jumping rules committee met to compile criteria for judging the style of competitors at the annual Holmenkollen ski-jump meetings. They honoured the origins of the two most skilful groups by affixing their names to the two turns then executed by ski jumpers to come to a stop after landing from flight. The turn in which the skis are held parallel throughout was named the Christiania, while the bent-knee stance with one ski trailing became the Telemark.

In modern Telemark skiing, the heel is free to lift up from the ski, and turns are steered, with one ski trailing and at an angle to the other. From the side, the manoeuvre looks like a genuflection in motion. Although competitive Telemark ski races are now held on packed slopes, as are alpine ski races, true Telemark skiing is a throwback to the skiing of Sondre Norheim's time. The rebirth of the Telemark turn has revived another old skiing practice – skiathlon – in which competitors must ski-jump, ski through a slalom course, and run a cross-country ski race, all on the same pair of skis.

The name is new, but the combination of manoeuvres dates back to the times when the men from Morgedal first mastered the ski-jumping meets in Christiania some 130 years ago. Then a ski jumping performance required the competitor to jump through the air, come to a stop after landing, ski back uphill to the top of the ski-jump, and jump again before finishing. ❑

LEFT: Telemark skiing uses one stick only.

International competition

From the broad base of people for whom sport is a major leisure time activity come the elite, competitors who enter the many national championships and represent Norway in international sports meetings. The results speak for themselves. For a country with such a small population, Norway has always been disproportionately strong in sports. Traditionally, Norwegian competitive prowess has been in winter sports and in sailing, but Norwegians have also won international medals in a wide range of events including marathon running, cycling, boxing, wrestling, handball, karate, canoeing, 40 percent of their income. Wherever you go, you are besieged by young people selling lottery tickets to support the local sports club.

However, recently recreation-type activities have gained in popularity at the expense of more strenuous sports. The Ski Association, Handball Federation and Athletics Federation are losing members while golf, billiards and amateur dancing federations are growing.

Football figures first

As elsewhere in Europe, football is Norway's number one sport, with some 1,800 clubs and a total of over 280,000 players. It is also the best

rowing, shooting, weight-lifting, women's football and ballroom dancing.

Such pervasiveness and prowess have their price. The annual turnover in sports, excluding the sports equipment sector, is more than NOK1,400 million (£120 million), and sports are supported through many channels: the NIF receives 90–95 percent of its revenue from central government, and sport receives one-third of the profits of the state-run football pools and Lotto, the national lottery. In addition, the 5,000-odd clubs use extra-curricular activities, such as bingo and local lotteries, to raise up to

supported, through funds from the football pools and from the sale of players to the major European leagues, in particular the English Premier League. While Norwegian football struggles to drop its amateur status (the population is too thin, too self-engaged, and too-busy to generate serious gate money), foreign coaches and eager agents find rich pickings among the home-grown talent. Even Rosenborg (Trondheim's football team) players have permanent jobs. Footballers such as Ronny Johnsen and Henning Berg (Manchester United), Tore Andre Flo (Chelsea) and Stig Inge Bjørnebye (Liverpool), to name but a few, provide the national coach with a good selection for his team.

ABOVE: the Norwegian football team in action.

Individual sports

Number two in the statistics and, its supporters contend, spiritually number one, is the country's traditional stalwart, skiing, with more than 1,500 clubs and a total membership of over 200,000. Together the four skiing disciplines – cross-country, alpine, ski-jumping and biathlon (cross-country skiing and rifle shooting combined) – are funded as well as and sometimes better than football. Third is gymnastics, with more than 500 clubs and over 100,000 members. Then follow handball, track and field athletics, orienteering, shooting, swimming, sailing and volleyball. Of these top ten only three, football, handball and volleyball, are team sports. The balance is almost the complete reverse of most countries, where team sports dominate, a possible reflection of the Norwegian mentality.

Grass roots support

The backbone of Norwegian sports is, of course, Norwegian involvement. A great deal of work on sports facilities is local and voluntary. Approximately half of the country's 1.4 million families with children are involved in sports in some way other than direct participation. Father is an official of the local club, and mother helps on the stalls at the annual club flea market. The older children sell club lottery tickets. In fact the whole family helps to run the annual club meets. Most families have one member who is either a certified coach or is training to become one.

One persistent reminder of this involvement is the seeming ubiquity of sports facilities and sports instruction. There are 10,000–12,000 sports centres in Norway, from the most modest local football field to major stadiums and indoor halls. In summer and autumn, they are hatcheries for future football and track-and-field athletic talents. In winter, their iced surfaces swarm with figure and speed skaters and serve as mini-arenas for ice hockey and *bandy*, a related sport played with a ball instead of a puck, to rules more closely resembling those of field hockey.

This high involvement has some drawbacks. In the more popular sports, competition has become so fierce that the criteria for doing well have been elevated to seemingly unattainable heights. Youngsters pushed into competition by overzealous parents can burn out prematurely, and this has become a recognised problem in almost all sports.

Such intense involvement, though, doesn't diminish the everyday enjoyment of sport. Internationally renowned violinist Arve Tellefsen's prime lament is that his infrequent sports ventures – his boyhood skills of ski-racing and football – invariably rate more media coverage than his violin virtuosity. But that doesn't prevent him from putting on a pair of skis or kicking a football at the weekend. ❑

WINTER OLYMPICS

Norway can claim more Winter Olympic medals than any other country apart from the former Soviet Union, and winter sportsmen and women are among the country's heroes. In the 1988 Olympics in Nagano, Norway came second to Germany – winning 10 golds, 10 silvers and eight bronzes – but ahead of Russia, Canada and the United States. The Norwegain cross-country skier Bjørn Dæhlie has printed his name indelibly on Winter Olympic history with the highest number of individual medals ever. In recent years Norwegian alpine skiers Ketil Andre Aamodt and Lasse Kjus have both won the Alpine World Cup.

LEFT: kayaking in Arctic waters.
RIGHT: climbing a frozen waterfall.

FISHING: SPORT AND SUSTENANCE

Norway's fjords, rivers and coastline are a veritable anglers' paradise. And when it comes to eating fish, Norwegians have a dish for every occasion

To Norwegians, fish is the standby staple. Even in modest markets, the variety of fish and fish products is amazing, and Norwegians look on a proper fresh fish shop as an asset to a community. Fish is both humble fare and holiday cuisine. Fish balls in white sauce are the Norwegian dining-table stalwart, and steamed

cod is a favourite for Sunday dinners. On festive occasions, herring in myriad forms takes its place with other delicacies such as *gravlaks* (cured salmon), *rakørret* (half-fermented trout), and *lutefisk* (dried codfish marinated in a lye solution, a dish few foreigners appreciate).

It is not surprising that Norway is a country of fishermen of all kinds. The language differentiates between them accordingly: *fisker* means "fisherman", one who lives by commercial fishing; while *sportsfisker* is the amateur variety, an "angler". But there the similarity stops. Angling in Norway is done both for the sport itself and as part of other outdoor pursuits. Fishing tackle is among the paraphernalia of

camping trips, just as it is the prime equipment for avid anglers.

The long coastline is a mecca for saltwater angling, yet freshwater angling is the more popular pastime, and there are a quarter of a million fishable inland lakes and ponds. The most common of around 40 freshwater species are trout and char; in the northernmost parts, and in lakes and ponds at higher elevations, they are the only fish. Grayling and pike are more common in larger lakes and rivers in eastern and central areas. Local legends about lakes rich in pike hold that the fish are descended from stocks set out in the late 18th century by the ruling Danes.

Bream, whitefish, perch and carp are found in most lower lakes in the southern part of the country, as well as in eastern Finnmark in the far north. Reliable varieties in saltwater include cod, coalfish, haddock, whiting, halibut, herring and mackerel.

The stars on the angling scene are the Atlantic salmon and sea trout, related varieties which are both popular game and commercial fish. The commercial varieties now come largely from fish farms, but the game fish still swim the rivers until they are two to six years old, migrate to the sea, and then return to spawn in some 400 rivers. Norwegians argue about the best rivers, but five in the northern part of the country stand out – the Alta and Tana rivers in Finnmark, and the Gaula, Namsen and Orkla rivers in Trøndelag, all of which draw anglers from around the world. There, the sport is so popular that you have to apply for licences as much as a year in advance.

Gaining a licence

You need two types of angling licence to keep within the law. The first one is the annual *Fiskeravgift* (fishing fee) that helps to offset the costs of overseeing fishing and the aquatic environment (particularly adding lime to the water). The *Fiskeravgift* can be obtained at the post office at NOK90 (£7.50) for freshwater fish and crabs (excluding salmon and sea trout). These, however, are included in the annual fishing licence which is dearer at NOK180. Fishing in sea water is free whereas fishing in lakes and rivers requires a further local licence. Freshwater fishing licences come from the owners of the fishing rights, usually the property owners along the banks of a river or the shores of a lake, whether private persons or communities. These vary in price, and are valid for specific dates and periods, ranging from one day to several weeks. You usually buy them from local hotels, sports shops or tourist offices.

Fly fishing is popular, so much so that Norwegians compete in the sport, including the annual world championships in fly casting.

Other countries do better in fly-casting competition, but the Norwegians pride themselves on their versatility. Lure fishing leads, and spoon-hook fishing and trolling are also widespread.

Baiting the hook

Even youngsters start fishing using artificial bait. Theories abound as to why this is so, but the most plausible ascribes it to Norway's location and topography. In the north, there are few insects large enough to use as bait, and worms are hard to find on rocky shores. Minnows and other live fish are prohibited as bait, primarily to curtail the spread of parasites and diseases.

MAXIMUMS AND MINIMUMS

The question of size, whether with a record in mind or to protect juvenile fish, is never far away. Norwegian angling records include 32.5 kg (71.6 lb) for freshwater salmon and 37.5 kg (82.6 lb) for cod caught in the sea. Although trout average 0.5 kg (1 lb), the freshwater trout record currently stands at 15.3 kg (33.7 lb). As for the minimum permissible sizes for keeping fish caught, they are 25 cm (9.8 inches) in length for salmon, sea trout and sea char, and 30 cm (11.8 inches) for all other fish.

LEFT: the strange fascination of ice–fishing.
ABOVE: cleaning the catch outside the family *hytte*.

For the same reasons, the transfer of live fish, water, or wet fishing boats or other equipment, from one watercourse to another is prohibited.

Just as winter does not deter Norwegians from walking (they switch to cross-country skis), frozen lakes do not halt fishing. Ice fishing is a prime wintertime hobby, a simple and straightforward form of angling, which requires only a baited hand line or short pole and line, warm clothing, and lots of patience. Ice anglers must hew holes in the ice by hand as motor augers are prohibited. It's a sport for the hardy, and ice angling contests, such as the popular Ice Fishing Festival at Vangsvatnet in Voss, are for the very dedicated.   ❑

THE TRADITIONAL ARTS

Tradition is strong in Norway, especially when it comes to the folk arts; but to an inquisitive eye, that tradition contains some unexpected influences

In the year AD 793 "dire portents appeared over Northumbria and sorely frightened the people. They consisted of immense whirlwinds and flashes of lightning, and fiery dragons were seen flying in the air. A great famine followed those signs, and a little after that in the same year, on 8 June, the ravages of heathen men miserably destroyed God's church on Lindisfarne, with plunder and slaughter."

So the *Anglo-Saxon Chronicle* documented the destruction of the monastery at Lindisfarne, now Holy Island, just south of Berwick-upon-Tweed in Northumberland in the north of England. It was the first major impact on Christendom by the Vikings, the pagan men of the North who were to set their mark on European culture for the next three centuries. But in the end, it was a reciprocal cultural exchange. An early Viking king, Olav Haraldson, converted to Christianity, was baptised in Normandy, and returned to his homeland to introduce the faith. By the year 1030, when he fell in battle, he had firmly rooted Christianity in most areas as Norway's future religion.

Today, the legacy of the Vikings is neither blurred nor buried, but still highly visible in a myriad of forms, collectively termed the folk arts. Wood carving, rustic painting, colourful national costumes and decorative painting are the most obvious forms.

Wood carving

The Viking Age owed its very being to superior sea power. The Viking craft, or longships as they became known, were at once extremely seaworthy and boldly beautiful. They were clinker built (overlapping planks held together with iron rivets) on long keel planks that swept up to a stem at either end. The Vikings carved elaborate decorations on the prows down to the waterline, often with dragon heads and figures.

PRECEDING PAGES: traditional rose painting.
LEFT: a detail from Tidemand's *The Grandmother's Bridal Crown.*
RIGHT: jewellery on a national costume.

They also carved elaborate designs on everyday items, from the handles of implements to the lever of the aft-right mounted *styrbord*, or steering board. On land, the details of buildings were similarly enhanced. Pillars were carved, not just at their capitals, but over their entire surfaces. There were ornate friezes, inte-

rior mouldings were decorated and gable ends became display points. Wood carving was a highly developed art, executed primarily for, and partly by, the Viking aristocracy.

Stave churches

By the 12th century, Christianity had supplanted the aristocracy as the prime patron of the arts, and the wooden *stavkirke* (stave church) became the major outlet of wood carving as an art form. About 750 of these magnificent structures were built, most in a 100-year period from 1150 to 1250, and 32 survive to this day, making them among the world's oldest wooden buildings. Their ornately carved

portals serve the same purpose as old book illu-
mination in England. They are one of the country's manuscripts. First, there are the animal
heads of Nordic mythology, documenting the
remnants of the Viking Age; then the classical
tendril of Christian art appears, springing from
the jaws of a beast. Finally, tendrils and flowers
assert themselves, sometimes solo and sometimes interwoven with other motifs, partly but
not completely replacing the beasts. Aside from
the stave churches and their various artefacts,
these early people decorated chairs, beds,
tables, ladles, bowls and other household items
with ornate carving. Some of the best-preserved

for peasant pieces of native spruce or pine, the
more ornately carved the better.

"Collecting old houses is something of a
family mania," says one shipowner (the nearest
Norway comes to an aristocracy). "My father,
brother and I have been combing the back
country for 40 years for handcrafted dwellings
and objects, homesteads, barns, cabins and huts
complete with their country beds, chests, bas-
kets and cupboards. Each must be unique to its
own valley and period."

Typical of the national mania for folk art, this
family's collection began simply by bartering
with valley farmers for small items, such as

examples of the work of Norwegian medieval
artisans are the carved portals, window sur-
rounds and other details of farm buildings.

A passion for the past

The traditions survive to the present day. The
timber *hytte* – even the ultra-modern *hytte* built
in the 20th century – must have some exterior
carving and the Frognerseteren Restaurant,
which was built in 1891 on a hillside overlooking Oslo and remodelled in 1909, is one of
the best examples of the more modern dragon
style of decorated wooden buildings. Today's
nostalgia in home furnishings is not for the lavish designs of the courts of the past, but rather

handcrafted butter and porridge *tine*. These
colourful, wooden caskets, often a first gift to a
betrothed, form an unbroken tradition from
Viking times to the present. Always highly decorated, the *tine* are still used by country lads to
show off their carving and rose painting skills.

Rose painting

Much as wood carving evolved from the urge
to decorate functional items, the art Norwegians
call *rosemaling* or "rose painting" sprang from
humble surroundings. The two were often used
together: carved building details and household
furnishings and implements were frequently
painted, both as enhancement of, and in con-

trast to, the carved wood. The name misleads: roses appear only in a few of the traditional patterns; it would be more correct to term it "rustic painting", which denotes its agrarian roots, far removed from the cities. True *rosemaling* is not limited to flowery designs, although variations of the tendril motif are its strongest themes. It also includes geometric figures, portraits, and an occasional landscape.

The earliest decorations have survived less well than the carvings on which they were painted, so the beginnings of rose painting remain an enigma. The oldest surviving examples date from around 1700, centuries after the necessary paints were first available.

Theories on its origins abound. One school of thought holds that originally it was used to add colour to drab interiors. From medieval times on the typical rural dwelling was an *årestue* (hearth house), a windowless room with an opening in the roof to let the smoke from the open fire in the centre to escape. Rose painting could have been the peasants' reaction to their otherwise grey interior environments.

Another line of thought, with some substantiation in contemporary historical records, is that the peasants emulated the ornate decorations of churches, which were then also the major civic buildings in rural areas.

Imported styles

Whatever its origins, rose painting evolved and, in its own right, became a record of its times. The earlier rose paintings of interiors and household articles clearly show that the art of the Renaissance reached as far as the Norwegian countryside. The colours are the peasant stalwarts, blue, green, red and yellow, but the patterns are definitely imported.

The prosperity of the late 18th century brought more clerics and more functionaries to rural districts and with the new professionals came their belongings, decorated household furnishings and implements. What the peasants saw they replicated as best they could in their own style.

Most were untutored and the commonest way of learning the skills was either from travelling artists or from local practitioners. The

relative isolation of the valleys, cut off from their neighbours by the high mountain ranges, meant that every valley became its own art centre for a particular style of painting.

Too conservative to borrow directly from outsiders, Norwegian farmers carefully extracted only those aspects that fitted their own sense of colour and decoration. Hallingdal farmers were partial to delicate S-curves applied to everything from walls to spoons and bowls. In affluent Gudbrandsdal, the locals carved their decorations into built-in benches and box beds. The most isolated districts, such as Setesdal, have a very simplified *rosemaling* tradition. So indi-

vidual were the styles, today's experts can identify the age and origin of almost any item with uncanny accuracy. Their knowledge is currently in much demand as rose-painted period furniture commands the highest of prices for Norwegian antiques.

Rose painting survives today, like wood carving, as a nostalgic link with the past and throughout the country amateur rose painters keep that link alive. For most it is a hobby with the occasional spin-off of small profits from sales to local handicraft shops. But for some it offered more. One of the antique business scandals of 1989 concerned cleverly faked, rose-painted "antique" furniture.

LEFT: rose painting used to decorate a set of shelves.
RIGHT: Einar Holte at work on one of his famous miniature wooden boats.

The national costume

Norway's *bunad* is as colourful as the national costumes of any country. It is not just worn by folk dancers or for fancy-dress parties, but is in regular use as formal attire at weddings, official ceremonies, and at gatherings on national holidays. Many claim that the *bunad* is Europe's most often worn national costume.

The *bunad* is a throwback to the everyday clothing of times past, and the word itself means simply "clothes". It has developed variations in style, cut, colouring and accessories according to locality and the skills and tastes of its makers. There were costumes for men,

women and children, everyday *bunads* and dress *bunads*. As with rose painting, every area of the country had its own style.

Despite these differences, the *bunad* has common characteristics that identify the dress as Norwegian. Women's costumes characteristically have skirts or dresses of double-shuttle woven wool and bodices or jackets of similar or contrasting material worn over blouses with scarves. Sashes, purses, the beautiful silver accessories and traditional shoes and stockings complete the costume. Men's *bunads* are essentially three-piece knickerbocker suits, with matching or contrasting waistcoats, white shirts, long socks and traditional shoes.

Like wood carving and *rosemaling*, the design of a *bunad* is in itself a historical record. For example, those from coastal areas often reveal a stronger Continental influence than those from the remote valleys, where housewives spun, dyed and wove their own woollens to local patterns.

Folk revival

In the mid-19th century, factory-made cloth and garments began to replace homespun products. As people moved from farm to town, the *bunad* seemed to be heading for extinction. It was rescued single-handed by Hulda Garborg, a prominent author who saw a need to preserve the rural traditions. Shortly before the turn of the century, she founded a *leikarring*, or folk dance group, in Oslo. Folk dances should, she maintained, be performed in folk costumes which led her to compile the first anthology of *bunads*, published in 1903. It was a best seller and Garborg and one of her dancers, Klara Semb, succeeded in starting the folk dance movement and a *bunad* renaissance which continues to the present day.

Although *bunads* are no longer daily wear, the number of known types and varieties is greater than ever. Some, like those from Setesdal, date back 300 years or more. Others, such as the costume from Bærum, a suburb of Oslo, have been designed in the past 40 years.

Its current popularity is matched only by the range of opinions about how it should be worn. Traditionalists contend that a *bunad* from a particular district should be worn only by a person born and bred there. Moderates maintain that correct style outweighs the circumstances of the wearer's birth and upbringing, and the radicals view the *bunad* as a style to be copied piecemeal in modern clothes.

While the standard dark suit has, like in so many other countries, become the bastion of the Norwegian male wardrobe, women still face the dilemma of what to wear for formal occasions. In Norway, a *bunad* is always correct. It is timeless and may be passed on from generation to generation, while the traditional silver belt is often a gift from a father and mother to their son's wife. ❏

LEFT: Hulda Garborg (left) photographed in 1899 dressed in a traditional *bunad*.
RIGHT: the 13th-century Heddal stave church.

TRADITION, NOT HAUTE CULTURE

Norwegian artists, writers and musicians dug deep into the country's
rural past in search of a new national identity

Culture in Norway? Well, certainly it exists, in its own fashion. Just take a look at your fellow travellers in the Oslo Central Station. Half of them trudge around in boots and a backpack; the other half have only the backpack. They are all heading for isolated cabins – Norway's holy *hytte* – far away from the city and its pleasures. The Munch Museum and National Theatre take second place to trekking the highlands, searching mountain valleys for *rosemaling*, the indigenous folk art.

That is all culture certainly, though not of the grand, *haute* culture sort. Although Norway does not foster glittering opera soirées, galas do, of course, occur, a notable example being the awarding of the Nobel Peace Prize. But such parties are just the icing on the cultural cake and ever so slightly foreign, imported glamour (Nobel, after all, was a Swede).

Home-grown culture

Real Norwegian culture is something far more fundamental – folksy, a reaction to foreign domination. As a political entity, Norway was established in 1905 after centuries of Danish and Swedish rule. All Norwegian "dialects" were forbidden by the Danes for official documents and communications. The national constitution, which was drawn up at Eidsvoll in 1814, was in Danish. Such cultural imperialism was crushing to Norwegian self-esteem and national identity.

Ordinary Norwegians were driven away from the centres of power to rural farms. Tradition, folk costume, the old ways became a cultural refuge and eventually the treasuries of Norway's national personality. Culture with a capital "C" was something the overlords brought with them from foreign capitals. And it was something they took away with them when they left. Norway today has no noble families excepting the king and his household.

LEFT: Henrik Ibsen.
RIGHT: murals by Per Krohg and Henrik Sørensen in the main hall of Oslo's Rådhus (City Hall).

While politicians could elect a king and parliament, it fell to cultural workers, especially writers and painters, to revive the national identity. They turned for inspiration to the traditions of those isolated valleys with their ancient farmsteads and their equally ancient verbal traditions, telling heroic sagas about an expansive

Norway of earlier days and of the greatness of native Viking lords.

Henrik Wergeland (1808–45), a richly talented poet and prose writer, became an early and passionate propagandist of this sort of Norwegian nationalism. Following the same call, artist J.C. Dahl (1788–1857) left his studio for the wilds of Norway's hinterland. His shimmering, majestic views of the mountains are major attractions at the National Gallery which he helped to found in 1836.

On the dark side, the epoch's fears of isolation and rampant anxiety of the future inspired the violent, emotionally charged style of painter Edvard Munch (1863–1944). Death and desolation are his recurring themes most strongly expressed in *The Scream* (1893), *The Kiss* and *The Vampire* (both 1895). Munch's fears of enslavement come so close to the national heart that his works have been enshrined in their own museum in Oslo as well as on an entire floor of the National Gallery.

Equally loud cries for freedom came from Henrik Ibsen (1828–1906) whose poetic drama *Brand* was a spirited indictment of Norwegian authority at home. It put Ibsen on the cultural map for the first time even outside Norway.

At the same time, the close of the 19th century, other authors turned homewards for inspi-

ration. Alexander Kielland (1849–1906) abandoned a promising international career to write about old Norway. Nobel laureate Knut Hamsun's (1859–1952) chilling novel *Hunger* (1890) is an exposé of the abuses of bourgeois Swedish rule. His masterpiece, *The Growth of the Soil* (1917), reflects a deep love of nature and concern for the effects of material conditions on the individual spirit, themes that still dominate Norwegian writing.

Even architects abandoned continental idioms to embrace a native "Viking Romanticism". They began building in heavy timber and turfed roofs. Eaves and gables sprouted carved and polychromed dragon heads. An

excellent example of the style is Troldhaugen, the last home of composer Edvard Grieg (1843–1907). Just outside Bergen, the house fits perfectly into Grieg's unabashed folkloric, wildly romantic style. He titled his creations after national heroes such as the much loved *Peer Gynt Suite* (1876, words by Ibsen).

A century ago, new plays by national playwright Henrik Ibsen, works by major authors such as Amalie Skram (1847–1905) and Kielland were front-page news in Oslo, Bergen and Trondheim. Critics and politicians publicly debated new works; plays became issues, even national causes. Literature became the smithy where the nation's identity was being forged.

Dramatist Bjørnstjerne Bjørnso (1832–1910), championed the Norwegian cause, working his entire life to free the Norwegian theatre from Danish influence. While director of Bergen's Ole Bull Theatre (1857–59) and the Oslo Theatre a few years later, he commissioned new, saga-like dramas drawing on Norway's epic past, such as the *Sigurd Slembe Trilogy*. His efforts helped to revive Norwegian as a literary language. He became poet laureate and his poem, *Yes, We Love this Land of Ours,* became a rallying point in the struggle for political independence from Sweden. The poem is now the national anthem of Norway.

New Norse vs *bokmål*

The political and extremely didactic approach in Norwegian literature finally disappeared in the 1980s. But there are still many attempts to emancipate individual languages. Norway boasts three languages: Sami, used almost exclusively by the Sami (Lapps) in the north; then there are *bokmål* (book language) and *nynorsk* (new Norse), two variations on a theme that have developed since independence.

Bokmål grew out of the gradual exchange of Danish loan words for words discovered in native dialects, by the substitution of Danish syntax with Norwegian, and by turning soft Danish consonants into hard Norwegian ones. It became the official language, used today by about 80 percent of the towns and throughout the entire northern districts.

New Norse is only used by about 15 percent of Norwegian primary school children. It draws heavily on the archaic Old Norse of the central-western dialects. Since this is a language based on rural culture, *nynorsk* has suffered by

20th-century urbanisation, losing ground to *bokmål* – though to complicate matters, *nynorsk* literature is very popular.

New concerns

The 1980s produced a sort of realistic novel, written in sociology textbook style, directly opposed to the older, bourgeois psychology novels, "a die-hard heritage from Hamsun, Cora Sandel and Torborg Nedreaas". Most readable among these "revolution" works are Dag Solstad's (born 1941) trilogy about World War II, *Svik* (Betrayal), *Krig* (War) and *Brød og Våpen* (Bread and Arms). This revival of problems using "street language" and spoken modes of expression. Løvied's lyrically erotic *Sug* (Suck) rocked the staid Oslo critics but has brought her international recognition. Live Køltzow's (born 1945) third novel, *The Story of Eli*, explores sex roles in society.

The 1990s saw a general literature boom. Whodunnits by Gunnar Staalesen, Kim Småge, Ingvar Ambjørnsen and Anne Holt are well known and popular. The first prize, however, must go to a book on the history of philosophy written for adolescents: *Sophie's World* by Jostein Gaarder. He is quite easily the most famous Norwegian writer since Knut Hamsun.

social realism allowed an author such as Asbjørn Elden (1919–90) to produce essentially modern yet "back to our roots" sagas about the inconspicuous lives of ordinary people, such as his *Rundt Neste Sving* (Around the Next Bend).

Women have come to the fore of Norwegian writing. Cecilie Løveid (born 1951) and Kari Bøge (born 1950) crashed on to the literary scene in the late 1970s with audacious, even shocking works. Ignoring male-dominated social realism, they picked apart purely female

LEFT: detail from Edvard Munch's *The Vampire* (1895).
ABOVE: writer and nationalist Bjørnsterne Bjørnson at the dinner table.

Post-war art

As with other cultural forms, Norwegian art began to drop its nationalist style after World War II. Gone (but certainly not forgotten) were the fairytale illustrations of Theodor Kittelsen (1857–1914) and morbid subject matter of Edvard Munch and in came the modernists. Impressionism inspired such landscape artists as Gladys Nilssen Raknerud (born 1912) and Thorbjørn Lie-Jørgensen (1900–61); expressionism found its place through the likes of Arne Ekeland (born 1908) and Rolf Nesch (1893–1975); and abstract expressionism appeared in the early 1960s through the work of Sigurd Winge (1909–70) and Jakob Weidemann (born 1923).

However, the old nationalist style continued well into the 1950s with such artists as Hjalmar Haalke (1892–1964) and Søren Steen Johnsen (born 1903) and the team responsible for the Oslo Rådhus murals. There was also the inevitable reaction to the modernists. When Odd Nerdrum (born 1944) applied for a place at the National Academy of Fine Arts he submitted three works; two of these had been long-term projects, but he was selected on the basis of his third work, an abstract image thrown together the night before. With his scepticism towards the establishment and doubts about abstract art reinforced, the young Nerdrum

Leading the way

If there is one area where Norwegians have the edge it is in furniture; consider Peter Opsvik's classic TrippTrapp chair for kids or his sculpture-like Cylindra Objects, and architecture, which in recent years has responded to increasing demands for sustainable development. Probably the most internationally renowned Norwegian architect is the "concrete poet" Sverre Fehn (born 1924), whose main materials have been concrete, wood and glass, and Nordic light. In 1997, Fehn became the first Nordic architect to win the American Pritzker Architecture Prize, the "Nobel Prize" of archi-

turned to the great masters, in particular Rembrandt, in whom he saw "eternal tranquillity". However, his subject matter was always on the controversial side – see *Amputation* (1974) or *Hermaphrodite* (1976–81) – and it took until the late 1980s for the Norwegian public to catch on to his post-modern classicism.

There is growing interest in the moderns, which had hitherto been the domain of the avant gardist Swedes. The focal point of the Norwegian art calendar is the Autumn Exhibition in Oslo, and in recent years the city has seen the opening of three new contemporary art galleries, all exhibiting the works of national and international artists.

tectural awards, and the award cited "a marvellous, lyrical and ingenious architectural form… both forceful and extremely rational". To see his work visit the Norsk Bremuseum (Glacier Museum) in Fjærland, built in 1991, or the Hedmarksmuseet (Museum) in Hamar.

There is also a wealth of talent to continue the traditions of the prolific sculpture Gustav Vigeland (1869–1943). There are more 20th-century sculptures/statues per capita in Norway than in any other country in Europe: see *inter alia* Joseph Grimeland's Sailors' Memorial, Bygdøy; Arnold Haukeland's "dynamic" structure, Strandpromenaden, Oslo; and Knut Steen's Whaling Monument, Sandefjord.

Norway's Paganini

Norway has a long tradition in music. The skaldic poems of the Viking Age provide a medieval link to the music traditions of Central Europe; Gregorian chants used in the worship of St Olaf are very similar to the Parisian school of the 13th century.

While higher forms of music stagnated during the 450 years of Danish rule, folk music unfolded freely, encouraged by the ecclesiastical centres and travelling musicians of the time.

Norwegian music developed for the first time in the early 1800s, mainly as a result of the union with Sweden and the influence of the Royal Swedish Court, but also because of the international breakthrough made by violin virtuoso Ole Bull (1810–80) in 1834. "The Nordic Paganini", as he was called, became a model for musicians and writers such as Grieg, Bjørnson and Ibsen. The 1870s and 80s became know as the Golden Age of Norwegian music with such prominent composers as Halfdan Kierulf (1815–68), Edvard Grieg and Johan Svendsen (1849–1911). Music took on a national flavour, urged on by Ole Bull's promotion of the Hardanger fiddle and Ludvig Mathias Lindeman's collection of Norwegian folk tunes. Most of the composers of the second half of the 19th century incorporated some element of folk music in their works.

With the end of the union with Sweden in 1905, Norwegian composers found the need to define a national identity, which they achieved by reverting back to the music of the Norwegian Middle Ages. Seeking inspiration in medieval poetry, German romanticism and French impressionism, David Monrad Johansen (1888–1970) tried to create a monumental kind of music based on musical archaisms. This national romanticism continued until just after the war. Germany was out; a new generation of composers went to study in Paris or the United States, consciously aware of the need to internationalise their musical language.

Today, Oslo, Trondheim and Bergen all have philharmonic orchestras, and the latter hosts the Bergen International Music Festival each May.

> ### FESTIVAL CULTURE
> Norway has a festival for almost everything, from the midnight sun and trolls to the winter and emigration.

The Norwegians' yearning for culture is most explicit, however, in the myriad of festivals, especially folk festivals, that are organised each year. If you wish to find the real soul of Norway visit the country in May. It's a month when little gets done, much to the chagrin of foreigners who arrive on business. But it's the prime time for observing the patriotic emotions that lie at the centre of Norwegian culture. The month starts with the May Day festivals; but the high point comes on the 17th, Norway's National Day. ⊔

NORWEGIAN CINEMA

Based around a unique system of municipal cinemas and the state-run Norsk Film, Norwegian cinema has come a long way from its first feature *The Perils of the Fisherman*, made in 1907. It gained a considerable amount of international attention in the 1970s with such films as Anja Breiens' *Wives* (1974) and Lasse Glomm's *The Second Shift* (1977). The prevailing style of social realism began to fade in the 1980s, and was replaced by a variety of approaches, including Roar Skolman's surrealist *Junior Heads* (1981) and the Oscar-nominated *Pathfinder*, made in 1988 by Nils Gaup.

LEFT: the Breheimsenteret (Glacier Centre), Jostedal.
RIGHT: Live Køltzow.

NATURE'S LARDER

*Wild nature and a mild climate are the main
sources of the ingredients from which
Norway's culinary traditions have evolved*

Magnificent landscapes
and climatic contrasts
have helped to create a
natural larder from which
Norwegians have helped
themselves for centuries.
Norway's long, varied
coastline has provided
ample opportunity for
harvesting both "wild"
and farm-raised fish; the slow ripening process of
everything that grows during the light summer
imparts an extraordinary aroma to berries, fruits
and vegetables; and the animals that graze on the
verdant grass provide meat with a distinctive full
flavour. Today Norwegian comestibles such as
Chinese cabbage, apples, pears, cherries and strawberries are in demand the world over. Although
eyebrows are raised when the nation's chefs win
international awards, it is not the first time that
foreigners have been impressed by Norway's fare.

PAPAL SURPRISE

When papal envoy Cardinal Wilhelm Sabina
attended the coronation of King Håkon V in
Bergen in 1247, he arrived with apprehension
having been forewarned about the food. However,
in his speech following the banquet he lavished
praise on the meal he had been served. Sadly, the
historical record of his speech makes no mention
of the menu, but visitors to Norway in the 18th
and 19th centuries speak highly of the salmon,
fowl, game and strawberries with cream – treats
which modern-day tourists may also experience.

▷ **MARKET TRADING**
The famous Bergen fish
market was once the place
where locals gossiped about
the latest catch: now they
come here to catch up on
the latest gossip!

△ **WILD PASSION**
Cloudberries (or *multebær*)
are found in mountain marsh-
lands in late summer/ early
autumn. Rich in vitamin C,
multer is used as a jam, a
liqueur and in desserts.

◁ **GONE FISHING**
Fish of all shapes and
sizes, including cod
(*torsk*), haddock (*hyse*)
and plaice (*flyndre*), are
landed daily in the ports
along the West Coast.

△ **SUPERIOR BREAKFAST**
Probably the most
important meal of the day in
Norway is breakfast (*frokost*),
with copious amounts of cold
meats, cheeses, crispbreads
and black coffee.

AKEVITT – THE WATER OF LIFE

Akevitt (aquavit or "water of life") is the national spirit of Norway. The most famous aquavit, Løiten Linie, is matured through a century-old process which includes a sea voyage in oak casks across the equator and back (each bottle carries details of its "voyage" on its label). This story originates from 1840, when the Norwegian ship *Preciosa* rounded Cape Horn; on board was aquavit, which the crew swore had improved in flavour.

Distilled from Norwegian potatoes, this blend of spirit, caraway and other herbs and spices is matured for several months in sherry casks. The result is a smooth spirit of about 45% proof by volume. Norwegians regard Linie as an accompaniment to pork (*ribbe*); It also goes well with seafood and the Christmas *lutefisk* dish.

▽ **LOFOTEN TRADITIONS**
Klippfisk (dried, salted split-cod) is a major Norwegian export and *rorbuer* (fishermen's huts) now accommodate tourists in Lofoten.

▷ **PRAWN COCKTAIL**
Fresh prawns (*reker*) are a favourite among Norwegians, served with white bread (*loff*), mayonnaise, lemon and an ice-cold pils.

▷ **MAGIC MUSHROOMS**
Chanterelle mushrooms are found in the forests north of Trøndelag and are a delicious complement to reindeer and game.

WHY DOES EVERYTHING COST SO MUCH?

Norway's high standard of living has its price, but it isn't as expensive as it used to be

L et's get this straight right from the start: day-to-day living *used* to be exorbitantly expensive in Norway, about 25 years ago, but there has been a gradual levelling out of prices in comparison with other European countries. Today, some food items are generally less expensive than elsewhere, such as cof-

fee and butter, but these are the exception rather than the rule. Visitors are often surprised at the relatively high prices for meat and, amazingly enough, fish. Staple vegetables are reasonable; exotic types, for which there is less demand, are expensive. Fruit follows the same pattern. You can find imported apples or tomatoes at normal European Union (EU) prices.

This is partly explained by high taxes: Norway adds 22 percent VAT to all grocery items. However, the European Economic Area (EEA) Agreement with the EU, signed in 1992, has meant that the old restrictive import practices are slowly being eroded away, and supermarkets are gearing up accordingly.

"Made in Norway"

Somewhat surprisingly Norway boasts a reasonable tomato crop, less because of sunshine and high temperatures and more because the Norwegian Ministry of Agriculture sees independence from other countries as its main aim.

Norway's desire to be self-sufficient has blossomed in unusual areas. The farmers in some tiny valleys in the west of the country live in grand style because their tomatoes, cucumbers, Chinese cabbages or cattle are highly subsidised. Only three percent of the land is used for agriculture, so variety is essential.

Cattle farmers are proud of their beef and pork, vegetable farmers praise their organically grown produce; and it's true that meat scandals are unheard of in Norway. But it's equally true that Norwegian tomatoes don't taste of anything much other than water. However, 95 percent of the grain consumed is harvested in the country and cattle is almost entirely reared in the domestic market. As far as foodstuffs are concerned, the logo "Made in Norway" is therefore more an expression of a political principle than of exceptionally high quality.

Things are changing. The higher standard of living has stimulated a demand for a richly laid table. Admittedly, prices in Norwegian hotels are high – but so is the standard of the breakfast buffet. Anyone sampling a fully laden breakfast table can only start the day in a good mood: fruit juice, smoked salmon, pickled herring, fresh bread, fruit and muesli. This meal can easily get you through the day and save you the expense of lunch. So why bother about money?

Taxed to the hilt?

Not so long ago, it was fashionable to blame rich farmers and a false subsidy policy for high taxes. In reality these subsidies are cut each year, more and more smallholdings have been given up and the tax burden is now bearable.

The average income of around NOK200,000 (£17,000/US$27,000) is subject to 30–45 percent income tax. But that's it. Social security, health insurance and pension payments are all included, and even the Church is funded by the state. Other state revenue comes from oil and gas sales as well as taxes on various luxury items – which explains the high prices for cars, alcohol and cigarettes.

Luxury costs money and Norwegians aren't supposed to enjoy luxury items – or at least they should do it in a different way. The debate on cigarette and alcohol prices is an inevitable item in the annual budget discussions and only two of the eight political parties in the Storting vote to reduce these taxes. The rest squeeze yet a little bit more out of them every year: a packet of cigarettes costs more than NOK60 (£5/US$8).

long learned to live with the link between vice and illness, have stopped arguing about prices, and drink their beer in peace.

To drink or not to drink

As the alcohol takes affect, and especially if there are visitors present, many Norwegians feel obliged to explain why they are drinking. It is, they will say, because they can't remember when they were last in such good company or, as the case may be, feeling lonely and neglected. Before a dark cloud of Nordic gloom settles on the proceedings the subject is likely to broaden to why Norwegians drink so much, or,

Beer and wine prices are also on the increase. As Norwegians resignedly comment: "That's as certain as Christmas comes in December." But what is the reasoning behind a price of NOK40–50 (£3.30–4.20/US$5.30–6.80) in a restaurant and NOK18–22 (£1.70/US$2.75) in the supermarket for half a litre of beer? The government insists that the treatment of alcohol and cigarette-related illnesses costs billions. And the budget discussions are also enlivened by the Christian Democratic Party, which rallies against these vices. Norwegians, however, have

not much at all. The question of alcohol and its corollary, teetotalism, have long been burning issues in Norway and are discussed so keenly that visitors, who are bound to become involved, might like to familiarise themselves with the background.

The climate is often blamed for Norwegian drinking. There may be some truth in this, since long winters used to put a premium on the art of preserving and storing food. Salt was the key, and it was therefore consumed in such quantities that great thirst necessarily followed. The "normal" consumption of beer and mead was six to 10 litres (10 to 18 pints) per day. The aristocracy drank wine from the earliest times.

LEFT: Torget, the fish market in Bergen.
ABOVE: plenty of choice, but at a price.

The 19th century produced a rash of travel books about Norway, and all of them drew attention to a weakness for drink. Even boys of 12 and 14 years, according to the Reverend R. Everest, indulged in the "odious vice", drinking quantities of brandy "that would have astonished an English coalman". Pontoppidan, whose *Natural History of Norway* was published in 1755, admired the Norwegians: "so hospitable ... liberal ... willing to serve and oblige strangers." Not, however, when they drank: "When a peasant with his

> **TRICKY ISSUE**
>
> Since independence in 1905, the prohibition issue has been responsible for the downfall of three governments.

only hosts who travel abroad or live near the coast can offer famous names. One thing visitors should not expect is the Viking drink of mead. This tradition has nearly died out – because honey is dear and it's difficult to make.

Statistics prove, it is said defensively, that Norwegians actually consume less alcohol than almost any other European nation. These statistics also reveal that beer and wine have supplanted harder spirits. But unreported numbers are a lot higher: Norwegians like to travel and certainly buy the complete quota of duty-free items. Also not included in the statistics is HB, home-made schnapps made from sugar and potatoes. Even in this high-tech age, there are still quite a few moonshine distillers at work, and *sprit* (96 percent raw alcohol) smuggling is big business.

It would be unrealistic to seek reliable information about smuggling along Norway's long coastline, although there may be a clue in the fact that when a strike closed the state-run *Vinmonopol* shops for months on end in 1986, there were no apparent shortages and, as soon as the suppliers had geared up for the unexpected windfall, the price of alcohol went down to levels unknown before or since.

family was invited to a wedding, the wife generally took her husband's (funeral) shroud with her; on these occasions they seldom parted before they were intoxicated with liquor, the consequences of which was fighting, and those battles seldom ended without murder."

Home brew

Although the Norwegians are extremely hospitable they will only offer alcoholic beverages once proper friendship has been established. Those who like the odd tipple can normally present a well-stocked bar but many of these drinks are often home-made. Every large town has shops selling winemaking equipment, so

A history of prohibition

The first attempt to curb drinking in Norway, possibly in the world, was made by King Sverre in Bergen in the 12th century. He was the leader of a rapacious bunch of ruffians called the *Birkebeiner*, who might have won the Battle of Fimreite for him against the rival Magnus Erlingsson except that they were too drunk to fight on his behalf. Sverre's attempt failed.

The strident minority in favour of total prohibition saw World War I, in which Norway remained neutral, as an opportunity to press their case. The excuse was to conserve the raw materials that went into the making of beer and spirits. When the war ended the restrictions were not lifted; on the contrary, they were extended to cover all alcoholic drinks except wines below a certain, modest strength.

Unfortunately for the prohibitionists, France, Spain and Portugal were among the largest customers for Norway's important fishing industry, and they paid for the fish with wine, none of which qualified under the new regulations for sale or consumption in Norway. Under pressure from the fishing industry, the limit was lifted just enough to admit the French wine, but the country was also saddled with 400,000 litres (88,000 gallons) of French brandy for which it had no possible use, having given an undertaking not to re-export it.

The government immediately declared prohibition permanent, a signal to Spain and Portugal that it would not be hoodwinked in similar fashion again. Two years later, they let it be known that 500,000 litres (110,000 gallons) of fortified Spanish wine were nevertheless on their way, shortly to be followed by 850,000 litres (185,000 gallons) of Portuguese. The government resigned rather than face a country awash in untouchable drink. The new government lifted the ban on wine, and in so doing put the skids under national prohibition.

State control

Since 1923 and until recently the import and sale of wines and spirits had been a state monopoly. Government buyers decided what was to be made available (and the price) in the chain of *Vinmonopolet* shops, as well as in most hotels and restaurants. It was said that by this act the Norwegian state had made itself the biggest single buyer of alcoholic drinks in the world, a painful irony for the numerous prohibitionists who were still beating the drum.

In 1997, however, the Norwegian government made a major concession to the EU by deregulating the import, wholesale and distribution side of the market. The effect of this means that hotels, restaurants and bars may now do business with independent importers, and *Vinmonopol* has been forced to privatise its distribution function. Although maintaining their monopoly on retail sales (and prices), the *Vinmonopolet* shops are slowly revamping their image (they used to be as uninviting as a dentist's waiting-room), and the stigma attached to walking around with chinking wine bottles in a plain plastic bag is fast disappearing.

One of the results of this, as visitors find out, is that drinks are freely available in major cities, albeit at numbing prices (typically NOK40–50 (£3.30–4.20/US$5.30–6.80) for a half litre of beer, NOK120 (£10/US$16) for the cheapest bot-

LEFT: a *Vinmonopol* shop.
RIGHT: home brewing in the attic.

tle of wine in a bar – beer and spirit prices are fixed at low profit margins, so poor wine-drinkers are in effect subsidising all the others.

Today, it is easier to be served a drink in Oslo at 2am than it is, say, in London. Laws affecting the sale of alcohol, however, are decided at the *kommune* level (i.e. by town and rural councils), so outside the cities, and especially on the west coast *bibelbelte*, it is a matter of luck whether a particular place is completely dry and without a legal drink within 100 km (60 miles). Between Sognefjord and Ålesund there are only two *Vinmonopol* outlets but dozens of hotels who didn't apply for a licence.

Paying for the roads

It's no exaggeration to claim that car drivers have financed their own infrastructure. Here, as with alcohol and tobacco, Norwegians believe in the principle of cause and effect, which is paid for through high car prices (Norway doesn't have its own car industry), a large tax on petrol and toll charges: if you want to drive through Oslo (and there are few ways to circumnavigate it) you have to pay a toll of NOK12 (£1/US$1.60). Bergen, Trondheim and Stavanger have similar, though less costly systems. The road system, on the other hand, now with numerous bridges and tunnels (including under the sea), reaches the tiniest villages. ❑

PLACES

*A detailed guide to the entire country, with principal sights
clearly cross-referenced by number to the maps*

Norway is a long narrow strip of a country, stretching north from mainland Europe far into the Arctic. In the ancient capital of Trondheim, you are 500 km (350 miles) from the modern capital of Oslo, yet only a quarter of the way up the country's jagged coast. Oslo is as far from Monaco as it is from Nordkapp (North Cape), with Norway's northernmost outpost, the islands of Svalbard (Spitsbergen), hundreds of kilometres further on. With a population of only 4½ million, Norway has, above all else, space.

Yet travel is not difficult. From early times, the Norwegians (as Vikings) were magnificent sailors, and this old way of travel continues today through the Hurtigrute coastal steamers and other ferries that link coastal communities. On land, the Norwegians have achieved in 100 years the seemingly impossible, connecting even the most isolated settlements by building railways, roads and bridges across their fjords and by tunnelling deep into the mountains and under the sea.

This is one of Europe's most beautiful countries. The scenery is dramatic and the land changes constantly, from mountain to sea, fjord to forest. Oslo, Stavanger, Bergen, Trondheim and Tromsø are small manageable cities that make good use of the surrounding countryside. Neither the Norwegian climate nor the people are as chilly as the northern latitudes might suggest. The Gulf Stream warms the western coastline so that the seas are ice-free all the year round, and the great distances and long journeys between villages, towns and farms have encouraged an age-old tradition of hospitality.

In the 1970s, oil brought wealth to Norway and now these stubborn, self-sufficient, deeply patriotic people enjoy one of the highest standards of living in the world.

Norwegians are an outdoor people, and Norway a country where inhabitants and visitors alike can make the most of limitless space for walking, skiing, touring and just breathing in the clear air. As a visitor you are advised to "explore" the amenities on offer, but do not expect all the man-made attractions to be as monumental as the country itself. The relatively small domestic market and short summer season are unable to finance major "Disney-like" attractions, and many of the museums, especially those in rural areas, exist more because of local enthusiasm and voluntary effort than to any supreme tourist policy and national funding. When you see a national heritage symbol our advice is to go and investigate – you'll probably be pleasantly surprised. ❏

PRECEDING PAGES: Storm over Borgundfjorden; a "light circle" in the Arctic city of Tromsø; Gamlehaugen.
LEFT: drying fish in the Lofoten Islands.

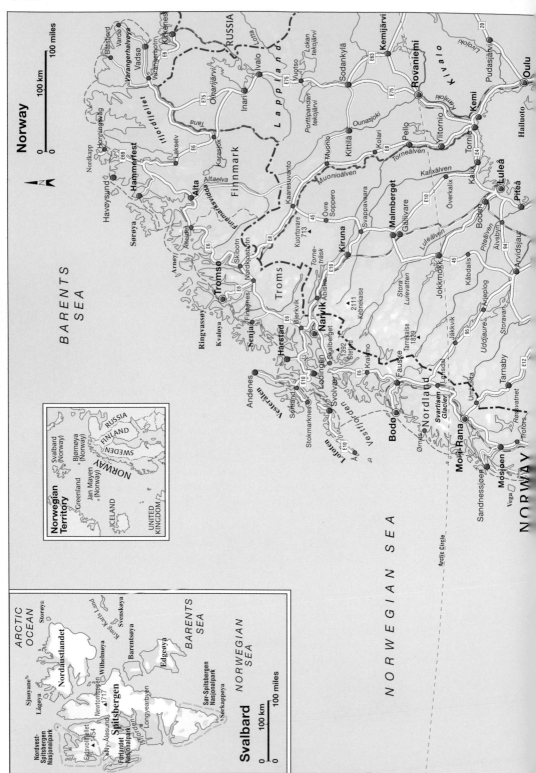

Norway

N

0 — 100 km
0 — 100 miles

BARENTS SEA

RUSSIA

Lappland

Finnmark

Troms

Tromsø

Narvik

Nordland

NORWEGIAN SEA

Arctic Circle

NORWAY

Norwegian Territory

Svalbard (Norway)
Bjørnøya (Norway)
Jan Mayen (Norway)
Greenland
ICELAND
RUSSIA
FINLAND
SWEDEN
NORWAY
UNITED KINGDOM

Svalbard

Spitsbergen

ARCTIC OCEAN

BARENTS SEA

NORWEGIAN SEA

0 — 100 km
0 — 100 miles

Nordaustlandet

0 — 100 km
0 — 100 miles

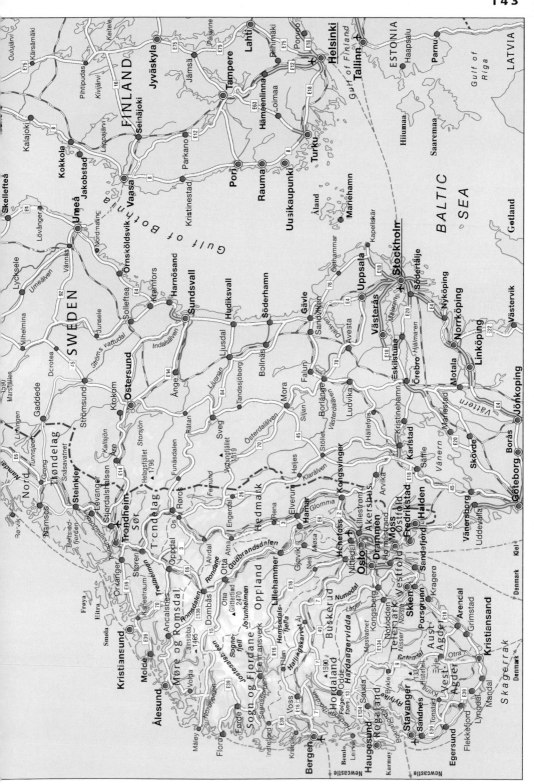

OSLO, NORDIC CITY OF LIGHT

*Oslo has shaken off its dowdy image and emerged full of new street
life, with a multitude of galleries and museums. And Oslo's fjord,
the Nordmarka forest and a Viking ship are just a short ride away*

Map on
pages
156–7

I n the 1880s and 1890s, Edvard Munch drew and painted an Oslo seemingly
inhabited by spectres. Men and women were dressed all in black, their hat
brims pulled down low, their faces chalk. To him they were like "the living
dead who wend their tortuous way down the road that leads to the grave".

This is the Oslo that was, a dour city lacking the vitality of Copenhagen or
Stockholm; Munch left it to live in Berlin and Paris. Nearly 100 years later, until
the mid-1980s, many of Oslo's cultural attractions were still imported, while
native talent left for the brighter lights elsewhere. The only real cultural diversions
were a few museums based around explorers and skiers.

Expensive and remote, Oslo also bore another black mark. Nights were once
meanly trimmed of their fun by laws that severely curbed drinking hours, a tes-
tament to the influence of that side of Norwegian Lutheranism which brings the
mentality of the small village to the big city. And so travellers to Norway used
to give Oslo no more than a passing nod as they steamed through on their way
to Bergen and the more spectacular scenery of the west coast fjords.

Coming alive

To call Oslo the Nordic City of Light would be too pat a way of saying that Oslo

PRECEDING PAGES:
outside Oslo's
parliament building
on National Day.
LEFT: Gustav
Vigeland's great
Monoliten.
BELOW: Aker
Bryggo.

has come of age. But in a short space of time it has,
and Oslo today bears little resemblance to the dim
place that Munch so hated – or even to the Oslo of
the early 1980s. Norway, despite all its interest in the
past, has awakened to the attractions of city fun. The
small capital by the fjord has developed into a metrop-
olis with a revitalised cultural life, not to mention a
diverse and lively night life.

Oslo's cultural rebirth in the late 1980s has been in
part conscious, in part a natural outcome of infusions
of money in the right places. If the talent were to be
lured back home, things would have to change dra-
matically – they did. On the back of the oil boom came
more and more money for the arts. A lot of artists still
used their stipends to work abroad, but suddenly there
was sufficient going on at home to make them curious
enough to return. (One famous Norwegian who stayed
faithful to Oslo throughout her artistic career was
actress Liv Ullman, who came back again and again to
play in Ibsen here.)

Best by boat

Oslo is at the head of a fjord shaped like a swan's
neck; it is surrounded by low hills. Your initial impression will depend entirely on how you arrive. The ideal
way is by boat, for then you get the most complete
picture, though arriving by car from the south along
the Mosseveien also offers some impressive views.

There are now a few tall buildings in Oslo, but your view from the fjord will still be dominated by the **Rådhus** ❶ (City Hall; open all year; free). It is a large, mud-coloured building topped by two square towers, not a favourite among Oslonians but a useful landmark. Opened in 1950 to commemorate the city's 900th anniversary, the building improves on closer inspection. The courtyard is adorned with fantastic figures and symbols from Norwegian mythology; note the **astronomical clock**, the **Yggdrasill frieze** by Dagfin Werenskiold and Dyre Vaas' **swan fountain**. The mosaics inside the main hall are based around more modern themes. The south-facing clock, at over eight metres (30 ft) in diameter, is one of the largest timepieces in Europe.

In defence

To the right, abutting the fjord, is the medieval **Akershus slott og festning** ❷ (Castle; open all year; free access to grounds). Built originally in 1308, it helped protect Christiania (as Oslo was called until 1925) from marauders throughout the periods of Danish and Swedish rule. The Nazis took over Akershus during

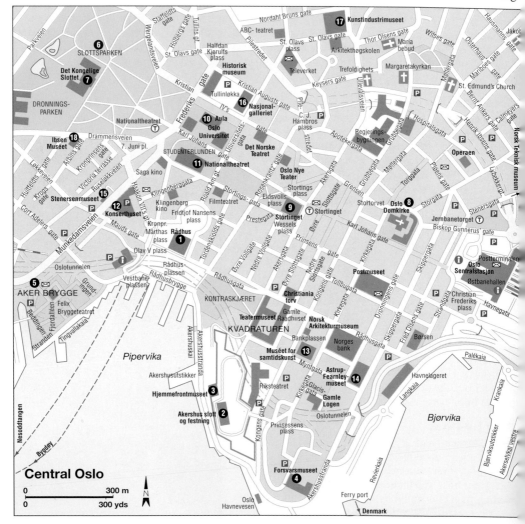

Central Oslo

0 ——— 300 m
0 ——— 300 yds

World War II and shot several resistance fighters by the old magazine. When the war was over, the traitorous Norwegian chancellor, Quisling, was shot on the same spot. The **Hjemmefrontmuseet** ❸ (Resistance Museum; open all year; entrance fee) in the grounds illustrates the intense story of occupied Norway, while the **Forsvarsmuseet** ❹ (Armed Forces Museum; open all year; free) covers Norwegian military and political history from the Vikings to today.

Thrusting up on the opposite side of the Pipervika inlet are the glass, chrome and neon traceries of **Aker Brygge** ❺. Centred around an open-air sculpture court, this modern harbourside development contains shopping arcades, bars, restaurants, food stalls, theatres and galleries.

In summer, greenery encroaches on Oslo from every side. From the fjord approach you'll see the tops of the trees of **Slottsparken** ❻ (Palace Gardens), and several parks stretching north beyond it to the wooded hills at Oslo's back. There your eye will inevitably be drawn to the giant white curlicue of the Holmenkollen ski-jump arched against one of the city's highest hills.

Compact centre

Oslo city centre is large enough to be interesting yet compact enough to get around on foot. The main axis is **Karl Johans gate**, originally designed in 1826 by the Royal architect H.D.F. Linstow, it was widened some 30 years later to become Oslo's answer to the Champs Elysées. Its western end merges into the broad avenue leading to the doors of **Det Kongelige Slottet** ❼ (Royal Palace), and the focal point of the National Day celebrations on 17 May. In the east it runs to Jernbanetorget, the location of **Oslo Sentralstasjon** (Oslo S station). To the south, the centre extends to the natural boundary of the fjord.

Map on page 148

TIP

An easy way to travel around the city is to invest in an Oslokortet (Oslo Card), available from tourist offices, most hotels and some newsagents, which is both a city-wide travel pass as well as a parking and musuem discount ticket.

BELOW: the Rådhus (City Hall) at night.

A statue of Karl XIV Johan stands on the steps of Det Kongelige Slott, the Royal Palace.

Parallel to Karl Johans gate to the north is **Grensen**, another busy, shop-lined street. The **Oslo Domkirke** ❽ (Cathedral; open all year; free) dominates Stortorvet (square) at the east end of Grensen. Completed in 1697, its exterior is of darkened brown brick, while inside artists of the 18th, 19th and 20th centuries have contributed to the cathedral's adornment, making an eclectic but nonetheless important display of Norwegian church architecture and interior design. Behind Domkirke is a round, colonnaded market with food and handicraft stalls.

Grensen becomes **Khristian IV's gate** as it passes the **Stortinget** ❾ (Parliament; open all year, with public gallery and guided tours) and **Eidsvollplass** then runs alongside the old university. Studenterlunden, the small park around the university, contains the main university building, **Aula** ❿, which is decorated with murals by Edvard Munch. The **Nationaltheatret** ⓫ (National Theatre) is just opposite Studenterlunden, and **Slottsparken** is immediately west.

Artistic attractions

Norwegians, with their seagoing past, have always had a fine awareness of faraway cultures. But it has always been hard to entice foreign artists they admired, not just their work, to their own shores: Norway was too remote, the population too small. Riotously enthusiastic receptions can make up for a lot, however, and that's how Oslo now gets its favourites back year after year. The Oslo Philharmonic, whose home is the **Konserthuset** ⓬ (tel: 22 83 32 00) on Munkedamsveien, performs with a dazzling sequence of guest conductors and soloists. Away from the classical, the variety of music to be heard in Oslo's clubs and concert halls is vast, from South American to punk rock. Even the mega-stars such as Michael Jackson or The Rolling Stones add Oslo to their

BELOW: inside the Rådhus (City Hall).

world tour calendar. Every August there is an international jazz festival, and in September it's the international Gjøglerne Kommer (The Clowns Are Coming), a performing arts festival with venues throughout the city.

The simple need for space to accommodate all these artistic ventures has also played a role in reviving neglected parts of Oslo. It has helped breathe life back into **Christian IV's town**, "Kvadraturen", an historic area bounded to the north by Rådhusgata and to the south by Akershus Slott, and characterised by old customs and shipping houses and grand open plazas. Until recently, this area was frequented only by streetwalkers and their pursuers, who could be assured of empty streets to use as pick-up points. The town's history as a redoubtable part of Oslo is reflected in its former nickname, "Little Algerie" – see the painting in Engebret Café on Bankplassen, an artists' haunt since the early 1900s.

But **Gamle Logen** on Grev Wedels Plass is a now a serious concert venue and there's also the **Cinemathèque** (repertory film theatre). The **Norsk Arkitekturmuseum** (Norwegian Museum of Architecture; open all year; entrance fee) is found in Kongens gate just over from the newly opened Clarion Bastion Hotel. The **Muséet for Samtidskunst** ⓭ (Museum of Contemporary Art; open all year; entrance fee) is housed in the original Norges Bank (Central Bank) building, on Bankplassen, and has an extensive collection of 20th century Norwegian art. Just around the corner is the **Astrup Fearnley-museet** ⓮ (Modern Art; open all year; entrance fee) which focuses on international artists, although it too contains Scandinavian works. Galleries across the city are full of art in every medium, and established museums have opened their doors to the works of contemporary, living artists. Try the **Stenersenmuseet** ⓯ (closed Mon; entrance fee) near the Konserthuset.

Map on page 148

BELOW: Akerhus Slott (Castle).

A multitude of museums

The **Nasjonalgalleriet** (National Gallery; open all year; entrance fee) is for anyone who has never heard of any Norwegian artist apart from Edvard Munch. The sheer size, if not the content, of the forest and fjord paintings of the Romantic artist J. C. Dahl (1788–1857) will impress you. You'll also see the work of his prolific contemporaries, Adolph Tidemand (1814–76) and Hans Frederik Gude (1825–1903). There is a wonderful series of etchings depicting barn dances and village scenes and festivities. The international display, especially of Impressionists, is also excellent. And don't forget the Munch room.

A little further north is the **Kunstindustrimuseet** (Museum of Applied Art; closed Mon; entrance fee). It is graced by two earthen urns at its entrance and has superb displays of Norwegian textile, fashion and furniture design. The most famous tapestry in its possession is the *Baldishol*, dating from 1180, and one of the most popular exhibits is of the royal costumes. On the uppermost floor is a collection of Scandinavian design for the home ranging from bent-wood chairs to streamlined kitchen gadgets.

A short way up Drammensveien from the National Gallery and next to the Royal Palace is the small **Ibsen Muséet** (entrance from Arbiens gate; open all year; guided tours; entrance fee) set in Henrik Ibsen's apartment where he lived from 1895 until his death in 1906.

For the technically minded there is the **Norsk Teknisk museum** (Museum of Science, Technology and Telecommunications; open all year; suburban train, trams 11 or 12, bus 37 to Kjelsås; entrance fee). This is a great day out for the kids with lots of hands-on exhibitions about energy, industry, transport and telecommunications. There is also a shop and cafeteria. Nearby is a water mill and weir which feeds the Akerselva river.

Life on the streets

Along with the upturn in the arts, Oslo's streets feel tangibly alive these days, especially in summer: festivals come fast and furious, opening hours are greatly extended, and the crowds at restaurants and cafés brim over on to the pavement.

Oslo's growth in nightlife owes much to the lifting of restrictions on licensing hours. In the late 1980s and early 1990s it was possible to drink (legally) virtually round the clock. But this led to problems of rowdiness and so licensing hours were restricted to 3am – still not bad for a Lutheran society with a monopoly on retail sales of wines and spirits. So alcohol is more widely available, even if still brutally expensive. The number of new **bars** and **clubs** that have sprung up in order to take advantage of late-night traffic is astounding. Even more astounding is that they draw people seven nights a week.

Restaurants too have flourished: the influx of immigrants has resulted in a variety of ethnic kitchens being opened, though they still tend to cater for the Norwegian palate by being rather conservative with the spices. Included among these "foreign" restaurants are typical north–west Norwegian fish restaurants which serve traditional dishes according to age-old recipes.

TIP

There is a large choice of museums in Oslo and the best source of detailed information about them, and other cultural events in the city, is the *What's On/Hva Skjer* Oslo Guide, available free from tourist offices and hotel foyers.

BELOW: in summer everything happens on the streets.

Map on
page
148

Norwegians are serious coffee drinkers and nowhere in the city should you find yourself far from a café to take respite in. There are **cafés** that are simply cafés (sometimes spelled *kafé*). Then there are *gjæstgiveris, kros, bistros, spiseris* and *kafeterias*, which all tend to be a bit more casual than restaurants; in other words, they are likely to serve smallish meals plus snacks all day and into the night. Seattle-style coffee shops are also popular: if you are travelling by train via Oslo S or just passing nearby try the authentic Rooster Coffee Bar in the nearby **Østbanehallen**.

Most eating and drinking places start to fill slowly after working hours and turn more boisterous after supper. Bars and clubs are spread throughout the city, and range from underground to upmarket – consult the *What's On* Oslo Guide (see Tip, opposite page), or consult someone who knows Oslo. Nightlife in Oslo changes every month. What used to be a disco is now a music pub. The "in" scene changes every year, but can normally be identified by the long queue in front of the building which will certainly not disperse after 1am. This phenomenon seems to be an intrinsic part of Norwegian nightlife and is therefore the best insider tip for visitors: the longest queue somewhere near Stortinget, that's your best bet.

The Fram, Fridtjof Nansen's Arctic exploration boat, took Roald Amundsen to the South Pole in 1912.

Come the weekend

The Norwegians tend to divide their evenings out into three different parts. Since restaurants are expensive friends are invited to the home. Once the richer crowds leave the cinemas, theatres or restaurants, then the real nightlife starts and the high price for a beer is no longer important. From 2am the pubs empty and act three is about to begin. Friends and neighbours (not necessarily the

BELOW: enjoying a drink on Karl Johans gate.

ones who were with you at the beginning of the evening) are invited in and offered the remaining contents of the house bar. Despite all the fun of enjoying Oslo till the last bars close, natives still pull on their boots and head for the hills next day. Love of nature and folklore are inbred in today's Norwegians.

Come Sunday evening, it's a good idea to book tickets early if you want to see a film, since Sundays are Oslo's favourite time to go to the movies. The price of seats is reasonable, at around NOK35–55 (£3–4.5), and most cinemas show films in their original language with Norwegian subtitles.

There is no English language theatre but Norwegians are devoted theatre-goers, and companies perform everything in Norwegian, from Eugene O'Neill to Andrew Lloyd Webber. You will find international drama festivals across Norway in summer, which would be your only chance to see something in English. However, if there's an Ibsen play on that you know well, it might be worth seeing it in Norwegian – the emotiveness of Ibsen should get through any language barrier. Tickets to the theatre start at NOK120 (£10).

How to stay solvent

When it comes to budgeting for a stay in Oslo, there are a number of ways to save your kroner. Norwegian hotel breakfasts usually offer a large, help-yourself selection. The better assortments are likely to include toast and crispbreads, cheese, marinated and smoked salmon, herring, cereals, fruit, eggs, juice, tea and coffee. (The *Kaldtbord*, which is the lunchtime variation, will have some hot dishes added.) If you can make a hearty breakfast your main meal of the day, and avoid eating a large evening meal in a restaurant, then you'll manage to keep to a reasonable budget.

BELOW: the rich pattern surrounding Vigeland's Monoliten.

The most common street snack is the *pølser* – a long, skinny hot dog served either with *brød* (bread) or rolled in a *lompe* (potato pancake). But there are now a lot of cafés, brasseries and pizzerias where you can get small to medium-sized meals that won't break the bank. Full meals can be reasonable, too, as long as you don't order a lot of alcohol.

Alas, the high cost of alcohol is unbeatable. Bringing in your full duty-free allowance helps, but you can't really tote your own bottle around the streets or in restaurants, so that provides a limited solution. Drinking costs will be high enough even if you stick to beer; but if you choose wine or spirits, they'll rocket.

In summer, hotel rates are deeply discounted to make up for the lack of business and conference traffic. In winter, you can sometimes do fairly well with weekend rates, but watch out for school and ski holiday weeks when hotels are crowded and rates higher again. Pensions, mission churches and youth hostels are usually reasonably priced. Camping is another option in such an outdoor city as Oslo: the site at Ekebergsletta, a hilly park suburb with extensive paths and wonderful broad views over Oslo and the fjord, is just over three kilometres (two miles) from town.

From Munch to minorities

Combining a museum visit with a stroll is a relaxing and usually a cheap way of spending part of a day or evening. Once you leave behind the bigger hotels and restaurants where business people wine and dine, food and drink prices drop significantly. The exploring suggestions below focus on sights outside the very heart of Oslo; the sights within the city centre area are easily found and fairly close together so no special planning is needed to reach them.

Map on page 148

BELOW: sculpture and echo in the Vigeland-museet.

Nordmarka

Strømsdammen Lake
Tryvannstårnet ㉗
Øvresetertjern
Lillevann
Skøgen
Voksen-kollen
Utsyten
Frognerseteren
Nordmarka
Sørkedalsveien
VESTRE GRAVLUND
Voksenkollveien
Holmenkollveien
Bogstad camping-plass
Voksenlia
Holmenkollen kapell
Skimuseet
㉖ Holmenkollen-bakken
Midtsuen
Holmenkollen
Ankerveien
Oslo
Besserud

0   750 m
0   750 yds

Borgenveien
Diakonveien
Thaulows vei
Tårnveien
Frøen
Apalveien
Kringkastingen
Grefsen
Wilhelm Færdens vei
Suhms vei
Gyldas vei
Gardeveien gate
Trudvangveien
Hammerstads gate
Kirkeveien
Majorstuen
Ole Vigs gate
Colosseum senter
Sporveismuseet
Misjons-kirken
Volvat
168
Stendalsveien
Sørkedalsveien
Valkyrie
Jacob Aalls gate
Majorstuen
Aalls gate
Suhms gate
Schønings gate
Fagerborggata
Lyder Sagens gate
Colosseum kino
Essendrops gate
Bogstadveien
MAJORSTUEN
Fagerborggata
Sorgenfri gate
Industrigata
Døvekirken
VIGELANDSPARKEN
Monolitten ㉔
FROGNERPARKEN
㉓
Frogner stadion
Kirkeveien
Majorsstuen
Gjørstads gate
168
Vibes gate
Rosenborggata
Sporveigata
HEGDEHAUGEN
St. Dominikus
Fearnleys gate
Industrigata
Underhaugsveien
HOMANSBYEN
Oslo Bymuseum ㉕
Professor Dahls gate
Fougnerbaugata
Munthes gate
Uranienborgveien
Prof. Dahls gate
Oscars gate
Hegdehaugsveien
Josefines gate
Vigelandmuseet
FROGNER
Nordraaks gate
Gyldenløves gate
Eckersbergs gate
Tidemands gate
BRISKEBY
Briskebyen
Sundts gate
Hoegda
Josefines gate
Uranienborg
Grønnegata
Hegdehaugsveien
Kunstne
Werge
Kristinelundgata
Hafrsfjordgata
Eckersbergs gate
Nobels
Thomas Heftyes gate
Gimleveien
Odins
Levenskiolds gate
Arno Bergs plass
President Harbitz gate
Briskebyveien
Hotgata
Skovveien
Camilla Colletts vei
Oscars gate
Hegder veien
Kontngata
Olav Kyrres plass
Bygdøy allé
Elisenbergveien
Frognerveien
Gyldenløves gate
Niels Juels gate
Skovveien
Oscars gate
Nobels
Tostrups gate
Thomas
Frogner
Gimle kino
Bygdøy
Gabels gate
Colbjørnsens gate
Meltzers gate
SLOTTSPARKE
Frøyas gate
American Lutheran Church
Sophus Lies gate
Mogens Thorsens gate
Bygdøy allé
Oslo Energi
Slottet
DRONNINGS-PARKEN
Nati th
Thomas Heftyes gate
Stangs
Hydro
Drammensveien
Parkveien
Drammensveien
SKILLEBEKK
Drammensveien
Universitets-biblioteket
Sollgata
Cort Adelers gate
RUSELØKKA
Observatorie terrasse
Ridstrygdeverket
Munkedamsveien
P.A. Reichwens gate
Observatoriegata
Huk
Oslotunnelen
Mauds
B y g d ø y
Frognerkilen
Båthavn
Munkedamsveien
AKER BRYGGE
Oscarshall slott ㉝
Kongen
Ferry port
Filipstadveien
Filipstadkaia
FILIPSTAD
Piper
Dronninghavnveien
Dronningen
Filipstadutstikker
Tjuvholmen
㉜ Norsk Folkemuseum
Melbyedalen
Langviksveien
Huk åveny
Christian Bennechees vei
Langviksbukta
Kon-Tiki museet
㉘ Vikingskipshuset
Løchenveien
㉚ ㉙
㉛ Frammuseet
Norsk Sjøfartsmuseum
Oslo
Bygdøyneset

0   500 m
0   500 yds

O s l o f j o r d
page 148

Denmark, Germany
Nesoddtangen

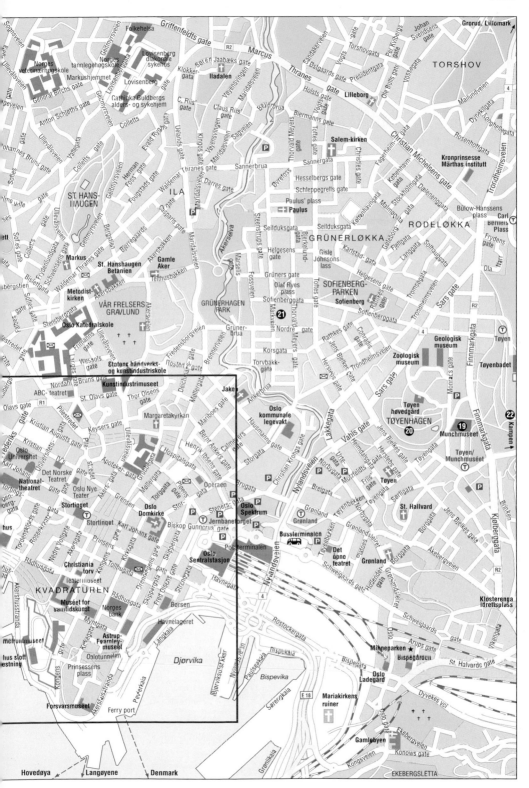

One of Oslo's many statues, overlooking the water in Eidsvollplass.

One of Norway's best-known museums is **Munchmuseet** (Munch Museum; T-bane Tøyen; open all year; entrance fee). A tremendous collection of Munch's work is housed there, all donated by the artist himself. Edvard Munch (1863–1944) was a doctor's son. As a child he often accompanied his father on calls, a time of his life reflected in numerous paintings of the sick and dying. Festive renderings of gypsy families and blazing autumn landscapes counteract these gloomier works. The famous *Skrik* (*Scream*) is darkly riveting, as is the *Marats død* series (*Death of Marat*, 1907) in which Munch portrays himself bleeding from gunshot wounds inflicted by an angry mistress. After a series of breakdowns, Munch returned to Norway, having spent most of his adult, artistic life in Paris and Berlin. He sought peace, but continued working, in his cottage at Åsgårdstrand in Vestfold.

The Munch museum is flanked by parks. The one to the east contains the **Tøyenbadet** (public swimming baths), including a lido, water slide and saunas. To the west is the **Tøyenhagen** (Tøyen Botanical Gardens) with the Zoological, Mineralogical, Geological and Palaeontological Museums at its north end (open all year; free). In September and early spring, this is the site of Norway's largest traditional circus.

A few streets northwest of Munchmuseet, across Trondheimsveien, is the **Grünerløkka** district. It is a former working-class neighbourhood, now densely populated with artists and writers. At the intersection of Trondheimsveien and Thorvald Meyersgate is the former Schous Bryggeri. The most interesting street in Grünerløkka is **Markveien**, painted in muted pastel colours and lined with galleries and boutiques. In the courtyard near Markveien 42 is a brick building housing various artists' studios. Continuing north on Markveien, you'll

BELOW: enjoying a meal outside, down by the harbour at Aker Brygge.

find a cross street called Grünersgate. From here up to Schleppergrellsgate are some magnificent residential courtyards. The gates are usually open. Peer inside for a look at how tranquil urban living in Oslo can be.

Kampen ㉒, whose northern limit is Kampenspark (on the southeast side of Munchmuseet), is a district of gorgeous wooden houses brilliantly painted in siennas, golds, pastels and vibrant blues. Some of the streets in lower Kampen are overhung by trees and are supremely quiet; look up, too, at the dormer windows above the street corners, hung with macramé and lace curtains.

Directly west of Kampen is Oslo's largest Pakistani neighbourhood. It is an interesting sidelight on to a largely mono-ethnic city, but in truth there is not much to do or see here unless you are hankering for a Pakistani meal. There are a few good, cheap grill restaurants, and local grocers sell fresh market produce.

Oslo is not as ethnically diverse as Copenhagen or Stockholm, but the immigrant community has grown rapidly over the past 15–20 years. Some 15 percent of the capital's inhabitants are immigrants, mainly from other European countries and Asia. Large numbers of Poles come in the summer months for seasonal work. While Sweden and Finland have prominent populations of Romany gypsies, and of Turks who came in the 19th century as fur and skin dealers, Norway's most noticeable older ethnic group is the Tartars. They have been in Norway for centuries and are smaller of stature and darker than the pure Scandinavian.

Vigeland's vision

West of the city centre is **Frognerparken** (park) or **Vigelandsparken ㉓** (sculpture park; open all year; free). The park, containing the life's work of the famous Norwegian sculptor Gustav Vigeland (1869–1943), is a 40-minute walk from the

Map on pages 156–7

BELOW: kindergarten children.

Nobel's Peace Prize

One of the great ironies is that the Swedish armaments manufacturer Alfred Nobel should have been the founder of the world's most prestigious prize for peace. Was it the realisation that his invention of nitro-glycerine in 1866 could and had been easily turned from peaceful rock tunnelling to war that led him to include the peace category alongside prizes for physics, chemistry, medicine and literature? Or was his conscience troubled by the thought that his great riches were built on weapons of war? It could have been no more than a tribute to the Norwegian reputation as workers for peace. Nobody knows what went on in the mind of this introspective, isolated man.

It is almost as strange that when he set up his trust fund, Nobel chose the Norwegian Storting (Parliament) in which to make the peace award. It was a time when the near

century-old union between Sweden and Norway was collapsing. Perhaps Nobel hoped that, by giving the Peace Prize into Norwegian jurisdiction, he might help keep the two nations together. If so, he failed. The Union was dissolved five years after his death in 1901 and Norway was already a year-old sovereign state at the first ceremonies in 1906.

Except for the Peace Prize, the other five categories are judged in Sweden and presented in Stockholm to those who, in Nobel's words, "shall have conferred the greatest benefit on mankind". In Oslo, the Nobel Peace Prize ceremony is held in the Aula (Great Hall) of Oslo University, against a wall of murals, called *The Sun*, by Edvard Munch.

Nobel's early instructions were that the Peace Prize should be used to award efforts to reduce the size of military forces and standing armies, but the Prize broadened its remit to the promotion of peace in general. This vague brief can lead to controversy, as it did when the Israeli and Egyptian Prime Ministers, Menachem Begin and Anwar Sadat, received the Peace Prize jointly for their 1978 efforts to open up talks and communication between their two countries. Dr Henry Kissinger's award in 1972 also aroused controversy, particularly when his Vietnamese co-recipient, Le Duc Tho, turned down his own award for their joint efforts in ending the Vietnam war. However, few begrudged Nelson Mandela and F.W. de Klerk their joint award in 1993.

There were no dissenters when the Red Cross received the prize in 1917 for its work amid the battlefield carnage of World War I. The explorer Fridtjof Nansen regarded the Nobel Peace Prize as the greatest of the tributes to his years as internationalist, humanitarian and head of the Norwegian delegation at the League of Nations.

Among the many other recipients were Martin Luther King, Dr Albert Schweitzer and Amnesty International, but most popular of all was Mother Teresa in December 1979. In the cold of a Norwegian winter, she appeared in her customary habit and sandals, standing out as a tiny figure of a woman in white against the guests' sombre suits and the rich colours of Munch's great mural. ❑

LEFT: Alfred Nobel (1833–96).

centre. One way of getting there would be by continuing on from the Royal Palace to Hegdehaugsveien, which becomes Bogstadsveien – a long, lively street of art galleries and enticing shops – or pick up a bus or tram (12 or 15) in the direction of Frogner. Any west-bound T-bane from the Nationaltheatret stops at Majorstuen, the end of Bogstadveien, from where it is only a short walk to the beginning of the park.

Map on pages 156–157

Once inside the intricate wrought-iron gates, you'll come across **Vigelands-broen** (bridge), bedecked with 58 bronze figures of men, women and new-born infants, including the famous *Sinnetagen* (*Angry Boy*). Next is **Fontenen** (Fountain); six male figures raising a giant bowl. Vigeland was obsessed with the cycle of life which he depicts here in 20 reliefs around the edge of the fountain pool. Above the fountain on a raised plateau, and surrounded by 36 groups of granite figures, is **Monolitten ㉔**, a great spire 17 metres (55 ft) high and comprising 121 figures sculpted out of one solid block of a whitish granite. The last of the major sculptures, the **Livshjulet** (Wheel of Life) is a continuum of human figures in a kind of airborne ring dance. The **Vigelandmuseet** (open all year; entrance fee), containing the rest of his work is at the southern end of the park. Some Norwegians love the park, others despise it. Vigeland spent 40 years of his life designing and constructing the park, all financed by the taxpayer, something which Munch found reprehensible, and proved it by donating all his own work to the city.

A living exhibit in traditional dress in Oslo's Folkemuseum at Bygdøy.

Frogner Park also contains the **Oslo Bymuseum ㉕** (City Museum; closed Mon; entrance fee). Founded in 1050 by Harald Hardråde, Oslo was originally bounded by the (now subterranean) Bjørvika, Alna and Hovin rivers. It took another 250 years before it attained capital status during the reign of Håkon V (1299–1319). The town had just 3,000 inhabitants at the time.

BELOW: Norwegians are generous in a good cause.

Following a great fire in 1624, Christian IV decided to move the whole conurbation to where Akershus Festning (Fortress) now stands, and the town became known as Christiania or "Kvadraturen". What was the centre is now called **Christiania torv**, where in 1997 a statue of Christian IV's index finger was erected to commemorate the historic event.

With its strict grid plan pattern, Christiania had little in common with medieval Oslo. The greatest change, however, has happened over the past 150 years due to growth in its population. In 1880, Christiania had 120,000 inhabitants; by 1910 the population had doubled. By popular consensus the town reverted to its original name in 1925. From 1945 to 1955, Oslo went through a new period of growth, and finally surpassed the half million mark in 1997.

Norway's national jump

For **Holmenkollen bakken ㉖** ski-jump and **Skimuseet** (Ski Museum: open all year; entrance fee) take T-bane 1 and get off at Holmenkollen. The jump is only used in February and March, and the crowning event in the ski-jump season is the competition on the second Sunday in March (see "The Great Ski-Jump", page 105). Built in 1892, Holmenkollen is the world's oldest jump, and a national symbol. The

Away from the city centre, the domestic architecture in some of Oslo's suburbs reflects the tranquil side of urban life.

BELOW: from the top of Tryvannstårnet, Oslo's radio tower, the view stretches to Sweden.

adjoining Ski Museum is a small but fascinating monument to "One Thousand Years of Skiing". Very old skis and snowshoes are on display, as well as the trail-worn paraphernalia carried by such intrepid Norwegian explorers as Fridtjof Nansen, who crossed Greenland on skis.

For **Tryvannstårnet** ㉗ (Observation Tower; open all year; entrance fee), with its lift to a panoramic view of the city and surrounding area, take the T-bane one more stop to its end destination, Frognerseteren (with a restaurant of the same name, famous among other things for its home-made apple pie). The area is thickly forested and popular for walking and skiing. If you choose to go back to Holmenkollen on foot, the walk is signposted and takes 15 to 20 minutes.

Other exploring possibilities are provided by the islands and peninsulas of Oslofjorden, most of which are accessible by ferry from Aker Brygge quay. **Nesoddtangen** is at the tip of a hilly, wooded peninsula jutting from the east side of the fjord. Local artists exhibit at **Hellviktangen Manor** (open May–Sept, weekends out of season; entrance fee), where they serve coffee and waffles on Sundays. The house is surrounded by apple trees and gives directly on to the fjord. **Hovedøya** and **Lindøya** islands have beaches, but the best are on the western edge of Bygdøy. **Gressholmen** and **Langøyene** have free camping and good beaches. **Kalvøya**, on the western side of the fjord near Sandvika, is the site of big outdoor rock concerts in summer; access from Sandvika is by footbridge.

Bygone days on Bygdøy

Even if you don't arrive in Oslo by boat, it is not difficult to appreciate that the harbour is a pivotal point. Oslo hugs the fjord, and the city limits extend quite far down its sides. Just west of the harbour is the Bygdøy peninsula, where the old Viking ships and the more recent explorer ships are kept, and where Norway's maritime past is commemorated. It is home to the **Vikingskipshuset** ㉘ (Viking Ship Museum; open all year; entrance fee), the **Frammuseet** ㉙ (open all year; entrance fee), which houses Fridtjof Nansen's polar sailing ship *Fram*, and the **Kon-Tiki Museet** ㉚ (open all year; entrance fee) which contains, apart from the *Kon-Tiki* raft on which Thor Heyerdahl travelled to Polynesia, *Ra II*, a fragile-looking reed barque on which he travelled to Egypt. There is also a fine collection of his Easter Island artefacts. The **Sjøfartsmuseum** ㉛ (Maritime Museum; open all year; entrance fee) concentrates on the history of the craft of boat-building, and includes the Panorama Super-videograph showing an odyssey through Norwegian maritime history.

Also on Bygdøy is the **Norsk Folkemusuem** ㉜ (Norwegian Folk Museum; open all year; entrance fee) and **Oscarshall slott** ㉝ (Castle; open May–Sept; entrance fee). The folk museum, established in 1894, is an indoor/outdoor museum devoted largely to Norwegian rural culture. The collection of outdoor buildings, including a stave church from Gudbrandsdalen, gives a good idea of what old villages and agricultural settlements looked like. Other exhibits include Ibsen's studio, Sami (Lapp) ethnography, and a pharmacy museum. Oscarshall was built in quasi-Gothic style as a summer residence by King Oskar I.

A summer ferry runs from Aker Brygge quay to Bygdøy. There is a bus to the Viking and Folk museums and Oscarshall, or you can walk to them in about 25 minutes. Alternatively, take bus 30 from Oslo S or the Nationaltheatrert.

Weekends out of doors

A typical city dweller from Oslo spends huge amounts of time outdoors. On workdays, many take their *matpakke* from home (a basic lunch bag stuffed with sandwiches and fruit) and sit outside, weather allowing, between 11.30am and 12.30pm to eat it. (Lunch is eaten later in restaurants, from 12–2pm.) The number of outdoor and pavement establishments has grown astronomically of late, so those without *matpakke* can also lunch out of doors.

The Oslo area gets very warm in summer – in 1989, the temperature reached nearly 38°C (100°F) – and very cold and snowy in the winter. So if it's summer, people are likely to plan outdoor activities after work, anything from swimming, berry-picking, walking, jogging, or cycling at home in the suburbs in the light of the evening sun. Norwegians treasure their space and contact with nature, and many people who work in Oslo live a fair distance from the city. In winter, this means they can get quickly on to the floodlit slopes and cross-country ski trails after work.

Come the weekend, there is a widely followed pattern for the 48 hours. Friday night is usually a night out on the town. This may begin after dinner and a change of clothes at home, especially for younger people, who don't start to fill the bars until well after 10pm. Saturday morning is given over to shopping,

BELOW: a statue of Camille Collett, one of Norway's earliest female writers, in Slottsparken.

Maps, pages148 & 156–7

followed by gardening or watching soccer, and Saturday evening tends to be dinner or a party at someone's home.

No matter how wild or calm the Saturday night, Sunday is *tur* day. The *tur* is a walk or ski-tour, and a formidable tradition. Depending on a person's age, fitness, and the number of accompanying children, the *tur* can be anything from a one-to six-hour affair. The *matpakke* provides lunch in the forest. Some walks will include café stops in one of the 70-odd cabin lodges in the **Nordmarka** area of Oslo; if not, coffee and hot chocolate come along in a vacuum flask.

Nordmarka

There is a great swathe of forest due north of the city centre. Larch, birch, pine, aspen and several deciduous species dominate; the colour contrast in autumn is worth a special trip. Den Norske Turistforening (Touring Association) at Stortingsgate 28 has free sketch maps of most routes in these areas; maps 1 to 12, the "Oslo og Omegn Turistforening" series, cover the Oslo region; they also sell more detailed survey maps. Access to these routes from the centre is easy and cheap via public transport. For **Grorud** and the **Lillomarka** area (northeast of the city centre), take either T-bane 5 (destination Vestli) or bus 30 from Jernbanetorget. Trails begin just west of the Grorud T-bane. Due north is **Grefsen**, along a suburban train line (information from Trafikanten at Oslo S), tram 11 or 12 (Grefsen/Kjelsås), or bus to Grefsenkollen.

For walks in the **Holmenkollen** area and northwest, part of the Nordmarka, take T-bane 1 to Frognerseteren (not to be confused with Frognerparken) and stay on until the end of the line. The Touring Association can recommend trails or, even better, ask a Norwegian to recommend a favourite *tur*. The trails are signposted, but if you get lost, seek help from other walkers. (Also, see the Oslo Guide under "Outdoor Activities" for other recommended routes.)

Many of the forest trails circumnavigate lakes, so a swimming break might be included if it's hot. Come winter, there's skiing, skating and sledging (also covered by the Oslo Guide) to add to the general flurry of activity on a Sunday. If a good snow cover has been established, walking trails double as cross-country skiing trails. The more daring head for Holmenkollen to practise their jumping and the best prepare for the annual jumping competition in March. Home then to change for an early dinner, then it's off to the cinema. And thereby hangs a weekend.

Something to take home

Handicrafts, textiles, woollens and pewter are favourites for visitors in Oslo. **Basarhallene**, one of the few "older" shopping areas at the back of the Domkirke, has a wonderful jeweller's, Elias Sollberg, and a hatshop. Glasmagasinet across the way (Stortorvet 9) and Steen & Strøm at Kongensgate 23 are big department stores. **Aker Brygge** on the waterfront and **Oslo City**, next to Oslo S, are two major malls. Grensen is the street for bargains, while Lille Grensen has stalls selling everything from sausages to skateboards. Hennes & Mauritz, the Swedish chain, has a bargain basement on Kirkeristen. ❑

BELOW: out sailing on Oslofjorden.
RIGHT: a traditional "loft" house (food store) in the Folkemuseum at Bygdøy.

AROUND OSLO AND ITS FJORD

The charms of Oslofjorden may need some searching out, for this is Norway's industrial heartland, but it is rich in natural beauty and Viking history, and the surrounding area echoes to its pulse

Map on page 170

At dusk the islands of Oslofjorden look like hunched prehistoric animals about to sink into a subaquatic sleep. In the colder months, the sky at sunset grows from lavender to purple while the islands turn slate-grey, then ominous and black. Summer sunsets bring twisted pink clouds underlit by a huge red sun that drops only briefly behind the fjord's western cliffs before rising again in the east.

Daytime along the 100-km (60-mile) long fjord reveals a high concentration of industry down both the eastern and western sides. With Oslo at its head, the fjord is the capital's workhorse, its roads travelled by juggernauts with cargoes of lumber and oil, its ports and waterways busy with yachts and barges. Outside its working ports, Oslofjorden is a magnificent expanse of water stretching into the Skagerrak. Sprinkled liberally with islands, skerries, natural marinas and swimming beaches, the fjord is popular with Oslo residents in summer.

The lungs of the city

Akershus, **Vestfold** and **Østfold** are the three main counties to touch Oslofjorden. Akershus county contains the Oslo conurbation plus a broad swathe of agricultural and forest land reaching to Sweden. At its northern reach lies the Mjøsa lake town of Eidsvoll, where the Norwegian constitution was signed and the modern state born in 1814. Østfold (east) and Vestfold (west) spread down from Oslo like a pair of lungs. Some of Scandinavia's oldest ruling families were found buried in Vestfold along with several sunken Viking ships loaded with booty; while Østfold is rich with ancient rock paintings and stone circles.

Both of these counties contain provincial cities of major historic significance: Fredrikstad in Østfold, a magnificent fortress town, and Tønsberg in Vestfold, the oldest extant Scandinavian city, founded in 872. Remains of **Kaupang**, the oldest Nordic town yet discovered, were found a couple of kilometres (one mile) from Tønsberg and are now in Oslo's Historisk (Historical) Museum. Corroboration of its early existence appeared in a world history by England's 9th-century monarch King Alfred the Great. Larger towns usually have an old section closely packed with superbly crafted wooden houses. Halden, near the Swedish border in Østfold, and Larvik in Vestfold, are the southernmost points on the fjord, each accessible within a couple of hours from Oslo.

Despite its rich history and good travel links (not to mention its seafood festivals), the Oslofjord area gets few tourists from outside Scandinavia. The scenery isn't as dramatic as the west coast's. There are however more habitable islands than in any other fjord,

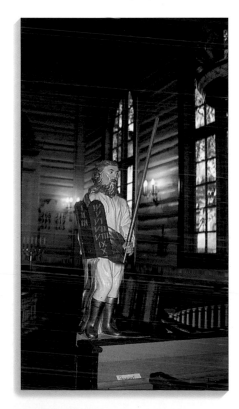

PRECEDING PAGES: old wooden houses on Oslofjorden. **LEFT:** a summer's evening on the fjord. **BELOW:** Moses with the Ten Commandments, Drøbak church.

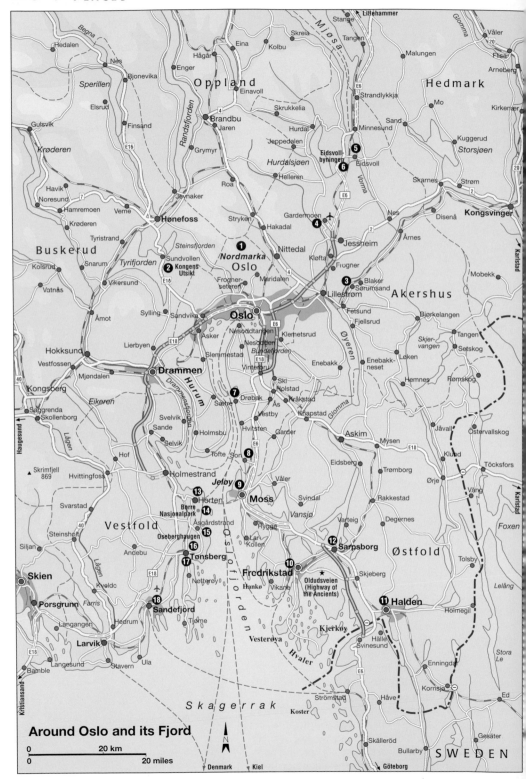

Around Oslo and its Fjord

0 ————————— 20 km

0 ————————— 20 miles

many with sports centres and hotels offering everything from tennis to wind-surfing and swimming. Inland is sloping countryside punctuated by forests, orchards and tilled fields which appeals to cyclists and those on short journeys or with children who want to avoid overland hauls.

Map on page 170

Walker's paradise

There are fantastic walks in the **Oslomarka** (the forests surrounding Oslo) accessible by bus, train or tram. Much of the **Nordmarka** ❶ (the area to the north of the city) is privately owned by lumber barons who have kept it open to the public and, in any case, Norway's "Outdoor Recreations Act" permits everybody to cross outlying property on foot. The "Oslo og Omegn" maps (Nos. 1–12, free from Den Norske Turistforeningen at Storgata 3, Oslo; weekdays only; tel: 22 82 28 00) cover the Nordmarka's network of cleared trails. Around Grefsen, south of **Maridalsvatnet**, is a luxuriant parkland (tram 11 and 12 or bus 37 to Grefsen, Grefsenkollen, Kjelsås). Maridalsvatnet is a tremendous lake fed by a series of charming clearwater brooks. **Sognsvann**, the lake west of Maridalsvatnet is at the end of T-bane 5.

By car you can explore further. If you're a fan of Norwegian rural architecture you'll have your fill in outer Akershus. Take route E16 in a westerly direction towards Tyrifjorden and at Sundvollen turn right and follow the toll road into the **Krokkleiva** district. The paths cross wooded hills 400–500 metres (1,300–1,600 ft) high. **Kongens Utsikt** ❷ (viewpoint) gives panoramic views across Steinsfjorden and Tyrifjorden.

Afterwards, rejoin the E16 northbound, direction Hønefoss. Leave it before Hønefoss to pick up Road 241 northeast from Bråk, and then strike east on to Road 242. South of this road is a **wilderness** of pine marshland, secluded lakes, oak forests and stream-bordered fields (map Oslo Nordmark – Nordre Del). There are some NOK10 tolls (10 krone coins only), but when you see how wild the area is you'll appreciate the fact that there are any roads here at all. Road 4 south returns you to Oslo and the junction with the E6; northbound it leads to Gjøvik on the western side of Lake Mjøsa.

Birthplace of the state

If you go east from the junction of Road 4 and the E6 along Road 170 you come to the small village of **Fetsund**, just past Lillestrøm, and the **Fetsund Lenser** (Log Floating Museum; open May–Sept; free), a logging museum celebrating the industrial activity on the banks of the Glomma river. The museum includes a nature trail and boat trips to the North Øyeren Nature Reserve, a haven for migratory bird species. The café here also specialises in serving grilled *gjedde* (pike) in burger form.

Further on, a road to the left will bring you to **Sørumsand** ❸, where there is a narrow-gauge "Tertitten" railway (open Jun–Sept, Sun only; tel: 63 82 69 70). From here, Road 171 north will bring you back to the E6. Travelling north you come to the unusual landscape of **Raknehaugen** (burial site; open all year; free) at Jessheim off the E6 near **Gardermoen** ❹.

BELOW: runic inscription at Skjeberg, Østfold.

The Norwegian constitution was signed in 1814 in this large wooden manor near Eidsvoll, home of the Ankers family.

Further north still, at the bottom of Lake Mjøsa, is **Eidsvoll ❺**, about 65 km (40 miles) north of Oslo. It is a lake town of old wooden houses and churches, and nearby, on the other side of the E6 at Eidsvoll Verk, is a national landmark: the **Eidsvoll-byningen ❻** (Memorial building; open all year; entrance fee), is a mini-museum to the Norwegian constitution and includes the room where the document was signed. The nearby **Eidsvoll Bygdetun** (Rural Museum; open Jun–Sept; free) consists of a collection of 26 old farm buildings and a World War II museum all set in beautiful countryside. Then tour Lake Mjøsa on the old paddle steamer *Skibladner*. The round trip takes 12 hours, with the halfway point at Lillehammer (*see page 181*).

Tranquil countryside, sleepy shore

Heading south out of Oslo, the quiet way to Fredrikstad is via the old **Mossveien**, which hugs the fjordline as near as topography allows. Having taken the E6 or E18 out of the city, turn right off the main road at Vinterbru and head for the tip of Bundefjorden. Take the road signposted to Nesoddtangen. Eventually you will come across a signpost to **Drøbak ❼**.

The village of Drøbak was once a fishermen's settlement. Fishing vessels still arrive here and sell fresh prawns and fish on the quayside. Places of interest include the **Follo Museum** (Heritage Museum; open May–Sept; entrance fee), **Oscarsborg Festning** (Fort) out in the fjord from where gunfire sunk the German cruiser *Blücher* in 1940 (guided boat trips from the harbour), a small aquarium and a coastal heritage museum (both open all year; entrance fee). Another point of pride is the cross-timbered **church** from 1776 (open all year; free). It has an elaborately carved model of a ship inside, a common piece of

BELOW: Sunday is *tur* day, a day to tour the countryside on foot or on skis.

Map
on page
170

church decoration in seafaring towns. Rococo touches include wooden busts of Moses and Aaron. The church has gospel and jazz concerts in summer. If you're in a Christmassy mood, visit **Jul (Yule) Hus** in the old meeting house, stacked to the rafters with handicrafts and toys.

Artist centre

The road out of Drøbak takes off just before the ferry terminal, from where small car ferries run every half hour or so to the Hurum peninsula. Soon the road passes through fertile farmland and forest first to Hvitsten and then to **Son ❽**, a fetching artists' village hugging the edge of a sheltered sound. The surrounding countryside and shoreline here provided inspiration for the likes of Theodore Kittelsen and Edvard Munch.

The **Son Kystkultursenter** (Coastal Heritage Centre; open May–Sept; free) explains how this one-time Dutch freeport (the original name was Zoon) has thrived variously on timber, ice and fishing. The unusual elevated building at the edge of the marina is the last remaining fishing net drying structure in the Oslo fjord. **Gallery X** and **Bakgården** are showrooms for local artists (open all year; free), while La Riviera next door is an excellent French restaurant with an authentic wood-burning oven. Son is a popular summer resort for boating enthusiasts and on a summer's evening, with a cold beer in hand, there is no better place to watch the sun set behind the billowing sails of a myriad of yachts.

Østfold is a long funnel through which tourists from Sweden pour. Despite its industrial towns such as Halden, Sarpsborg and Moss, Østfold buzzes with outdoor pursuits: canoeing and cycling are popular, and the area is dotted with hiking and skiing centres. There are also golf courses, and the Mysen race track.

Knut Hamsun, the Nobel prize-winning novelist, once lived in the Reenskaug Hotel in Drøbak, and the town became a rich source of material for his 1920 novel, Konene ved Vandposten (Women at the Pump).

BELOW: the view over Halden from the fortress.

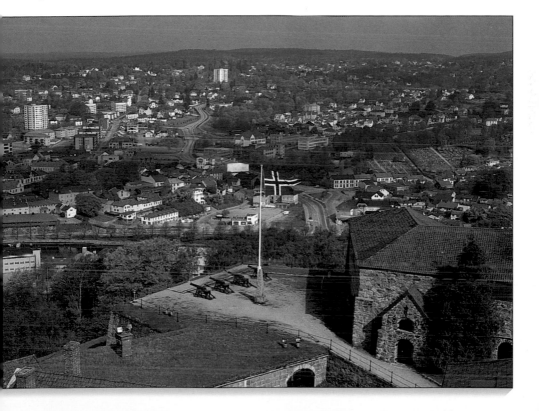

Then there's the draw of the fjord. Jeløy peninsula is the site of **Galleri F15** (open all year; entrance fee) at **Jeløy ❾**, which has fjordside trails and stupendous lawns. Exhibitions are laid out through a light-filled house. Its cafeteria is a beloved coffee pit-stop. Down the coast, the Royal yacht *Norge* is anchored at **Hankø**, Norway's regatta centre.

Old centres

Fredrikstad ❿ is a gem among Østfold towns, and Scandinavia's only completely preserved fortress town, dating from 1567. The cobbled streets of Gamle Byen, the old town, were laid by prisoners; wooden stocks face the former prison, now a bank (but with the prisoners' room preserved). Its restaurants and galleries keep their old façades. The stately Rådhus (Town Hall) was designed by the architect who built Oslo's Stortinget. The old-style Victoria Hotel serves fine meals; a speciality are their wild game dishes.

History and prehistory figure largely in Østfold's attractions. The **Oldtidsveien** (Highway of the Ancients), Road 110 between Fredrikstad and Skjeberg to the west, has runic paintings 3,000 to 4,000 years old and burial sites like **Hunn**, covered with stone circles. The area once had links with ancient Tuscany.

Halden ⓫, south of Skjeberg and close by the Swedish border, is dominated by **Fredriksten Festning** (Fort), a largely intact ruin with many of its buildings serving as small theme museums. The streets below were laid out along the cannons' blast lines to give the fortress's defenders freedom to fire. Halden's hosting of the 1991 International Amateur Drama Festival was the excuse for building a new open-air theatre in the fortress grounds. In summer, a passenger boat travels the inland waterway system, navigating through massive locks.

TIP

"Highway of the Ancients", free from the tourist board, is a useful guide to the ancient history associated with the road between Fredrikstad and Skjeberg.

BELOW: edible fungi are a welcome addition to a meal.

Throughout Østfold, St Olav's day (29 July) is celebrated with a great show of folk costume, music and dance. One of the best displays is at the **Borgarsyssel Museum** (open all year; entrance fee) in **Sarpsborg** ⓬, north of Skjeberg. Sarpsborg is the site of one of Østfold's two youth hostels, on Tune lake (the other is at Moss), and it has brewery tours and trips on the jazz boat Krabben. (For information, call Sarpsborg Tourist Office; tel: 69 11 70 00).

Across to Vestfold

There is much shared history between Østfold and Vestfold. It was the fast action of troops on both sides of the fjord that led to the sinking of the *Blücher*, scuppering Hitler's plans for an easy invasion.

The Moss-Horten car ferry connects Østfold and Vestfold; it crosses in under an hour. The **Marinemuseet** (Naval Museum; open all year; free) at **Horten** ⓭ documents this event and hundreds of others in displays bulging with weird and wonderful artefacts. Multiply the experience a hundredfold if you meet retired Commander Steinar Sandvold here. There are also museums of photography and veteran cars in Horten (both open all year; entrance fee).

Heading southwards, tranquil **Løvøy** island has a solemn medieval stone church. This was Viking country, and **Borre Nasjonalpark** ⓮ (open all year; free), en route to Tønsberg, contains enormous turf-covered humps concealing Viking kings' graves. Borre is Norway's oldest national park, with an extensive network of trails, and the largest collection of Iron Age burial sites in Scandinavia. Keeping to the coastline along Road 311, **Åsgårdstrand** ⓯ (open May–Sept; entrance fee) is where Edvard Munch lived when he returned to Norway from abroad, and he used it as a setting for many of his paintings. This

Map on page 170

BELOW: in summer, berry-picking in the garden or forest is a popular activity.

Learning to sail on Oslofjorden.

tranquil village's white wood houses merge into the sky on misty mornings; set back from the harbour are a huge old meeting hall and public baths on a square at its centre. Near the promontory where Munch painted *Three Girls on a Bridge* is Åsgårdstrand Hotel, the town's only hotel. In summer a great gush of activity emanates from here: boat trips, barbecues, and the Åsgårdstrand Festival, when there are dance and piano concerts – and a great Wiener schnitzel cook-up. You can spurn these organised activities to cycle, swim in the fjord, fish in Borre's lake, or watch the fishermen come in each afternoon with the fresh catch.

Viking burial

Between Åsgårdstrand and Tønsberg is **Oseberghaugen** ⑯ (burial mound), the most important Viking site yet discovered (open all year; free). Oslo's Vikingskipshuset (Viking Ship Museum) contains the finds, including the 20-metre (65-ft) arch-ended wooden ship. Only the mound itself, near Slagen church, remains, but as a symbol Oseberghaugen has a subtle, magnetic power.

Just south is history-rich **Tønsberg** ⑰, established in the 9th century. On the 65-metre (200-ft) high **Slottsfjellet** are the fortress remains and tower. The main street, Storgata, is flanked by Viking graves. These were excavated and incorporated, under glass, into the ground floor of the new library. Across the street are the walls of one of only two medieval round churches in Scandinavia.

The most renowned king to hold court in Tønsberg was Håkon Håkonson IV (1240–63. The ruins of his court can be seen on Nordbyen, a street with old houses hunched along it. A more recent native son is Roald Amundsen, the polar explorer. Less known outside Norway is Svend Foyn, the Tønsberg whaling captain who invented the explosive-powered harpoon.

BELOW: one of the many popular bathing sites around Oslo's fjord.

The steamship *Kysten I* (built 1909), moored on Byfjorden near the old customs house, does a three-hour islands tour. North of the *Kysten*, you can pick up Nordbyen which will bring you back into town.

To the south of Tønsberg, along the eastern side of the fjord, the islands of **Nøtterøy** and **Tjøme,** and the skerries, are fantastic summer hangouts. **Rica Havna** is on a gorgeous natural haven carved from rock. **Verdens Ende** (World's End) is at the end – but for a few boulders – of the chain. The old lighthouse here is a beautifully simple structure made of stone.

On the other side of Tønsbergfjorden lies **Sandefjord** ⑱, a famed whaling town and its **Hvalfangstmuseet** (Whaling Museum; open all year; entrance fee) is excellent. The sea still dominates life here. One of the main industries is marine paint production. The town centre is compact, and the cosy old Kong Carl Hotel is one of its handsomer buildings. Near Badeparken are the former spa and the old town, along Thaulowsgate. Preståsen is the hilly park above it.

Just outside Sandefjord are **Gokstadhaugen** (burial site; open May–Sept; guided tours), in which the Gokstad ship, now in the Vikingskiphuset (Viking Ship Museum) in Oslo, was discovered in 1880 and **Vesterøy** peninsula, ideal for walking, biking and boating. It's a supremely peaceful place – the film star Liv Ullman's summer house is in the vicinity.

Map on page 170

Larvik was home to two legendary boat lovers: Thor Heyerdahl, and Scotsman Colin Archer, designer of the polar ship *Fram*. Archer's first house was at Tollerodden, on the fjord. At Larvik's back is the huge lake Farris.

There are many fine waterside spots around Larvik, such as **Mølland** beach, stacked with sea-rounded pebbles, and **Nevlunghavn**, an exquisite fishing cove tucked around the bay west of Stavern. The fish and shellfish festivals in the Larvik area are renowned. Hotels often host them; the Grand in Larvik has both excellent seafood and a superb "wild" menu including pheasant, ptarmigan and elk in their seasons.

Inner Vestfold's rivers run with salmon and trout. **Brufoss** is a favourite anglers' haunt (accommodation and day licences available). In winter, this is a popular downhill ski district, particularly now that Svarstad's Ski Centre, off Road 40 near the Lågen river, is fully operational. You will find a lot of ceramic works which offer tours in outer and inner Vestfold and, in common with Østfold, every little hamlet seems to have an art gallery. The area tourist board office is at Tønsberg (tel: 33 44 36 60).

Knut Steen's Whaling Monument at Sandefjord.

Local pride

People who live around Oslofjorden have a strange modesty-pride complex. They are the first to point out the area's shortcomings – smallish mountains, the stink of the pulp and paper plants – but once these are out of the way, the superlatives begin to flow. The birthplaces of the most intrepid explorers are here, as are the best sailing races, the warmest summers, the finest archaeological discoveries, the best drinking water, summer resorts… the list goes on; for when it comes to this part of Norway neither the modesty nor the pride is false.   ❑

BELOW: a refreshing beer in historic Tønsberg.

THE HEART OF NORWAY

Away from Mjøsa and its lakeside towns, central Norway extends east into the wilds around the old copper-mining town of Rorøs, and north towards the quintessentially Norwegian Dovre mountains

Map,
pages
182–3

Norway's heartland is centred on the counties of Oppland and Hedmark, and is characterised by three main features: Lake Mjøsa, the country's largest lake, the great massif of Dovrefjell to the north, and the long slanting valleys of Gudbrandsdalen and Østerdalen. In this widest part of Norway, these great valleys lie straight and narrow from southeast to northwest, their rivers like veins cutting between the mountain ranges. Alongside the rivers are fertile farms, which climb up the valley sides to forests. Then, above the tree-line come the bare slopes of tussocky grass and rocks, a playground for skiers and walkers.

Despite Norway's busy network of rural buses, it can be difficult to get into some of the remoter corners; but this region makes wonderful country for touring by car. Each new vista is more magnificent than the last as the road climbs, dips and circles. Nevertheless, for some of the higher plateaux, it can be simpler and quicker to push further into the wilderness by train, which stops at many small stations along the main line between Oslo and Trondheim – almost as spectacular as the famous Oslo–Bergen route in the west.

PRECEDING PAGES: the opening ceremony of the 1994 Winter Olympics, Lillehammer. **LEFT:** a decorated *stabbur* (food store) from 1863. **BELOW:** Hafjell, near Lillehammer.

Mjøsa and Mjøsabyen

Lake **Mjøsa** ❶ also lies southeast to northwest some 160 km (100 miles) north of Oslo. One of the best ways to enjoy the lake and its surroundings is a trip on the old paddle steamer *SS Skibladner* (May–Sept; varying tours on alternate days excl. Sun; tel: 62 52 70 85). Built in 1856 as a continuation of Norway's first railway line between Oslo and Eidsvoll, she now plies the lake carrying tourists and is based in Hamar on the east of the lake.

Around Mjøsa lies some of the most fertile agricultural in Norway and throughout the gently undulating countryside are large farms, encircled by thickly forested hills. Where Mjøsa is at its widest, some 17 km (10 miles) across, is the attractive island of **Helgøya**. At its southern tip, the island has a burial mound, part of the historic Hovinsholm, a Royal estate from Viking times until 1723.

Three main towns lie along the lake: Hamar and Lillehammer are on the eastern shore and Gjøvik on the west. A bridge across the lake roughly half way between Hamar and Lillehammer, links the municipalities and, in a commercial sense, has combined the area into what has been christened **Mjøsabyen**. All three backed Lillehammer's successful bid for the 1994 Winter Olympics.

In the Middle Ages, **Hamar** ❷ was the centre of Roman Catholicism in Norway and the seat of the bishop. It enjoyed great prosperity and had an impres-

Heart of Norway

0   50 km

0   50 miles

N

NORWEGIAN

SEA

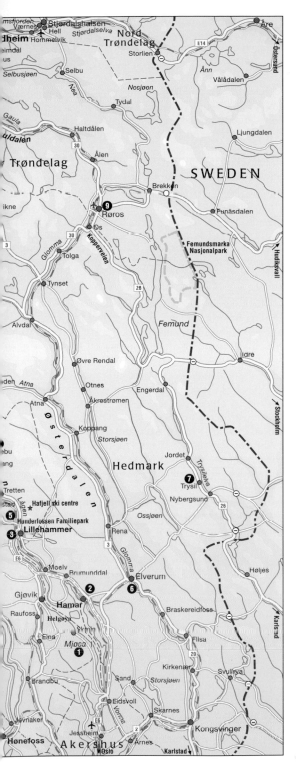

sive cathedral. However, Hamar's downfall came in 1537 when the Danes carried off the bishop, and 30 years later when the Swedes burned the town to the ground. The cathedral ruins at Domkirkeodden (Cathedral Point) are now part of the **Hedmarksmuseet** (open May– Sept; entrance fee). Not until the 19th century and the coming of the railway did Hamar regain a measure of importance, as a railway junction with a locomotive building works. It was not surprising, therefore, that it became the site of the **Jernbanenuseet** (National Railway Museum; open May–Sept; entrance fee;) in 1896, which moved to its present lakeside location in 1956. A highlight of this large collection is the early steam engine, Caroline, built by Robert Stephenson in 1861.

A lasting reminder of the 1994 Winter Olympics is the rather unusual "Viking ship" Olympic **skating arena** (open all year; entrance fee). Roughly 18 km (11 miles) east of Hamar towards Elverum is the **Løiten Brænderi** (Distillery; open summer only; entrance fee; tel: 62 59 12 19) famous for the Løiten aquavit.

Sandvik's collection

The largest of the three Mjøsabyen towns is **Lillehammer ❸** situated at the northern end of the lake where it narrows to become the River Lågen and crosses Gudbrandsdalen (valley). Lillehammer is called the capital of Gudbrandsdalen and its success in gaining the 1994 Winter Olympics confirmed its popularity for winter sports. A whole new downhill skiing area on nearby **Hafjell** was added to 500 km (300 miles) of cross-country skiing tracks. An ice-hockey and speed-skating rink were built into the hillside at Gjøvik and Hamar got its skating arena. But, after its moment of not inconsiderable glory, the town returned to normal.

For summer visitors, the biggest attraction is **Maihaugen** (open-air museum; closed Mon in winter; entrance fee), remarkable even in a country of many open-air museums. Maihaugen has some 120 buildings brought into the 40-hectare (100-acre) site from all over Gudbrandsdalen, to show life as it once was. The

The old paddle steamer, Skibladner, on Lake Mjøsa goes between Hamar, Eidsvoll, Gjøvik and Lillehammer during the summer months.

museum was the life work of Anders Sandvig. A dentist by profession, he came to Lillehammer in 1885 suffering from tuberculosis and with a life expectancy of a mere two years. Whether it was the interest of the museum he founded in 1887 which kept him alive or not, Sandvig achieved another 65 years and died in 1950.

He is the town's only honorary citizen with his statue prominent in the market place. Apart from the buildings, which range from the medieval to the 19th century, Maihaugen has some 30,000 artefacts, all collected by Sandvig, and the many demonstrations of old skills and rural crafts give the museum a real sense of being alive.

If Hamar attracts the railway fan, then Lillehammer, not to be outdone, has something for the motoring enthusiast. The **Norsk Veg Museum** (Museum of Vehicle History; open all year; entrance fee) has everything from horse-drawn sleighs, gigs and carioles to motor cars. There are some unusual examples, including steam and electric vehicles, a strange six-wheeled Mustad and a 1922 Bjering, which seated two people in tandem and could have its front wheels replaced by skis in winter. There is also the Troll, the last car to be manufactured in Norway, which ended its production run of 16 vehicles in 1956.

Artistic light

The quality of light in Lillehammer and its surroundings has attracted numerous artists to the area, including Fredrik Collett, Lars Jorde, Alf Lundeby, Einar Sandberg, Kirsten Holbø, Erik Werenskiold and Henrik Sørensen. As a result, the town has an impressive art gallery, the **Kunstmuseum** (Art Museum; open all year; entrance fee), which includes works by Jacob Weidemann, and Norway's most famous artist, Edvard Munch.

BELOW: Odalen man's best friend, a *dølahest* (eastern Norwegian horse).

One of Lillehammer's most revered names is Danish-born Sigrid Undset, winner of the 1928 Nobel Prize for Literature, who took up residence at nearby Bjerkbæk in 1921. At **Aulestad** ❹ (open May–Sept; entrance fee), about 11 km (7 miles) from Lillehammer, is the home of another famous Norwegian writer, Bjørnsterne Bjørnson, who was one of the writers who inspired the nationalist movement in the 19th century and who wrote, among other things, Norway's national anthem. Bjørnson, too, won a Nobel Prize and his house is exactly as it was when he died in 1910.

Alongside these literary attractions, Lillehammer has not neglected its younger visitors. On the outskirts of the town, at Øyer, is **Lilleputhammer** (open May–Sept; entrance fee) with its quarter scale version of the centre of Lillehammer as it was in 1900. You walk down the main street, peer in the shop windows and find some are open to the public. There is also the popular **Hunderfossen Familiepark** ❺ (open May–Sept, entrance fee) north of the town, with a whole range of things to do and the world's largest (fibreglass) troll; Norway's figure of fable is said to have an evil disposition and a face as gnarled as the mountains and rocks where trolls have their homes. Nearby is the **Huseskogen bob track** (tel: 61 25 92 99) built for the 1994 Winter Olympics and which offers dry runs for tourists during the summer.

Østerdalen

To the east of Lake Mjøsa lies **Østerdalen**, which cuts through the mountains on a line roughly parallel to Gudbrandsdalen. At times the valley is narrow, with seemingly endless forests on either side, broken only occasionally by patches of farmland. It starts at **Elverum ❻** in the south and continues northwards for 250 km (150 miles) becoming broader and more open further north. Throughout its length flows Norway's longest river, the **Glomma**, kept company by the railway and the E3.

Elverum is one of the essential crossroads of Norway, and lies at the junction of many valleys, with routes to Hamar to the west, Kongsvinger to the south and Trysil to the northeast. It has the well-preserved **Terningen bastion** built in 1673, and a climb to the top of the water tower provides a good view. The town's most famous episode is commemorated in a monument to the fierce battle fought in April 1940, which delayed the German army for long enough to allow the king and members of the government to escape further north before finally crossing to Britain to continue the fight in exile.

By far the most important of the town's attractions are two major museums. The **Glomdal Museum** (open June–Sept; entrance fee), opened in 1911 on a large natural site, has 88 old buildings of many kinds, brought in from Østerdalen and Solør. The indoor exhibition is divided into three sections – the farming year, transport and communication, and handwork and crafts – and it shows what life was like in Østerdalen from 1870 to 1900. There is also a collection from the Neolithic age and Viking era, as well as an open-air theatre.

The second museum is the **Norsk Skogsbrukmuseum** (Forestry Museum; open Jun–Aug, entrance fee) and encompasses forestry, hunting and fishing.

Built for the 1994 Winter Olympics, Hamar's skating arena was designed along the lines of an upturned Viking ship.

BELOW: Lake Mjøsa at sunset.

The main building also has exhibits devoted to geology and wildlife, and children will head for the aquarium. The outdoor collection is mainly situated on the small island of Prestøya in the middle of the Glomma river.

Early skiing

To the northeast, **Trysil ❼**, in Hedmark near the Swedish border, is a popular winter sports area. It has the distinction of being home to the world's oldest ski club, the Trysil Shooting and Skiing Club founded in 1861. In summer, Trysil is a centre for paragliding, rafting, canoe tours and mountain tours with pack dogs to carry the luggage. But it goes without saying that almost anywhere in the heart of Norway you only need to go a short way for the sort of outdoor recreation that mountain, river and lake can provide.

North from Elverum along the E3, there are few places of any size or importance, but the whole of this area is well off the tourist track and ideal for exploration. At **Koppang**, about half-way along the length of Østerdalen, you can take an alternative route north, along Road 30 past the long thin Storsjøen (lake), rejoining the E3 at **Tynset**. Northwest of Tynset, you come to Kvikne and near it the rectory at Bjørgan, the birthplace of Bjørnsterne Bjørnson.

Alternatively try Road 219 which turns west at **Atna**, some 30 km (20 miles) north of Koppang, for a drive into the foothills of the wild and mountainous region of **Rondane**, where the peaks rise up to 1,800 metres (6,000 ft) high. At Enden, the road is joined by Road 27, which has taken the parallel route north from Ringebu. Called the **Rondevegen ❽**, the road climbs steeply from Gudbrandsdalen to some superb views of the Rondane mountains. After coming this far, it is well worth continuing from Enden to Folldal, past the great peaks

BELOW: as this selection shows, each area has its own design of *bunad*, Norway's traditional national costume.

that include Rondeslottet at 2,178 metres (7,144 ft) high, with the **Rondane Nasjonalpark** (National Park) to the west. Established in 1962, this was Norway's first national park and offers a wide range of trails of varying difficulty.

Road 27 ascends to nearly 915 metres (3,000 ft) before reaching **Folldal**, itself one of the highest permanently inhabited communities in Norway. Folldal's history begins from when copper was discovered in the area in the 18th century. Although the mine is no longer worked, the mining company is still based here to serve a new mine at Hjerkinn about 30 km (20 miles) away. The old Folldal mine, and some of its buildings, now form a **museum** (open all year; entrance fee) with guided tours in summer.

Along the copper road

From Folldal, if you head east you return to the Glomma river valley and the E3 at Alvdal, all connected to and part of the system of valleys and rivers that spread out from Østerdalen. Along the way abandoned mine works indicate how important minerals were and, to some extent, still are to this area. North of Alvdal, rail, road and river head northeast, through Tolga and Os – which is the start of the **Kopperveien** (Copper Road) – before coming to the old copper-mining town of **Røros** ❾ (*see page 188*). Here, you can visit the old smelter in the **Rørosmuseet** (open all year; entrance fee), the impressive **church** (open Mon–Sat, June–Sept; Sun only, Oct–May; entrance fee), and a disused mine at **Olavsgruva** (open all year; entrance fee) out east along Road 31.

Røros is also a junction for roads which lead through an eastern wilderness with little habitation: the first is Road 31 to the Swedish frontier, only 45 km (30 miles) away to the east, past several lakes, some artificial, dug to provide water

Map, pages 182–3

BELOW: autumn colours come early on the fjords.

Røros and the Old Copper Country

Røros was the archetypal company town with life and society revolving around the mining of copper. Isolated, exposed, nearly 600 metres (2,000 ft) above sea level and surrounded by mountains and enduring winter cold, its existence was entirely due to the discovery of copper, which was first mined here over 300 years ago and was worked until 1972. The town was hardly beautiful, and slag heaps (*slegghaugen*) and the smelter (*smelthytta*) provided the backdrop to the miners' houses. These were usually small and overcrowded, but many workers also possessed a small patch of land and one or two animals as a source of food.

Further away from smelter and slag lived those higher up the company pecking order – in the executive area. By some miracle, Røros escaped the fires which so often laid waste the wooden buildings of Norwegian towns.

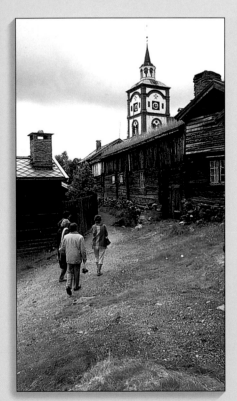

Today, Røros has a unique townscape and almost the entire older part of the town is preserved by law. Doors, windows and colour schemes all have to conform, buildings have to be lived in and there is strict control of advertising signs and notices. As a result, Røros is in a time warp, retaining much of its mining town atmosphere, and is on the UNESCO World Heritage list.

The most noticeable feature in Røros is the stone church – "the pride of the mining town" – which was dedicated in 1784 and replaced a wooden one built in 1650. The interior reflects the mining society, with paintings of clergymen and mining officials, while prayers were said every Sunday for the company and its directors.

The smelter was the heart of the copper-mining company and the focal point of the town. Its bell was rung at the start and end of each shift and is still there today. The smelter has been restored as a museum: the exterior still resembles the building in 1889 but the interior is now given over to a series of exhibitions depicting life in the town, mining techniques in Europe in the 18th and 19th centuries, cultural features of the southern Lapp society and aspects of Røros society and its environs.

One of the most interesting elements in the museum is the series of working models to one-tenth scale which demonstrate the arduous methods called for when the only power available was water, horses and human muscle. In the past it was usual to make such scale models to see if a new technique or piece of equipment would work so today's replicas are following an old tradition.

Thirteen kilometres (8 miles) from Røros is Olavsgruva (the Olav mine), which was opened as a mining museum in 1979. A guided tour takes visitors 50 metres (165 ft) below ground. Up until 1880, when dynamite was introduced, the miners used the heat from wood fires stacked against the rock face to crack the rock. Back on the surface, the bare and bleak scenery surrounding the mine, even in the summer sun, is the most telling way to emphasise the wretched existence of those early miners. ❑

LEFT: both Rorøs church and the town's characteristic turf roofs are now preserved.

for mining operations; another north to Ålen (Road 30) which has a small open-air museum, then through the fast-flowing gorge of the Gaula river until the valley broadens out near Støren; yet another is an alternative route to Fæmund lake, Norway's third largest, which offers good fishing.

In search of Peer Gynt

After Østerdalen, **Gudbrandsdalen** is the second longest valley in Norway. The Lågen river runs its full length and the valley stretches for 140 km (90 miles) northwest from Lillehammer to Dombås, the starting point for climbing trips into the Dovre rock formation. This huge plateau is very popular with walkers, not least because it is framed by impressive peaks such as the **Snøhetta** 2,286 metres (7,498 ft).

Perhaps because it was surrounded by mountains, which emphasised its sense of identity, the Gudbrandsdal valley has a long tradition of folk dancing and folk music; it is famous for its wood carving and rose painting, and you can find good craftwork to take home. North of Lillehammer at **Ringebu** ❿, you can visit the 13th-century **Ringebu Stavkirke** (Stave Church; open May–Sept; entrance fee). Built of enormous upright timbers, it has a statue of St Laurentius, crucifixes and a baptismal font all from medieval times.

Peer Gynt, as depicted by P.N. Arboe.

Vinstra ⓫ is the heart of Peer Gynt country and his farm, Hågå, now privately owned, is nearby. One of the Gynt cottages serves as the information office in Vinstra, another has gone to the Maihaugen open-air museum at Lillehammer, and the third remains above the farm. In the cemetery at **Sødorp**, a couple of kilometres (one mile) from Vinstra, is a monument to this strange, legendary Norwegian figure. Though Peer (or Per) Gynt is legendary to many,

BELOW: low-lying farmland offers rich pastures.

Map,
pages
182–3

he is real enough to Norwegians as a marksman, ski-runner and something of a braggart who was often "economical with the truth". Yet he inspired the poet and dramatist Henrik Ibsen to write the play which he called Peer Gynt and the music of Edvard Grieg's Peer Gynt Suite. Each year the play is performed (July–Aug; tel: 61 29 01 66) along with Greig's music in the amphitheatre at Golåvatnet to the southwest of Vinstra.

Today, Peer Gynt is a handy legend to use in the promotion of tourism, hence the creation of the **Peer Gyntveien** (Way), a minor road which goes round in a huge semicircle through Golå and returns to the E6 at Tretten. It reaches an altitude of over 900 metres (3,000 ft) and presents a near continuous panorama of desolate mountains and lakes – stark but appealing. There are a number of mountain hotels in this area which are popular in both winter and summer.

Scottish visitors should make a point of stopping at **Kringen** to see the memorial to a battle of 1612, when an army of Scottish mercenaries was defeated by local farmers. Despite their defeat, the Scots (said to be Sinclairs) have another memorial in the checked cloth used in one local costume, which looks remarkably like Sinclair tartan.

Solid as a rock

BELOW: Dovrefjell.
RIGHT: Maihaugen open-air museum, Lillehammer.

Travelling north from Vinstra, the E6 passes through Otta (where Road 15 heads off west to the western fjords) on its way to Dombås. Here it turns north-east, accompanied by the railway, and climbs up and over **Dovrefjell ⑫**. To many Norwegians, the Dovre mountains represent the strength of their country, something that brings their nation together. With admirable brevity, they sum it up in the old phrase *"Enig og tro til Dovre faller"* ("United we stand until the Dovre mountains fall").

The train stops at small stations such as Fokstua, Hjerkinn, Kongsvoll and Drivstua to disgorge walkers with boots and backpacks. The summit of Dovrefjell is at Hjerkinn, reputed to be the driest place in Norway, and for the rest of the way it is all down hill across the **Dovre Nasjonalpark** (National Park) en route to Oppdal. Dovrefjell is one of the three places in the world where you find musk ox in the wild.

Oppdal ⑬ sits looking up towards the Dovre plateau, and to Trollheimen (*see page 286*) to the northwest. In winter, it is a centre for skiing and in summer for walking, fishing, rafting and riding. The new **cable car** takes both walkers and skiers high above the village.

Not far from Oppdal, off Road 16, a small path leads to a peaceful place with trees and uneven mounds which are Viking graves. This is **Vang**, once the centre of the community until the railway brought Oppdal to life. There are 758 graves dating back to the early Iron Age. A track branches off to **Gjevilsvassdalen** and its lake. It is here that Anders Rambech, an 18th-century country attorney and one of the negotiators of the 1814 constitution, built **Tingstua**. Today the wooden building is a popular upland inn. Small and simple though it is, the inn has been favoured by Crown Princess Sonja who made it her base for walking into Dovrefjell. ❏

Map, pages 182–3

PEAK AND PLATEAU

Whether on foot or by car, the peaks of Jotunheimen and the flat rocky expanse of the Hardanger plateau both mesmerise and stun the senses with their sheer size and magnificence

Jotunheimen ("Home of the Giants"), which includes Norway's mightiest mountain range, and Hardangervidda (*vidde* means "highland plateau") together form an extensive area of outstanding natural beauty. Centres of population are few, places of interest are also thin on the ground, but of superb scenery – mountains, glaciers, lakes and rivers – there is an excess.

The attraction of **Hardangervidda** resides in its wide open spaces. On average 900 metres (3,000 ft) above sea level, it lies south of Jotunheimen with three main valleys – Begnadalen, Hallingdalen and Numedalen – cutting across it. The centre of the plateau with its lakes and streams (a paradise for anglers) forms the source of the mighty Hallingdal and Numedal rivers. There are a number of magnificent waterfalls in the area, including **Vøringfossen** (see page 238) and **Valursfossen** , which drops 90 metres (300 ft) into Hjelmodalen. To the south, Hardangervidda broadens out from **Hallingskarvet**, a rocky wall rising to a height of 1,700 metres (5,700 ft).

Crossing the plateau

Hardangervidda is in many ways unique as Europe's largest mountain plateau, covering an area of 10,000 sq km (3,860 sq miles) nearly a third of which lies within the **Hardangervidda Nasjonalpark** ⓯. The flora and fauna of the plateau is Arctic and very varied: several thousand reindeer roam freely, around 120 species of birds breed on these upland moors, and there are in excess of 400 different species of plants, an abundance due to the two distinct climates of Vidda – the gentle western coastal climate and the harsher inland climate of the east. There are tracks and trails galore and isolated cabins provide basic overnight accommodation.

The **Oslo–Bergen railway line** ⓰ cuts across Hardangervidda keeping Road 7 company as far as Haugastøl, where it goes north of the Hardangerjøkulen through Finse (see page 102), Myrdal and Mjølfjell. The road takes a different course, heading southeast across the wide, empty landscape with distant views of mountains, passing lakes and streams, before making a dizzy descent to sea level via a series of brilliantly engineered tunnels to Eidfjorden.

Travelling northwest from Haugastøl, both road and railway are initially dominated by Hallingskarvet. The immediate surroundings become somewhat softer as you reach **Geilo** ⓱, which has a good strategic position at the head of the Hallingdal valley and the gateway to Hardangervidda. Though it lies at a height of 800 metres (2,650 ft) above sea level, Geilo has grown into one of Norway's most popular winter sports resorts with 18 lifts, 34 well-groomed downhill runs

LEFT: view from the top, Jotunheimen.
BELOW: keeping traditional tunes alive.

TIP

Apart from Torpo
Stavkirke, other stave
churches worth
visiting in Buskerud
county are to be found
further south at Uvdal,
Nore, Rollag and
Flesberg.

BELOW LEFT:
summer skiing in
Jotunheimen.
BELOW RIGHT: the
first frosts turn the
leaves red.

and 220 km (135 miles) of cross-country tracks. With its range of hotels, Geilo has also become popular as a summer holiday centre and as a base for exploring the region by car (although the choice of roads is limited), on foot or horseback. In summer it still looks like a typical winter resort minus snow, with its spread out, slightly unfinished appearance.

From Geilo, Road 40 goes southeast past **Hol Bygdemuseum** (Rural Museum; open June–Aug; entrance fee) which takes the usual form of a collection of old buildings. In this case it includes the Mostugua from 1750, the Hågåstuga from 1806 and a mill from 1774. Road 40 continues along the eastern edge of Hardangervidda before it follows the Numedal valley to Kongsberg.

Road 7, meanwhile, continues northeast to Hagafoss where **Road 50** turns off it towards Strandavatn (lake). It leads along the north side of the long, clear lake dotted with small mountain huts. The landscape soon changes, however, allowing a magnificent view and a summer skiing centre is located nearby. Suddenly the road begins to descend through a series of tunnels, including spirals, until the motorist is decanted into the Aurlands valley which continues to the village of Aurlandsvangen at the head of Aurlandsfjorden.

After being separated by Strandfjorden, Road 7 and the railway meet up at **Ål** ⓲, where the Norwegian-German artist Rolf Nesch (1893–1975) lived and worked for 25 years. The **Nesch Museum** (open all year; entrance fee) contains the largest exhibition of his work in the country. **Torpo** has no museum but a stave church (open June–Sept; entrance fee) which is the oldest building in Hallingdal. It dates back to the second half of the 12th century and has a unique painted ceiling from the 13th century. The motifs include scenes from the life of St Margaret, to whom the church is dedicated.

Just past Gol, Road 7 turns southwards towards Nesbyen, Norway's oldest outdoor museum. Founded in 1889, the **Hallingdal Folkemuseum** (open Easter and June–Aug; entrance fee) has 22 buildings, the earliest – Staveloftet – dating from 1340. All come from different parts of Hallingdal. Some interiors are rose painted and the exhibition building houses collections of furniture, textiles and weapons.

The two other roads at Gol both lead the traveller through more attractive scenery. Road 52 goes northwest along the Hemsedal valley through **Hemsedal**, another winter sports centre (13 lifts, 26 runs, 90 km (55 miles) of cross-country tracks) with a church (open Mon; free) which has an altar piece from 1775 and a painting of *The Last Supper* from 1716. From the village a minor road goes past a small open-air museum near the village of Ulsåk and, further on, a private toll road winds its way across superb scenery to Ulnes on Road E16. This is the **Utsiktsveien** ⓲ (Panorama Way; summer only), a popular route which links the Hemsedal and Valdres valleys. Although narrow and rough in parts it lives up to its name, threading its way between lakes and providing fine views of the Skogshorn, known as the "Queen of the Hemsedal".

Home of the Giants

The **Jotunheimen** was, in Norwegian mythology, the home of trolls and giants and it is here that the mightiest mountains are to be found. In the east is the **Jotunheimen Nasjonalpark** ⓴ which includes the two highest mountains in the country: **Galdhøpiggen** at 2,469 metres (8,098 ft) and **Glittertind** ㉑ at 2,470 metres (8,101 ft). In west Jotunheimen is another group of crevassed mountains, the **Skagastølstindane**, which reach to over 2,000 metres (8,000 ft).

Map, pages 182–3

BELOW: the mountain massif of Jotunheimen.

The southern part of the Jotunheimen has some major lakes, including Gjende which is particularly beautiful with its greenish glacier water and flanked by impressive peaks. Other major lakes are Bygdin, Tyin and Vinstri, while glaciers add to the superb natural attractions.

Northern approaches

The northern border of Jotunheimen is the Otta river valley which acts as a natural boundary. From **Otta** in the east the river and Road 15 go through fertile countryside, with farms and forests, but beyond **Lom** the scene gradually changes. The green and lush surroundings give way to forests and rocky outcrops and the river grows more turbulent. Eventually at the tree line the scenery becomes bare and inhospitable.

Grotli, which consists of little more than a large roadside hotel, cafeteria and souvenir shop, marks the beginning of the Breidalsvatnet (lake). Shortly afterwards at Langevatnet, Road 63 turns off and becomes a spectacular mountain road which skirts Djupvatnet and then descends steeply to Geiranger. Road 15 continues on its course through 15 tunnels until it reaches Stryn on Innvikfjorden. An alternative to Road 15 from Grotli is the old **Road 258 ㉒**. Twenty six kilometres (16 miles) long, it climbs to a height of 1,139 metres (3,736 ft) and although narrow and unsurfaced in parts provides a thrilling journey. West of the summit it passes a summer ski centre and **Snowland**, a summer activity area for the family – with snow thrown in.

Between Otta and Grotli there are only two roads that go south, bold enough to penetrate the heart of Jotunheimen. Road 51, the most easterly, leaves the Otta–Grotli road at Randen and heads into the **Valdres** region. It starts by climb-

Having attacked a guard with an axe, the Valdres knight Sigvat Kvier kidnapped Ivar of Sandbu's betrothed. Sigvat, hotly pursued by Ivar, and with the beautiful lady in his arms, escaped by jumping the River Sjoa at Riddderspranget or "Knight's Leap".

BELOW: fish-farming in Sunndalsfjorden.

ing into a area of upland pastures with a distant backdrop of mountains. A further climb to Darthus brings **Ridderspranget ㉓** ("Knight's Leap") close at hand, where the river Sjoa is channelled into a narrow gorge.

Lakes lie scattered across to the west while beyond can be seen the peak of Glittertind. The most important stretch of water is **Lake Gjende ㉔**, long and narrow and curving slightly to the southwest. Beyond Bessheim there are more inspiring views and this scenic feast continues for kilometre after kilometre.

Bygdin lies between two lakes: Lake Bygdin which stretches like a long finger pointing to more distant mountains in the west; eastwards is the major expanse of Lake Vinstri. There are boat trips on several of the lakes and Lake Bygdin has northern Europe's highest scheduled boat service, in waters 1,060 metres (3,477 ft) above sea level.

The River Sjoa is good for white-water rafting.

The heart of the Valdres

Between Bessheim and Bygdin the road reaches its highest point – 1,389 metres (4,557 ft). From here it descends, first to the tree line, then to more gentle scenery at **Beitostølen**. This winter sports resort got its first ski lift in 1964 and now has 8 lifts, 16 runs and more than 325 km (200 miles) of cross-country tracks. It is a typical village of its kind with several hotels, very popular for cross-country skiing, and with a school for handicapped and blind skiers, who plunge down the slopes with unbelievable confidence.

Fagernes ㉕ is in the centre of the Valdres area. The focus of attention is the large **Valdres Folkemuseum** (open all year; entrance fee) which features some 80 buildings from between 1200 and 1900. Of particular interest are a 16th-century tapestry, medieval chests, a collection of antique silver, folk music instru-

BELOW: the visitors stare at the goats, and the goats stare back.

Map, pages 182–3

Mountain seter
(summer farms)
in autumn.

BELOW: summer
on Lustrafjorden.
RIGHT:
Borgund Stavkirke
near Flåm.

ments and hunting weapons. On a modern note, Fagernes has one of Norway's newest airports, opened in 1987. This area is also scattered with **stave churches** including Hedalen, Reinli, Lomen, Høre, Øye, Hegge and Garmo.

In one direction the E16 goes southeast through the Begnadal valley and eventually to Hønefoss. In the opposite direction the road goes west through more exciting scenery on the southern edge of Jotunheimen. At Tyinkrysset a road goes off to Øvre Årdal on Årdalsfjorden while the E16 turns south, descending through forested scenery to **Borgund** ㉖. Apart from the stave church at Heddal in Telemark, the one at Borgund is regarded as the most typical and best preserved in Norway. Built in 1150, it is dedicated to St Andrew.

At **Sæbø** a **minor road** goes to **Aurlandsvangen** ㉗. It starts to climb almost immediately, through lush scenery but this gradually changes as the narrow road ascends higher and higher, unfolding a series of stunning panoramas until the summit at 1,305 metres (4,284 ft). It then begins an increasingly steep descent to the village of Aurlandsvangen. "Breathtaking" is an over-used description but on this road it is justified, especially the view over Aurlandsfjorden from several thousand feet above it. Not for the fainthearted.

Across Sognefjell

The second route south from the Otta–Grotli road is Road 55 from Lom to Lustrafjorden, which is the part of Sognefjorden farthest from the sea. **Lom** ㉘ is a typical Norwegian "junction" village with its two or three hotels, shops and garages, but it also has a fine stave church. The **Fossheim Steinsenter** (Stone Centre; open all year; free) in Lom contains stones, rocks and gems from all over Norway and it also has a collection of minerals from Jotunheimen, while the associated **Norsk Fjellmuseum** (Mountain Museum; open May–Sept; entrance fee) focuses on mountain life throughout Norway.

Starting out from Lom, you drive through the deceptively placid Bøverdal valley, passing small farms and villages, but the view gradually changes as it gains height and the mountains become more noticeable. At **Galdesand** there is a toll road to Juvashytta, which is the nearest point by car to the Galdhøpiggen mountain.

At 640 metres (2,100 ft) is **Elveseter** ㉙, one of Norway's most unusual hotels. The Elveseter family has owned the property for five generations, gradually converting it into an hotel but retaining many of the old buildings. The oldest is from 1640 and has survived as a wooden building because of the dry mountain air. The first visitors arrived in the 1880s, but it was the opening of the Sognefjell road in 1938 that lead to the expansion of tourism.

The road continues its upward ascent past the isolated Jotunheimen Fjellstue to the summit at **Krossbu** at a height of 1,400 metres (4,590 ft) amidst superb mountain scenery. From there, make the steep descent to **Turtagrø** where the hotel (which is about all there is to Turtagrø) is a popular base for walkers and climbers; continue the downward course to softer surroundings at Fortun and, a few miles on, to sea level, at the end of **Lustrafjorden** at Skjolden. ❏

TELEMARK AND THE SOUTH

Map, pages 204–5

Norway's southern coastline is a magnet for summer visitors with its beaches and picturesque seaside towns. Inland, the scenery is starker and life in the mountain valleys lingers in the past

As they are proverbially advised to do "when in Rome", visitors to Oslo – or, equally, to Stavanger and Kristiansand – could usefully do what the locals do for recreation. The fundamental choice is either mountains and lakes, in which case they steer a course for **Telemark**, or the sea, which draws them to **Aust Agder** and **Vest Agder**, jointly known as Sørlandet.

Locals would usually travel in their own cars, a definite advantage in trying to make the most out of Telemark but not so necessary on the coast, along which it is possible to leapfrog from port to port on ferries which are sufficiently frequent to permit an improvised itinerary.

Oslo, Kristiansand and Stavanger, the principal cities along the southern rim of Norway, have good inter-connections, including flights, so they all serve as practical starting or finishing points for a tour, and you can combine Telemark and Sørlandet on one of several coach excursions. One from Oslo, for example, covers nearly 1,200 km (750 miles) by road and ferry and lasts five days.

Designed by a king

In 1639 King Christian IV of Denmark-Norway had the sort of whim which is the privilege of kings and very few others. He wanted to found a town and name it after himself. In the event, the choice of the site where **Kristiansand ❶** now stands was not entirely capricious. It was an admirable base from which to control the approaches to both the North Sea and the Baltic. The town had to be fortified, and much survives of the first of many forts to be built on the site, **Christiansholm Festning** (Fortress; open May–Aug; entrance fee for exhibitions). Through nearly three turbulent centuries, however, none of the forts ever fired a gun in anger (not until 9 April 1940), and gradually Kristiansand changed from being a military town to a trading and administrative centre.

Kristiansand has had its problems: with witches, one of whom confessed (in 1670) to having flown to Copenhagen to pour poison into the mayor's ear, fire (in 1734), syphilis (in 1782) and a "privateer" period (1807–14) marked by such wholesale swindling, bribery and corruption that it caused "violent upheavals in the economic life of the country".

Present-day Kristiansand has managed to put all that behind it. It is a pleasant city, laid out in squares according to Christian IV's directive, and the sort of place which invites visitors simply to stroll about. The weather is more reliably sunny than anywhere else in Norway, the port and central market are always busy, the **Kvadraturen** is a picturesque quarter of old wooden houses, and one never has to look far for a spot to sit down and watch the world go by. "A total

PRECEDING PAGES: Norway's Sørlandet (south land) is rich farming country. **LEFT:** Brevik on the Telemark coast. **BELOW:** a farmer assesses his grain harvest.

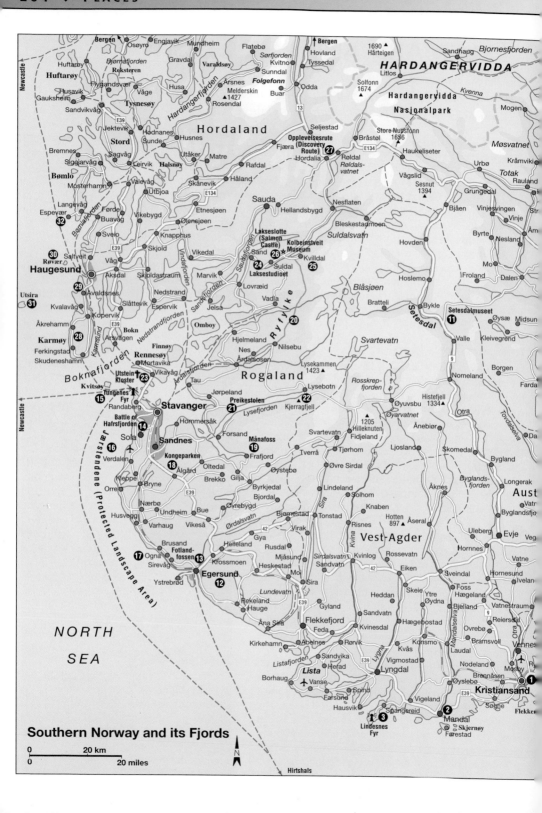

Southern Norway and its Fjords

0   20 km
0   20 miles

N

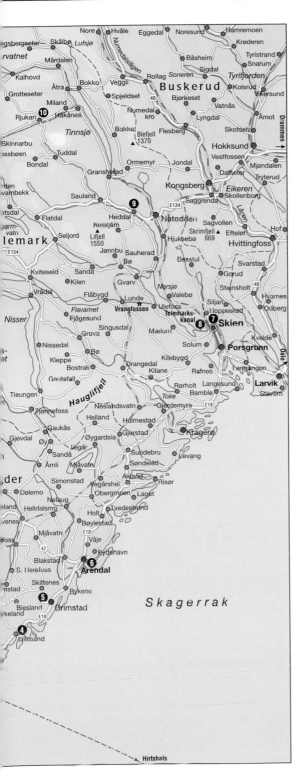

of more than 10,000 seats in cafés and restaurants" is the city's proud claim.

The city's zoo **Kristiansand Dyrepark** (open all year; entrance fee), which includes the miniature town of Kardemomme By, is "the most visited family park in Norway". The fictional town is out of a popular children's story by Torbjørn Egner and besides the large zoo there are water chutes and other attractions. Just north of the centre the **Ravnedalen Nasjonalpark** (National Park) is set in attractive, hilly grounds. The **Gimle Gårde** (Mansion; open May–Sept; entrance fee) across the River Otra is a magnificent symbol of 19th-century Norwegian capitalism. It was built by a shipping and trading tycoon, Bernt Holm, and passed down the family (with a five-year interruption while it was occupied by the German army) until finally it was bequeathed to the town and opened to the public in 1985. The **Setesdalbanen** (Railway Museum; varying times; tel: 38 12 13 14), with its narrow gauge steam railway is a short way north of the city.

Dutch port

About 45 km (28 miles) west of Kristiansand is **Mandal ❷**. A busy port long before Christian IV felt the urge to build Kristiansand, it suffered from the competition afterwards. A 1799 traveller remarked that "the houses are jammed together so tightly that a careless pipe-smoker at any open window could spit into his neighbour's parlour". This is due to the nostalgia of foreign residents: Dutch who were there to trade and Scots. The point known as **Kastellet** is where a wealthy Dane, who once reached into his pocket to make a personal loan to the notoriously empty-pocketed King Frederik IV, installed cannon to keep pirates away from his estate.

The nearby lighthouse at **Lindesnes Fyr ❸** (open all year; entrance fee to museum) marks the southernmost point of Norway, and in bad weather is buffeted by ferocious winds. The small islands about 5 km (3 miles) offshore are often mentioned in ancient Norse sagas as a refuge for Vikings ships waiting for better

A possible sighting of the Seljord Monster, as depicted here in an early illustration, draws many to the small Telemark village of Seljord.

weather before turning the corner into or out of the Skaggerak. **Farsund**, a little further up the coast and once a privateer centre, has suffered the misfortune of being destroyed by fire so often that there is hardly a building left pre-dating the present century. Nevertheless, the relatively modern houses are painted white and present a pleasing spectacle.

The region is rich in rock carvings and ancient sites including, near **Vanse**, the remains of nine Iron Age homes surrounded by 350 burial mounds. Lomsesanden, a popular beach on the Lista peninsula, is all of 10 km (6 miles) of white sand. The last town before Vest Agder rises to meet Rogaland is the small port of **Flekkefjord**. This is mountainous country which, apart from necessitating the construction of some of Norway's longest railway tunnels (there are 46 between Flekkefjord and Egersund), has created several waterfalls, especially around Kvinesdal.

Coastal journey

The principal centres along the coast east from Kristiansand are, in order, Lillesand, Grimstad, Arendal and Risør. **Lillesand ❹**, apart from being a pretty holiday town with a pleasant selection of cafés and restaurants around the harbour, has a special place in Norwegian history as the centre of an 18th-century revolt led by a farmer named Lofthus, a Robin Hood figure who travelled to Copenhagen to confront the Crown Prince with a long list of grievances. On his return he collected a force of 2,000 men and caused panic among the Danish "establishment" in the coastal towns. The house where he was finally arrested still stands; he spent the rest of his life in chains. The **Lillesand Bymuseum** (Town Museum; open June–Aug; entrance fee) tells the whole story.

BELOW: a statue of Henrik Ibsen in Skien.

Grimstad ❺ is indelibly associated with Ibsen. It was here that he served his apprenticeship to a chemist. Ibsen was an unhappy young man and Grimstad, though a pretty place, must have contributed (together with Skien, where he was born) to his searing exposure of goings-on in small Norwegian towns. His works caused a scandal at the time, but years have healed the wounds and he is commemorated in the **Grimstad Bymuseum** (Town Musuem: open May–Sept; entrance fee) which holds the largest collection of Ibsen memorabilia in Norway.

Arendal ❻ is full of character, every ounce of which was needed to thwart King Christian's plan to close it down and transfer the inhabitants to his pet project, Kristiansand. One of his successors, Frederik IV, visited Arendal in 1704 and was puzzled about dinner with the local priest who "went to great trouble to explain in detail how the rite of circumcision was performed by the Jews". Arendal prospered in the 17th and 18th centuries as a conduit for timber shipments abroad, including much of the timber used for the rebuilding of London after the 1666 Great Fire.

In 1863, Arendal itself was struck by fire, losing the houses on stilts which had earlier given it the nickname of "Little Venice" but, overflowing on to a number of small islands, it retains its lovely setting. An unusual and recent addition to its attractions is a museum meticulously created by unpaid volunteers

Map, pages 204–5

out of the contents of a pottery factory that went out of business a few years ago. Located in the Regency style Kløcker's House (1826), the enthusiasm of the staff at the **Arendal Bymuseum** (Town Museum; open all year; entrance fee) is infectious. The **Rådhus** (Town Hall), previously the home of a merchant, is said to be one of the largest wooden buildings ever constructed in Norway.

Risør, the last town in Aust Agder, was also threatened by the creation of Kristiansand. Its traders were forced to maintain residencies in the new city but they kept their links with Risør. Mary Wollstonecraft, an English visitor in 1795, noted an addiction to tobacco. The men never took their pipes out of their mouths and absolutely refused to open a window. The women, she decided, dressed like tarts or, as she put it, "sailor girls in Hull or Portsmouth". Many of these women were probably Dutch since it was fashionable among young seamen to bring wives back from the Netherlands, the main trading partner. In Risør, as in other parts of Sørlandet, children may still be given distinctly Dutch names.

Ibsen completed his first play, Catalina, in 1850 while still serving his apprenticeship to the chemist in Grimstad. Soon after, he left behind his provincial existence and headed for Oslo.

The ice canal

The capital of Telemark is **Skien** ❼, which was the birthplace, in 1828, of Norway's greatest playwright, Henrik Ibsen. His **childhood home** (open May–Aug; entrance fee) is about 4 km (2½ miles) north of the town and has become a national shrine.

Skien originally came into existence on the back of an industry producing stone projectiles for military slingshots, even stranger than another industry which prospered in the nearby village of Ulefoss until the close of the 19th century, namely the production of ice. Ice was easily transported along Telemark's natural waterways which were later rationalised into a canal system.

BELOW: Kragerø, summer home of Edvard Munch, on Oslofjorden.

Inside the silver mine at Saggrenda not far from Heddal.

The impressive **Telemarkskanal** ❽ (canal) stretches from the Telemarks-sjærgården, an unusual skerry formation that stretches out from Oslofjorden along the southern coast, to the foot of Hardangervidda. Eight sets of locks raise boats a total of 72 metres (225 ft) up to Flåvatn, which in turn runs into Kviteseidvatn and Bandak all the way to Dalen. Completed in 1892, the canal cuts 110 km (70 miles) into the interior and is now used by pleasure boats such as the *MV Victoria* and *MV Henrik Ibsen* (both May–Sept; tel: 35 95 82 11). The Norwegian State Railways also offer inclusive tickets from Oslo, while Lindhjem Reiser in Skien (tel: 35 52 00 20) runs a variety of tours with bus connections. The canal is littered with attractions, including **Vrangfossen** (waterfall) above Ulefoss, and places to stay. The best way to keep abreast of what's on is through the information pack produced by the local authority, Statens Vegvesen Telemark in Skien (tel: 35 58 16 00).

Interior isolation

Throughout Telemark one senses an older Norway lurking just beneath the surface. The upper districts were, until recently, impenetrable except on skis, travel in winter being easier than in summer. Isolated communities were not inclined to take orders from interfering outsiders, although a lot of water has passed under the bridge since the people were described (in 1580) as "shameless bodies of the Devil whose chief delight is to kill bishops, priests, bailiffs and superiors – and who possess a large share of all original sin".

BELOW: typical "Sørlandet houses" near Farsund, Vest Agder.

Although a finger of Telemark reaches the sea at Kragerø, not far from the mouth of Oslofjorden, the province is associated in most minds with the inland terrain, which inspired an eccentric farmer named Sondre Norheim to turn the

pedestrian business of plodding about in snow on two planks into the sport of skiing. His discovery of the delights that could be achieved with planks that were properly shaped and had heel bindings made him overlook his domestic chores. It is apparently true that, when he ran out of firewood in winter, he simply hacked off another piece of his house and put that on the fire (*see "Morgedal and Telemark Revival, page 108*).

Morgedal, where Norheim lived (he later emigrated to America) deserves to be called the cradle of skiing but it is now only one of dozens of skiing centres in the province, many of which have ski-lifts to complement the traditional cross-country courses which do not need mechanical contraptions. Norheim's statue is a feature of the Norwegian Skiing Adventure Centre in **Kviteseid** (open Easter and May–Sept; entrance fee), near to Kviteseidvatn and the canal.

Rural arts

Visitors with their own transport in Telemark can hardly go wrong: pick any of the winding roads that head inland and the scenery is bound to be breath-taking. For those who do not have a car, the waterways are a wonderful alternative: Skien is on a main line from Oslo and a good place to pick up boats going north through Sauherad to Notodden (Road 36 then 360 covers the same route). Schedules change according to season – in some parts the boats press on with the help of a small ice-breaker – so it is advisable to check with the tourist office (tel: 35 58 16 00) in Skien.

West of Notodden, along Road 11, lies **Heddal ❾** with its famous **Stavkirke** (open May–Sept; entrance fee), the largest in Norway. Built between 1147 and 1242, it has a richly carved doorway with animals and human faces. But Hed-

Map, pages 204–5

BELOW: the popular bathing beach at Mandal.

Map, pages 204–5

dal is more than that. The Telemarkers are masters at expressing nature through art and nowhere is this more evident than in the rose paintings in the Ramberg room of the **Heddal Bygdetun** (Farmhouses: open May–Sept; entrance fee).

Further on, Road 37 branches off to the north past Tinnsjø (lake) towards **Rjukan ⑩**. The stretch between Rjukan and Rauland is particularly lovely and can be covered by public bus. Keep an eye open for highly decorative wooden houses and double-storey barns, sometimes bigger than the house itself, with a ramp leading to the upper floor.

The obvious attraction of Rjukan itself is the heavy water plant, now the **Norsk Industriarbeidermuseum** (Norwegian Industrial Workers Museum; open May–Sept; entrance fee) but in 1943 the target of a daring sabotage attack by the Norwegian resistance (see "The Heroes of Telemark", page 54). The town library, incidentally, has a good collection of literature about the operation, including some books written by those who participated. A few of these are in English and the charming librarian could not be more helpful.

Rjukan is generally rather gloomy because the sun is nearly always blocked off by surrounding mountains. On top of those mountains, though, another world of vast vistas opens up, and it is said that on a good day it is possible to see one-sixth of Norway. You can take the cable car (open June– Aug, weekends only Sept–May; entrance fee) from Krosso to the top of Gvepseborg at 860 metres (2,800 ft) for just such a view.

Medieval life in the 20th century

An alternative route inland is Road 39 from Kristiansand, which climbs sharply up the Otra valley and runs north along **Byglandsfjorden** to **Setesdal**. Until modern times this area was very remote. The inhabitants sent their timber down to Arendal by pushing it into a river which plunged 700 metres (2,300 ft) over a distance of about 150 km (90 miles). Otherwise, contacts were few and Setesdal preserved its own almost medieval way of life, including a distinct dialect, dress and cuisine, right into the 20th century.

Setesdal is a haven for those in search of rural culture. The most famous dwelling is Rygnestadtunet, a 16th century windowless tower of three storeys with an amazing collection of relics, such as leather hangings depicting St George's battle with the dragon. The tower was built about 400 years ago by Vond-Asmund who, on discovering that his fiancée was about to marry someone else, snatched her away from the wedding procession. From the upper floor of his fortress, he fired off arrows at anyone who approached and in so doing killed at least four people. His descendants still farm in the area. Rygnestadtunet is part of the **Setesdalmuseet ⑪** (Heritage Muesum; open all year; entrance fee), which is 15 km (9 miles) to the south.

If all this is too boring for the kids you can visit the Sommarland family park at **Bø** (open Jun–Aug, entrance fee). Other attractions near to this inland route include the Setesdal Railway Museum north of Kristiansand (see page 205), and the **Setesdal Mineralpark** (Mineral Park; open May–Oct; entrance fee) based around an old mining complex near Evje. ❑

BELOW: collecting the honey in summer.
RIGHT: *Lindesnes fyr* (lighthouse) on the southernmost tip of Norway.

FJORDS

*The Norwegian fjords are a defining feature of both country
and culture – the difficulty is to decide on a favourite*

To create a fjord, take a mountain and a river, and mix in an Ice Age many thousands of years ago. To describe the fjords is to find yourself running out of superlatives: the deepest water, the highest mountains, the narrowest, the most beautiful, the stillest, the most peaceful... each fjord has its own special characteristic, from the Sognefjord (the longest) to the Geiranger, which many people think the most beautiful. But who would argue? With so many fjords, everybody is entitled to their own opinion.

The fjords gave Norway its great seafaring tradition. From the early Vikings who found Scotland, Iceland and the rest of Europe easier to reach than the area around Oslo, to the modern traveller who chooses a ship as the most comfortable way to travel this magnificent coastline, the sea has provided the link.

The fjords begin at Stavanger in the south, now Norway's oil capital, not far from Preikestolen, the great slab of rock standing a dizzy 600 metres (2,000 ft) above Lysefjorden. They stretch north to the Hardanger, one of the largest in the country and an early favourite where the old traditions of music and storytelling influenced travellers such as the composer Edvard Grieg. On the way, they encompass Bergen, the fjord capital, Sognefjorden and Nordfjorden, in an area of glaciers, lakes and mountains massifs, Storfjorden, parts of which bite far into the land, and, finally, the calm of the Geiranger.

From their high mountain sides, waterfalls cascade into the fjords, and small farms cling to every ledge and hectare of green. The fjords are beautiful, timeless, and everyone's idea of the soul of Norway. ❏

PRECEDING PAGES: passing through Trollfjorden, in the Lofoten Islands, is a delicate operation for the Hurtigrute ship.
LEFT: small coastal freighter at Femrissundet (sound) in the north.

ROGALAND

Map, pages 204-5

This often overlooked corner of the country contains many delights, from the picturesque fishing harbour of Egersund to an eagle's-eye view over Lysefjorden from the top of Preikestolen

Many people believe that Norway's fjord country begins at Hardangerfjorden and the city of Bergen, and stretches north. If so, they are missing all the southern fjords and islands, where Norway first became a nation. Today this area of Rogaland is centred on Stavanger, the centre of Norway's international oil industry, and contains some of the fjord country's most spectacular natural sights: what a pity to miss Preikestolen ("the pulpit"), a flat slab of rock swooping some 600 metres (2,000 ft) up from Lysefjorden, which offers a 180° view over *fjell* and fjord.

Rogaland has the mildest climate in Norway and the beauty of the coast is unsurpassed. These coastal and outer fjord areas have the highest average temperature in the whole country, but pay the penalty for their closeness to the sea in unexpected showers and a higher rainfall. In winter, thanks to the Gulf Stream, there is little snow and the fertile fields are green for most of the year.

LEFT: Preikestolen, one of Rogaland's best-known landmarks.
BELOW: goat's cheese made at Egersund.

Starting in the south

By air, the way in is Stavanger's international airport at Sola, or you might come by express boat from Bergen in just under three hours. From the south, the main road is the E18, which crosses into Rogaland south of the old town of **Egersund ⑫**, now Norway's largest fishing harbour. There is also a coastal route (the scenic Road 44), which hugs the coastline all the way north to Stavanger. At the southern corner of this route, small fjords bite into a rough, rocky coast, which lead to green valleys and a myriad of shining lakes.

The best view of Egersund's sheltered harbour, with its dozens of yachts both big and small, is from the top of the lighthouse. The town itself has a fine **cruciform church** (open Jun–Aug; entrance fee) from 1620 (renovated in the late 18th century) and the **Dalane Folk Museum** (open all year; entrance fees; tel: 51 49 14 79) which includes the **Egersund Faiyance Museum** (displaying painted earthenware crockery, once the town's main industry).

Inland is the waterfall **Fotlandfossen ⑬**, and further north on the E18 you come to the southern end of **Ørdalsvatn**. From here, Rogaland's last remaining inland waterway boat, *Ørsdølen*, sails the 20 km (13 miles) to Vassbø at the far end of the narrow lake. Near there you can have a simple home-made meal before the boat returns. A few miles further on is Vikeså, where Road 503 to Byrkjedal runs past **Gloppedalsura**, where the boulders are as big as houses.

The flat and fertile country above Egersund is Norway's main area for the production of meat, dairy products, poultry and eggs, but it was not always as peaceful as it is today. In AD 872, it was the scene of

TIP

The walking trail to the top of Preikestolen starts from the Preikestolhytte and takes takes two hours each way.

BELOW: Månafoss waterfall.

the **Battle of Hafrsfjord** , where King Harald Hårfagre (Fair hair) won his final and most important battle to unite the warring Norwegian kingdoms. That battle is marked at the edge of Hafrsfjorden, the near circular fjord to the southwest of Stavanger, where three huge sculptured swords rise out of the ground.

In 1977, by royal decree, a narrow strip some 70 km (43 miles) long, from Raumen Island at the southern end to **Tungenes Fyr** (Lighthouse; open Jun–Aug; entrance fee) northwest of Stavanger, became **Jærstendene Landskapsvernområdet** (Protected Landscape Area), which includes offshore islands. Raumen itself is one of eight bird sanctuaries where, at different times of the year, you can find turnstones, ringed plovers and knots taking a brief rest on the long flight to or from southern Europe or Africa; offshore are wintering eider and long-tailed ducks, and the islands provide nesting places for seabirds, often in protected areas closed to visitors during the breeding season.

In the eight botanical reserves you find such delights as the spear-leaved fat hen saltbush, and the rare marsh orchid grows in the reserve near **Ogna**. There are also four geological sites and no less than 150 monuments listed and protected. But this does not mean that Jærstrendene is given over solely to flora and fauna. **Beaches** with white-gold sand are popular picnic spots and, though the water can be chilly, this does not deter swimmers.

Bicycle land

Sandnes on Sandfjorden, is Norway's "bicycle town", where the famous DBS bicycles are made and, whether this is the reason or not, where cycling is popular and you can hire bikes to explore the surrounding countryside. Another delight for youngsters is **Kongeparken** (open May–Sept; entrance fee), Norway's biggest leisure park, not far from Sandnes at the little town of Ålgård. At 80 metres (260 ft) long, Kongeparken's Gulliver is hard to miss. Inside, Gulliver's body is full of unusual playthings and the park has Scandinavia's longest bob-sleigh ride.

In many of the mountain areas around the fjords, waterfalls cascade hundreds of feet below. One of the most famous is **Månafoss** on the Frafjord, the innermost finger of the Høgsfjord, reached by Road 45 south from Ålgård to Gilja. At Gilja, turn down the steep road to Frafjord, which gives a fantastic view of the fjord. There are directions to Månofoss in the car park at the foot of the mountain.

Fjords once more

The **Ryfylke area** northeast of Stavanger is true fjord country, one of the least known parts of Norway despite the drama of its scenery. In the south, due east of Stavanger, Ryfylke starts with **Lysefjorden** and stretches north past long narrow lakes that once were open fjords, until it reaches **Vindafjorden**, **Saudafjorden** and **Suldalsvatn**.

Although he never saw it, Victor Hugo described Lysefjorden in *The Toilers of the Sea* as "the most terrible of all the corridor rocks in the sea". Hugo probably meant "awesome" and that the fjord still is. Every visitor to Norway should try to walk out through heather moor and scrubland to stand on the top of

Preikestolen ㉑, a rock platform high above the fjord. On the way you might see golden eagles, willow grouse, ptarmigan and other birds as well as reindeer and the angular shape of an elk. The great height of Preikestolen gives a view towards Stavanger and the fjords to the west, and upwards to the treeline and the rocky heights above. Everywhere there are lakes, waterfalls and rushing torrents.

From the village of Forsand at its mouth, Lysefjorden is 40 km (25 miles) long and, at its innermost end, has one of Europe's most remarkable feats of civil engineering: the road to the hydro-electric power station (closed Mon; entrance fee) at **Lysebotn**, which is hidden hundreds of metres inside the mountain. This road, which seems to defy gravity, snakes up and down more than 750 metres (2,500 ft) with 27 hairpin bends and connects Lysebotn to Sirdal and Setersdal to the west along the Lyseveien. If you dare to keep your eyes open as the bus takes its near perpendicular route down, the view is magnificent.

Near the end of the fjord on the south side towers **Kjerragfjell** ㉒, an enormous granite mountain around 1,100 metres (3,550 ft) high. Lie on your front and look down through the wedge cut out of the mountain plateau to the fjord below. To get there takes about two hours' walking from several spots along the Lyseveien.

Wedged between two rocks, the famous Kjerragbolten offers a breathtaking vantage point from which to view Lysefjorden below.

Inshore islands

The sheltered bay north of Stavanger, and the outer islands such as Karmøy, protect Ryfylke's inshore islands from the North Sea. Christianity flourished early here under the protection of the bishops of Stavanger and the islands have many churches. In summer, the 12th-century **Utstein Kloster** ㉓ (Cloister; open

BELOW: Gulliver at Kongeparken.

Sandvesanden beach on the island of Karmøy.

May–Oct, closed Mon; entrance fee) on **Mosterøy** makes a beautiful setting for concerts which are mostly classical. It offers the traveller a refreshing break on the way from Stavanger to Boknafjorden. The cloister's setting, acoustics and the palpable sense of history give these concerts a very special atmosphere.

The many **lighthouses** are not only landmarks for islanders and seafarers but make excellent bird-watching sites, with the hunched outlines of cormorants and other seabirds on wave-washed rocks below. The waters around these peaceful islands are a sea kingdom for sailors of all kinds with enough coastline to give every boat a bay to itself and many yacht harbours. Most of the island grocers also provide boat services and it is easy to hire rowing boats and small craft with outboard engines.

Northeast highlands

Here fjords, lakes and rivers are rich in fish and fine for sailing and canoeing, and all these inland, eastern areas of Rogaland have good cross-country skiing tracks in winter as well as some fine alpine slopes. Among the best holiday areas is the **Suldal district**, stretching from Sand on the Sandsfjorden, along the Suldalslågen (river) – where the rushing waters have produced huge salmon (the largest so far weighed almost 44 kg (75 lb) – to the long narrow Suldalsvatn. At the Sand end of Suldalslågen is **Laksestudioet** ❷ (open all year, Mon–Fri, plus weekends Aug–Sept; entrance fee), an observation studio, built under a waterfall where visitors look through a large window at the salmon resting before their next leap up the fish ladder on the way to their spawning grounds. Where river meets lake is **Kolbeinstveit Museum** (open May–Sept; entrance fee) with the old Guggedalsloftet Bygdetun (farm) which dates back to the 13th century.

BELOW: Utstein Kloster (Cloister) on Mosterøy.

From Sand, a bus follows the line of the river to the giant **Kvilldal** ㉕ station , opened in 1982 by King Olav, who chiselled his signature into the mountainside, a popular royal tradition in Scandinavia. On the way to this cavernous power station the bus stops at the **Lakseslotte** ㉖ (Salmon Castle) at Lindum, built by Lord Sibthorp in 1885, when the British "salmon lords" looked on a few weeks in Norway as part of the fishing season. River and lake still draw anglers from many countries and the castle is a popular guest house.

From Stavanger and Jæren, ferries and express boats reach this fjord country and its islands, and it is easy to combine bus and ferry. Vindafjord, Saudafjorden and Suldalsvatn look up to 1,500-metre (5,000-ft) peaks that lead the way to the great mountain massif of Hardangervidda, in the next county of Hordaland. In summer you can take the exciting **old mountain road** north from Sauda to Røldal; the new road now has tunnels to keep it open all year. At Røldal, and on the road from Suldalsvatn, you pick up the **Opplevelsesrute** ㉗ (Discovery Route; E11), which has come all the way over the Haukeli mountains from Telemark, and you can continue along until it becomes Road 13 towards Odda.

Back to the coast

The sea route north to Bergen is one of the most popular ways to see the northern coast. By taking an express boat (a cross between a catamaran and a hydrofoil) you can drop off at any of the harbour stops and stay a night or a week according to your whim. **Karmøy** ㉘, the island at the south of the outer islands chain, is big enough to merit its own boat service, which goes to **Skudeneshavn** in the south, an idyllic old port with white, wooden houses along narrow

Map, pages 204–5

Norway's largest hydro-electric scheme is to be found in Sudalen. The Ulla Førre plant contains five power stations linked to 13 separate dams on the enormous Blåsjø (lake).

BELOW: typical "seahouses" in Skudeneshavn.

Map,
pages
204–5

Following claims by the Norwegian film critic Pål Bang-Hansen that Marilyn Monroe's father was a Norwegian emigré from Haugesund, the town erected a statue to the Hollywood goddess on the quayside.

BELOW: young buskers in Haugesund during the Film Festival.
RIGHT: fish market on the island of Utsira.

streets (tours from **Mælandsgården Museum**; Jun–Aug; tel: 52 82 72 22). The north of the island is linked to the mainland just south of Haugesund, the first sizeable coastal town north of Stavanger, fast becoming prosperous through oil and the last mainland town in the county.

Karmøy's known history dates back to saga times, when it was the "North-way" shipping lane that gave Norway its name. Harald Hårfagre made his home at **Avaldsnes** ❷ after the battle at Hafrsfjord. Also here is **St Olaf Kirke** (Church) which was built between 1248 and 1263 by King Håkon Håkonson and restored in 1922 as the parish church. Near its north walls stands St Mary's Sewing Needle, a strange 6.5-metre (21-ft) high stone pillar leaning towards the church wall. Legend tells that the Day of Judgement will come when the pillar touches the wall; many priests are said to have climbed the pillar at dead of night to pare away the top to make sure that the Day was not yet nigh.

On the west coast at **Ferkingstad** are historic boathouses with walls made of stone blocks 1.5 metres (5 ft) thick. Further north on the west coast, outside the town hall at **Åkrehamn**, stand two stone pillars from the Iron Age. Crossing to the east coast, near the town of **Kopervik** are burial hills and mounds and stone pillars. The largest burial mound, Doøa Hill, was restored in 1978 and, though it has not yet been fully excavated, it dates back to the Bronze Age. Further north, on the mainland side of the bridge to Haugesund are **Dem Fem Dårlige Jomfruer** (Five Bad Virgins), stone monuments some 2.5 metres (8 ft) high, where excavations in 1901 revealed a Roman bowl dating from AD 300–400.

Fish, festivals and UFOs

Haugesund has long been a centre for fishing, shipping and farming. Today its harbour is filled with pleasure boats; the town has also become a festival and congress centre and plays host to the International Trad Jazz Festival and the Norwegian Film Festival (both Aug; dates and prices vary).

Numerous fjords and lakes cut into the roughly shaped peninsula, like a piece of well nibbled cheese, ideal for fishing, sailing, rowing, canoeing, sports diving and walking. Further out to sea a boat trip to the idyllic group of islands of **Røvær** ❸⓪, around 10 km (6 miles) to the west, occupies a half or whole day and offers shore fishing, interesting flora and fauna and, in summer, a wharfside café.

For the adventurous, **MS** *Utsira* (tel: 52 72 50 55) provides a daily service to the island of the same name ❸❶, familiar from European shipping forecasts and Norway's western outpost. The 90-minute journey out makes a wonderful tour for bird-watchers, as does the island itself. Fishing is also excellent and Norwegian saltwater fishing is free to holders of a national licence (*see pages 112–13*). Day licences for lakes in Rogaland and for salmon and sea trout in the many rivers vary from around NOK30 (£2.50/US$4) to NOK150 (£12.50/US$20).

To the north of Haugesund the **Espevær** ❸❷, a fishing village at the mouth of Bømlafjorden, is well-endowed with heritage sites. The village itself is one of the best preserved sites in Norway; there is a maritime and fisheries museum, and a bathing house. ❑

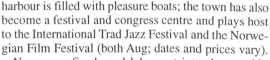

STAVANGER

Once the port from which thousands emigrated to the United States, today Stavanger attracts an international crowd – and cuisine – as the centre of Norway's thriving oil industry

Map on page 226

Strange though it may seem in a city which has devoted nearly 1,000 years to the sea, the best way to arrive in Stavanger is by overnight train from Oslo. As the dawn arrives, the train slips along the side of the fjord with black mountain peaks outlined on either side, past the huge latticework of oil rigs and drilling towers which have made Stavanger Norway's oil capital. Enormous though they are, somehow they do not intrude on the landscape because the size and grandeur of mountain and fjord dwarfs even these industrial giants.

Stavanger has been lucky because the sea has always been good to the city. As one source of prosperity disappeared, another arose. Shipping, fishing and trading have taken the city's ships and people all over the world, and brought seamen to Stavanger, to give it an easy-going relationship with other nations. Today, the city is as international as ever: nearly a tenth of its 100,000 inhabitants are foreigners.

International eating

This international community has demanded high standards and Stavanger has good restaurants, hotels, entertainment and a cosmopolitan atmosphere out of all proportion to its size. As well as the traditional **restaurants**, which specialise in good Norwegian food, there is a choice of Indian, Italian, Greek, Portuguese, Mexican and Japanese, and at least half a dozen Chinese restaurants, the latter a popular cuisine in most Norwegian cities.

Restaurants, and particularly alcohol, are expensive in Norway, but a great many cafés, bars and pubs have sprung up, sometimes with live music, plus a handful of youthful discos, which do not necessarily serve alcohol. In the **fish market** on the quayside, where fresh crabs eaten on the spot are the favourite buy, and the **fruit and flower market** nearby you will hear many languages, and in the heart of Stavanger's shopping streets behind the market almost all the assistants speak English.

Apart from the prosperity and development brought by oil industries, Stavanger is also the principal town, and the seat of local government, of Rogaland.

An American connection

In the 19th and early 20th centuries Stavanger was the exit port for Norway's extensive emigration programme to the United States (*see page 44*) – every Norwegian seems to have an American relative. Not surprisingly, therefore, the city is host to **Det Norske Utvandrersenteret Ⓐ** (Emigration Centre; open daily; free; tel: 51 53 88 60), where Norway's emigration history is documented and commemorated. For a fee, genealogical researchers will help you find your Norwegian

LEFT: Stavanger's past prosperity was based on sardines.
BELOW: winter in Stavanger.

roots. In midsummer the Centre arranges the Emigration Festival with exhibitions, concerts, folk dancing, crafts market, seminars, fjord cruises and city sightseeing. The highlight of the festival is the re-enactment of the 1825 sailing of the *Restauration*, the boat which carried the first emigrants across the Atlantic.

The smell of sardines

The Stavanger *siddis* (the colloquial name for a person from Stavanger) claims to be the oldest true Norwegian, dating from 872 and the Battle of Hafrsfjord, which took place just south of the city, and in which King Harald Hårfagre won his final battle to unite the kingdom.

When work began on the Domkirken (Cathedral) in 1125, Stavanger was simply a cluster of small wooden houses at the end of the narrow inlet called **Vågen**. It was chosen as the heart of the bishopric, nevertheless, because it was the only recognisable settlement along this south–western coast. From then on Stavanger was the most important town in the area. It grew slowly; the population was only 2,000 at the start of the 19th century, but jumped to 30,000 by 1900.

In the 18th and 19th centuries, the city depended on fishing and maritime trade and faced the world with an unbroken row of wharves and warehouses dedicated to these industries. Around the 1870s, at a time when fishing and shipping were beginning to face decline, the fishermen turned their attention to brisling (small herring), which were cured and canned in the town and sent as Norwegian "sardines" all over the world.

At one time Stavanger had as many as 70 canneries and nearly three quarters of the population worked in the industry. In the first half of this century, the smell of oily fish hung over the town, permeating every breath. But Stavanger was

Following chemical analysis, it has now been confirmed that the copper used to cover New York's Statue of Liberty came from one of the old Visnes copper mines on the island of Karmøy southwest of the city.

BELOW: an oil rig under contruction dwarfs the city.

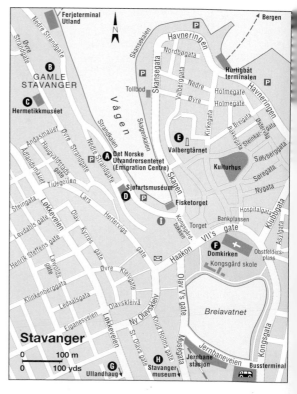

Stavanger

0 100 m

0 100 yds

never in doubt about the value of that smell. When, on a particularly odiferous day, a cheeky youngster wrinkled a disdainful nose, a mother would say: "Don't scorn it, that's the smell of money." It was, and Stavanger thrived on sardines until, after World War II, that all-pervasive tang began to fade along with the demand for sardines. For nearly 20 years, Stavanger knew difficult times. Then, in the 1960s, came oil – once again the sea had provided.

Map on page 226

Present-day reminders

Many traces remain of these fluctuations in the city's fortunes. From the late 17th and early 18th century is **Gamle Stavanger** Ⓑ (Old Stavanger) more than 180 early 19th-century, white, wooden buildings looking down towards Vågen, with cobbled streets lit by old-fashioned street lamps. But this is no museum. There may be a preservation order on the exteriors, and the owners take pride in keeping them in character, but the interiors have every comfort and gadget that modern Norwegians expect, and Gamle Stavanger is one of the most coveted areas to live in.

Nor have the canning factories been lost. Many are converted into modern offices, without destroying their scale and shape, and buildings that once canned sardines may now be the headquarters of an international oil company. One factory at Øvre Strandgate, near the harbour, has been preserved in its original state as the **Hermetikkmuséet** Ⓒ (Canning Museum; open all year; entrance fee). In the big open room with its curing ovens, the guides explain the life of the men and women who worked long hours in the intricate process of threading the sardines on to long rods, smoking, then packing them, almost all of it being done by hand.

Artefacts from Stavanger's old canning industry are kept in the Hermetikkmuseet (Canning Museum).

BELOW: Gamle (Old) Stavanger is still a living community.

On the waterfront at night.

Even nearer the harbour and the centre of the town is the **Sjøfartsmuséum** (Maritime Museum; open all year; entrance fee) in one of the old mercantile houses on Nedre Strandgate, with its warehouses towards the sea. It traces the history of Stavanger's maritime links over the past 150 years. Today, large windows have replaced the warehouse doors and you turn your head from the history behind you to the modern town outside.

On the Nedre Strandgate side, away from the harbour, is the general store, full of the provisions and supplies that it would have held before World War II. On the upstairs floor, where the owner lived "over the shop", is an office just as it might have been when a young crewman called in during the 1930s in search of a berth, or the skipper came to pay his respects. The owner's flat shows the comfortable life of a shipowner in the late 19th century, with much of its furniture and ornaments in a style that has returned to popularity today.

On the other side of the harbour facing the Maritime Museum is the site of the original Viking settlement. At its highest point is the **Valbergtårnet** (Tower; open all year, closed Sun; entrance fee). Built in the 9th century as a fire lookout, it is the best point from which to get a view over the whole city, old and new.

BELOW LEFT: old wooden houses.
BELOW RIGHT: Stavanger Domkirke, the only remaining building from the city's medieval past.

Centre of worship

The heart of modern Stavanger is the area around **Breiavatnet**, the small lake in the middle of the city, near the oldest and biggest building, the beautiful 12th-century **Domkirken** (open all year, closed Sat; free). Built in the Anglo-Norman style, it can claim with justification to be among the best-preserved medieval cathedrals in Europe. Alongside is the **Cathedral School** built in 1758 on the 12th-century foundations of the Bishop's Residence.

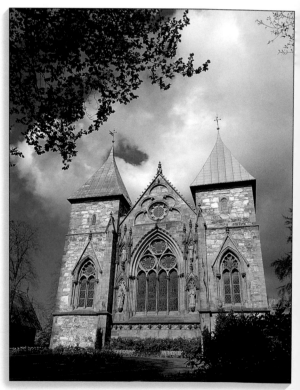

Map on page 226

Inside, this stone cathedral has a feeling of austere strength in the massive pillars which contrast with the elegant arches of the chancel and a remarkable tapestry (made by Frida Hansen in 1927) in the vestibule. Both chancel and vestibule were rebuilt after 1272 in a style similar to the Scottish Gothic of the times, a reminder of Stavanger's international connection even in those early days. One of the finest pieces in the cathedral is Andrew Smith's ornate 16th-century pulpit.

Even earlier is the Iron Age farm at **Ullandhaug** (open daily; entrance fee), about 2 km (1 mile) or so to the southwest of the centre. Here archaeologists unearthed and then reconstructed part of the farm to show three houses, parts of a cattle track and the original encircling stone wall from AD 350 and 550. This was a golden age in Norway, and the city's **Arkeologisk Museum** (Archaeological Museum; closed Mon, entrance fee; tel: 51 84 60 00) is gradually furnishing the houses to show how people lived then.

From Ullandhaug, it is well worth visiting the nearby **Botanisk Hage** (Botanical Garden; open daily; entrance fee) which has a herb and perennial garden with more than 1,500 species from all over the world. Rogaland is rich in birds and fauna from coast to mountains and the **Stavanger museum** (open daily; entrance fee) has an excellent exhibition, not only of Rogaland wildlife but also displays of cultural history and the history of fishing, which covers the industry and its creatures, including whales and seals.

Water buses

The inhabitants of the city jump on to a boat as unconcernedly as most of us jump on a bus. There are tours to the islands and fjords and fast ferries northwards as far as Bergen, where business travellers sit in their city garb alongside holidaymakers' picnic boxes and fishing gear. Color Line operate a passenger ferry service between Newcastle (England), Stavanger and Bergen, and Sola International Airport has flight connections to several European capitals as well as a busy domestic service. If you a travelling via the airport, you may care to drop in at the **Aviation Museum** (open May–Nov; entrance fee).

Within the city itself almost everywhere is within easy walking distance, and there are good walking tours of Stavanger organised from near the harbour.

Outdoor activities

The city is right on the doorstep of the Jærstendene Landskapsvernområdet (Protected Landscape Area), which stretches 70 km (43 miles) down the southern coast and its offshore islands, with nature reserves and wonderful silver beaches, ideal for swimming and picnicking. Sport at any time of the year is good: swimming, sub-aqua diving, sailing, wind-surfing and fishing, but there is also an active hiking club plus tennis and horse riding in Jærstendene.

In winter you can have the best of both worlds. Thanks to the Gulf Stream, Stavanger remains mild and the fields around the city are rarely covered by snow, yet it is not much more than an hour from good ski slopes. ❑

BELOW: much of Norway's food is grown in the area south of Stavanger.

HORDALAND

An inspiration to generations of Norwegian artists, the mighty Hardangerfjorden lies at the heart of this region, which mixes wild coasts with sheltered islands, spring blossoms with dark fjord waters

Nobody knows how many hundreds of islands lie off the coast of Hordaland. Deserted skerries, green islets, prosperous small harbours and busy communities, stretch out along the coast like a knotted skein, from the southern island of Bømlo to the beautiful small island of Fedje not far from the mouth of Sognefjorden.

Many of the inner islands around the fjord capital, Bergen, are linked by bridges and causeways in a pattern of islands and sea that seems all of a piece with the many branched fjords, including the famous Hardangerfjorden. Inland, the further east the higher the ground becomes until it reaches Hardangervidda, the great mountain plateau which stands 1,300 metres (4,500 ft) above sea level.

The beginning of Christianity

The southwest district of **Sunnhordland** has islands, skerries, sounds and straits, good harbours and sheltered bays. Though the North Sea is its neighbour, the climate is surprisingly mild. The main islands are **Bømlo**, **Stord** and **Tysnesøy**, and even so close to the sea they have a variety of scenery. An upland ridge on Stord reaches nearly 750 metres (2,500 ft) and the view stretches east to Hardangerfjorden and the white sheet of the Folgefonn Glacier, and south towards Haugesund. Everywhere are sails of all colours, the white wake of an express boat from Stavanger to Bergen and the smaller trails of pleasure craft.

Stord also makes a good paddling-off point for sea canoeing, either from island to island, or into the mouth of the Hardanger. It is an "oil island" too, where the gigantic outlines of oil platforms take shape, some rising nearly 380 metres (1,250 ft) out of the water.

The sagas tell that in 1024 St Olav first introduced Christianity to Norway in these islands. Today, an annual outdoor performance (late May or early Jun, tel: 55 32 14 80) of the historical play *Mostraspelet*, held at **Mosterhamn** ❶ on Bømlo dramatises this ancient saga. Nearby is a stone cross erected in 1924 on the 900th anniversary of the arrival of Christianity, and Mosterhamn has the **oldest stone church** in Norway (open all year; entrance fee) built around 995–1100. The church bells bear images of St Olaf.

Gateway to Hardangerfjorden

The mouth of the Hardanger fjord is as beautiful as anywhere in the fjord itself, but the irony is that Sunnhordaland as a whole tends to be overshadowed by the fame and drama of Hardangerfjorden. Too many visitors travel through quickly on their way to other places. The discriminating know it deserves a longer look. **Leirvik** on Stord is a good starting point with short ferry connections to most of the surround-

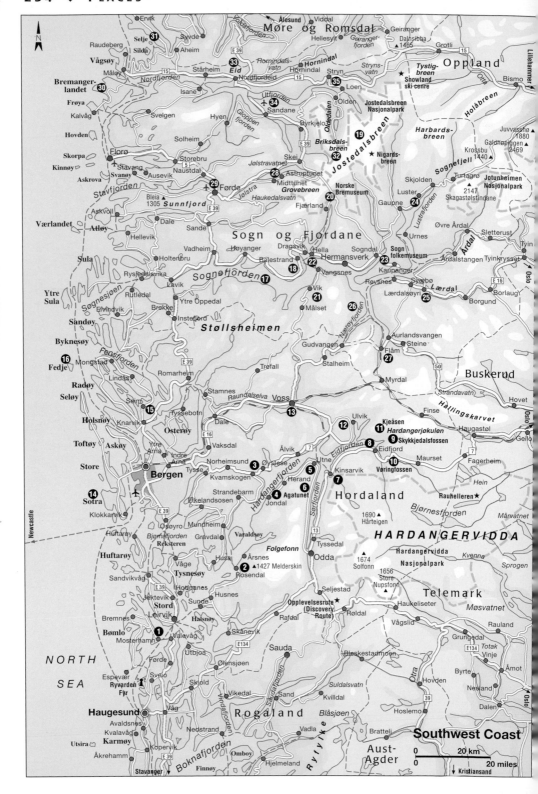

ing islands and to the mainland. It is also the location of the **Sunnhordland Folkemuseum** (open all year; entrance fee) which was established in 1913 as the local history museum. To the south, the ferry to **Valevåg** puts you on the right track for **Ryvarden Fyr** (Lighthouse; open Apr–Dec; free) at the mouth of Bømlafjorden, the home of the innovative composer Fartein Valen (1887–1952). There is also a museum, art gallery and café at nearby Møstrevåg.

To the east, a ferry to Sunde on the mainland brings you to where the cold waters of Hardangerfjorden begin to seep into the warmer tides from the west and the lovely 17th-century **Baroniet Rosendal** (Rosendal Barony; open May-Sept; entrance fee), in **Rosendal ❷** the only one of its kind in Norway, which largely lost its aristocracy with the departure of the Danes. The manor house was built in 1665 by Ludvig Rosenkrantz. He is buried in the nearby medieval Kvinnherad Kirke (Church), snuggled into the shelter of a rock face and once owned by the Barony. The Barony today has a peaceful park and a large carefully tended rose garden and is held in trust by Oslo University. Throughout the summer there are lunch time concerts, and the **Rosendal Music Festival** during May and June.

Map on page 234

A national inspiration

Hardangerfjorden is part of the Norwegian legend, the fjord that gave its name to Norway's national musical instrument, the eight-stringed Hardanger fiddle, and provided inspiration for the composer Edvard Grieg (1843–1907), the musician Ole Bull (1810–80) and, indirectly, for the 19th-century nationalist movement that eventually led to Norway's independence. Among these mountains and fjords, Grieg and Bull travelled on foot and horse, learning old melodies and dipping into centuries-old cultural traditions and customs.

Tourism came to the Hardanger district as long ago as the 1830s when the poet Henrik Wergeland (1808–45) wrote about "wonderful Hardanger", and foreign as well as Norwegian artists, scientists, and other travellers began to arrive; first in a trickle, then in a flood when, 30 years later, the steamers began to run regularly from Bergen or Stavanger.

Like the visitors of today, they came to Hardanger for its waterfalls, for the secret beauty of smaller fjords that lead almost to the massif of Hardangervidda, and for glaciers and mountains that rarely lose their snow-caps, contrasted with orchards lining the fjordside. Nearly half a million fruit trees grow here, turning the fjord pink and white in spring as the blossom reflects in the deep, still water. At blossom time the waterfalls are in full spate, shooting over the sides of the mountains, and the Hardanger has two of Norway's highest and best known: Skykkjedalsfossen, which falls 300 metres (1,000 ft), and Vøringfossen, lower but famous for its beauty.

Crossing to the north side, Road 49 runs along the sunny side of Hardangerfjorden towards the fjord villages of **Norheimsund** and **Øystese ❸**. Alternatively, they can be reached through day or longer excursions from Bergen either by boat or road (E16 and then Road 11). Both of these villages offer excellent trips for exploring the fjords by car and ferry, and marked paths here and at **Kvamskogen** further inland make

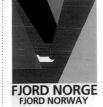

FJORD NORGE
FJORD NORWAY

Hordaland is at the heart of Norway's fjord country.

BELOW: the beautiful Vøringfossen (waterfall) lies at the end of Eidfjord.

for safe walking. But take time out to visit the **Ingebrigt Vik Museum** (open Jun–Aug; entrance fee) at Øystese, one of Norway's most distinctive museums containing virtually all the works by the sculptor of that name.

Not to be passed by is the **Hardanger Fartøyvernseter** (Hardanger Ship Conservation Centre; open all year; free) at Norheimsund where conservationists are patiently restoring the wooden craft that made Norwegian boat-building famous. They range from small rowing boats to the Centre's most prestigious restoration, the S/Y *Mathilde*, a 22-metre (73-ft) Hardanger yacht launched in 1884. This superb yacht has regained her former splendour under the guidance of Kristian Djupevåg (who also restored Roald Amundsen's yacht, *Gjøa*) and it has the world's largest authentic yacht rigging. The *Mathilde* sleeps 25 passengers in bunk benches or hammocks and is available for cruises and day excursions, when she can take 50 people to sail fjord and sea as they might have in days past.

Jondal ❹, on the other side of the fjord, is the entrance to the Folgefonn glacier, and the **Folgefonn Summer Ski-centre**. The safe but exciting road to the new ski centre is clear from June to September. With snow all year round, there are three mobile ski lifts, alpine and cross-country skiing tracks (you can hire all the necessary equipment), a cafeteria and guided walks on the glacier.

Jondal itself has a country museum, in the old **Lensmannshuset** (Sheriff's House; May–Sept; entrance fee), and Hardanger Cathedral (the largest church in the Hardanger region). Not far away at **Herand** you will find Bronze Age rock carvings and, at Herandsholmen, Hardanger's first guesthouse which opened in 1754. By now, into the inner fjords, the road suddenly turns sharply southeast along the short straight sides of Utnefjord to Utne village, part of Ullensvang kommune, which also includes both sides of Sørfjorden.

Edvard Grieg used to visit a small hytte poised on the edge of Hardangerfjorden near to the village of Ullensvang where, with piano and writing desk at hand, he would compose surrounded by the beauty of the Norwegian fjords.

BELOW: the old fjord village of Utne.

Five generations

When the fjords were West Norway's main "roads", **Utne** ❺ was an important junction between east and west and had the first post and telegraph offices in Hardanger, in 1836 and 1876 respectively.

Two establishments in Utne which sum up Hardanger life over the past centuries are the **Hardanger Folkemuseum** (open daily; entrance fee), and the **Utne Hotel** (tel: 53 66 69 83), founded in 1722, the oldest hotel in Norway still in operation. Since 1787, five generations of the same family have owned the hotel and it first became famous internationally during the time of Torbjørg Utne (1812–1903), known with affection as Mor (Mother) Utne. Her picture hangs on the sitting-room wall. The family is represented today by her great granddaughter, Hildegun Aga Blokhus. It has always been a favourite spot for artists who have donated many paintings and the hotel also holds exhibitions of national costumes and characteristic embroidery.

Since it opened in 1911, the Hardanger Folkemuseum has collected old houses and farm buildings for its outdoor museum, formed into a "cluster farm" as it would have been before the Norwegian agricultural reforms in the middle of the 19th century. Along the shore are old boathouses and a merchant's shop, which was in use in Utne not all that long ago, and an orchard preserves many old varieties of fruit which have now disappeared from other parts of the Hardangerfjord. Inside, the museum has a modern exhibition, other rooms showing old crafts and folk art, and the famous Hardanger fiddle, and changing exhibitions on special fjord themes.

Past Utne, the fjordside road turns due south into the **Sørfjorden**. Once you are used to the narrow road and would like to enjoy the magnificent view, you

Map on page 234

BELOW: traditional wedding at Voss led by a fiddler and toastmaster.

A traditional "children's wedding" at Voss.

should stop at **Agatunet** ❻ (open May–Aug; entrance fee), the farm of a 13th-century local sheriff. From the Middle Ages to the recent past, Agatunet grew into a nine-family village with a cluster of some 30 buildings. Today, the families no longer live there but the buildings are preserved by law.

On the eastern side of Sørfjord, a short ferry ride away, is the area's main amusement park, Ferieparken at **Kinsarvik** ❼. A favourite with children, it has a water chute, trampoline, a miniature zoo, a boating lake, and lends out surf boards, water mopeds and water skis. Kinsarvik was also part of the main eastwest route and its market place attracted merchants from both sides of Hardangervidda to exchange bog iron and furs for sea salt. The **old stone church** is said to have been built by Scottish builders around 1200, and has a 17th-century pulpit painted by Peter Reimers. Until Utne Kirke (Church) was consecrated in 1896, Kinsarvik had for centuries drawn its congregation from all around the fjords, and many worshippers arrived in church boats.

Falls, farm and forest

Heading northeast from Kinsarvik on the E13 and then Road 7 you will find one of the area's most beautiful stretches of water, **Eidfjorden** ❽. It cuts far into the dramatic landscape which includes the **Hardangerjøkulen** and below it **Skykkjedalsfossen** ❾, Norway's highest waterfall, and **Vøringfossen** ❿, which falls 150 metres (490 ft) down into the wilds of Måbødalen. There is a path at the top overlooking the fall which is not for vertigo sufferers. Alternatively, you can walk down to view this great outpouring from below, and fitness fanatics might welcome the challenge of the age-old packhorse track up Måbøfjell, with 1,500 steps and 125 bends. From June to August look out for signs to the **Måbødalen Kulturlandskapsmuseum** (Cultural Landscape Museum; open Jun–Aug; guided tours available) which provides a network of trails all signposted and with information boards explaining the various points of interest. The public barbecue areas make fabulous picnic stops.

BELOW: snowman outside Vangskyrkja (Voss Church).

Above tiny Simadalsfjord is **Kjeåsen** ⓫, a mountain farm which claims to be the world's most isolated settlement. It lies like an eagle's nest 620 metres (2,000 ft) on near vertical rock above the distant waters of the fjord. Those feeling strong and brave can tackle the old path to the top and marvel that this was how the villagers struggled up with their every need. For frailer spirits it is possible to reach Kjeåsen by car through a magnificent new tunnel. Inside the mountain is the **Sima Kraftverket** (Hydro-Electric Power Station; open Jun–Aug; entrance fee) which arranges guided tours three times a day.

Crossing Eidfjorden at Brimnes you enter a farming and forestry district. Instead of taking the E13, take a right turn onto Road 572 which will bring you to **Ulvik** ⓬. Artists and other visitors have been coming here for longer than almost any other place in Hardanger and the village has permanent exhibitions by artists such as Tit Mohr (born 1917) and Sigurd Undeland (1903–1983). No one should miss the fine examples of **rose painting** in Ulvik's 19th-century church, painted in 1923 by Lars Osa (1860–1958).

Hang-gliding to skiing

Continuing on in a loop back to the E13 you come to **Voss** ⑬, which lies next to a lake, **Vangsvatnet**, in the middle of rich farmland. The Voss kommune (district) makes full use of its surroundings to attract visitors. In summer they come for touring, fjord excursions, mountain walking, parachuting, hang-gliding and paragliding from **Hangurfjell**, and fishing and watersports on Vangsvatnet. In winter, everything changes and Voss becomes one of the best centres for alpine and for cross-country skiing of the more energetic touring variety.

Voss is also a good place for mountain touring and sport fishing in the 500-or-so lakes and innumerable mountain rivers and streams, with the Vosso river famous for the size of its salmon. Even in summer the high mountains call for boots or very strong shoes and plenty of extra clothes – temperatures drop quickly; this applies in all upland areas.

The top station of the **cable car** up Hangurfjell gives one of the best prospects of Voss in its bowl-shaped valley. As the ground drops away below, the two gondolas, "Dinglo" and "Danglo", take only four minutes or so to lift you 610 metres (2,000 ft). On a sunny day, a coffee on the platform outside the cafeteria is magnificent, with the occasional excitement of a paraglider soaring into the sun and over Vagnsvatnet, spread out below.

At the beginning of World War II, Voss was badly damaged by German bombing and not much remains of the old town centre except the **Vangskyrkja** (church; open every day, Jun–Aug) which dates back to 1277. The inside is certainly worth seeing with a colourfully painted ceiling liberally adorned with flying angels. Outside, a great stone cross stands in a field south of the church which, according to tradition, was raised two centuries before the church was

Map on page 234

Apart from its artistic associations, the village of Ulvik has the unlikely privilege of being where the first potatoes were grown in Norway, back in 1765.

BELOW: moonrise over the island of Fedje.

built by the proselytising King Olav Haraldson. The church walls are 2 metres (7 ft) thick and the wooden octagonal steeple is unique in Norway.

Below Hangurfjell, about half an hour's walk above the town, is **Voss Folkemuseum** (open all year, varying times; entrance fee; tel: 55 51 00 51), a collection of 16 old wooden buildings standing in traditional form around a central courtyard. The houses date from 1600 to 1870 and contain implements and furniture in use until 1927, incredible though it may seem. Yet somehow, despite the heavy farm work and meagre evening light, farm people like these managed to produce some beautiful embroidery, wood and other craft work. One of the most delightful is a traditional wood carving of a Voss bridal party riding to church, with the bride's horse led firmly by her father as though he feared she might gallop away. The carving is by a local sculptor, and is based on a bronze relief in the little park below Voss station in which the main figure, the bridal fiddler, is the legendary Ola Mosafinn who died in 1912.

Artistic tradition

Voss has long been a centre for artists and musicians, and their monuments are scattered around. The 1957 Sivle monument marks the centenary of the birth of the author and poet Per Sivle (1857–1904), who grew up on the mountain farm of Sivle, in the great Stalheim Skleive (Gorge); the monument behind Voss church commemorates three Bergslien artist brothers, Brynjulf, Nils and Knut; near Voss Fine Arts Society is a memorial to actor Lars Tvinde born and bred on the farm of Tvinde, which lies below the Tvindefossen (a waterfall to the north of Voss) and on the same road the 1958 Sjur Helgeland memorial commemorates another local fiddler and composer.

BELOW: midday snack at the Hangur ski centre.

This artistic tradition continues and Voss is one of the best places to hear the Hardanger fiddle and see the old dances performed in beautiful costumes. On the main street is a shop where you can see, or even buy, the ornate silver belts and jewellery that go with the traditional Norwegian costume.

Around Bergen and north

From Voss the E16 is the quickest way to Bergen. Back in the city, Bergen's islands are linked so closely together that sometimes it is hard to realise that you have crossed water, but islands such as **Askøy** and **Osterøy** to the north of Bergen have their own character, and the area round the **Bjørnafjorden** (the Bear fjord) to the south is particularly mild and green, and full of boats of all sorts.

After an hour's drive to the long narrow island of **Sotra ⑭** which shelters the city from the North Sea, there is no doubt that this is a different world. Sotra is a good base for sea canoeing in and out of its small offshore islands and rocks and, in good weather, as far as the open sea to combine canoeing with ocean fishing. In any case, shelter is never far away.

North of Bergen is a second island district, **Nordhordland**, that stretches as far north as Sognefjordenen and includes the islands of Holsnøy, Radøy and Sandøy. At weekends, it is a favourite area for Bergensere who go sailing, swimming and fishing.

Although this region depended on ferries for a long time, today taking the car is no problem: most of its fjords and sounds can be crossed via modern suspension and pontoon bridges.

In Nordhordland the sea can be at its wildest, smashing against the western coast, yet the area has been inhabited for some 8,000 years. Håkon den Gode (the Good) is buried at **Seim** ⓯, near Knarvik (around half an hour from Bergen by express boat). Another rare reminder of the Vikings is a beech wood, also at Seim, 1,000 years old and the northernmost beech wood in Europe.

Today, fish farming is important to Nordhordland, which exports vast quantities of salmon and trout all round the world, and the fish farmers are now attempting to rear cod, halibut and other species. Some fish farms are open to the public. There is good sea fishing for cod and coalfish, and special rosy coloured trout inhabit many of the lakes. Diving and sub-aqua fishing, as well as treasure-hunting, are easy in these transparent waters. Oil is a modern, though not conflicting industry in this widespread area with the night gleam of the light from Mongstad one of the few reminders of this large refinery.

Dangerous waters

Most remote of all, and a target for both sailing picnics and holidays, is the island of **Fedje** ⓰, an important navigation point for many centuries with two 19th-century lighthouses still in use today. In these ever-changing waters, Norwegian sea laws insist that all ships must carry a Norwegian pilot, and all tankers destined for Mongstad refinery are navigated from here through the unreliable waters. Stay overnight on Fedje in one of the guesthouses in Kræmmerholmen or in the Pensjonat there and sample the idyllic bird and flower habitat.   ❑

Map on page 234

BELOW: the Stalheim Skleive (Gorge) was the scene of fierce fighting during World War II.

NORWAY IN A NUTSHELL

If you have only a day to spare in this region, this tour which, but for the lack of an island or two, might well be called "Hordaland in a Nutshell", covers many of the sights. Organised by Norwegian State Railways, it runs from June until mid-September and combines bus, ferry and train. Starting from outside Voss station, the first stop is at the Stalheim Hotel. The hotel parapet looks down over the great depths of the Stalheim Skleive (Gorge), scene of fierce fighting in World War II. A hairpin descent leads to the fjord and Gudvangen below.

The next leg is by ferry, which travels through Norway's narrowest fjord, Nærøyfjorden, where the rocky sides of the fjord are twice as high as the water is wide, before turning right and heading to the end of Aurlandsfjorden and the pretty village of Flåm.

After a break for lunch, it is then time for one of the steepest train journeys in the world, the 40-minute panoramic trip up 850 metres (2,800 ft) of mountain gorge to Myrdal at the top, stopping – thanks to one of the five separate sets of brakes – on the way to photograph the torrent of Kjosfossenen and to pick up passengers and rucksacks at one or two of the tiny stations. From the mainline station at Myrdal it is back to Voss.

BIO-DIVERSITY AND SUSTAINABILITY

About 20,000 years ago Norway was covered in ice and barren tundra. But, as the climate changed and ice melted, flora and fauna began to thrive

The first species to arrive in Norway, following the melting of the glaciers, were the Arctic animals such as reindeer, fox, wolf and wolverine. Trees came later, accompanied by a rich flora and fauna including bears, lynx, elk, marten, hare, beaver and otter, and small rodents including the lemming. The forests were filled with grouse, owls and woodpeckers. The lakes provided a habitat for geese, grebes, ducks and cranes; shadowed closely by birds of prey. The coastline teemed with kittiwakes, guillemots, auks, puffins, cormorants and gulls. The coastal waters were awash with arctic fish such as cod, haddock and halibut, and the rivers offered spawning ground for salmon, trout and char. Perch, powan, pike and grayling joined the eco-system via the freshwater Baltic. Mankind entered the scene about 10,000 BC, with a strong hunting instinct. Whales, seals, lynx, bear and wolf almost became extinct, replaced by sheep and about 200,000 domesticated reindeer.

FROM PREDATOR TO PROTECTOR

Today large areas of Norway have been designated as national parks to protect special habitats and support bio-diversity. Hunting is strictly controlled: wolves are regularly sighted in East Norway and the last of Europe's wild reindeer, about 15,000 in total, are now found on the Hardangervidda. Norway promotes sustainable management of ocean resources and has resumed commercial whaling based on studied whale counts. The elk, on the other hand, has benefited from commercial deforestation and numbers have grown.

∇ **WATER BIRDS**
The clownish-looking puffin (*Fratercula arctica*), with its parrot-like bill, is an expert diver and adroit fisherman.

∇ **WORKING MAMMALS**
Reindeer often serve as a substitute to cattle or horses and are used to draw sledges and logs. They thrive on lichen moss.

▷ **WILD CATS**
The Eurasian, or Northern lynx (*Felis lynx*), is an agile climber and often hides in trees ready to pounce on small animals and birds. Lynx are also highly valued for their fur.

◁ **BEAR NECESSITIES**
Brown bears (*Ursus arctos*) are now restricted to the Nordland region. A protected species, many bears are electronically tagged.

△ **LORD OF THE FOREST**
The European elk (*Alces alces*) may stand up to 2.4 m (8 ft) high. The males' flattened, broad antlers are shed each year after the mating season.

COMMERCIAL WHALING

Norway was once a great whaling nation: northern towns grew up around the prosperous whale oil industry. With the advent of electric lighting, the whaling industry declined but, by then, the global whale population had been decimated, leading to international legislation.

However, Norway continues to hunt in order to maintain its coastal communities. It argues that minke whale stocks can support sustainable harvesting and annually sets itself a modest quota (671 animals in 1998). The hunt is held in summer when fishing activities are low and much effort goes into teaching and pursuing correct hunting methods.

◁ **GREAT WHALES**
Although Norway is one of the few countries to pursue commercial whaling, sightings are now rare. Minke and beluga whales are more common in Spitsbergen.

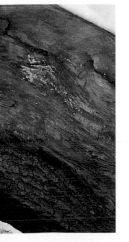

△ **ARCTIC KING**
The polar bear (*Ursus maritimus*) is Europe's largest predator and chooses his habitat where there is an abundance of seals.

▷ **MOUNTAIN GIANT**
The musk ox (*Ovibos moschatus*), once close to extinction, is found in Arctic regions and feeds on grass, moss and sedge.

BERGEN

With its relaxed atmosphere, stunning setting and vibrant cultural life, the city is an appealing mix of the cosmopolitan and the outdoor, with easy access to the western fjords

Map on page 248

There's always a sense of symmetry and order about a city built on hills. If it also stands on a peninsula and has a harbour at its heart, it is bound to be beautiful. Bergen, the capital of West Norway, has all these things. Built on seven hills, the city grew outwards from the coast and harbour in the quaintly named Puddefjorden and spread across the steep slopes and over the bridges that link islands and headlands.

The best place to get a feel of this natural shape is to take the funicular, **Fløybanen** Ⓐ (every half hour, 7.30–midnight, May–Aug, until 11pm Sept–Apr; fee), that climbs more than 300 metres (1,000 ft) in just eight minutes from the centre to **Fløyen**, high above Bergen. On the downward journey, you seem to be tipping headfirst into the city.

At the top is the lovely old-fashioned building that houses Fløyen Restaurant, built in 1925, and the start of eight marked walking routes, the longest no more than around 4 km (2½ miles), though this does not mean they do not contain steep hills through woods and open moor.

A leisurely coffee or lunch on the verandah of the restaurant gives a chance also to drink in the superb view over hundreds of islands, many with the small *hytter* (wooden cabins) and a couple of boats tied up to a landing stage that sums up a Norwegian's ideal summer. All around are mountains and hills that cradle the city – Fløifjellet, Damsgårdfjellet, Løvstakken, Sandviksfjellet, Rundemånnen, Blåmannen, and the highest of them all, **Ulriken** at around 600 metres (2,000 ft) reached by a cable car (open May–Sept, some weekends off-season depending on the weather; fee). The Ulriken mountain café is open when the cable car is running and offers evening concerts during the summer. There is a bus connection from Torget, the site of the famous Bergen fish market.

A long tradition of international trade has made this city the most outgoing in Norway and given the Bergensere a jauntiness in their walk that hints at generations of sailors, quick wits, worldliness and a sense of their own worth. Bergensere are certain they are the best, secure in the knowledge that, although Oslo may now be the capital, it is historically a mere toddler compared with Bergen.

Olav Kyrre's city

King Olav Kyrre is credited with founding Bergen in 1070 at Torget. But it would be naive to believe that, long before, the perfect natural harbour and sheltered fjords were not a home for people who depended on the sea. During the 13th century, Bergen became the first capital of a united Norway, and a great ecclesiastical centre, with a cathedral, 20 churches and

PRECEDING PAGES: Bergen harbour. **LEFT:** "Jacob", the street sign for Jacobsgården. **BELOW:** Fløibanen on its way to the top of Fløien, one of Bergen's seven hills.

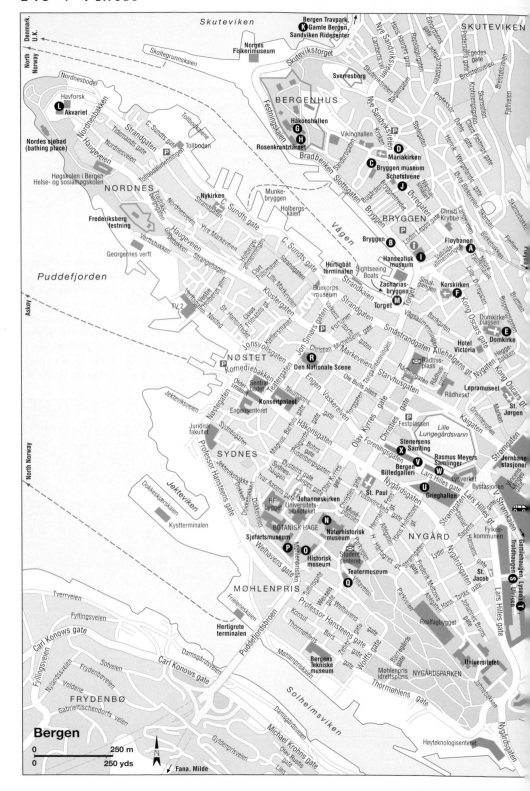

chapels, five monasteries and two hospitals for the poor. Bergen lost its capital status to Oslo during the Middle Ages, but still dwarfed the new capital. In medieval times, it was the biggest city in the Nordic countries and, until 1830, the largest in Norway. Today, with a population exceeding 200,000, it is roughly half the size of Oslo.

Map on page 248

Much of this early size and success came when Bergen was chosen as the hub of the medieval German Hanseatic League in the north. Their trading base on the north side of **Vågen** became the power house of all trade on the northwest Norwegian coast. But the Hansa began to grow too powerful all over Scandinavia and, at last, Norway broke the tie that kept the west in thraldom.

As in all wooden cities, fire has swept through Bergen on many occasions, often devastating it. The result is that the oldest surviving buildings are noticeably built of stone, and the present streets, following the last fire in 1916 when a gale fanned the flames to an inferno, are wide and designed as fire breaks.

During World War II, Bergen was a centre of the resistance movement and many young people from the town took the perilous route out through the islands to Scotland. There they trained for resistance work and then smuggled themselves back to West Norway to become members of sabotage groups. The actions of the movement are commemorated by the **Theta Museum** in Bryggen (open May–Sept; entrance fee).

Bergen city logo.

Yet the major disaster of this unhappy period came not directly from war but through accident caused by war. In 1944 a Dutch ammunition ship in the harbour blew up, damaging many of the oldest buildings on the northern promontory, including Håkonshallen and Rosenkrantztårnet. Anti-German feelings ran high at that time, and well into the 1980s the usually talkative Bergensere would be extremely reserved towards German visitors. The famous **Tyskebryggen** (quay named after Hansa merchants) has been tactfully renamed **Bryggen ❸**.

BELOW: trolls guard the entrance to a souvenir shop.

Starting with the past

The earliest archaeological remains are in **Bryggen Museum ❸** (open all year; entrance fee), past the Hansa houses on the north side of the harbour. It is also the Erling Dekker Næss Institute for Medieval Archaeology and contains the medieval remains uncovered between 1955 and 1972. There are also many artefacts and re-creations of medieval rooms. Together it gives a picture of the time when Bergen was a small fishing and sailing community that clung to the shallow slopes above the shore.

Nearby is the oldest building still in use, **Mariakirken ❹** (St Mary's Church; open all year, closed Sat, reduced opening off-season; entrance fee during the summer) built in the early years of the 12th century and justly proud of its rich Baroque pulpit. The only other medieval churches to survive periodic fires are the present **Domkirke ❺** (Cathedral; open all year; free), once dedicated to St Olaf's but now a blend of many different periods, and **Korskirken ❻** (Holy Cross; open all year; free), most of it now in the Renaissance style of the 17th century. The latter two are relatively close to the harbour and all three merit a visit.

National Day celebrations in Bergen.

Holmen was the site of **Bergenhus**, the old timber-built royal palace used when Bergen first became a capital. At a time of much building in the 13th century, it was converted to a fortified stronghold of stone, and the restored remains are close to where the original cathedral and bishop's residence stood. There are two particularly notable buildings: **Håkonshallen** Ⓖ (open all year, closed during Bergen International Festival; entrance fee), built by King Håkon Håkonsson between 1247 and 1261, which was used for the wedding of King Magnus Lagabøte (the Lawmaker), who was Håkon's son and co-ruler; and **Rosenkrantztårnet** Ⓗ (open all year; entrance fee) which was the work of a Danish governor of Bergenhus, Erik Rosenkrantz, who grafted it on to Håkon's original "Keep of the Sea".

Håkonshallen is the largest secular medieval building still standing in Norway. When both it and Rosenkrantztårnet were badly damaged in the 1944 explosion, Norwegian historians took the opportunity to reconstruct them as closely to the originals as possible. Today, Håkonshallen makes a magnificent concert hall, with gallery and café on the floor below, so that you can still see the massive pillars that support the Great Hall. Rosenkrantztårnet is now a museum, with both permanent and special exhibitions. In both buildings, the remnants of different periods make it possible to trace something of the history in stone.

The power of the Hansa

BELOW: Bergen's sheltered harbour.

Guides from Bryggens Museum also conduct tours through the row of **Hansa houses** that line Bryggen. These Hansa homes and warehouses were all built after the great fire of 1702, which destroyed many buildings, and are on the UNESCO World Heritage list. One key to understanding the Hansa way of life is

a visit to the **Hanseatisk Museum ①** (open all year, reduced opening off-season; entrance fee), furnished in the style of the time when the merchant had his accounting room within the main office on the first floor. This small room enabled him to keep an eye on the liquor room next door. The adjoining room, decorated with a Royal Cod, distinguished by a bump on its head and said to bring luck, served as dining and sitting room for merchants and apprentices. On the floor above are the apprentices' tiny box beds, one above the other. Although apprentices were merchants' sons, sent to learn their business with a colleague, they were locked into their tiny "prisons" each night.

As a fire precaution – all too often in vain – no heating was allowed in these Hansa houses and the Germans must have suffered torments of cold in the biting damp of a Bergen winter. No wonder that **Schøtstuene ②** (open all year, Sun only Oct–Apr; entrance fee), the assembly rooms nearby, were so popular during winter when trade was slack and few ships in the harbour. The long central table held both beer jugs and the Bible, exemplifying the two religions of the Hansa. In a drawer was the cane used to discipline the apprentices who had their schooling there. On one wall, written in German, are the "rules of the club".

At Elsesro, further out along the coast road, past Bergenshus and the North Sea quay, is **Gamle Bergen ③** (Old Bergen; open all year, guided tours only; entrance fee), the obligatory open-air museum beloved of Scandinavia. Here there is a collection of 40 wooden buildings from the 18th and 19th centuries, the interiors decorated to show different styles. Along the cobbled streets, guides in traditional red calf-length costumes and black shawls lead tours which range from the French Empire splendour of the official's drawing room to the tiny house where the seamstress plied her diligent needle in the 1860s.

Map on page 248

Historic wooden sign in Gamle (Old) Bergen.

BELOW:
Torget, the city's famous fish market.

KS OG ØRRET

LMON AND TROUT

LACHS UND FRISHE FOR

Nearby is the popular **Sandvik Sjøbad** (bathing area; free) which looks out over Byfjorden to the city. Back along Vågen, a short ferry trip from below Rosenkrantztårnet to the Nordnes peninsula gives a good opportunity to view the beautiful lines of the sailing ship *Lehmkuhl*, which trains youngsters in sailing techniques and gleams with polished brass. A short walk towards Nordnes point reveals another castle, **Fredriksborg**, and further on is **Nordnes sjøbad** (free) which includes a heated outdoor pool. Here, you are also within easy reach of the **Bergen Akvariet ⓛ** (Aquarium; open all year; entrance fee), which gives the feeling of having dipped below the surface of the sea.

Morning must

Early each weekday morning, **Torget ⓜ** is the site of Bergen's fish, fruit and flower market. Middle-aged women, elegant even at this time of the day, engage the fishermen in serious conversation about the day's catch, watched by an interested circle, and the stalls sell *gravlaks* (cured salmon) and other delights to take home. This busy scene is the heart of Bergen, where there is always something going on and where people linger to watch the transactions or peer into the boats tied up at the quay after a night's fishing.

Not far away from the fish market is another square where people like to linger, **Torgalmenningen**, with many of the best shops in the city. The square also holds the **Sailors' Monument**. Carved figures march round the base of this memorial dedicated to all Norwegian sailors who lost their lives at sea.

Alternatively, just up the hill from the fish market in another old section of the city is the **Gamle Rådhuset** (Old Town Hall). Originally built as a private house in 1558, it was presented to the town in 1562 and served the city for several centuries until, in 1974, the city administration moved to an inelegant high-rise modern block not far away. Another attractive old building in the area is the **Hotel Victoria**.

Museum cluster

Bergen is a good walking city and, if you fix your eye on the tall steeple of **Johanneskirken** (St John's Church; open all year, varying times; free), a two-minute walk up Vest Torggate from Torgalmenningen takes you to the top of **Sydneshaugen**, near the university area and a clutch of museums: the **Naturhistorisk Museum ⓝ** (Natural History) standing in the fine **Botanisk Hage** (Botanic Garden), the **Historisk Museum ⓞ** (Cultural History), and the **Sjøfartsmuseum ⓟ** (Maritime) which traces the history of this seafaring area from the Old Norse period to the present day (all three museums open all year, closed Mon; entrance fee).

Not far from these, near the Student Centre, is Bergen **Teatermuseum ⓠ** (open all year; entrance fee). This is right in the centre of the university area which consists of beautiful merchants' villas from the turn of the century. The old building on the hill which housed the museum is now also part of the university. Here the famous Arctic explorer Fridtjof Nansen spent his early career, and it was also a base for the father of weather forecasting, Vilhelm Bjerknes.

BELOW: "underwater" at the Bergen Aquarium.

Famous names

It is not surprising that this lively city, with its close European links, should have been the birthplace of many famous people. It was also a strong base for 19th-century nationalism which culminated in 1905 in Norway gaining its independence from Sweden. The Prime Minister who led Norway then was Christian Michelsen, whose home **Gamlehaugen** (open Jun–Sept, Mon–Fri; entrance fee) at Fjøsanger (near the happily titled southern suburb of Paradis) is now the residence of the King when he is in Bergen.

Nationalism had strong roots in the 19th-century revival of Norwegian culture, led by the playwright Henrik Ibsen, the violinist Ole Bull, the composer Edvard Grieg, and writers like Bjørnstjerne Bjørnson. Though Ibsen and Bjørnson were not natives of West Norway, Bjørnson was for a time director of Bergen's **Den Nationale Scene** ® (National Theatre; open Aug/Sept–June) founded by Ole Bull in 1850, and Bjørnson's statue stands on the steps in front.

The virtuoso violinist Ole Bull contribution to Norwegian culture came through his wanderings in the villages of West Norway and the great Jotunheim mountain plateau east of the fjord country. Here he collected many old folk melodies which were played on the Hardanger fiddle, the area's traditional instrument. Later, Grieg transcribed some of these folk tunes for piano, saving them from being lost.

Edvard Grieg (1843–1907).

Musical homes

Every year, thousands of visitors come to Grieg's summer home at **Troldhaugen** ⑤ (closed in Dec and at Easter; entrance fee; tel: 55 91 07 10) some 8 km (5 miles) south of Bergen on a high point above the fjord. Here Grieg also had

BELOW: a procession along Bryggen.

Map on page 248

Fantoft stavkirke (stave church), now in the Paradis district of Bergen, was brought from its original home on Sognefjorden in 1879, when it was decided to replace it with a new building.

BELOW: view from the top of Fløien.

a *hytte* where he could find peace to compose. The house is just as Grieg left it; his manuscripts are scattered around and even his piano is in working order in the comfortable drawing room. In the past, this room was the venue for many musical evenings; today, if you are lucky, the curator will play some of Grieg's music on it. The size of the room inevitably limited the possibilities and in 1985 Troldhaugen opened a special **Chamber Music Hall**, seating 200, built into the hillside so that it is barely visible among the tall trees. The latest addition is the **Edvard Grieg Museum** close to the concert hall and villa.

Troldhaugen is a wonderful setting for a concert and a continuation of the summer evening tradition when Grieg and his wife, Nina Hagerup, a Danish singer, would entertain their friends in the quiet garden outside the drawing room. Any bus for the Fana district goes to Hopsbroen, then a 15-minute walk leads to Troldhaugen; many city excursions also include Troldhaugen.

Ole Bull built his home on the island of **Lysøen** ❶ (open May–Aug, and Sun only in Sept; entrance fee) in 1873, when his fame had long spread throughout and beyond Norway. Bull turned the whole island into a park with woodland and walking routes and the house itself is unlike any other in the country. Made of traditional Norwegian wood, the decorated and screened balcony and the pointed arches of the windows on the front of this timber building have an almost Moorish flavour, and the tower topped by a minaret is reminiscent of St Basil's in Moscow's Red Square.

To get there, the bus (gate 19 or 20 at the bus station on the bus marked Lyse-fjordruta) takes about 50 minutes. It's a good idea to combine the visit to Lysøen with a stop on the way at **Lysekloster**, the ruins of a 12th-century Cistercian abbey, a daughter monastery of Fountains Abbey in Yorkshire, England.

Artistic legacy

Whether as a result of the fame of people such as Bull and Grieg, Bergen has a lively artistic and cultural life. The **Bergen International Festival of Music**, held each May and early June, attracts international artistes and thousands of visitors. At the end of the 1970s, the Festival led to the building of a new concert hall, **Grieghallen** , with marvellous acoustics which may or may not owe their quality to its strange architecture. The outside of the building looks remarkably like that of a concert grand piano, perhaps as a tribute to the composer whose name it bears. This is the heart of the 12-day festival but the whole city is involved, with events in Håkonshallen, Troldhaugen, Lysøen and Mariakirken.

Bergen also has several strong art collections, mostly centred on **Lille Lungegårdsvann**, the octagonal lake in the middle of the park, not far from the statues of Edvard Grieg, and of Ole Bull playing his violin, and near Grieghallen. Here are the **Bergen Billedgalleri ⓥ** (Municipal Art Gallery), with a large collection of Norwegian painting over the past 150 years, the **Rasmus Meyers Samlinger ⓦ** (Art Collection), which also specialises in Norwegian paintings with many by Edvard Munch, and the **Stenersens Samling ⓧ** (all three open all year, reduced opening in off-season; entrance fee; tel: 55 56 80 00), which has works by Munch, Picasso and Klee amongst others. Bergen, like many Scandinavian cities, is also strong in private galleries, many of which specialise in modern painting.

Shops often offer opportunities to see traditional crafts. Best known is **Husfliden** (on Vågsalm), which has richly decorated Norwegian costumes, woven textiles and woodwork, including the famous *rosemaling* (rose painting). For Norwegian glass try **Irgens** in Markeveien and Bergen's **Glasmagasin**.

BELOW: a concert in the ornate music hall of Ole Bull's house on Lysøen.

Map on page 248

Tradition in action

During the summer (mid-June to late August) the open-air stages at Lille Lungegårdsvann and Torgalmenningen are used almost daily for music and dance performances. Folk dancing and music from rural Norway are particularly popular with the Bergensere and visitors alike. Nearest to the real thing is **Fana Folklore** (tel: 55 91 52 40), in the district of Fana to the south. This is designed as a country wedding with typical Norwegian food, such as *rømmegraut*, a rich celebration "porridge" which bears little resemblance to the breakfast variety, cured mutton and sausage, flat bread and other traditional dishes.

By bus, you travel from Festplassen to **Fana Kirken** (varying opening hours), the 800-year-old church, worth a day visit in its own right, for a short recital of old hymns and old melodies by the organist; then on to **Rambergstunet**, and a traditional welcome by the *lur*, a folk instrument something like a coaching horn, and then to the long trestle tables for the wedding fare, accompanied by folk dancing displays where the dancers weave and jump in the prescribed steps that almost died out during the 19th century. Later, guests get a chance to join in and there are also displays by children and songs accompanied by one of Norway's most haunting musical instruments, the *langleik*, a one-string zither used to accompany traditional songs. You return to Bergen full of good food and memories of colour and music.

Outdoor city

Naturally the most popular pastime in this city of the sea and fjord is **sailing**. Not far behind are sea fishing and swimming. There are plenty of opportunities to be active in all three, or you could simply take a fjord cruise, sometimes lasting more than a day. The hills above Bergen, just ten minutes away from the centre by the Fløienbane, are ideal for walking, and **Sandviken Ridesenter**, not far from the Gamle Bergen Museum, organises horse riding tours both long and short.

For something different, try an evening (Thur) at the trotting course **Travpark** (tel: 55 24 79 00) at Åsane, around 16 km (10 miles) from the city. This is a peculiarly Scandinavian sport and excitement is electric as the horses and their drivers race round the track.

Apart from the gardens at Troldhaugen and Lysøen, the Norwegian Arboretum at **Milde** (open daily; free), founded in 1971, is busily planting up shrubs and trees from many parts of the world, and this pretty area along the shore has rocky gorges, hills and a small lake. The Fanafjord also provides good swimming. To get there take the bus to Mildevågen, and then a 15-minute walk through an area that looks out to islands and sea brings you to the arboretum.

Too many people make the mistake of allowing only a day or even half a day for Bergen at the start and end of a visit to the western fjords, which doesn't give the city a chance. Much better to use it as a base for a fjord holiday, combining the cosmopolitan delights of the city with the splendid scenery of the fjords. Bergen has plenty to do and see, or you can simply spend some time just soaking up the atmosphere down by the busy harbour. ❏

BELOW: Ole Bull nicknamed his house "the Little Alhambra".
RIGHT: old houses in the maze of narrow lanes behind Bryggen.

THE MOST BEAUTIFUL VOYAGE

Map on page 262

This is one of the great sea journeys of the world: from Bergen to the end of Norway and back again, the vessels plying the Hurtigrute are mail boats, freight ships and passenger liners in one

The ship slips out of **Bergen**'s hill-ringed harbour at 10.30pm, day in day out, all year round. In winter, it has been dark for hours and passengers linger no longer than to wave goodbye to the lights of the city before scuttling below to the warmth of saloon and cabin. In summer, it is a different matter: the deck is crowded as the big steamer sweeps out towards the fjord, leaving behind the small houses where the Hansa merchants once lived.

The coastal express heads north through Byfjorden and Hjeltefjorden, past the islands of **Askøy** and **Holsnøy** for the open sea, at the start of a trip of 1,250 nautical miles round Nordkapp (North Cape) and then to Kirkenes near the Russian border, crossing the Arctic Circle en route.

Nowadays, this coastal voyage has become one of the most popular journeys for visitors, but it is much more to the Norwegians themselves. From earliest times, this long and beautiful coast has been the main link in Norway for communication and trade, connecting communities hundreds of kilometres apart; the western and northern Norwegians once regarded Scotland and Iceland as being easier to reach than the region around present-day Oslo. In winter, it was the only way to travel because the Gulf Stream kept, and still keeps, the seaways open all year round.

PRECEDING PAGES: sunset at sea.
LEFT: resting on the aft deck.
BELOW: the view from on board *MS Nordlys* between Rørvik and Brønnøysund.

The swift route

The first steamship, the *Prinds Gustav*, set out from Trondheim to Tromsø in 1838. In time, other steamers also began to ply between the coastal towns and in 1893 a local steamship company, Vesteraalens Dampskibsselskab, opened the Hurtigrute (literally "swift route") between Trondheim and Hammerfest, in the far northwest. As the line extended to Bergen and Kirkenes, several ship-owners became involved. Following various mergers, just two companies now run 11 ships (ranging from the grand, old *MS Lofoten* to the *MS King Olav*, built in 1997) for a round trip that takes 12 days from Bergen to Bergen.

The Hurtigrute makes 34 ports-of-call along this ever-changing coast, some at places no bigger than a handful of houses around the harbour, with local people waiting on the quayside to collect a car or a container, to greet friends who have hopped a short distance between small towns where the alternative is a long difficult drive, or just as a social occasion where locals wave to the passengers looking down from the rails when the stop is too short to go ashore.

Part of the charm is watching a working ship going about its business: the efficient mooring as the crew shout down to the dockers; the crane winching over a

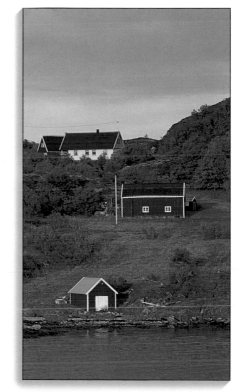

Vardø
Berlevåg
Mehamn
Båtsfjord
Kløllefjord
Vadsø
NORWEGIAN
SEA
❻ Nordkapp
Honningsvåg
Kirkenes
RUSSIA
Havøysund
Hammerfest
Øksfjord
Skjervøy
FINLAND
Tromsø ❺
Finnsnes
Risøyhamn
Vesterålen
Sortland
Harstad
Stokmarknes
Gulf
of
Bothnia
Stamsund
Svolvær
Lofoten
❹
Kjerringøy
Bodø
Ørnes
Arctic Circle ❸
Nesna
Sandnessjøen
SWEDEN
Brønnøysund
Rørvik
❷
Trondheim
Kristiansund
Molde
Ålesund ❶
Torvik
NORWAY
Måløy
Floro
Oslo
NORTH
SEA
Bergen
Skagerrak
Hurtigrute
Stavanger Kristiansand
0   100 km
0   100 miles
DENMARK

tractor which has been chained fast to the deck during the voyage; and the nervous face of its owner as a car is winched up.

The first stop for going ashore is **Åle-sund ❶**, one of the three Møre towns. It has all the natural design of a town built round a harbour and, because of a disastrous fire in 1904 , it was rebuilt all of a piece, with the wooden houses in an Art Nouveau style, carefully preserved and painted in brilliant colours.

The next main stop is **Trondheim ❷**, further up a magnificent coast with 87 peaks, snow-capped for much of the year. When it was the ancient capital of Norway, Trondheim was called Nidaros, and **NidarosDomen** (Cathedral) is a national shrine; it contains a memorial to King Olav Haraldson, who became St Olav the Holy after his death at the Battle of Stiklestad. The Trondheim stop is long enough for a morning tour of this historic city, with its busy harbours and bays, and wide streets lined with small wooden houses and old warehouses.

Early next morning, as the ship steams north again, it crosses the **Polarsirkel ❸** (Arctic Circle) and sails into "the land of the Midnight Sun". This used to be Norway's great tourist slogan until an inconvenient honesty forced Norwegians to drop it because not all Norway enjoys midnight sun! But, as far north as this, in summer you can stand on deck at midnight and admire the coast as it passes by the ship. On the way south, at the Arctic Circle crossing, **King Neptune** joins the celebrations on deck to award Arctic Circle certificates.

Hamsun's Nordland

Into the **Lofoten Islands ❹**, the ship is now in Nordland, the territory of one of Norway's most famous writers, Knut Hamsun. Hamsun named the old trading centre of **Kjerringøy** "Sirilund" in his novels, which describe the surprisingly outward-looking lives of these northern fishing and trading families around the turn of the century. A Ham-

Map
on page
262

sun novel (particularly *The Wayfarers*) is a good accompaniment to a voyage that illuminates his own characters and their thinking, and gives an insight into life in these northern lands today.

On deck, as the steamer weaves in and out of the islands, bird-watchers find it difficult to go below even to eat or sleep, in case they miss one of the numerous seabird colonies, the congregations of colourful exotic ducks in winter harbours and, particularly, the comical little puffins in their hundreds of thousands.

Between **Solvær** and **Stokmarknes**, the ship makes a brief detour into **Trollfjorden**, something no big cruise liner could do because the sheer faces of rock and scree press close in this narrow fjord. This, too, calls for a celebration and the ship's chef serves a special Trollfjorden soup to the accompaniment of Grieg's most troll-like music and the arrival of a troll to delight the passengers. In winter, ice makes entry impossible, but instead there is the endless fascination of the **Aurora borealis** (Northern Lights) – sometimes white spears, at others a brilliant blue-green aura across the sky, or a multi-coloured spectacular that gleams and sparkles. The high mountains of the fjord country further south have disappeared by now but, during the brief light of a winter day, the low slanting sun picks out the white cones of snow-covered hills.

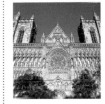

There is time to see the Norwegian Crown Jewels on display in Trondheim's Nidaros Domkirke (Cathedral).

Watching the seasons go by

In spring and autumn, the 12-day journey feels like a voyage through the seasons. Leave Bergen in May, when the fjord valleys are brilliant with blossom, and the hills and mountains of the north will still be white as snow flurries scurry across the fjords and mountains. The return journey is the reverse. Just as the north is beginning to slip out of its winter grip, the swift Norwegian sum-

BELOW: a steamer dwarfs the dockside at Øskfjord.

Map
on page
262

Arriving at Sortland.

BELOW: heading
north near Skjervøy.
RIGHT: late evening,
during the midnight
sun, north of Bodø.

mer marches north and will have already reached Bergen and the mountains around it, and it could be warm enough to lie out in a sheltered corner of the deck as the ship nears the end of its long journey.

The northern city of **Tromsø** ❺, set on an island in a rugged landscape, has a relaxed cosmopolitan atmosphere that fits with its nickname "Paris of the North" and can be enjoyed in its numerous restaurants and street cafés. The city is also a base for scientists at a polar institute, who study the polar regions and for the Arctic fleets. Returning south to Tromsø in summer, there is time for a midnight excursion by cable car to the summit of **Mount Storsteinen**. At 410 metres (1,350 ft) above the sea below, there is a wonderful sunlit view of coast and country.

Into Finnmark the ship sails past a coast of scoured hills and watercourses with forests along the valleys, to **Hammerfest**, Norway's most northerly town. In summer, the steamer, working ship or not, makes a concession here and slips through the Margerøy Sound to Honningsvåg and the start of an excursion by coach to **Nordkapp** ❻ (North Cape) – a highlight of any visit to Norway.

North Cape also marks a change of direction to the east across the very top of Norway on the way to **Kirkenes** ❼, five kilometres (three miles) from the **Russian border**, a coast where the place names begin to show Sami (Lapp) and Finnish origins. Kirkenes itself is a mining town in a strange no-man's land between East and West, which is also influenced by the local Sami culture.

Nowhere missed

On the way south again, the ship stops by day at the places it visited when northbound passengers were fast asleep below decks, so nowhere is missed.

Nor is it generally a rough voyage: the Hurtigrute hugs the coast or weaves in and out of islands that shelter the ship from the excesses of the Atlantic Ocean and the Norwegian Sea, even in the far north.

In the most popular summer months the ship takes on some of the trimmings of a cruise ship with dancing, film shows, and cruise guides to point out the sights in good time and organise excursions ashore. But this coastal steamer is always a working ship and part of the charm out of season is that it reverts to its traditional role of carrying west-coast Norwegians, who treat it as a bus, for business and pleasure. As they come on board, they pile their rucksacks on to the luggage racks near the gangway entrance, spend a few hours on board, play cards or music, talk among themselves and to the crew as people they already know, and step off with no more than a casual wave.

Although the network of small aircraft linking scattered communities has done much to reduce this traffic, the coastal steamer is still there when airports are closed and roads blocked. For supplies and deliveries to distant industries and traders, ships are invaluable and can carry things too big for the plane. Even so, with the ever-increasing tourist traffic this emphasis is likely to change somewhat in the future. For now, though, the "swift route" along Norway's jagged coastline continues to be a unique mix of the workaday and the spectacular. ❑

FROM SOGN TO NORDFJORD

Map on page 234

The presence of the last Ice Age is felt strongly here, in the shape of the great Jostedal glacier; but humans have also left their mark, in the form of ancient rock carvings and a plethora of stave churches

From a seat in one of the small planes that somehow contrive to land on the narrow strips along the fjords or the tiny green patches between the mountains, it looks an impossible territory. Yet the land that runs from Sognefjorden in the south to Nordfjorden to the north has all the features that made Norway famous: the world's longest and deepest fjord, Europe's largest glacier and Jotunheimen, Scandinavia's greatest mountain massif

The large *fylke* (county) of Sogn og Fjordane lies between a zigzag coastline drawn by the waters of the North Sea and the start of Jotunheimen's heights. Narrow fingers of water push inland from the main fjords to reach far into the mountains, and waterfalls tumble hundreds of metres into the fjord below. The force of all this water feeds powerful hydro-electric power stations, tucked away inside the mountains. Aluminium plants also make use of the spouting waterfalls to generate power and, among other things, produce the road barriers for many of Europe's mountain roads.

In the past, fjord, mountain and valley could be near impassable in winter. Today, though journeys often take longer than elsewhere, travel is made easier thanks to the network of ferries, tunnels and bridges. From Bergen, an express boat (a catamaran with water jet engines) reaches deep inland as far as Sogndal on Sognefjorden, almost half-way to Sweden.

LEFT: Flåm village.
BELOW: St Olav's Kirke (once the English church) in Balestrand.

Deepest and longest

At 200 km (120 miles) long and 1,300 metres (4,260 ft) deep **Sognefjorden** ⓱ is unmatched anywhere in the world. After British visitors discovered it in the 19th century, royalty too endorsed the fjord's delights. As Crown Prince, Edward VII came over from Britain as early as 1898, and Kaiser Wilhelm II was on holiday in Sogn when he learned of the assassination of the Archduke at Sarajevo which triggered World War I.

In spring, the fjord is pink and white when this apparently ungrateful soil puts up umbrellas of fruit blossom in orchards and gardens. In the warm summer days, far above the fjord, cattle and sheep cling to the small grass plateaux, the mountain farms or *seter* where once women and young girls spent the summer making cheese. The majority of the 100,000 people in the county still make their living by farming or fishing, forestry and fruit growing.

On both sides of the fjord small villages cling to every square metre of land, each with its own atmosphere. **Balestrand** ⓲ has been a favourite since the 19th century and has an English church, St Olav's, founded by one of those fearless Victorian Englishwomen who travelled the world. German artists from the Düsseldorf Academy were also quick to appreciate the beauty of Sognefjorden and built Swiss-style

BELOW: a solitary
boat on
Sognefjorden.

houses, decorated with dragon heads in deference to their hosts' Viking past, to add to the charm of this picturesque village. The area is renowned for having a particularly mild climate and across a small neck of water at **Dragsvik**, a local pastor-botanist planted exotic trees which thrive in the sheltered bay.

Ice spectacle

A narrow side-fjord leads to the little community of **Fjærland**, reached by ferry or car, a dairy farming centre near the two southernmost offshoots of the great **Jostedalsbreen** ⓳ (glacier). Nestling at its base on a large, flat esker deposited there thousands of years ago is the **Norsk Bremuseum** ⓴ (Norwegian Glacier Museum; open Apr–Oct; entrance fee). Tourists come to Fjærland every year to climb (or merely gaze at) the awesome glacier. From a distance, the concrete and glass building designed by Norwegian architect Sverre Fehn looks like part of the glacier itself. The museum includes a special cinema salon for viewing panoramic shots of Norwegian glaciers.

The ferry from Dragsvik runs to **Vangsnes** on the south side and, from there, it is only a few kilometres south to **Vik** ㉑ and the 12th-century **Hopperstad Stavkirke** (Stave Church), with dragon heads on the outside and rich decorations within. Vik also has a stone church, **Hove Kirke**, that is only 20 years younger than Hopperstad (both open May–Sept; single entrance fee). On the way back, stop at the statue of the Norwegian Viking hero, Fridtjof, a gift from Kaiser Wilhelm II in 1913.

Going east from Balestrand, a short crossing takes you to **Hella** ㉒ and past the glistening arc of **Kvinnfoss** (Lady's Waterfall) close to the main road. At the head of the fjord, **Sogndal** is the centre for trade and administration in an area

of forestry and farming. The pretty little town swells considerably during term time because it is also a centre for education, with university colleges and Norway's oldest folk high school. To the north, farms are dotted along Sognadalen's narrow lake. This is a popular spot for walking in summer and skiing in winter.

Map on page 234

Kaupanger Stavkirke (open Jun–Aug; entrance fee), a little further along Road 5, was built towards the end of the 12th century, its plain dark wood exterior has been restored to its early form, and it is a lovely place to listen to the organist's summer recitals. **Sogn folkemuseum** (open May–Sept; entrance fee) was set up in 1909 by the then landowner Gert F. Heiberg as a living museum with animals, including 35 houses and farm buildings, to show how people lived in Sogn from around 1500 right up to the present. Best of all, the museum is used as a setting for folk music and dancing.

Standing tall beside the fjord at **Nordnes** is a stone to mark the Battle of Fimreite in June 1184. That was when King Sverre and his peasant Birkebeiner (so-called because of their birchbark leggings) defeated King Magnus Erlingsson and the nobility, a turning point in Norwegian history.

Taking a break on the Flåm to Myrdal mountain railway.

Cool, green waters

In **Luster** , to the northeast of Sogndal, is another of Sogn's bumper crop of stave churches: **Urnes Stavkirke** (UNESCO World Heritage Site; open May–Aug; entrance fee) is thought to be the oldest in Norway and is linked with the coming of Christianity. Also within easy reach is yet another icy tongue from Josterdal glacier, called **Nigardsbreen**, where one of the delights is a boat trip over the ice-cold, green waters of a glacier lake.

BELOW: Urnes Stavkirke (Stave Church) high above Lustrafjorden.

South of Sogndal, Sognefjorden ends in the two most easterly fjords leading to Årdal and Lærdalsøyri, lovely valleys with mountain farms, plently of opportunities for walking, climbing, or fishing in upland lakes and streams. The **Norsk Villakssenter** (Wild Salmon Centre; open Jun–Aug; entrance fee) at **Lærdalsøyri**  provides a unique observation pool for wild salmon. Lærdal's one-time importance as an eastwest trading route is evident at Gamle (Old) Lærdalsøyri, an area of beautifully restored 18th and 19th-century listed building (open May–Sept, entrance fee).

Aurlandvangen, Flåm and Gudvangen lie along the innermost recesses of the fjord, which stretch south from the main fjord like an upside-down "Y". **Nærøyfjorden** provides the most dramatic fjord cruise in West Norway, the mountains pressing so close that you wonder if the boat will squeeze through. Also not to be missed is the **mountain railway** from Flåm to Myrdal, which spirals up the steep mountain gorge (*see "Norway in a Nutshell", page 241*).

Life on the lake

If from Balestrand instead of heading inland you turn northwest, along Road 5/13 towards Förde and the coast, you come to one of the regions many lakes – **Jølstravatnet** – that penetrate the foothills of the high tops in the east and feed into the fjords in the west. On

The replica Viking knarr (freighter) Saga Siglar in Sognefjorden before leaving for a two-year, round-the-world voyage.

the south side lies the farm **Astruptunet** ㉘ (open May–Sept; entrance fee), home of the artist Nikolai Astrup (1880–1928) who found themes for his art in his own surroundings. Astruptunet is just as it was during the painter's life, though the barn has been replaced by a new art gallery with a permanent exhibition.

From Jølstravatnet, it is easy to reach **Grovebreen** (glacier), some 1,600 metres (5,400 ft) high, and Haukedalsvatn to the south is quite close to the far side of the glacier. Walkers can reach the great icefields of Josterdalsbreen. A series of valleys, lakes and fjords links these high plateaux into the Nordfjord system to the north.

After leaving Jølstravatnet the Jølstra, said to be one of the best salmon rivers in the area, drops hundreds of metres by the time it reaches **Førde** ㉙ on Førde-fjord. Here you find the main **Sunnfjord Museum** (open all year; entrance fee), a collection of 24 historic buildings, 17 of which are reconstructed as a farmstead from around 1850.

Along the coast

The best way to get a view of Sunnfjord's hundreds of islands is from the high peaks in the east, though the coast itself is by no means all flat. **Bleia** rises straight from the north side of Førdefjord to more than 1,300 metres (4,300 ft), the summit of the Sunnfjord Alps, and many of the islands have high peaks. These islands stretch the length of the coast, from Fensfjord and the island of Sandøy, north to Vestkapp (West Cape) where the Hurtigrute (coastal steamer) turns northeast to its next stop at Ålesund.

It's an odd thought that **Florø**, the only community in this large county big enough to be called a town, should lie on the remote edge of the sea, but not so

BELOW: sunset lights up the slopes of Sognefjell.

strange when you remember that Norway has always depended on the sea for food, trade and transport. The **Sogn og Fjordane Kystmuseet** (Coastal Museum; open all year, entrance fee) in Florø has a fine collection of old boats. This most westerly town had its birth in the herring industry which flourished in the middle of the 19th century. Today, it still depends on the sea for fish, while oil and gas fields away to the west have, nevertheless, turned Florø into an oil centre.

Map on page 234

Offshore sights

There are many places to see: rock carvings at **Ausevik**, southeast of Florø; the nearby island of **Svanøy** has the ancient stone cross of St Olav, covered in runic inscriptions, a manor with an old garden and magnificent trees; there is a Romanesque medieval church on **Kinnøy**, where the Kinna Play, *Songen ved det store djup* (*The Song of the Great Deep*), is performed by the county theatre group and local people, and draws thousands to the island each June.

To the north of Fløro, at the mouth of Nordfjorden, is the island of **Bremangerlandet ㉚** with its **Vingen carvings** which are even older than Ausevik's and show the lives of the fishing-settlers of Nordfjorden. Further north, the village of **Måløy** on **Vågsøy** is one of Norway's largest fishing and trading ports, and at Raudeberg fish of all kinds is salted and dried. But size is relative, and industry does nothing to detract from the rural quietness of this hilly island. Måløy features the Allied Monument, a 6-metre (20-ft) high granite obelisk raised in memory of 52 Allied soldiers who died during the Måløy raid in 1941.

North of Vågsøy and Raudeberg is **Silda**, a tiny island for sea-anglers, sports divers and bird-watchers. It has only 80 inhabitants, no cars and, on an islet in the middle of the harbour, a restored fish salting works serves a feast of seafoods.

In summer, it is possible to see sea eagles along the coast of Sogn og Fjordane. This is the farthest south that this magnificent bird of prey builds its nest.

BELOW:
the sturdy *fjording* (fjord horse), typical of the region.

On the nearby island of **Selje** ❸ are the medieval ruins of **St Sunneva Kloster** (Monastery). On the northernmost tip is **Vestkapp** where winds blow fierce. Its closest neigbouring land is the Shetland Isles off the north of Scotland.

Inland along Nordfjorden

Hornindalsvatnet is Europe's deepest lake. Following the melting of the ice at the end of the last Ice Age, the Hornindal valley flooded to a depth of 514 metres (1,680 ft).

Nordfjorden is 100 km (60 miles) shorter than the Sognefjord. With so many side-fjords, lakes and valleys it is easy to get into the mountains or make the journey up **Briksdalsbreen** ❸, one of the most beautiful glaciers in the fjord country. Even better is that you can climb up to the base of the glacier in the two-wheeled farm carriages, *stolkjaerrer*, pulled by small sturdy, cream-coloured *fjording* (fjord horses).

The traditional home of the *fjording* is the Eid district, centred around **Nordfjordeid**, where Nordfjorden proper has already divided itself into Eidsfjorden and Isefjorden. **Eid** ❸, which is also connected to the coast by Road 15, is famous for **Firdariket**, the seat of the last Viking chief, and the town has traditional white-painted buildings. The church, which dates from 1849, is decorated with beautiful **rose painting**.

To the south of Eid, Road 1 crossed Utfjorden and then runs along Gloppenfjorden, which ends at **Sandane** ❸, the main town of Gloppen, the biggest farming district in the whole county and also a large fur-breeding centre. The **Nordfjord Folkmuseum** (open Jun–Aug; entrance fee) started in 1920 with five turf-roofed houses but now has more than 40 historic buildings, including a mountain *seter*. At the fjordside is a 100-year-old **sailing barge**, *Holvikjekta*, the last of the traditional freighters that served coast and fjord. There is also a fine adventure centre, **Glopen Camping og Fritidssenter**, which offers a week's

BELOW: summer swimming in the cold fjord waters.

programme of riding, canoeing, wind-surfing, mountain and glacier walking, mountain cycling and sight-seeing to various beauty spots.

Continuing along Road 15 from Eid you come to Hornindalsvatnet, which leads to the biggest community, Grodås, sited where the ground begins to climb. Hornindal valley has long traditions in handicrafts and folk music, and musicians wear the black breeches, or the long black skirt and green bodice of the area. The most famous artist was Anders Svor (1864–1929), first a wood carver and then, after a time at the Copenhagen Academy of Art, a sculptor. The **Anders Svor Museum** (open all year; entrance fee) contains more than 400 of his sculptures.

Map on page 234

Fjord end

Further along you reach the Inner Nordfjorden, where the fjord system ends at **Stryn** ❸, **Loen** and **Olden**, the start of three spectacular valleys stretching up to the northwest edges of the Jostedalsbreen. Nowadays, three tunnels out of the Stryn valley cut right through the mountain to the renowned Geirangerfjord to the north. Stryn is famous for summer skiing on the northeast of Strynsvatn, where the ground rises to Tystigbreen. Until you watch, it is hard to imagine skiers in swimsuits or shorts and teeshirts with deep tans, but there they are enjoying every moment.

Oldedalen is the route to Briksdalsbreen (Glacier) from the Briksdalsbreen Fjellstove by horse-carriage or on foot and then a half-hour walk to the great cascade of ice which hangs above the ice flows and the green waters of the glacier lake. Small birds flutter over the water and, in olden times, farmers from eastern Norway drove their cattle over these great icefields down into the kindlier valleys of the west. ❑

BELOW: the Briksdals glacier, part of the great Jostedalbreen.

MØRE AND ROMSDAL

Map
on page
278

*The county of Møre og Romsdal has a bit of everything: a jewel of
a fjord, Geirangerfjorden; the Art Nouveau Ålesund; the peaks
of Trollheimen, Home of the Trolls; and delightful islands to spare*

For nearly a century the coastal steamers of the Hurtigrute have called at
Ålesund, Molde and Kristiansund along the sea route that leads to Trondheim and the north. This part of Norway's jagged coastline is 6,000 km
(3,750 miles) long and more than 10 percent of the county's population lives on
islands. It's scarcely surprising then to learn that, even today, the sea is still the
great provider for Møre og Romsdal. Apart from fish, prospecting and providing for the oil industry are important activities, and North Sea oil and gas are
likely to become even more significant as Norway seeks new fields.

Looking at the jumble of coastline, islands and fjord mouths on a map, it is
sometimes hard to distinguish where sea and islands end and fjord and mainland
begin. Yet move inland and half the area lies above 600 metres (1,800 ft). In the
southeast, the highest peaks reach over 1,800 metres (6,000 ft). The county is
divided into three municipalities: **Sunnmøre**, **Romsdal** and **Nordmøre**, of
which the main centres are Ålesund, Molde and Kristiansund.

Sea trade has always been important and, from the Middle Ages, the accolade
for a settlement was to be given *kaupang* (market) status. At that time there
were just two: Borgundkaupangen, five kilometres (three miles) from the centre of Ålesund, in Sunnmøre; and Veøykaupangen, in Romsdal. Both were centres for northsouth and eastwest trade routes on sea
and land. Today buses 13, 14 and 24 from Ålesund
will take you to the **Sunnmøre Museum** (Open Air
Museum and Coastal Heritage Site, Borgundkaupangen and Medieval Age Museum; varying opening
hours; common entrance fee; tel: 70 15 40 24).

Rare harmony

Ålesund  is Norway's largest fishing town but best
known for its Art Nouveau architecture, built in 1904
after a great fire which destroyed the centre and which
gave rise to the Norwegian saying: "I've never heard
anything like it since Ålesund burnt down."

First to the rescue came the Norvegophile, Kaiser
Wilhelm II of Germany, who sent four ships laden
with supplies and building materials (the stained-glass
windows in the gable end of the **church** were an inau-
guration gift from the Kaiser). With help and dona-
tions from all over Europe, the people of Ålesund
completed the rebuilding of their town by 1907 in the
now carefully preserved Art Nouveau style. **Ålesund
Museum** (open all year; entrance fee) features exhibitions on the 1904 fire and subsequent rebuilding.
Towers, turrets and medieval-romantic frontages,
often with more than a trace of Nordic mythology,
give the town a harmony which extends to the painted
wooden warehouses along **Brosundet**, the deep inlet
of the inner harbour.

PRECEDING PAGES:
around Olden.
LEFT: looking
down into
Geirangerfjorden.
BELOW: Art Nouveau
detail on a door in
Ålesund.

Hauling the catch aboard just off the island of Rundøy.

Until the 1950s, Ålesund, was a veritable Klondyke for fish, fishermen and their boats, and *klippfisk* (traditional Norwegian split, dried cod). But as fishing changed so did Ålesund, which added fish processing and fish farming. Many former warehouses are now offices and restaurants, pleasant places to try out one of the more unlikely local specialities such as *bacalao*, made from boneless *klippfisk*, or the more traditional *brennsnute*, a potato and meat stew.

From the top of the 418 steps up **Aksla** hill in the centre of the town – if the climb doesn't leave you breathless, the view certainly will – the view stretches over several islands, now all linked by 12 km (8 miles) of deep underground tunnels. With great practicality, the builders used the rock from the tunnels to extend the airport on the nearby island of **Vigra**.

Every book and brochure that describes the county's thousands of islands shows similar happy pictures of people in, on or under the sea, and anglers with magnificent catches. There are sea caves, tunnels and bird cliffs, little harbours, campsites, clean, white beaches and *hytter* to rent. Some have relics of the Vikings, many have summer festivals. What these sea islands have to offer is almost unlimited: the difficulty is which to choose.

Bird island

Near Ålesund is one island not to miss. **Runde ❷** attracts professional and amateur naturalists from all over the world. More than 200 bird species have been recorded but this small island is best known for breeding birds, which line the cliffs in their hundreds of thousands. When they fly, it looks as if a gigantic swarm of insects has darkened the sky. One of the best ways of seeing the island is by taking a four-hour tour on board the *Charming Ruth*, which departs

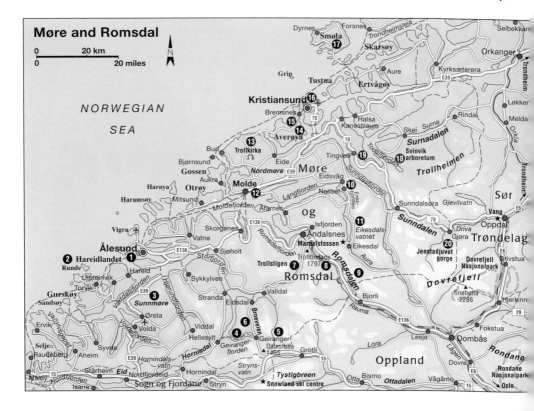

from Ulsteinvik harbour daily from June to August. As a bonus, the waters round the island close over interesting wrecks; not so long ago divers found a cache of gold from a Dutch ship, *Ackerendam*.

Map on page 278

Gateway to the Geirangerfjord

South from Ålesund between the Vartdalsfjorden and the Hjørundfjorden, the **Sunnmøre mountains** ➌ plunge straight into the fjord near Ørsta, one of the early targets for the many British climbers who first made Norway's mountains known. Ålesund is also the main entrance to **Storfjorden**, where the cruise ships turn in to reach their goal of **Geirangerfjorden** ➍, claimed by many to be Norway's most beautiful fjord. One road (No. 60) to Geiranger goes through Stranda, main town of inner Storfjorden, another (No. 1) via Ørsta, both ending at **Hellesylt**. From there you can travel to the inner end of Geirangerfjorden by boat or, in summer, there is a path along the fjord's high southern wall.

In this most secret of fjords far from the sea, great waterfalls tumble hundreds of metres in such delicate cascades that they are given names – **De Syv Søstre** (The Seven Sisters) and the **Brudesløret** (Bridal Veil). Lofty mountains reflected in the mirror-still water give the fjord a gentle grandeur and, in some places, farms cling to unlikely pockets of green. A small landing stage or two indicate that people climb up and down to these distant farms.

It is much too beautiful to miss and everyone stays on deck until the boat reaches **Geiranger** ➎ village, which huddles under the half circle of mountains. Half-way up the winding road behind the village is the appropriately named **Hotel Utsikten Bellevue**, which must have one of the best views in Norway, and further on the road passes by **Dalsnibba**, the highest peak in Sunnmøre.

One way of sampling the full range of Norwegian cuisine is to visit Ålesund in August, when it plays host to the annual Den Norske Matfestivalen (Food Festival; tel: 70 12 10 09).

BELOW: the coastal town of Ålesund seems to float on the water.

Along the troll road

Heading north once more (along Road 63) towards Åndalsnes, the first stretch to Eidsdal on the Norddalsfjord is known as the **Ørneveien** (Eagle's Road), and it is not difficult to see why as it winds ahead to **Ørnesvingen**, another vantage point. Over the fjord is the start of an even more spectacular road across the **Gudbrandsjuvet** gorge. Mountains rise into the distance of the west, until you reach the top of **Trollstigen** ❼ (the Trolls' Ladder or Trolls' Causeway). This is the heart of inner Romsdal. To the east is **Trolltindane**, around 1,800 metres (6,000 ft), and this fascinating mountain range can be admired before or after the journey on Trollstigen. From vast amounts of snow up here (even in July) it is only a short but exciting 15-minute journey down through 11 gigantic bends hewn out of solid rock into the green valley towards Åndalsnes.

Åndalsnes is known as "the village between fjell and fjord". It sits on a promontory in a circle of fjord and mountain, looking up to tops that challenge climbers of every nationality. They arrive by the score to tackle **Trollveggen**, part of craggy **Trolltindane** ❽, which rises almost vertically from Romsdalen in the east, to its summit bowl of permanent snow. Trollveggen itself has more than 1,000 metres (3,300 ft) of vertical and overhanging rock, first climbed in 1965. New routes are still being discovered. By less hazardous paths, the climb up Trolltindane takes around four hours and calls for boots and strong clothing.

Åndalsnes is the terminus for the train from Oslo through **Romsdalen** ❾ which brings thousands of visitors each year to double or treble the population. A 19th-century British traveller, Lady Beauclerk, described Romsdalen as "precipitous, grey rocks ending in points apparently as sharp as needles… emerging into the sunniest, and the most lovely little spot… sheltered from every wind by the snowcapped mountains that surrounded it, while a most tempting river ran through the dale". It is as true today as it was then.

Famous climbers

The pleasant valley was the base camp for early climbers such as William Slingsby and Johannes Vigdal who, in 1881, made the first ascent of **Store Vengetind**. In the same year, another early pioneer, Carl Hall, made the second ascent with two local climbers to the sharp point of **Romdalshornet**. It had first been conquered 50 years before by two local farmers.

To cater for all this early interest, a local police sergeant, Anders Landmark, opened a simple wooden inn at **Aak**, regarded as Norway's first tourist hotel, and many of Europe's mountain addicts stayed there. Some five kilometres (three miles) into the valley from Åndalsnes, it has recently reopened as a mountain sports centre, with summer courses in climbing and scrambling and, in winter, instruction in ice climbing and mountain (or Telemark) skiing. Rafting and canoeing are also good possibilities on the Rauma river, one of Norway's well-known fishing rivers, which runs through the valley. But it is not necessary to be a rock climber to get high into these mountains. Most have easy alternative routes, and roads reach more than 850 metres (2,500 ft).

TIP

For keen walkers, instead of taking the road down Trollstigen to Åndalsnes it is now possible to follow the well-marked Kløvstien, the old mountain track that was the only way through the mountains before the road.

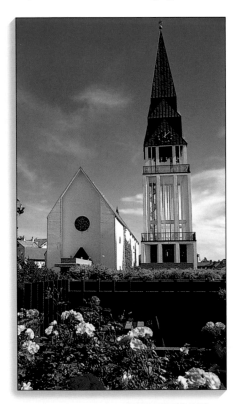

BELOW: Molde, the city of roses.

Back to the coast

Proceeding back towards the coast and Molde along Road 64, it is worth taking a detour into Langfjorden until you reach **Nesset** on Eresfjorden, deep into the mountains. Norway's prominent 19th-century writer and patriot Bjørnstjerne Bjørnson, who had a summer home in the area, described the Nesset mountains: "some standing white, others standing blue, with jagged, competing, agitating peaks, some marching along in ranking row."

The view today from the ferry along the **Eikesdalsvatnet** ⓫ shows you what he meant. The mountain peaks rise abruptly out of the fjord sides, and you get a glimpse of **Mardalsfossen**, a waterfall over 650 metres (2,000 ft) high. In the 1970s, hundreds of people chained themselves together near the waterfall, to prevent the building of a hydro-electric power station. It became a hot political issue and, though they did not win the final battle, the protesters ensured that the summer falls still exist. The struggle also brought the unexpected gift of making Nesset famous and encouraging climbers and other visitors.

Molde ⓬ is part of a collection of islands and peninsulas sheltered from the Norwegian Sea; its mild climate, green vegetation and rose gardens earn it the title "the Town of Roses". The statue of the Little Rose Seller stands in the market place, which has stalls selling everything from fruit and flowers to clothes and, of course, roses. This pretty, easy-going town makes an excellent base for touring on fjord or road.

From **Varden**, Molde's best vantage point, you look over fjord and island to the snowcaps of the Sunnmøre mountains – townspeople claim you can see 87 peaks and half an hour away to the north are small fishing villages which brave the worst of the west winds.

Map on page 278

BELOW: transporting hay the traditional way on a mountain farm.

When rough weather comes in from the west, the coastal Atlanterhavsveien (Atlantic Road) lives up to its name.

Molde has the inevitable outdoor museum – the **Romsdalsmuseet** (open all year; entrance fee), which includes the Hjertøya Fishery Museum – in a particularly beautiful spot where the timber houses, national costumes and folk dancing seem to fit in with the landscape. The museum's collection of *bunads* (national costumes), showing the fine details of shawl, head dress, bodice, jewellery and embroidered purse, is one of the most appealing. The Fishery Museum, 10 minutes by boat from the market place, illustrates the life of local fishing families over the past 100 years.

Yet there is little that is traditional about Molde's entertainment. The modern stadium is well used, with an all-year football ground (Norway largely plays football in the summer) located, spectacularly, by the sea, and the streets are often full of musicians, particularly each year during the famous **Molde International Jazz Festival** (mid-July; many free concerts; tel: 71 21 60 00).

Another fine route is to take Roads 64 and 664 from Molde to the 16th-century village of **Bud**, right on the west coast. Here a boat trip goes to the old fishing-station of **Bjørnsund**, now only inhabited in the summer. Before Bud, a walk from Road 64, reveals **Trollkirka** ⓭ (the Troll church) – a cave, some 70 metres (235 ft) long, divided into three sections, with a great waterfall tumbling down from the upper opening into a white marble basin in the mountains.

Travelling the Atlantic Road

BELOW: the harbour at Torvik on the island of Averøya.

From Bud a small coastal road leads back to Road 64 and the **Atlanterhavsveien** (Atlantic Road) to Kristiansund, over **Averøya** ⓮, the biggest island in the area. As this road heads north across the rim of the ocean, it's a bit like driving on the sea itself.

Averøya deserves more than the view from a car window. Archaeologists believe that this was one of the first places to be settled after the last Ice Age, and their finds in 1909 are unique remnants of the early **Fosna Culture** that existed around 7000 BC. ("Fosna" was the original name of Kristiansund.) One of the best ways to get around is a 50-km (30-mile) tour which varies from seaward skerries and small islands linked by bridge or causeway, to hills around 500 metres (2,500 ft) high in the centre, and there is a fine stave church at **Kvernes** (open Jul–Aug; entrance fee) with an unusually richly decorated mid-17th century interior.

Near **Bremsnes** ⓯, on the northeastern tip of Averøya, is the Viking **Horgsteinen** (Stone of Horg), where the victor of Hafrsfjord, Harald Hårfagre, had his famous hair cut and washed, having fulfilled his vow not to touch it until Norway was united. It is just 15 minutes by ferry from Bremnes to Kristiansund.

The *klippfisk* capital

Unlike Ålesund and Molde, **Kristiansund** ⓰ has little protection from the worst the North Atlantic can do. It is right on the coast, with weather-beaten rocks pounded by the sea, yet not far inland are grassy areas and small woods. This is the *klippfisk* town, for long the biggest exporter of Norwegian dried cod. There are only 18,000 inhabitants but, because of the centuries-old links with other countries of its sailors and fishermen, and the foreign merchants who settled here, the atmosphere is quite cosmopolitan.

Like most Norwegian towns with "Kristian" in their title, Kristiansund was named after a Danish King, Christian VI, who gave it town status in 1742. An good introduction is by *sundbåtene*, the harbour boats which for more than 100

BELOW: the Vågen Kystkultur Museum (Coastal Culture Centre) on the waterfront at Vågen, Kristiansund.

Map on page 278

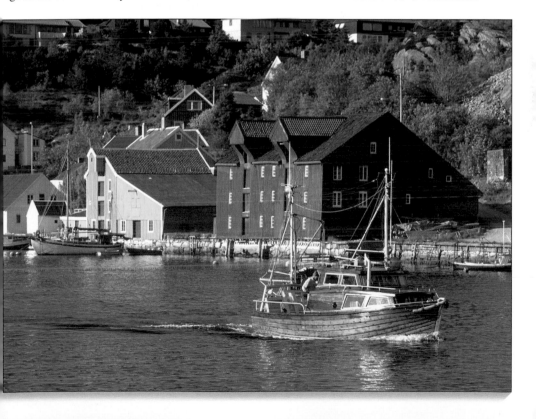

A Country Afloat

To the world, Norway and seafaring are synonymous; the very word Viking means "Men of the Bays". From the age of sail until after World War II, the Norwegian merchant fleet was one of the world's largest, and Norwegian could be heard in ports worldwide.

The country's most popular museums by far are the Sjøfartsmuseum (Maritime Museum) on the Bygdøy peninsula in Oslo, along with the Vikingskipshuset (Viking Ship Museum), with magnificently preserved long ships, the Kon-Tiki Museum, with the rafts used by ethnographic explorer Thor Heyerdahl, and the Frammuseet (Fram Museum), built around the sturdy vessel that carried Fridtjof Nansen and Roald Amundsen on their heroic polar explorations.

Norwegians seem happiest when they are in, on or around the sea. Each year, over a third of the population spend their summer holidays partly or completely in craft that

range from small dinghies to large motor launches and ocean-going yachts. Even the most conservative estimates place the number of pleasure craft in Norway at 650,000, about one for every seven Norwegians. The sea is a natural part of life.

Geography and topography are the deciding factors. There are thousands upon thousands of islands, and the fjords and coastal archipelagos are a paradise for competitive and recreational sailors, king and commoner alike.

King Olav V was the country's foremost sailor in more than name only. He won a Gold Medal in sailing in the 1928 Olympics, making him the world's only Olympic medallist monarch. He also won medals in the Sailing World Championships in 1971 and 1976.

In founding its first sailing club in 1868 in Tønsberg, then a major merchant fleet port, Norway triggered a long latent urge. In 1883 Den Kongelige Norske Seilforening (the Royal Norwegian Sailing Association) was formed in the capital, and in 1900 sailing became an Olympic sport. For years, Norwegians were a major force in Olympic and championship sailing and in regattas worldwide.

By chance, Norway's leading position in international sailing coincides approximately with the country's yacht production. In the days of wooden yachts, Norwegian yards and naval architects were among the world's best, and Colin Archer (1832–1921) stands out. Born in the port of Larvik, Archer grew up with boats and at an early age started building craft to his own design. Among his best known are the stable, sturdy rescue schooners that bear his name and the three-masted Arctic exploration vessel *Fram*, built in 1892. The tradition of boat building continues to this day, albeit somewhat altered: fibreglass hulls and masts changed the picture completely. Nowadays, Norway exports motor cruisers and imports yachts.

Wherever there's water, there are all manner of motor and sailing craft. Small boat harbours in and near major cities, particularly Oslo, Kristiansand, Ålesund, Stavanger and Bergen, never fail to impress visitors by the numbers and types of crafts lying there. From wind-surfing in fjords to major regattas, Norwegians love being on the water. ❑

LEFT: relaxing after a day's sailing.

Map on page 278

years have linked the town's islands. **Mellemverftet**, once one of four shipyards in **Vågen**, is working again as a centre for preserving the craft of shipbuilding, carefully restoring the beautiful lines of traditional Norwegian boats.

Kristiansund consists of three islands. One of them is **Innlandet**, the oldest preserved part of the town with its first customs house (1660–1748), hospital, school and other buildings which are gradually being restored. Walk to the **Sjursvika** on the east side for a look at the old warehouses. These interesting parts of the harbour are being amalgamated into an emergent coastal culture centre, to tell the history of the maritime people of old, alongside harbour life that continues today.

The **Nordmøre Museum** (open all year; entrance fee) includes archaeological finds from the Fosna culture and the history of *klippfisk* processing. But the town's oddest monuments are the tall pointed natural stones, tributes to town dignitaries. Bäckström, who built the reservoirs, Brinchman, the provider of the water supply, Bræin, the musical founder of a musical family, which gave birth to an annual Opera Festival, and Hanson, the Polar explorer.

Kristiansund's main church was destroyed by bombing in 1940. The architect responsible for its replacement named his creation "Rock Crystal in Roses", and whether you love it or loathe it, you cannot ignore this stark, white building. Inside the **Atlanterhavskatedralen** (Atlantic Cathedral; open all year; free), the choir wall is a 30-metre (100-ft) sweep of 320 stained-glass panels which at the foot symbolise the heavy, dark colours of the earth soaring up to eternal light.

"Fishwife", next to the harbour in Kristiansund.

BELOW: fishing for trout or salmon is a popular pastime in the country.

Island excursions

An entirely different church stands on the island of **Grip**, not far from Kristiansund. The island has a long and eventful history of flood and storm, and the islanders often took refuge in the small church. In 1796, a nor'wester tore down and washed away 100 houses and, when the same thing happened seven years later, the pastor recorded the piteous prayer: "Almighty God, spare us further destruction and misery". Whether it was that plea or not, the ancient little red stave church survived, only 8 metres (25 ft) above the sea. Once 400 souls lived on Grip, scraping a living from fish: today people live there only in summer when it metamorphoses into a holiday island and makes a popular excursion from the town. A wedding in the 15th-century church is a very special occasion.

To the north and northeast of Kristiansund, the last big island is **Smøla** ⑰ at the mouth of the Trondheimfjord, where the county ends in a gaggle of islands which retain something of the life of the old farmer-fishermen.

Sanden is one of several buildings that form Smøla's scattered museum, with the main 18th-century building, warehouses, barn and a store house on wooden pillars, just as it was when the last owners left a few years ago. A few of these old fishing grounds where cod was split, salted and dried on the rocks are now marinas with simple accommodation, seafood menus, and the atmosphere of earlier days. The idyllic island of **Kuli** off-

Map on page 278

Smøla is rich in relics, the most famous being the Kuli stone. On this stone the name Norway is mentioned for the first time in an inscription which dates to the first years after the coming of Christianity.

Land of the trolls

Inland, the northern part of the county ends in a criss-cross of fjords eating into the islands and peninsulas which lead to **Trollheimen**, the "Home of the Trolls", where the mountains reach nearly 1,600 metres (5,000 ft). This haunt of climbers and skiers is bounded by two important valleys, **Surnadalen** and **Sunndalen**, with between them the tiny **Todalfjorden**. Beside the last is the surprise of the **Svinvik Arboret** ⑱ (Arboretum; open May–Sept; entrance fee), beautiful gardens with thousands of rhododendrons, conifers and other plants. Despite the northern latitude, plants from all over the world grow at Svinvik, owned and run today by the University of Trondheim.

On the way to Sunndalen along Road 70 from Kristiansund, you come to **Tingvoll** ⑲, which has Nordmøre's oldest church, popularly known as the **Nordmøresdomen** (Nordmøre Cathedral; open Jun–Aug; entrance fee), in an area with a surprisingly large selection of churches from different centuries and styles. The Tingvoll church is believed to date from the 12th century and is a well preserved granite and brick structure surrounded by a stone wall with an arched entrance way.

Sunndalen is deep in the Nordmøre wilderness, with narrow valleys between the mountain ranges forming sheltered farming country which supplies grain for most of the county. At the end of the fjord, lies the industrial town of Sunndalsøra, once a mecca for the British "Salmon Lords": the **Leikvin Kulturminnepark** (Heritage Park; open May–Oct; entrance fee) at Grøa records their privileged position in society up to the end of the 19th century. The river Driva debouches into the fjord and the surrounding mountains are of breathtaking beauty – a magnificent area for walking, skiing as well as fishing.

Road 70 follows the course of the valley to Oppdal on the third side of Trollheimen. On foot, there are more energetic routes over the mountains, with a mountain centre in Innerdalen and ski lifts as well. The **River Driva** is one of the most famous in a country of good salmon and trout rivers. Between the head of Sunndalen and Grødalen, next-door at Åmotan, the spectacular **Jenstadjuvet** ⑳ (gorge) is the place where five valleys and their watercourses meet in two furious waterfalls. Grødalen has an oddity in **Alfheim**, a small hunting lodge from 1876 built in Scottish Highland style by a Scot, Lady Arbuthnott, who became something of the "laird" of the valley. Her old farm at Elverhøy is now the **Sunndal Museum** (open May–Sept; entrance fee).

Surnadal has another good salmon river, the **Surna**; side valleys lead up to the heart of Trollheimen, and to signposted trails from mountain hut to mountain hut, in what seems like the top of the world. At valley level, the road through Surnadal is the inland route out of West Norway, straight on to the city of Trondheim, the gateway to the north. ❏

BELOW: in autumn, mountains and forests are bright with berries.
RIGHT: De Syr Søstre (Seven Sisters), Geirangerfjorden.

TRONDHEIM

Map on page 292

Although the city has lost its political role, to many Norwegians it remains the country's historical, cultural and religious capital, and is host to the annual celebrations of its patron saint, St Olav

A thousand years ago, Trondheim, then Nidaros, was the capital of Norway, and the resting place of King Olav Haraldson. Founded in 997 by King Olav Tryggvason, a reminder of Trondheim's early days and of the old harbour is provided by the **wharves** and the narrow streets (*veitene*) which run between the wooden buildings. Though they date back only to the 18th century, these coloured warehouses echo the architecture of medieval times and it is not too difficult to feel what the atmosphere must have been around that busy harbour when fish and timber dominated the city.

Today, Trondheim is the home of SINTEF, Scandinavia's largest foundation for scientific and industrial research, and is at the forefront of Norwegian education and church affairs. Not far from SINTEF is the Norwegian University of Science and Technology (NTNU), the country's second largest university. The city has been a scientific centre since the 18th century – the **university museum**, from 1760, is Norway's oldest scientific institution – and today both SINTEF and the university attract high-tech businesses to Trondheim, with the advantage of being able to turn to the research establishments for help.

Modern though it may be, Trondheim has kept much of the charm of the past, with the heart of the old city lying on what is virtually an island between the **Nidelva** river and **Trondheimsfjorden**, joined only by a narrow neck of land to the west, once the western fort. One building that unites past and present is the **Nordenfjeldske Kunstindustrimuseum** (National Museum of Applied Art; open all year; entrance fee) on Munkegata.

Saint and martyr

Though King Olav Tryggvason had attempted to introduce Christianity to Norway in the late 10th century, many Norwegians still clung to their pagan gods, and it was only after the death of his successor, Olav Haraldson, at the Battle of Stiklestad some 30 years later (*see page 297*) that Christianity acquired a focal point in Norway. Olav's men buried him in sandy ground near the river but when miracles began to happen he was moved to the town's only church. Then, according to the sagas, a spring began to flow near his first grave and "men were healed of their ills by the waters". The king was declared a saint and martyr.

His nephew, Olav Kyrre, built the great stone church over the place where the saint's body had lain which is now **Nidarosdomen** (Cathedral; open all year; entrance fee) and Trondheim's finest building. Once again, the saint's body was moved and the cathedral became a place of pilgrimage. For centuries, pilgrims came from the south of Norway, from Sweden and Finland, and from Iceland, the Faro Islands

PRECEDING PAGES:
Trøndelag countryside in autumn.
LEFT: gutting the catch.
BELOW: looking out over the city to Trondheimsfjorden.

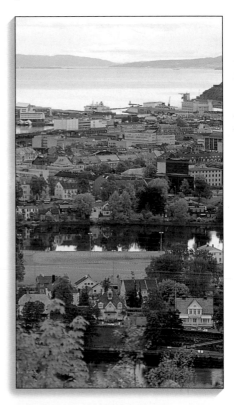

and Greenland to pay homage to St Olav. When the Reformation came to Norway in 1537, the cult of the ancient relic was abolished and pilgrimages to Nidaros ceased.

Royal tradition

Until the Reformation, Nidaros Cathedral was the seat of the archbishop, and the setting for the coronation of Norwegian monarchs, a tradition revived after 1814, when Norway shrugged off its 400 years of Danish rule and united with Sweden. In 1991 King Harald V was also crowned in Nidaros Cathedral which pleased the monarchists no end. In 1988 the Norwegian **crown jewels** were placed in the cathedral in a special ceremony and the modest but beautiful regalia for King, Queen and Crown Prince are now on display in a side chapel.

The **great arched nave** is in a Gothic style and, looking back to the west end, the most striking feature is the brilliant stained-glass **rose window** above the main entrance, the work of Gabriel Kjelland in 1930. Both inside and out are many statues of saints and monarchs; but the beautiful interior lines of the cathedral, built in a green-grey soapstone, are its finest feature and do not call for over-ornamentation.

Next door to the cathedral is Scandinavia's oldest secular building, once the **Erkebispegården** ❶ (Archbishop's Palace; open all year; entrance fee), later the residence of the Danish governors, and eventually a military establishment. The oldest part is used for official receptions, and the palace includes the **Rustkammeret** (open Jun–Aug, weekends out of season; entrance fee), an army museum which includes exhibits on World War II and the resistance movement. Nearby is **Waisenhuset**, a beautiful timber building from 1722.

In 1997, the old pilgrim routes from the south of Norway and Sweden to Nidaros Cathedral were reopened as part of the city's 1,000th anniversary. So far, the Prosjekt Pilegrimsleden (Pilgrim Way Project; tel: 22 11 19 05) has marked routes from Oslo and the Swedish border east of Trondheim, with more planned.

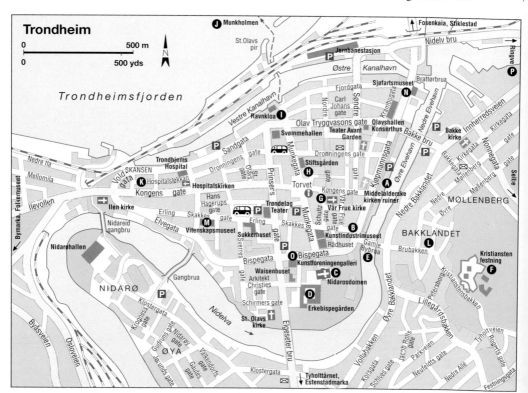

All around the original medieval city are the remains of fortifications, which were reinforced or built in the late 17th century by a military architect from Luxemburg, General Johan Caspar de Cicignon, after the great fire of 1681 devastated most of medieval Trondheim.

From the cathedral area it is just a short walk to **Gamle Bybrua** – the old town bridge – also erected after 1681 when de Cicignon was constructing **Kristiansten festning** (Kristiansten Fort) on a hill to the east, at that time outside the city proper. The first bridge had a sentry box and excise house at either end and the western building still remains, now used as a kindergarten. The present bridge and gates were built in 1861. **Trondheim Aktivum** (the local tourist office; tel: 73 92 94 02) organises guided tours to these sites.

View over the city

Kristiansten Fort, now part of the city, provides one of the best views of Trondheim, spread out below like a map. From here you can see the old stone walls of the 13th-century **Vår Frue kirke** (Church of Our Lady; open Jun–Aug, Tues–Fri; free) and **Stiftsgården** (open Jun–Aug, closed Mon; entrance fee), Scandinavia's largest timber mansion which was built as a private house in the 1770s. Today it is the official residence of the Norwegian Royal Family when visiting the city. Both church and residence are near the main city square, **Torvet**, on **Munkegata**, which looks up to the cathedral.

Further away, and not far from the bustle of the **Ravnkloa** at the lower end of Munkegate and past the ornate railway station, is **Fosenkaia**, where sightseeing and other boats tie up. At midday, the Hurtigrute coastal express will be lying at one of the two main quays, with a half-day to spend in Trondheim

Gamle Bybro (Old Town Bridge) offers good views of the warehouses along Kjøpmannsgate.

BELOW: colourful old buildings along Trondheim's waterfront.

before it heads north. Returning south on a summer evening, the ship is outlined against the late sun as its passengers make an excursion to see the midnight sun from the summit of **Mount Storsteinen**. The remains of Trondheim's old defences, **Skansen**, lie to the west where the city gate once stood. Skansen is now a park. Also near the harbour is a curious warehouse built out on iron stilts over the sea; its shape is explained by the fact that it was a World War II U-boat bunker when German forces occupied the city.

Well out into the fjord is the islet of **Munkholmen ❶** (hourly ferry from Ravnkloa; open May–Aug; entrance fee) where Benedictine monks built a monastery very early in the 11th century, one of the first two monasteries in Norway. Even earlier this had been Trondheim's execution ground and in 1658 it became a prison fort. You can make a tour of the fort and the island offers good sea bathing and a restaurant.

St Olav.

Walking around

Trondheim is an easy walking city where many people still live in the centre. Two places best toured on foot are **Hospitalsløkkan ❿**, the area around the old Trondheim Hospital, and **Bakklandet ❶**, on the eastern side of the Nidelva, not far from the old town bridge and opposite the riverside warehouses.

In the grounds of the hospital, which was founded in 1277 and is Scandinavia's oldest surviving hospital, lies the first **octagonal timber church** (1705) to be built in Norway. The surrounding area is full of typical old timber houses, lovingly restored by their present owners. Bakklandet is another area of old wooden houses, and was originally the working-class section of the town. It and the Mollenberg and Rosenborg districts, were restored relatively recently as complete communities of houses and shops.

BELOW: a good way to get around the city in the snow is by *sparkstotting* (kick-sledge).

Looking into the past

For an understanding of the past of this ancient area of Trøndelag, two museums are invaluable. At the **Vitenskapsmuseet ⓜ** (Museum of Natural History and Archaeology; open Jun–Aug, Sundays only out of season; entrance fee), the main exhibits trace the history of the area up to the Middle Ages and the development of church art from the 13th to the 18th century. There is also a natural history display covering Trøndelag flora and fauna. **Sjøfartsmuseet ⓝ** (Maritime Museum; open Jun–Aug, closed Sat during Sept–Dec; entrance fee), situated in an old penitentiary from 1725, covers shipping, fishing and whaling.

Folkemuseet (Buses 8, 9 from Dronningensgate; open May–Aug, Sun only Sept–Dec; entrance fee.) in Sverresborg, on the west side of the city, looks at rural life in days gone by. There are old tools used to scrape a meagre living, a ski museum and recollections of old trades and crafts, such as the *passementerie* which made trimmings and lace for women's Sunday best. Within the museum are the remains of King Sverre's palace, **Sion**, from around 1180, and the 18th-century tavern has a good restaurant.

With all the "oldests" and "firsts", it is no surprise that Trondheim has Norway's oldest theatre building, **Trøndelag Teater** in the centre of the old town, as well as **Teater Avant Garden**. Other arts are represented by institutions, galleries and centres such as the **Trøndelag Kunstforeningengallerei**  (Academy of Art; open all year; entrance fee), galleries showing and selling contemporary paintings, the Trondheim Symphony Orchestra and, almost more interesting than anything else, the **Ringve Museum** (Museum of Musical History at **Ringve** ❷; buses 3, 4 from Munkegaten; open May–Sept, Sun only out of season; entrance fee).

The Ringve museum is near the Lade district to the northeast, an ancient manor still run as a farm. Since the late 19th century, it belonged to the Bache family. In 1946, the last representative, Christian Anker Bache died and his widow, Russian-born "Madame Victoria", worked steadily to build up the couple's collection of musical instruments from all over the world. Her persuasiveness in prising relics from many countries is legendary and when the museum opened in 1952 the collection had grown magnificently.

Madame Victoria decreed a living museum; almost all the instruments in the beautiful rooms of the main building can be, and are, played by the music-student guides during the tour. In addition to the more formal, classical instruments, there are examples of music boxes, old folk instruments such as the *langeleik*, a sort of Norwegian zither, and clay flutes shaped like birds and soldiers, which delight children.

Just before her death in 1962, Madame Victoria opened the museum's concert hall, which can seat 350; it was built into the old cow sheds and is used for more formal musical occasions. After the museum, leave time for a stroll around the **Ringve Botaniske Hage** (Botanic Gardens; open every day; free), just next door, and the most northerly botanical garden in the world.

The Ravnkloa clock down by the fish market.

BELOW: Trondheim is a major stop for the Hurtigrute coastal steamers.

Map on page 292

TIP

For a bird's-eye view of the city from the 120-m (400-ft) telecommunications Tyholttårnet (tower; open all year; entrance fee) take buses 20 or 60. There is also a revolving restaurant.

BELOW: an old view of Stiklestad by Johannes Flintoe for an 1839 edition of the *Norse Sagas*.

Outdoor life

As with all Norwegian cities, it doesn't take long to escape to the great outdoors. Trondheim's back garden is **Bymarka** to the west, where Gråkallen (Old Man) at some 520 metres (1,700 ft) is the city's favourite skiing area. In summer, it is a good spot for walking. Its counterpart to the east is **Estenstadmarka**.

Fishing is good in the River Nidelva, which is renowned for the size of its salmon. The Gaula to the south is another fine fishing river, while the fjord itself is ideal for sea-fishing from boat or shore.

As well as the hourly boats to Munksholmen, in summer the tourist office runs two-hour tours of Trondheim from the sea, which leave from Ravnkloa; there is also a half-day tour to the 17th-century manor and gardens at **Austråtborgen** (open May–Aug; entrance fee) at Ørland on Trondheimsfjorden, which includes a catamaran tour along the fjord to Brekstad, a tour of the castle and coffee and waffles to finish. Another idea is to take a short leg of the Hurtigrute and return by coach or train.

Alternatively, you can travel southeast to the **Strikkemuseum** (Knitting Museum; open all year; entrance fee) at Selbu, which shows the history of the famous Selbu knitwear from 1853. Road 705 to Selbu features a particularly scenic route marketed as **Ferieveien** ("holiday road"; tel: 72 49 63 44 for details) and the trip to the museum can easily be combined with a cruise on Selbusjøen.

But for most people Trondheim means history and culture. Like the pilgrims of old, visitors come to see the cathedral, the Archbishop's Palace and de Cicignon's 17th-century city, and for historical events such as the annual 10-day **St Olav festival**, known as Olsok (Olav) Days, centred around 29 July, the anniversary of the Battle of Stiklestad. ❏

Stiklestad

Stiklestad is a name which means nothing to the majority of visitors to Norway but it is known and revered by Norwegians. The ancient battlefield is a milestone in Norwegian history and a church marks the spot where King Olav Haraldson died. For Stiklestad, north of Trondheim, saw the foundation of Norwegian national unity and the adoption of the Christian faith.

In the 11th century Norway was a country constantly disrupted by disputes between rival chieftains, and Olav's ambition was a united Norway. He also aimed to create a Christian country with Christian laws and churches and clergy.

He was not the first to attempt this. In the previous century Olav Tryggvason (a descendant of Harald Hårfagre) had been converted to Christianity in England and confirmed by the Bishop of Winchester. He returned to his native land in 995 with the express purpose of crushing the chieftains and imposing his new-found faith. But Olav Tryggvason's conversion had not swept away all his Viking instincts and in his religious zeal he used great cruelty to convert the populace. As a result, he fell in the Battle of Svolder in the year 1000, due to the defection of some disenchanted Norwegian chieftains.

Olav Haraldson was also a descendant of Harald Hårfagre and he ascended the throne in 1015. But, like his predecessor, Olav foolishly made too great a use of the sword to establish Christianity. The result was the same: with his eye on the Norwegian throne, King Canute of Denmark and England gave support to discontented factions within the country and in 1028 invaded Norway, forcing King Olav to flee to Russia.

Undaunted, King Olav returned with a few followers but whatever loyalty he had once inspired had been lost through his ruthless methods. He died on 29 July 1030 at the Battle of Stiklestad. Olav's corpse was taken to the then capital, Nidaros, and buried on the banks of the river Nidelva. When the body was disinterred a year later, it showed no signs of corruption: his face was unchanged and his nails and hair had grown, at that time taken as a sign of sanctity.

Following this revelation, Olav was proclaimed a saint and his body placed in a silver shrine in Nidaros Cathedral. Faith in the holiness of King Olav – or St Olav as he now was – spread and, until the Reformation, his shrine became a goal of Christian pilgrims.

Canute's triumph at the Battle of Stiklestad was but brief. He ceded the reins of power to his son Svejn but, as the rumours of Olav's sanctity grew, popular support for Canute evaporated rapidly and Svejn was exiled to Denmark in 1035. All the while, St Olav's son, Magnus, had also been in exile in Russia, but Norway now invited him to return and accept the crown.

From that time, Stiklestad has been a place of steady pilgrimage. They still come at the end of July to commemorate the battle. Stiklestad now also has a beautiful open-air theatre, and on the anniversary of the battle, a cast of over 300 – actors, choristers, dancers and musicians – re-enact the events of July 1030. ❑

RIGHT: a statue of St Olav in front of the Stiklestad open-air theatre.

Map on page 302

NORTH, INTO THE ARCTIC

*North of Trondheim lies a beautiful but often harsh landscape,
caught between the warm sea and the mountains inland, and cutting
across it an imaginary border into the vast expanse of the Arctic*

T he city of Trondheim is a marker on the map of Norway, the gateway to the north. But anyone who looks for an immediate change in scenery will be disappointed. The first county north of Trondheim, Nord Trøndelag, has wide areas of rich agricultural land with prosperous-looking farms.

Running right up the middle of the county is Norway's north – south jugular, the E6 highway, which lures a driver ever further north. But this is also rail country, and the Nordland railway follows much the same route. Just north of Trondheim, a branch line (with a companion road) reaches over the border into Sweden. It veers off at the small village of **Hell**, whose station must be one of the most photographed in the country and whose tickets are collectors' items.

From a motorist's point of view, there is not a great deal of interest along this section of the E6 and the inclination is to keep going north; but make time for **Værnes** ❶, which has an interesting church from the Middle Ages with a fine Baroque pulpit. Adjoining that is the **Stjørdal open-air museum** (open June–Aug, weekends only May–Sept; entrance fee). The **Frostatinghaugen rock carvings** at Frosta is the site of the first Norwegian legislative assembly (AD 600–1000) with rock carvings going back a further 3,500 years.

Six kilometres (4 miles) east of Stjørdalshalsen on the E14 heading towards Sweden is the **Falstad Museum** (open Jun–Aug; entrance fee) at Levanger. Located in the main building of Norway's only SS concentration camp, the museum includes two execution sites and a cenotaph in the Falstad forest. Four kilometres (2½ miles) further on lies **Hegra Festning** (Fort; open May-Oct; entrance fee). Built following independence, it was the site of several tough battles during World War II as well as a 25-day German siege. The fort has been restored, with guns in place, and includes the obligatory Resistance museum.

St Olav's battleground

Just north of Verdalsøra is the road to **Stiklestad** ❷, the battleground where King Olav Haraldson was killed in 1030, and revered by Norwegians as the birthplace of Norwegian national unity (*see page 297*). It is near here that the **Nasjonale Kultursenter** (National Arts Centre; open all year; entrance fee) in Verdal produces the annual open-air play about St Olav (late Jun; two hours long; entrance fee), a spectacular dramatisation of the battle and Olav's death. The centre also has exhibitions about local natural and cultural history, and includes a Resistance museum, a folk museum and Stiklestad Church from 1180.

The first town of any size north of Trondheim is **Steinkjer**, which has been a centre of commerce for more than 1,000 years. Like so many northern Nor-

PRECEDING PAGES:
Arctic reflections.
LEFT: the turbulent waters of the giant maelstrom south of Bodø.
BELOW: a favourite subject for English-speaking photographers.

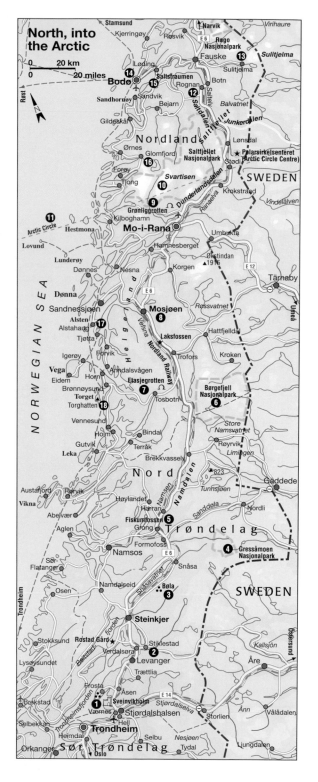

North, into the Arctic

wegian towns, Steinkjer was destroyed in World War II. After the German invasion in 1940, the king and government moved north, eventually to Tromsø, before they left to continue the government in exile from London. This meant that these sparsely populated northern areas suffered dreadful destruction through the bombing which followed the German invasion.

The Nord Trøndelag county museum has two branches near the town, one of which is sited in the former factory of **Dampsaga** (open all year; entrance fee) and features some works by the Norwegian painter Jacob Weidemann (born 1923), who also decorated Steinkjer church with murals and a beautiful stained-glass window.

North of Steinkjer it is worth branching off the E6 onto Road 763, which runs along the eastern side of Snåsavatnet (lake), to take a look at the impressive rock carvings near **Bøla** ❸ (open May–Oct; free). Of these, the best is the 6,000-year-old Bøla reindeer. The scenery around the lake is remarkably soft and gentle for a latitude between 63 and 64 degrees north, and at its northern end is **Snåsa**, the centre of South Sami (Lapp) culture. It has a Sami school and cultural centre which includes a museum (open Jun-Aug; entrance fee).

To the east, about 50 km (30 miles) away and close to Sweden, the **Gressåmoen Nasjonalpark** ❹ (National Park) contains an area of typically thick Trøndelag forest and mountain landscape.

Dotted throughout Norway – and particularly in the north – are small towns or villages which are essentially crossroads for many forms of transport. Typical is Grong, where the E6 runs north – south and the road and railway to Namsos on the coast goes off to the west, while just south of the town a secondary road runs east through wild countryside to the Swedish frontier at Gæddede. It is also the junction of two rivers, the Namsen and the Sanddøla, both popular with anglers. Each river has an impressive waterfall not far from

Grong: **Fiskumfossen** on the Namsen and **Formofossen** on the Sandøla. You can learn all there is to know about salmon at the **Namsen Akvariet** (Aquarium; open Jun–Aug; entrance fee) at Fiskumfossen.

Map on page 302

Touched by the Gulf Stream

This is the beginning of the long valley of **Namdalen**, while to the northeast is **Røyrvik**, a huge mountainous area which stretches to the Swedish frontier. Half this region is above the tree line and there are three major lakes: Tunnsjøen, Limingen and Store Namsvatnet. The first has an island peak soaring to 820 metres (2,700 ft), and was once a Sami place of sacrifice to their gods.

The Bøla reindeer.

Here the contrast between the east and west of Nord Trøndelag is very marked. The frontier mountains to the east, which bulge into Sweden, have a harsh beauty but much of the land is desolate and empty. To the west, the coastal scenery is a pleasant surprise, green and fertile. All year round, the Gulf Stream warms the western coast to the very north of Norway, making the climate much gentler at the same latitude than it is further inland and allowing the Hurtigruten (coastal steamers) to continue working even in the depths of winter.

The north end of Namdalen valley marks the border with the county of **Nordland**, the beginning of the real north. This border is straddled by the **Børgefjell Nasjonalpark** (National Park), a district of high mountains, lakes and numerous watercourses, a backpacker's idyll for walking and to see nature.

In these northern territories, distances are long, and Nordland stretches 500 km (300 miles) north to Narvik. The Polarsirkel (Arctic Circle) runs through the middle and the county includes the long, narrow islands of Vesterålen, and the grey peaks of the Lofoten Islands (*see The Far North, pages 315–18*). Nordland

BELOW: a picnic on the coast by the light of the midnight sun.

has immense variety. If you take in all the fjords and islands, it contains a quarter of Norway's coastline, as well as mountains of over 1,900 metres (6,000 ft), countless islands and skerries, the second largest glacier in Norway, Svartisen, and the largest inland lake, Røssvatnet.

Near the Helgeland coast is **Bindalen** (valley), green with forests. At one time, the discovery of gold turned it into a mini-Klondike. Today, it has gone back to sleep. Close to Bindal, on the side of the fjord that bears its name, is the mountain massif of **Tosenfjellet**, a favourite haunt of potholers and cavers. The biggest cave is **Etasjegrotten** ❼, which is 1,400 metres long, where cavers have discovered an underground lake.

Between Trofors and Mosjøen on the E6, is the wide but shallow **Laksfossen** (waterfall) which has a 16-metre (50-ft) drop. At **Mosjøen** ❽, an industrial town where a splendid location fights for domination with a large aluminium works, there is **Dolstad** church, built in 1734 and the oldest octagonal church in north Norway. Look closely at the traces of the old ornamental decor and at a wooden angel in the ceiling which is lowered for use as a baptismal font. Near the church is the **Vefsn open-air museum** (open Jun–Aug; entrance fee). Founded in 1909, it brings together 12 buildings from the surrounding district and a collection of some 5,000 objects from the olds days of farming, fishing, hunting and domestic life. There is one old area of the town where some wooden houses and warehouses have been preserved and restored.

Last stop before the Arctic

Beyond the town the scenery changes as farmland gives way to bare *fjells*. There are camping sites with tents and cabins on both sides of the road north to cater for the outdoor holidaymakers who especially love these northern regions. **Mo i Rana** is also on a fjord and, like Mosjøen, is dominated by industry – in this case, the steelworks of Norsk Jernverk. These industries in small remote towns may displease the casual visitor but they illustrate a Norwegian determination to minimise the pull of the more populated south and to help people to find work locally.

Though Mo i Rana itself may be too modern for a visitor's taste, it is within reasonable distance of several "musts" on the list of many visitors to Norway – caves, a glacier and the Polarsirkel (Arctic Circle). The **Grønligrotten** ❾, (caves; open Jun–Aug; entrance fee) lie about 20 km (13 miles) north of the town and guides shepherd parties through a glittering underground world of stalactite-hung caverns. At **Sætergrotten**, the cave calls for care and is more suitable for enthusiasts, with unexplored caves, crevices and passages, and interiors of marble and limestone.

From Mo i Rana, it is also easy to reach Norway's second largest glacier, **Svartisen** ❿ which covers 370 sq. km (140 sq. miles) with ice up to 100 metres (330 ft) thick in places. Its is also the lowest-lying glacier on the European mainland, reaching down to within 170 metres (565 ft) of sea level. The route lies off the E6 just north of Mo i Rana, which heads northwest to Svartisvatnet. You then cross the water by boat, and walk about 3 km (2 miles) to the glacier.

TIP

The best time to see Norwegian waterfalls is in late May, or even June this far north, when summer creeps northwards melting the snow and ice to swell the rivers.

BELOW: on the edge of the glacier.

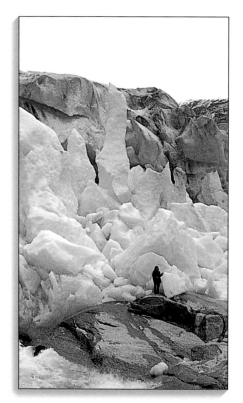

Crossing the line

Many try but few have managed to explain why it should be so exciting to cross a line you cannot see. But most people experience an inexplicable thrill and sense of achievement as they cross the **Polarsirkel ⓫** (Arctic Circle). It seems to mark the end of modern comforts and the beginning of the wild north, and nowhere is that sense of entering the unknown stronger than on highway E6 on its long trek north.

From Mo i Rana, the road makes its way through the temperate landscape of Dunderlandsdalen, past Storsforshei iron ore mine. Then, beyond Krokstrand, the scenery begins to change as the road approaches **Saltfjellet**, a wild and majestic mountain valley flanked by bare, brooding mountains. Apart from the road, railway line and river, there is nothing else until you come to the monuments that mark the Arctic Circle. Alongside the official markers are numerous small stone cairns erected by visitors who felt a common need to mark the event. A short visit to the architecturally pleasing **Polarsirkelsenteret** (Arctic Circle Centre; open May–Sept; free) is a good way of celebrating the moment. The centre provides information on the flora and fauna, the climate and Sami culture – and also sells souvenirs. Nature, it would seem, cannot be left to its own devices.

There is a darker and sadder side to this area, which dates back to World War II when thousands of prisoners of war, mainly Yugoslavs, were used to build the railway. Many perished in the bitter winter conditions, and their memorial stands in the wild mountains where they worked and died.

The summit of the Saltfjell road, at **Stødi**, is 700 metres (2,300 ft) high and these mountains also mark the limit for most temperate flora and fauna, though

Map on page 302

BELOW: reindeer have right of way on the roads.

a few brave exceptions survive. As the road begins to descend, first the trees re-appear at Lønsdal and then, as it races down towards sea level at Rognan, the vegetation becomes lush and abundant but flanked by impressive mountains on either side. About half-way down, a short detour to the right and a steep climb to **Junkerdalen** takes you to the "silver road", a historic route from Skellefteå on the Gulf of Bothnia in Sweden, to Bodø. This dramatic mountain scenery also leads to a unique botanical phenomenon. A bedrock of mica, which provides exceptional growing conditions, has led to a profusion of rare plants such as cyclamens, usually found only in lowland or more temperate regions. Nowhere else can you find similar growth at this height and nearly 67° north.

At **Rognan** ⑫, the **Saltdal Museum** (open all year; entrance fee) has been upgraded from the inevitable local museum to include the ominously named **Blodveimuseet** (Blood Road Museum), the only museum in Norway dedicated to the prisoners of war. The 1,657 Yugoslav and Russian prisoners who died here in World War II are buried in a cemetery a little further north at **Botn**. Though these prisoners slaved to build a road and not a railway, the result was the same and the stretch between Rognan to Fauske earned the name of the "blood road". In another cemetery nearby, 2,700 German soldiers are buried and a plaque commemorates the 2,000 who died in the battle cruiser *Scharnhorst*, sunk off Nordkapp (North Cape) in 1943.

Copper, silver and gold

Fauske, on the Skjerstadfjorden, is another crossroads town. The ever-present E6 goes north to south, while another road (No. 830) disappears east towards the mountains. It stops at **Sulitjelma** ⑬, which owes its existence to the discovery

The area around Fauske provides the unique reddish marble known as Norwegian Rose, which has been used to decorate major buildings all over the world including the United Nations building in New York.

BELOW: a herd of wild reindeer in Nord Trøndelag.

of copper by a Sami in 1858. The mines go down to 400 metres (1,300 ft) and produced half a million tonnes of ore a year. Copper pyrites, sphalerite and iron pyrites were extracted from the ore, plus a useful haul of silver and gold.

For many years, a railway was the only link between Sulitjelma and the outside world, but when that closed the road was built over the former trackbed. The wild and desolate mountain scenery of this remote area is dominated by the **Sulitjelma glacier**. Scenery like this and the mining museum (open Jun–Aug; entrance fee) at Sulitjelma make a detour worthwhile, and there is tourist accommodation and a camping site.

In this narrow part of Norway – and even more so as the road heads north – you are never far from either the sea or the Swedish border. At Fauske, midway between both, Road 80 and the railway turn west and run along the north of the fjord to Bodø, on the west coast.

End of the line

Bodø is another marker along the way to the far north. Like many of the coastal towns, it began as a small community, a safe place for boats and fishermen, and stayed small until the 1860s, when three changes brought prosperity: the herring fisheries developed fast, the Sulitjelma mines started production, and the first coastal steamer service began to link the towns of the west coast. It, too, was largely laid waste in attacks by German forces in May 1940 and today it is a spacious modern town with a population of around 32,000.

Bodø is the commercial and administrative centre. It is also a staging post for summer visitors, the end of the Nordland railway line, where the backpackers get down and continue north by coastal steamer or bus. The town is home to the

Map on page 302

The winter colours of the Arctic fox stand out against the summer landscape.

BELOW: sunset over the Sulitjelma mountains.

Among the planes on display at Bodø's Norsk Luftfartssenter (Norwegian Aviation Centre) is a British Spitfire and an old American spy plane that was shot down over Russia.

Norsk Luftfartssenter (Norwegian Aviation Centre; open all year; entrance fee), which includes a selection of planes, a flight simulator and even an old traffic control tower. Forty km (25 miles) to the north on the coast is the old trading centre at **Kjerringøy** (open Jun–Sept; entrance fee). Long overtaken by Bodø, Kjerringøy was one of the richest trading settlements in northern Norway in the 19th century. It has 15 preserved buildings, all with their furnishings, and some typical Nordland boats.

South, away from the E6

If you are travelling north by the E6, largely an inland route, when you reach Bodø again on your return journey, you might like to try another route south even thought it takes in innumerable ferry crossings. Road 17 starts by bridging the **Saltstraumen** , where the combination of powerful currents and a narrow channel twice a day creates a vast rush of water, and violent "kettles" or whirlpools. This is the most powerful maelstrom in Norway, some 370 million cubic metres (480 million cubic yards) of water pour through the sound which is less than 15 metres (50 ft) wide, at a rate of up to 28 knots. Saltstraumen is a joy to anglers and seabirds alike, as the current brings an abundance of fish. Nearby is the **Saltstaumen Opplevelsessenter** (Experience Centre; open May–Oct; entrance fee) which explains the phenomenon in depth.

The road follows coast and fjord on its way south, and passes **Våg** on the island of Sandhornøy, and **Blixgård** (manor house; open Jun–Aug; entrance fee) which has a memorial to the poet Elias Blix, who composed North Norway's national anthem *Å eg veit meg eit land*, (Oh, I know of a land).

At **Glomfjord** a chair-lift gives wonderful views and you can also reach

BELOW: puffins are very common on the northern coasts.

an arm of the Svartisen glacier. However, it is better to keep to Road 17 which goes through a major tunnel under the outer edge of the glacier and comes out alongside Nordfjorden, cross the Holandsfjorden and then walk to the base of the glacier.

Four ferries later, the road reaches **Sandnessjøen**, on the northern tip of the island of **Alsten**, a trading centre for more than 300 years. **Alstahaug** on the southern point has a 12th-century church and memorial stone to the parson-poet Petter Dass who lived there from 1689 until his death in 1708. Dass was so well known that, after his death, most Norwegian ships carried a black patch on their sails as a badge of mourning, a practice that continued for more than 100 years. Today, his life and work are commemorated by a biennial event organised by the **Petter Dass Museum** (open Jun–Aug; entrance fee) at Alstahaug.

A short ferry crossing takes you to the island of **Dønna**, where **Dønna Manor** has been an estate from saga times until the present day. The 13th-century stone church has secret passages cut into the walls which revealed a hoard of coins, some dating back to the time of King Håkon Håkonsson (1204–63).

On the eastern side of Alsten is a mountain range with seven peaks known as **De Syv Søstre** (The Seven Sisters). South of Sandnessjøen is **Tjøtta** which was the home of Hårek, one of the chieftains who killed King Olav at Stiklestad.

Map
on page
302

This entire area is full of burial mounds and monoliths. There is a cemetery for 7,500 Russian prisoners of war, and even more heart-rending is the **Riegel cemetery** which has the graves of over 1,000 of nearly 3,000 Russians, Germans, Poles, Czechs and Norwegians. They died when *Riegel* was sunk in 1945 outside Tjøtta, destroyed by Allied aircraft unaware of its human cargo.

Old hat

Further south near Brønnøysund and after two more ferry crossings, is another strange natural phenomenon. The high hat-shaped peak of **Torghatten** ⓲ is pierced 160 metres (520 ft) up by a great hole more than 40 metres (130 ft) high. Legend has it that the hole was made by a horseman, thwarted in love, who shot an arrow at his lady, the Maid of Leka. Just in time, the mountain king of Sømnafjellet saw what was happening and threw his hat in the air to intercept the arrow. At that very moment the sun rose and all were transformed into stone. The Maid of Leka stands petrified on the island of **Leka**; Torghatten has its hole; and to the north is the island of Hestmona to represent the horseman. A more prosaic explanation lies in the action of frost and sea towards the end of the last Ice Age when the island was much lower than it is today. A small road takes you to Torghatten, from which it is a 30-minute scramble up to the hole.

The Brønnøysund area has some of the most fertile land and the largest farms in northern Norway. The island museum of Leka has many curiosities, including boats and fishing equipment. South of Leka is **Vikna**, linked to the mainland by a bridge over the Nærøysund, which, so the old legends relate, was the battleground of giants and trolls. After one more ferry, Road 17 deserts the coast and moves inland through Namsos until it joins the E6 just north of Steinkjer. ❑

BELOW: Bodø lit by the midnight sun.

LAND OF THE MIDNIGHT SUN

Some of Norway's most stunning natural wonders lie within the Arctic Circle and are a prime target for tourists visiting the north in summer

The phrase "Land of the Midnight Sun" was originally coined by the French American explorer Paul Belloni Du Chaillu (*c.* 1831–1903) who published a travelogue by the same title in 1881 after travelling extensively in northern Europe. The name caught on: more than 100 years later, tourists still flock to the North Cape every summer to experience this natural spectacle.

The Midnight Sun is the appearance of the sun above the horizon at midnight. The phenomenon is due to the inclination of the Earth's axis, and to the fact that the axis points in the same direction during the whole period of the Earth's yearly revolution around the Sun. It may be witnessed at any point on the Arctic Circle on 21 June or on the Antarctic Circle on 21 December. Within these circles the length of time the sun is in the sky without setting gradually increases, being 65 days at latitude 70° and 134 days at latitude 80°. For six months, the sun never sets at the poles.

WINTER DARKNESS

Of course, the down side to the phenomenon is that during the winter the Sun never appears above the horizon and thus all regions within the polar circles are plunged into darkness as they experience a long polar night. In Tromsø this period of darkness lasts from 27 November to 15 January, while the Midnight Sun can be seen from 20 May to 22 July. For the people of the north, the Midnight Sun is not so much a phenomenon as a way of life.

▷ **AURLANDSFJORD**
At the head of enchanting Aurlandsfjord is Flåm and the start of the 10-km (6-mile) mountain railway up to Myrdal.

◁ PREIKESTOLEN

Preikestolen (the Pulpit Rock) soars 280 metres (600 ft) above Lysefjord. The view stretches towards Stavanger and the fjords.

▽ GLACIER WANDERING

The Jostedal glacier is the largest glacier on the European continent. The ice can be up to 230 metres (500 ft) thick in parts.

▷ BRIKSDAL GLACIER

One of Jostedal's more famous side-arms is the Briksdal glacier, accessible from April to October. The glacier lies at the end of the beautiful Olden valley

▽ FOLGEFONN GLACIER

Near Sorfjord (below) is the Folgefonno glacier, 500 metres (1,650 ft) above sea level. The glacier is growing at a rate of 1.5 metres (6 ft) per day.

◁ WATER POWER

Norway's rapids and waterfalls are very important commercially: Norway is self-sufficient in electricity from hydropower. They also provide recreation opportunities for fishing, kayaking and white-water rafting.

THE NORTHERN LIGHTS

The Northern Lights, or *Aurora borealis*, are a huge natural light-show, filling the winter sky with patterns of light and colour. This remarkable phenomenon originates from electric particles sent out into space by the sun. These are drawn into the Earth's magnetic field where they collide with other particles in our atmosphere. The resulting electric charges give rise to the greenish patterns of light which dance across the night sky.

The Northern Lights Planetarium in Tromsø provides a more precise explanation. The sun has a number of holes in its corona from which high energy particles stream out. These particles are ejected into the solar system as solar wind, which meets the Earth's magnetosphere, compressing it on the daylight side, while drawing out the tail at night. The solar wind particles accelerate down to Earth again along the open magnetic fields of the polar regions. When the solar wind particles collide with air molecules their energy is transferred into light. These processes occurring simultaneously result in the Northern Lights.

THE FAR NORTH

*For many, the aim of travelling this far north is to visit Nordkapp,
Norway's northernmost tip; along the way you can go island-
hopping in the Lofotens or cross the expanse of the Finnmarksvidda*

Viewed from the mainland across the broad expanse of Vestfjorden, the
Lofoten Islands present an imposing wall of jagged peaks rising up sheer
from the sea. On the west these mountains form a mighty breakwater
from the onslaught of the Arctic Ocean, a 112-km (70-mile) archipelago which
stretches from the tiny island of Røst in the south to the waters of the narrow
Raftsundet in the north. In winter the coast is one of the stormiest in Europe
while the unsurpassed summer beauty of the islands makes them one of Norway's major tourist attractions.

Between the mountains, which are composed of some of the oldest rocks in
the world, are stretches of fertile farmland, fjords and deep ravines while the
coastline is sprinkled with fishing villages and one or two small towns.

A phenomenon peculiar to the Lofotens is the annual cod fishing which in the
past involved up to 6,000 boats and 30,000 fishermen. Between January and
March these migrant fishermen lived in simple waterside wooden cabins called
rorbuer. By 1947 the number of fishermen was declining and today it is down to
2,000, and this seasonal event has been replaced by a year-round fishing fleet.

Svolvær ❶, the main town, is on the island of Austvågøy and has been a
trading centre since the 17th century. Virtually surrounded by water, and confusing to the visitor on that account, it is flanked by
sharp, pointed rocky peaks. Some of these rise almost
straight up from the gardens and the town has its own
special mountain Svolværgeita (the Svolvær goat).

The town is connected to the mainland by ferry to
Skutvik, and by coastal steamer to Bodø. It, like the
Lofotens as a whole, has attracted many artists and
craftsmen and is now the site of the **Nordnorsk Kun-
stnersentrum** (North Norwegian Artists' Centre; open
all year; entrance fee). Scenes like those described
above are captured on canvas by local artist Dagfinn
Bakke who owns and runs a gallery here (open
May–Aug; free), while at nearby **Kabelvåg ❷** there
is an art school and an impressive wooden church
which looks old but was in fact built in 1898.

Payment in fish

On the outskirts of Kabelvåg is the **Lofotmuseet**
(Lofotens Museum; open May–Aug; entrance fee)
sited where Vågar, the first town north of the Polarsirkel (Arctic Circle), existed in the Middle Ages. The
main museum building was originally in the centre of
the thriving fishing community and one room is furnished as a fish station owner's office from the 1880s.
He would own all the *rorbuer* and the fishermen who
rented them would pay in fish from their catches.
There is a typical *rorbu* from 1789, with its primitive
and crowded living conditions, and a boathouse with

PRECEDING PAGES:
Røst in the Lofoten.
LEFT: small boats
and *rorbuer* (old
fishing cottages) in
Stamsund.
BELOW: island
fisherman.

Many of the old rorbuer on the Lofotens have been restored and fitted with modern conveniences and are now rented out to summer visitors.

three traditional boats of various sizes. Another building is devoted to the development of the Lofoten fishing industry which in its modernised form plays a vital role in the economy of the islands.

Kabelvåg gained a new attraction in 1989 with the opening of the **Lofoten Akvariet** (Aquarium; open all year; entrance fee), which is designed as a small fishing village, and includes both salt-and freshwater fish and a seal tank.

Island hopping, Norwegian style

To journey south on the E10 means going from island to island, all of which, bar one, have gradually been linked by impressive bridges. The one remaining ferry connection was replaced by an undersea road tunnel in 1990. This route must rank as one of the most outstanding in Norway. At every turn the traveller is confronted with another seemingly haphazard series of jagged peaks and possessing a stark beauty which contrasts with the green scenery at sea level.

On the southern tip of Austvågøy is **Henningsvær**, one of numerous Lofoten fishing villages, while the imposing bridge over Gimsøystraumen, 840 metres (2,760 ft) long, provides access to the small island of Gimsøya. From here a second bridge takes the road across Sundklakkstraumen to Vestvågøy. **Stamsund**, on a secondary road, is a coastal village and a port of call for the coastal steamer.

The **Vestvågøy Museum** (open Jun–Aug, closed Sat; entrance fee) is at Fygle, near Leknes, and has exhibits showing how the fisherman-farmer's life has changed over the years. **Leknes** is the main centre of population on the island and a typical small Norwegian town with a long straggling main street. A few miles south at Lilleeidet was the ferry to **Flakstadøya**, which was replaced by a tunnel that goes 50 metres (165 ft) below the surface of Nappstraumen.

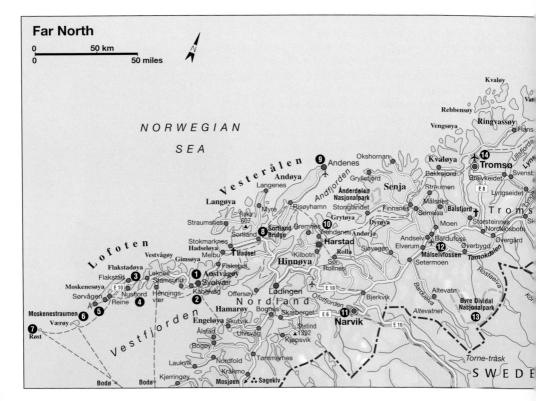

The west coast of Flakstadøya provides the surprise of wide **sandy beaches**. On a sunny summer's day, the sight of children paddling belies the fact that it is in the Arctic. The hamlet of **Flakstad ❸** has a pretty 18th-century church with an onion dome, while nearby are monuments to those who died in World War II and fishermen whose lives were lost at sea. **Nusfjord ❹** and Sund are two other fishing villages on the island. The former is on UNESCO's list of preservation-worthy environments while Sund has a small fisheries museum (open Jun–Aug; entrance fee). One section is devoted to early marine engines while the adjoining smithy is used by Hans Gjertsen, who is well known for his stylishly crafted steel cormorants. Also on the island is **Storbåthallaren**, the oldest known Stone Age settlement in northern Norway populated 6,000 years ago.

The last bridge takes the road across to the island of Moskenesøya. This also has its quota of fishing villages of which the most picturesque is **Reine**. The road clings close to the coast and looks across the Vestfjorden.

Ending at Å

The E10 finally runs out at Å ❺ – aptly named as "Å" is the last letter of the Norwegian alphabet – which marks the end of the line of peaks that make up the **Lofotenveggen** (Lofoten "wall"). It has one of the few trading posts to be preserved in its original condition. There is the small **Fiskevaersmuseum** (Fishing Village Musuem: open all year, closed weekends Sept–May; entrance fee) in a 19th-century barn, and a café opposite offers coffee and home-made cakes.

Beyond the tip of Moskenesøya is the **Moskenestraumen ❻**, a maelstrom which may not match the Saltstraumen near Bodø but which was once greatly feared by sailors. Even in calm weather it seethes and boils and was made

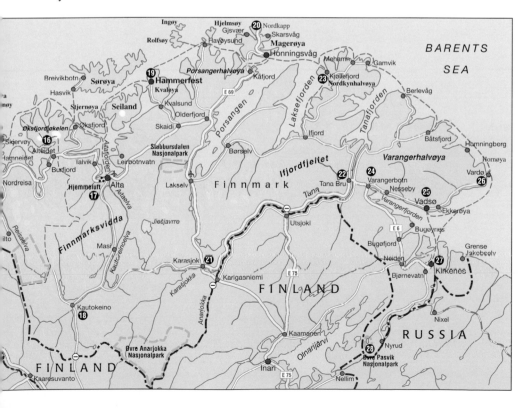

TIP

Whale safaris are very popular, so it is worth booking in advance. Trips leave daily from Andenes, Stø and Nyksund and last 3–5 hours. If you don't spot a whale on your first trip you can repeat the journey for free. For information and booking tel: 76 11 56 00.

BELOW: a statue looks out to sea from Leknes on the Lofoten island of Vestvågøy.

famous through the works of Jules Verne and Edgar Allan Poe. The maelstrom separates Moskenesøya from the small island of **Værøy**, beyond which is the even smaller island of **Røst** ❼. These are the "bird islands", which attract thousands of different species including puffin, auk, eider, guillemot, kittiwake and cormorant. Both islands have small airfields with scheduled flights to Bodø, obviating a sea trip which, because of the rapidly changing sea conditions, can be unpleasant. Thanks to the Gulf Stream, it never gets very cold on Røst or Værøy and sheep can graze on the meadows throughout the winter.

Vesterålen: home of the Hurtigrute

North of Svolvær the views may be splendid but they do not quite measure up to those in the south. In truth, this is only a question of degree because the Lofotens have such a richness of views that they almost give you scenic indigestion. Heading north, the road keeps close to the Austnesfjord, beyond which, to the northeast, is Raftsundet and the narrow, grim **Trollfjorden** which is used by the coastal steamer in summer. At Fiskebøl the ferry takes the visitor away from the Lofotens to **Melbu** on the first of the Vesterålen Islands, **Hadseløya**. As if to emphasise that you have left the Lofotens behind, Melbu has the **Vesterålen Museum** (open Jun–Sept; entrance fee), housed in an Empire-style manor house.

Between Melbu and Stokmarknes on the northern side of the island is **Hadsel Kirke** (Church; 1824), distinctive in style and with an altar piece from 1520. **Stokmarknes** is the headquarters of the Vesteraalen Steamship Company, founded by Richard With, sometimes called the father of the coastal steamer. Not surprisingly then is the **Hurtigrute Museum** (open Jun–Aug; entrance fee), where you may buy special Hurtigrute tickets for return trips to Svolvær.

From whaling to whale safaris

The Hadsel bridge carries the main road to the island of **Langøya**. Here the principal town is **Sortland**, a commercial centre with a fishing harbour that has a busy and pleasant atmosphere. The western side of the island has imposing mountains, the most unusual being the sway-backed **Reka** at 620 metres (2,000 ft) which is popular with climbers.

Map, pages 316–7

The **Sortland Bridge** ❽, 960 metres (3,150 ft) long, is the link to **Hinnøya**, Norway's largest island. Away to the northwest is the long island of **Andøya**, which is also connected by bridge and, unlike most other Vesterålen islands, is flat. Much of the land is peat, renowned for its cloudberries. **Andenes** ❾, at the northwestern extremity, is a large fishing village with the **Polarmuseet** (Polar Museum, open Jun–Aug; entrance fee). It was a fishing village in the Middle Ages and then a Dutch whaling base in the 17th century. Today, it is one of the starting points of the famous **whale safaris** (see "Tip" opposite).

The Sortland Bridge, one of the many stunning bridges between islands in the Lofoten and Vesterålen archipelagos.

Hinnøya's scenery varies: farmland along the coastal fringe, green valleys, rugged mountains and fjords. Following the E10 southeast from the Sortland Bridge you come to Lødingen on the eastern coast, with a ferry service to **Bognes** on the mainland and the E6. A little to the north is **Trondenes** ❿ which has a 13th-century stone church (open all year; free). In the bay below there are Viking burial mounds. Also here are the **Adolfkanonen** (Cannons; visits start from Harstad Tourist Office; tel: 77 01 89 89), massive long-range guns installed by the Germans during World War II to protect the approaches to Narvik.

A final lengthy bridge carries the E10 over **Tjeldsundet** and on to the mainland, although to the confused motorist it may appear to be another island as the road skirts along Ofotfjorden which provides deep-water access to Narvik.

BELOW: morning service at Hadsel Kirke (Church), Vesterålen.

If the Lofoten and Vesterålen islands are ignored the only alternative way north is by the inevitable E6. From Fauske it clings to the side of fjords, going through a succession of tunnels, with the **Rago Nasjonalpark** away to the east. This is a vast mountainous area with no roads, judged to be the most magnificent but least accessible of all Norway's National Parks.

A superb new section of highway has been built from Sommarset, where formerly there was a ferry, which cuts across exciting mountainous country. There are several tunnels, the longest being below the Sildhopfjell. North of Kråkmo, at **Sagelv**, there are 5,000-year-old rock carvings of reindeer (early man was a prolific graffiti artist in this part of Norway). At Ulvsvåg a road goes off west across Hamarøy to **Skutvik** for the ferry to Svolvær. The road continues on to Engeløya island which was a seat of power many centuries ago and there are numerous graves and burial mounds, the biggest being at **Sigarshaugen**.

Back on the E6, a little north of **Bognes**, are more rock carvings depicting 40 different subjects. To the east of Tysfjorden is a mountainous section popular with climbers, especially **Stetind**, 1,392 metres (4,600 ft) high which is called the "world's greatest obelisk". There are many caves for those who prefer to go down rather than up, the best known being **Råggejavie**, 620 metres (2,000 ft) deep. For the rest of the way to Narvik the road clings to the side of Ofotfjorden.

Narvik

The deep, ice-free waters of the Ofotfjord were the reason for **Narvik ⑪** becoming a major centre for the export of the iron ore mined in northern Sweden, and a railway was completed from the mining town of Kiruna to the port in 1883. In World War II Narvik was the scene of bitter fighting and these events are por-

BELOW: students celebrate graduation from the gymnasium in Sortland, Vesterålen.

trayed in the **Krigsminnemuseum** (War Museum; open all year; entrance fee). For an overview of Narvik and its surroundings take the cable car to the top of Fagernes, but at ground level Narvik is uninteresting, which is maybe why the local tourist office sells tickets for the "tourist train" (June–Aug), a three-hour guided tour between Narvik and the Swedish border, with photo opportunities and a chance to buy Sami souvenirs.

Troms

North of Narvik the E6 crosses Rombakfjorden over another major bridge, passes the junction with the road to Sweden, and joins with E10 at Bjerkvik. Then follows a climb up Gratangseidet county boundary into Troms. Troms has widely contrasting scenery, all typically North Norwegian: rugged mountains, with sharp peaks, countless islands and skerries, a softer landscape at sea level and fast-flowing rivers and numerous lakes. The county is split up by a number of major fjords and is also notable for its extensively forested valleys.

Setermoen, the first town north of Narvik, lies in the heart of a military area and has a large garrison. The military presence is also apparent further north at Bardufoss, with its major airbase. From Bardufoss the E6 follows the Målselv river until it turns abruptly east past Takvatnet where a major new cut-off provides some stunning views of distant mountains. Near **Balsfjord Kirke** (Church) about 10 km (6 miles) from Storsteinnes are rock carvings which are 2,500 to 4,000 years old. The area around Balsfjord has some of the richest farming land in Troms and goat farming is a major activity.

Alternatively, before you get to Bardufoss turn eastwards at Elverum onto Road 857 from which you can reach **Målselvfossen** ⑫ (waterfall). It may only have a drop of 15 metres (50 ft) but it extends over 600 metres (2,000 ft). There are salmon ladders and the Målselv river, which is renowned for its salmon, was discovered by English anglers as early as the 1840s. Further along at Rundhaug a secondary road follows the Målselv river to Øverbygd, then continues along **Tamokdalen** until it finally rejoins the E6 near Øvergård. To the south, adjacent to the border with Sweden, lies the **Øvre Dividal Nasjonalpark** ⑬, where all four of Norway's major predators – bear, wolf, lynx and wolverine – have their habitat.

City of the Arctic

Tromsø ⑭ occupies most of the island of Tromsøya and overflows on to the adjoining island of Kvaløya. With a population of 50,000, it is by far the largest city in Northern Norway and, until the opening of the bridge in 1960, everything had to be ferried across from the mainland. Today, there is a second bridge and an amazing network of road tunnels under the city, including subterranean car parks and roundabouts that appear to be formed around giant stalactites. The tunnel system links the city centre with Tromsø Langnes international airport: if you arrive by air and take a taxi the driver will gladly take you via the tunnel system (at the extra cost of the toll). The town has variously been called the Gateway to the Arctic, the Arctic Ocean City and the Paris of the North.

Map, pages 316–7

TIP

The rock carvings near Balsfjord Kirke (Church) are part of the Tennes Heritage Trail, which is one of the many trails included in *Fotfar mot Nord* (Trails to the North) available from tourist offices.

BELOW: *rallar* (railway men's) statue in Narvik.

Archaeological finds indicate settlements dating back 9,000 years. Tromsø became an ecclesiastical centre in 1252 and much of the subsequent development from 1300 to 1700s was influenced by the Hanseatic League. Trade restrictions led to strong dependence on Bergen throughout the Middle Ages. In 1794, the town was granted *kaupang* (market town) privileges and the right to independent trade, and became a focal point for the Pomor trade, with Russian ships bringing timber, rape, flour and other items from the White Sea in exchange for fish and goods brought by the Hanseatic traders.

In the early 19th century Tromsø was the natural starting point for trapping expeditions to the pack ice both to the north and the east to Svalbard (Spitsbergen). It has also been the site of a number of sea battles, including the sinking of the German battleship *Tirpitz*, pride of the German fleet, which was bombed by British bombers while guarding the entrance to Tromsø.

Heavenly winds

Though fishing (for shrimps, herring and other fishes) is of prime importance, Tromsø University and a new regional teaching hospital are also ranked as major employers here. The university is an important research centre and works closely with the **Tromsø Bymuseum** (City Museum; open all year; entrance fee), the **Polarmuseet** (Polar Museum; open all year; entrance fee) and the latest addition, the **Nordlysplanetariet** (Northern Lights Planetarium; open all year; entrance fee; tel: 77 67 60 00). The planetarium, located at Breivika on the island of Kvaløya, is really a must for anyone visiting the city. By means of a special projection system, you are taken on a ride through the universe, undersea or on a poetic journey through the four seasons; but the prime motive for vis-

Tromsø's nickname, Paris of the North, stems from the 18th century when traders brought the latest fashions from the French capital to sell to the wives of rich, local merchants.

BELOW LEFT: racks of drying fish have their own "guards" to deter hungry birds.
BELOW RIGHT: Tromsø Domkirke (Cathedral) in winter.

Map, pages 316–7

iting the planetarium is to study the Aurora Borealis or Northern Lights (*see pages 310–11*). In medieval Europe the phenomenon was thought to be reflections of heavenly warriors; we now know that it is connected to movements of the solar wind, but the Aurora is still not fully understood).

In the centre of the town is the **Domkirke** (Cathedral; open Jun–Aug, closed Mon; free) completed in 1861, which is one of the country's largest wooden churches. On the mainland is the modern **Ishavskatedralen** (Arctic Ocean Cathedral; open May–Sept; entrance fee), opened in 1965. Apart from its striking external appearance, the cathedral contains a huge stained-glass window and an unusual church organ. Near it is the cable car to the top of the **Storsteinen**, 420 metres (1,380 ft), from where there are magnificent views over the town and the surrounding area. Tromsø also contains Europe's northernmost brewery, Mack, established in 1845 and famous for its Arctic Ale. Is a short walk from the centre with a beer hall on the premises (tel: 77 62 45 00).

Where glacier and sea meet

To the northwest of Tromsø lie a number of islands which stand guard where the lengthy Ullsfjorden and **Lyngenfjorden** reach the sea. Between these two is a long wide peninsula with, on its eastern side, the range of mountains known as the **Lyngsalpene** ⓯ (Lyngen Alps). The full majesty of these snow-capped peaks and glaciers is best seen from the eastern side of Lyngenfjorden, and there is a short cut that avoids the main road while affording fine views of the mountains. Take Road 91 just south of Tromsø through the Breivik valley, a ferry across the Ullsfjord to Svensby then a drive to Lyngseidet and a second ferry across Lyngenfjorden to Olderdalen and the E6.

BELOW: the Ishavskatedralen (Arctic Ocean Cathedral), Tromsø.

The more obvious route is along the E8 to where it joins the E6 at Nordkjosbotn and then through Skibotn, keeping along the shore of the Lyngenfjord with its views of the mountains across the water. After changing direction along the side of the Rotsundet, opposite the island of Uløya, the road swings inland before meeting Reisafjorden. There are fine views to the west which are even better after climbing over the summit of **Kvænangsfjellet**. There is an impressive panorama of islands and mountains before descending to Burfjorden. Just past Alteidet, a minor road goes to the Jøkelfjord where the **Øksfjordjøkelen**  (Glacier) calves into the sea, the only one in Norway to do so. A little further on is the boundary into Norway's most remote county, Finnmark.

Finnmark

No-one describes Finnmark without a combination of superlatives and impressive statistics. It is Norway's most northerly county and the largest, covering 48,000 sq km (18,500 sq miles), equal to 15 percent of the entire country, and yet it has only 75,000 inhabitants, two percent of the population. Finnmark lies along the same latitude as Alaska and Siberia, but the Gulf Stream ensures that the harbours do not freeze even in the depths of winter. Inland, the temperature can drop to a chilling −50°C (−70°F); while during the short summer it may hit 32°C (90°F). Between mid-May and the end of July the sun never sets – you can read a newspaper outside at midnight – while in winter the sun stays snug below the horizon from the end of November to the end of January.

BELOW: contrasting styles at the Sami market in Hammerfest.

The scenery is spectacular with the highest areas in the northwest and a vast mountain plateau, the **Finnmarksvidda**, to the south and southeast. The bare grey rocks of the coast take the full force of the winter storms. It is the vastness of the uninhabited areas that make the greatest impression: ranges of mountains and fjells stretch away to the horizon, seemingly without end, silent and awe-inspiring. The coast has its own gaunt beauty with sudden patches of green which catch the visitor unawares.

Much of this wonderful county is now easily accessible by car or public transport on well-surfaced main roads, while there is an extensive network of air services which land at tiny airports dotted all over the area, and the ubiquitous coastal steamer serves towns and villages along the coast.

Despite the inhospitable nature of the region and the ferocity of the winter, the people of Finnmark are greatly attached to their part of Norway, which has been inhabited for 10,000 years. They include not only Norwegians and Sami (Lapps) but also many Finns. The Norwegians settled along the coast in the 14th century, but major changes in the 18th and 19th centuries brought in people from the south of the country. At the same time came a large migration from Finland and Sweden.

Scorched earth

World War II was a nightmare for the county when, as Soviet liberators crossed the northern border in the autumn of 1944, the German occupation forces began a "scorched earth" policy as they retreated south, burning towns and villages and even individual farms as they went. Signs of this can be seen in **Alta**, the first town across the country border from Troms and the biggest in the county, where some of the architecture is undistinguished, often the case in north Norwegian towns which had to rebuild rapidly after World War II.

But if parts of Alta are less than imposing, it does have a major attraction. On the southern outskirts is an outstanding collection of prehistoric rock carvings at **Hjemmeluft** ⓘ (signs from Alta; open May–Sept). Discovered in 1973 and added to UNESCO's World Heritage List in 1985, there are about 3,000 carvings on four different sites, with the biggest concentration at Hjemmeluft itself. These "stories in pictures" are estimated to be 2,500 to 6,000 years old and depict people, animals (particularly reindeer), boats, weapons, and some which have yet to be identified. Traces of these early inhabitants, the Komsa people, were discovered in 1925 on Komsafjell, which bulges out into Altafjorden. Here the dwelling sites go back some 10,000 years, a sobering reminder of how long human beings have lived in this apparently inhospitable region.

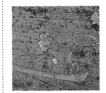

One of the prehistoric carvings at Hjemmeluft.

Sami culture

Finnmark has few roads, so it is easy to find your way. Going south from Alta is Road 93 to **Kautokeino** ⓘ and the Finnish frontier. Kautokeino is the largest Sami community in the county and the centre of Sami education. The **Kulturhuset** has the only Sami theatre in Norway, and the **Samisk Museum** (open all year; entrance fee) has exhibits showing Sami life in old Kautokeino.

Northwards from Leirbotnvatn (around the fjord from Alta) to the village of **Skaidi** is 45 km (28 miles) of sheer emptiness. The ever-present E6 takes a lonely course through this stretch of wild countryside. Almost the only building

BELOW LEFT: selling skins and other Sami goods.
BELOW RIGHT: an early print of a Sami women and child.

Reindeer hazard.

is the small **Sami chapel**, dwarfed by the immensity of its surroundings. The only signs of life away from the road are the vast herds of reindeer. On a first journey through this territory, you find yourself constantly aware of how little human activity has impinged on the grandeur of its great empty spaces.

History of disasters

Skaidi is a popular base for local anglers, hunters and winter sports enthusiasts. It is also the junction of the E6 and Road 94 to **Hammerfest ⑲**, 56 km (35 miles) away on the island of Kvaløya. Hammerfest, on its bare rocky island, is the world's most northerly town. Founded in 1789, for centuries it was the best ice-free harbour in these northern waters, although storms and hurricanes plus many man-made disasters have repeatedly wrought havoc on the town. In 1825, a hurricane destroyed houses and boats, and an even more ferocious storm in 1882 moved the German Kaiser, Queen Victoria and the Tsar of Russia to donate money to repair the damage. In 1890, the town had ambitious plans for a hydro-electric power station but, only a month after work started, fire again destroyed two-thirds of the town. In the following year, nevertheless, Hammerfest became the first European town to have electric lighting.

The harbour has always been of importance both commercially and strategically and ships have long called there. For more than 100 years it was also the principal Norwegian base for hunting and fishing. When Norway was invaded in 1940, it was a growing and flourishing community. The retreating Germans burned down the entire town and by 10 February 1945 it had been wiped out except for the **chapel** in the graveyard. Today, it is Norway's main trawler port, devoted to all aspects of the fishing industry.

BELOW: boats and warehouses in Hammerfest harbour.

Map, pages 316–7

Measuring the planet

Hammerfest clings to the shore line which is backed by a steep escarpment. Its most notable monument is the **Meridianstøtta** (Meridian Column), which was erected by King Oskar II to mark the first international measurement of the Earth, a joint enterprise by Russia, Norway and Sweden. On the highest point of a walk from the town up the escarpment is the Midday Pole, erected at the end of the 19th century and topped by a cannonball. When the shadow from the pole points directly to the Meridian Column, the time is 12 noon precisely.

In 1809, after Norway became involved in the Napoleonic wars, two British warships attacked Hammerfest. The town fell to the British who stayed for a week of plunder and destruction. The British cannonball on top of the Midday Pole is the permanent reminder of this unhappy event. To prevent any further attack the military built a redoubt or **Skansen** in 1810 with eight guns, which Hammerfest folk are happy to report never fired in anger. This walk also passes a beacon built by the young people of the town in 1882–83 "as they had no other amusements". The occupation forces pulled it down but the town rebuilt it in 1982–83, though by this time the young people had other amusements.

More noticeable today is the circular **Isbjørnhallen** (Polar Bear Hall) used for sporting events and exhibitions. At the other end of the town is the equally striking **church** (open Jun–Aug; free), its form inspired by traditional fish-drying racks. Its altar piece, which dates from 1632, comes from the town's first church.

In a shrewd move in 1963, Hammerfest created the Isbjørnklubben (Royal and Ancient Polar Bear Society), which offers one of the more attractive souvenirs of its kind. To get a certificate of membership, you must apply in person to the society's **museum** (open all year; entrance fee) in the Town Hall.

BELOW: Nordkapp (North Cape) in winter.

En route to China

From Skaidi the E6 goes northeast across another stretch of wild, uninhabited territory before the road descends to the sea at Olderfjorden. Here the majority of visitors turn north for Finnmark's overwhelming attraction: **Nordkapp**  (North Cape). This is for many the Holy Grail, the end of their pilgrimage by car, motor-home, motor bike, bus or even bicycle. The alternative is to fly to Honningsvåg or sail there by coastal steamer or cruise liner.

The road hugs the edge of the huge Porsangenfjorden, with rugged country to the landward side, and ends at Kåfjord, where a ferry runs to **Honningsvåg** on the island of Magerøya. In the summer season you can face lengthy delays, but take heart as an undersea tunnel is due to open in 1999. Between Honningsvåg and Nordkapp lie 35 km (21 miles) of the only genuine Arctic scenery in Europe. It may be bare and treeless but there is an unusual beauty about the island which, on a sunny day, is emphasised by the clarity of the atmosphere; too often, alas, misty conditions prevail.

The name North Cape was given to this imposing headland by an Englishman, Captain Richard Chancellor. In 1553, as master of the *Edward Bonaventure*, he was seeking a new route to China when he rounded Europe's most dramatic northern point; but it was not until the 19th century that Nordkapp began to attract visitors. In 1845, passengers from the *Prinds Gustav* were rowed ashore and then had to struggle up 300 metres (1,000 ft) to the plateau at the top. After a visit by the intrepid King Oskar II in 1873, Thomas Cook arranged the first organised tour for 24 Englishmen in 1875. By 1880, a path with primitive railings from Horn Bay to the top had appeared and you can still see the remains of the quay by taking the 11-km (7-mile) walk from the plateau. The coastal

Following Richard Chancellor's attempt in 1553 to find the Northwest Passage to China, it was to be more than 300 years before Nils Nordenskjøld finally succeeded in travelling from the Atlantic to the Pacific via the north in 1879.

BELOW: the children's statues at Nordkapp (North Cape).

steamers have provided the biggest impetus to tourist traffic and by 1920, the wild grandeur of the headland had learned to live with the incongruity of its first building. The road from Honningsvåg opened in 1956, as did a centre with the usual souvenir shop, cafeteria and post office. In 1989, this earlier building gave way to the new **Nordkapphallen** (North Cape Hall; open Apr–Oct; entrance fee), with its circular Compass Restaurant and, below, the Super-videograph, where a 225° screen and wrap-around sound bring the four seasons of Finnmark to the visitor, whatever the time of year.

An underground tunnel leads from the new hall and champagne bar, which is like an amphitheatre cut out of the rock and overlooks the Arctic Ocean. Even if you suffer from vertigo, look briefly from the balcony which provides a spectacular view straight down to the sea far below. Along the tunnel are tableaux depicting historical events at Nordkapp, such as the visit of King Oskar II, who also has a monument on the plateau (entrance fee) to commemorate the same occasion. On what is in danger of becoming a crowded plateau are seven circular, wheel-like sculptures. They are monuments to the children of the world, sculpted in 1988 by seven children from seven lands as monuments to "joy, friendship, and working together".

The comical puffin can be found all along the northern coasts.

"Haddock" English

Apart from the main road to Nordkapp itself, there is only one other road on the island, which leads to the village of **Gjesvær** on the west coast. On the eastern side of Magerøya is the little fishing community of Skarsvåg. Honningsvåg, where the ferry arrives, has been a fishing harbour for many years and an important pilot station. In the old days, the trawlers were the most frequent visitors, and up to 4,000 called each year at this remote northerly port. Most were British and, through their visits, Honningsvåg developed "haddock English", a mixture of sign language and occasional English words. Like other centres in the north, Honningsvåg burned down during hostilities and by the end of World War II the 1884 church was the only building left standing. Honningsvåg today also has a small local museum, the **Nordkappmuset** (North Cape Museum; open all year; entrance fee).

BELOW: one of the Nordkapp (North Cape) monuments.

Most villages and towns in Finnmark sit along the coast but the two main Sami communities are the exception: Kautokeino and **Karasjok ㉑** are deep inland. Returning from Nordkapp, continue south through Lakselv at the end of Porsangenfjorden to get to Karasjok. The town's 1807 **Gamle Kirke** is the oldest church in Finnmark, and was lucky enough to survive the war, and the **De Samiske Samlinger** (Sami Museum and Library; open all year; entrance fee) has a unique collection of Sami literature.

At Karasjok the E6 makes a massive U-turn and heads north again, keeping company with the **River Tana** through its every twist and turn, all the way to **Tana Bru ㉒**, which is at the first bridge across the river and is the meeting place of four roads. One is the alternative route east from Lakselv (Road 888), which veers away from the E6 at the head of the Porsanger fjord. This long road has few communities but an

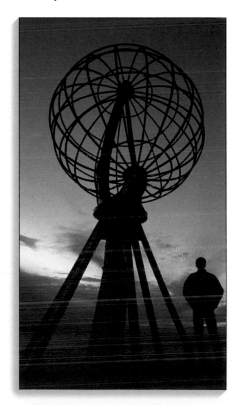

Mending fishing nets on the quayside.

BELOW: a good catch: Atlantic salmon at Honningsvåg.

abundance of beautiful scenery and it rolls ahead across two magnificent inland stretches – from **Børselv** to **Laksefjorden** and across the **Ifjordfjellet**. At Ifjord the road pushes further north to the Nordkyn peninsula and **Kjøllefjord ㉓**, Mehamn and Gamvik, across the very top of the country. About 15 km (9 miles) from Kjøllefjord, including a 30-minute ramble along a well-prepared trail, is the remains of the **Oksevåg whaling station**, which was used during the Finnmark whaling season from 1864–1905. Further walks are marked through the **Slettnes Nature and Heritage Reserve** at Gamvik (open all year; free).

Over the bridge at Tana Bru, the road divides; the E6 winds a long route east towards **Kirkenes**, only 5 km (3 miles) from the Russian border, while Road 890 heads north to **Berlevåg** and **Båtsfjord**, crossing the highest pass in Finnmark, the **Oarddojokke** at 400 metres (1,300 ft) above sea level. Berlevåg and Båtsfjord are fishing villages, both on the far coast of the Varanger peninsula, last of the three that stand out from the north of Norway. Places of interest include the **Løkvika Fiskehytte og Partisanhule** (Fishing Cabin and Partisan Cave; open all year; free).

Continuing east on the E6, you come to **Varangerbotn ㉔**. In this part of Norway, where the fjords and coastline bite deep into the land, you are rarely far from water. Varangerbotn has a small but interesting Sami museum, the **Samiske Museum** (open Jun–Aug; entrance fee), and it is worth making a detour along the north coast of the Varangerfjord on Road 98 to **Vadsø ㉕**, the administrative centre of Finnmark. On the way, at **Nesseby**, you find a small wooden church built in 1858 and Varanger's oldest log cabin, from 1700. The surprise of this whole remote area is that it is rich in archaeological finds, with graves and places of sacrifice to indicate human occupation as early as 9000 BC.

Finnish migration

A monument in Vadsø explains why many inhabitants are of Finnish origin and Finnish-speaking, and the local **museum** (open Jun–Aug, by arrangement the rest of the year; entrance fee) is housed in two buildings, one a Finnish-style dwelling, Tuoainengården, and the other, Espengården, a patrician house from 1840. Vadsø's **church**, built in 1958, is of striking appearance. In front, the King Stone bears the signatures of King Olav V of Norway, President Kekkonen of Finland and King Carl Gustav of Sweden, who all visited the town in 1977, to unveil the **Innvandrermonumentet** (Immigrant Monument) to the Finns who came to find food and work in Finnmark in the 1800s. Another landmark is the **Luftskipsmasta** (mooring mast) used by Amundsen's airship, *Norge*, in 1926 and by Nobile's airship *Italia*, two years later.

Beyond Vadsø there is only the town of **Vardø 26**, Norway's easternmost town and the only one situated in the Arctic climate zone. There have been fortifications at Vardø since around 1300, but the present octagonal star-shaped redoubt was built in 1734. The only remnant of the original fortress is a beam which bears the signature of King Christian IV and is dated 1599, while later monarchs have added their names: King Oskar II (in 1873), King Håkon VII (in 1907) and King Olav V (in 1959), which is in the **Vardøhus Museum** and **Festning** (Fortress; open all year; entrance fee).

Along the coast west of Vardø is the abandoned fishing village of **Hamningberg** with its old architecture and church, paradoxically one of the few not destroyed in World War II. As you return south again, you come to **Ekkerøya**, Finnmark's only bird rock accessible by car. Here bird-watchers gather to watch breeding kittiwake, black guillemot, Steller's eider and grey phalarope.

Map, pages 316–7

After two months of winter darkness, Vardø celebrates the return of the Sun, usually around 20 January, with a gun salute on the first day that the entire disk is visible above the horizon.

BELOW: the harbour at Vadsø.

Map,
pages
316–7

Beyond Varangerbotn, the E6 follows the coast through another huge, uninhabited area to the southeast and some beautiful views across the waters of the Varanger fjord. **Bugøynes** is an old fishing village on the coast which, like Hamingborg, escaped destruction in the war. Further east, **Bugøyfjord** is an old trading centre and birthplace of the Sami artist John Savio.

Only 8 km (5 miles) from the Finnish border to the southwest, the little town of **Neiden** has the only Greek Orthodox Church in Norway, where the Skollé Lapps worship. Each year since 1965, the church has held a service to bless the waters of the River Neiden to ensure that their reputed healing powers continue, a service which attracts believers from many areas. The restored Labahå farm at Neiden, built by Finnish immigrants, is part of the **Sør-Varanger Museum** (open all year; entrance fee) at Svanvik.

This easternmost wedge of Norwegian territory became important with the discovery of iron ore at Bjørnevatn and, since 1906, it has been mined and shipped from the port of **Kirkenes ㉗**. The region is also a centre for fishing, farming, forestry and reindeer husbandry. Kirkenes is dominated by the installations of the Sydvaranger Iron Ore Company. Although it has recently acquired a new luxury hotel, the Rica Arctic, the town's somewhat rough and ready appearance is explained and easily forgiven when you learn that the 20th century has brought no less than four wars fought in or near it. World War II brought the most suffering when, apart from Malta, Kirkenes acquired the unsolicited honour of being the most bombed centre in Europe. It was liberated by the Russians in 1944, which engendered a rare lack of nervousness of, and sympathy for, the "Russian Bear". Kirkenes is the final point of call for the Hurtigrute coastal steamer before it returns south to Bergen.

BELOW: post boxes brighten up the winter landscape.
RIGHT: winter in Kautokeino.

Unusual border post

The extreme eastern tip of Norway, at **Grense Jakobselv**, has a chapel built on the order of King Oskar II in 1869 as an unusual means of protecting Norwegian interests. The idea of a chapel rather than a fort at this strategic location came about when the Norwegians noticed that the Russians attended their own Orthodox church not far over the border. Faced with a Protestant church, the argument ran, the Russians would realise they had strayed into Norwegian territory and this somewhat unusual approach to maintaining the frontier was highly successful.

In the extreme north of Finnmark, Norway is sometimes only a kilometre or two wide between the border and the sea, and a long pocket of the country hangs south between Russia and Finland. Here the **Øvre Pasvik Nasjonalpark ㉘** includes the largest virgin forest in the country. This comparatively flat area has pine forests, bare rock, swamps and two watercourses which are tributaries of the Pasvik river (the official boundary between Norway and Russia). Wildlife in the park includes moose, reindeer, bear and wolverine; there are whooper swans, great grey owls, the bean goose, sea eagles, gyr falcons, spotted redshanks and cranes, the whole area is protected from development and pollution to form a peaceful border between East and West. ❑

SVALBARD

Map
on page
338

Nearly as close to the North Pole as to Norway, the Svalbard archipelago (more widely known by its English name, Spitsbergen) teems with bird, mammal and plant life in the short Arctic summer

NORWAY

PRECEDING PAGES:
rock formations on
Spitsbergen.
LEFT: a young polar
bear.
BELOW: the Russian
mining settlement
of Barentsburg.

From Tromsø in the north of Norway, the big airliner drones almost due north for an hour and a half. Far below is a seemingly empty sea, hidden here and there by banks of clouds. Suddenly the traveller becomes aware that through the clouds, stark, jagged mountain peaks project like huge fangs, and that the clouds in between are in reality great snow covered glaciers. This is Svalbard, the land of the pointed mountains.

The Svalbard archipelago lies 640 km (400 miles) north of the mainland of Norway and has two main islands, Spitsbergen and Nordaustlandet, with numerous smaller islands dotted around in the seas nearby. In winter, the pack ice of the Arctic is all around and only some 950 km (600 miles) separate the islands from the North Pole.

The smooth asphalt runway lies on the narrow coastal plain between the mountains of Spitsbergen and the sea of Isfjorden. With a minimum of formality, you are through customs and on to a land where the forces of nature are still in control. On the landward side, the mountain slopes darkly up in to the clouds, traversed by a row of pylons; now disused, they carried coal from the mines down to the loading jetties.

Why an airport?

The Svalbard coal mines are rare in that the mine shafts do not go down into the ground but are driven horizontally into the mountains. The township of **Longyearbyen**  was built solely to accommodate the people who came north, mainly from Norway, to work at the hard and dangerous job of winning coal from the inside of the mountains.

Coal was first discovered in the early 17th century, but for many years it was used only as a source of fuel for trappers. Only since around 1900 have serious attempts been made to exploit this resource, and the first to claim mining rights was a Norwegian skipper from Tromsø, called Zakariasen. He was followed by others including John Longyear, an American after whom the village is named.

Around 2,000 people live in the village, mainly in modern, well insulated houses, served by facilities such as shops, a bank, a café, and even a fine little **museum** which, as well as stuffed examples of typical Spitsbergen birds and mammals, displays many artefacts from the days when the only people to live in these Arctic islands were a few hunters and trappers.

As if to remind you that summer, if sweet, is short, in front of most houses you will see a parked skidoo, a motor scooter with rubber tracks and steering "skis", which is the only means of transport in winter when snow lies thick on the ground.

One of the
characteristically
spiky peaks that gave
Spitsbergen its
English name.

Mineral rights

After World War I, Norway was granted sovereignty over the archipelago, though the various countries who agreed to the treaty reserved the right to exploit minerals. Sweden already operated a coal mining business but sold out to a Norwegian company in 1934.

Today, Russia is the only one of the original signatories to the Svalbard Treaty to retain an interest in coal mining, and has a substantial operation at **Barentsburg ②**, only a few miles further down the fjord from Longyearbyen. Around 2,000 people, mostly Ukrainians, live in a coal-dusty village on the steep fjordside which, nevertheless, has an indoor farm of dairy cattle and chicken sheds. Kittiwakes scream from their nests on the window ledges and, on an esplanade below, well-dressed fur-hatted groups, once overlooked by a smiling portrait of Lenin, now sell cheap Russian souvenirs and, now and then, a family "treasure" to the occasional summer cruise-ship passenger.

Nature in the raw

Svalbard should not, and is unlikely ever to become, a place for mass tourism: the islands cannot support it and, in any case, the appeal is to people who like to find their own wildlife and explore nature in the raw. However, the cruise ships are beginning to threaten the peace. Longyearbyen has a hotel and hardly a day goes by without a luxury cruise ship depositing its passengers on the shore for a barbecue or a short trip around the area. For safety reasons, visitors are normally accompanied by men with loaded guns and may not leave the pre-set routes. Thus, the polar bear takes care that mass tourism never spoils the environment and only a few well equipped campers dare go further afield.

BELOW: cruise ships are an increasingly common sight in summer.

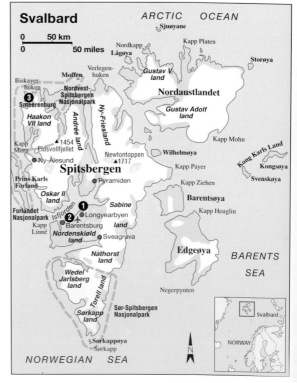

Svalbard

ARCTIC OCEAN

Map on page 338

The area around Longyearbyen is a pleasant place during the summer, the stark mountains offset by a valley which has meadows spangled with flowers. Here, you will find the tiny bells of cassiope mixed with purple saxifrage, *S. oppositifolia*, and, perhaps, a patch of boreal Jacob's ladder, *Polemonium boreale*, an Arctic rarity with beautiful flowers. Near the shores where the glaucous gulls congregate, look for the fleshy leaved *Mertensia maritima*, or oyster plant.

The polar winter is a different matter. The sun does not rise above the horizon and everything is locked in darkness, lit only by the moon and the multi-coloured rays of the **Aurora borealis**, or Northern Lights.

When the sun reappears and gathers strength, the ice pack retreats north, speeded by the warming influence of the Gulf Stream. Still with enough strength to exert pressure on the ice waters of the Arctic Ocean, this warm current flows up the west coast of Spitsbergen and ensures that, in summer, ships can have an ice-free passage right to the north shores of the islands.

Spitsbergen is mountainous and glaciated with around 60 percent covered in permanent ice. The highest mountain, **Newtontoppen**, is over 1,700 metres (5,500 ft) high. Farther from the influence of the Gulf Stream, the second largest island, **Nordaustlandet**, is almost completely covered in an enormous layer of ice, said to be more than 700 metres (2,300 ft) thick in places.

Unknown and unexplored

According to the old Icelandic annals, in 1194 land was found to lie "four days sailing from Langanes, at the northern end of the sea". They called it Svalbard but, after that first mention, the islands were forgotten for several hundred years. The next mention was in the journals of the great Dutch explorer, Willem Bar-

BELOW: a coal train in Ny-Ålesund.

The Norwegian botanist Hanna Resvoll-Holmsen took this self-portrait in 1908, while camping at Colbay.

BELOW: taking a really close look at an Arctic skua.

ents, in 1596. Barents, with two ships under his command, was trying to find a northern route to China when he sighted an island which, from the shape of its mountains, he named Spitsbergen. The two ships then parted, one to carry news of fjords filled with whales and walrus back to Holland, while the other ship with Barents on board continued eastward, only to become trapped in the pack ice and forced to spend the winter during which Barents and many of his crew died.

Story of the whales

By 1610 hunting expeditions had begun to arrive around the coast of Spitsbergen. News of the numbers of whales spread and soon the Dutch **whalers** were joined by English, French, Basques and Danes. Inevitably trouble flared as they disputed rights and fought pitched battles when warships came north to defend the claims of their whalers.

The English and Dutch at last agreed on a division of hunting territories and some peace was restored. The Dutch set up a shore base on **Amsterdam Island**, which grew to be almost a town with a fort, church and whale-oil refinery, and a summer population of a couple of thousand. They called it **Smeerenburg ❸**, the "Blubber town", and you can still find the outlines of stone buildings and the furnaces built to render the whale blubber into oil. The large numbers of bleached whale bones testify to the growing demands for whale oil and in some places further mute testimony in the graves of men who died, either in battles or from more natural causes. Under the pressure of all the killing, it was inevitable that the whale stock would decline and by around 1750 whaling ceased.

This intensive whaling was purely a summer activity. In winter the islands were deserted except by accident. In 1630, an English ship was wrecked and the crew managed to cling to life throughout the winter. In 1633, some Dutchmen wintered at Smeerenberg, but the following year those who attempted to stay on all died of scurvy. The English had intended to colonise the archipelago but even prisoners under sentence of death refused to face the prospect of the Arctic night.

Tough life

The Russians were made of sterner stuff, however, and in the early part of the 18th century a number of hunting parties built houses on Svalbard and continued to hunt bear, fox, walrus and seals throughout the winter darkness. Not until the late 18th century did Norwegian hunters first arrive. They too over-wintered and today their cabins still lie along the shores of many fjords. Though mainly deserted, scientists and explorers often make use of the huts and many are kept in a good state of repair.

A trapper led a tough and rigorous life. He had to set his traps, mainly for Arctic fox whose beautiful pelts were most valuable in winter, in a hunting territory that covered many square kilometres. He also shot or caught polar bears in baited "fell-traps" and hunted seals, not just for food and skins, but for the oil which he then extracted from the blubber.

Ever since its discovery Svalbard has attracted scientific expeditions. The first on record was in 1773 and included no less a personage than Horatio Nel-

son, then a midshipman. In 1827, the first Norwegian geological expedition took place under Professor B.M. Keilhau, and this was soon followed by expeditions from many nations. Today, the **Norsk Polarinstitut** is the clearing house for all expeditions which visit this fascinating Arctic outpost.

Map on page 338

Natural laboratory

Svalbard offers a unique environment for the study of ecology and **natural history** by scientist and amateur alike. Almost every visitor who makes the long journey north has more than a passing interest in wildlife in general and birds in particular, and Svalbard's short Arctic summer offers a rich feast. For though the archipelago can seem desperately inhospitable, in the 24-hour days of summer the tundra slopes between the mountains and near the sea offer enough thin soil to encourage and support a surprising number of plants. These, in turn, support other wildlife such as insects, birds and a few mammals. The surrounding seas, although cold, are rich in fish and invertebrates which attract sea birds and sea mammals who use the shores and cliffs for breeding and resting.

Kittiwakes, glaucous and ivory gulls push north as soon as daylight allows and are soon followed by Arctic terns, all the way from the southern hemisphere. The kittiwake is essentially an ocean bird which feeds almost exclusively at sea. At nesting time they set up huge noisy colonies on suitable cliffs, or even on window ledges in some places. Another ocean wanderer is the fulmar. Most of the Svalbard population is the dark grey phase, largely confined to Arctic waters, and this at first puzzles some bird-watchers from further south.

Four species of auks breed in Svalbard: Brünnich's guillemot, the little auk, puffin and black guillemot. While Brünnich's guillemot nest on open but inac-

The small yellow blooms of the Svalbard mohn.

BELOW: soil patterns in Sassendalen.

Map
on page
338

*The seal hunters who
once flocked to
Svalbard in the
summer months used
to refer to ringed
seals as "floe rats".*

BELOW: at the edge
of the pack ice
(with a rifle for
protection).
RIGHT: in summer
the Arctic ice
breaks up under
the influence of the
warm Gulf Stream.

cessible ledges, the others seek the safety of crevices or burrows, where predators such as Arctic fox and glaucous gulls have less chance of getting at their eggs or young. There are also some waders.

The large expanses of barren mountains do not offer much in the way of food for land birds, but try the slopes and valleys which are often carpeted in dwarf birch and polar willow, and you will find snow buntings foraging for seeds and singing from the rocks. The ptarmigan also uses this habitat and it is the only bird to stay through the winter. Three kinds of geese breed on Svalbard – pink-footed, Brent and barnacle – and the many naturalists who have studied the barnacle geese now realise that the entire Svalbard population travels to Scotland each year, to spend the winter in the Solway area in the southwest, then return in spring to breed. When you spot the plentiful flocks of common eider along the shores, look closely because you may be lucky enough to find a few king eiders, showing off their superior plumage to their less flashy kin.

Arctic monarch

There is only one kind of grazing mammal in the islands and that is the hardy Svalbard reindeer. Smaller than the Samiland reindeer, you come across groups, which seem quite tame, living a Spartan life off plants and lichens in the valley bottoms. The only other land mammals are the two carnivores, the fox and the bear. The Arctic fox is a very attractive looking little animal, with a coat of varying shades of white and grey in summer and pure white in winter. Though it was hunted heavily in the past, it is still remarkably tolerant and curious about humans and is not too difficult to find on the sea-bird cliffs in summer, where it digs out nests or picks up any young birds that have fallen from the ledges.

The undoubted king of the Arctic is the polar bear. Adult males especially lead a nomadic life on the pack ice for much of the year and live mainly on seals, while young males and females with cubs tend to spend the summer on the island feeding largely on a vegetarian diet. Though they were formerly hunted for their skins, polar bears are now protected and can be killed only if they threaten human life. They are not uncommon, especially on favourite breeding islands, such as **Barentsøya** and **Edgeøya**.

Though the fjords of Svalbard may no longer be "filled with whales and walrus", as they were said to be in the 15th century, you will certainly find sea mammals around the islands. Though it is now rare to see any of the great whales, species such as the lesser rorqhual or minke whales come into the fjord quite often. But the one you are most likely to spot is the beluga or white whale, easy to identify with its white body and lack of a dorsal fin. Now and then you might be lucky enough to sight the remarkable narwhale, with its spear-like tusk projecting out in front.

The immense herds of walrus which in days past thronged places like **Moffen Island** have never fully recovered from over-hunting, but sometimes small groups appear at Moffen or on the south of Edgeøya, where they feast on the clam beds or rest on the shore: a hopeful sign in an age when Svalbard is visited for its stark natural beauty and summer wildlife. ❑

INSIGHT GUIDES

Travel Tips

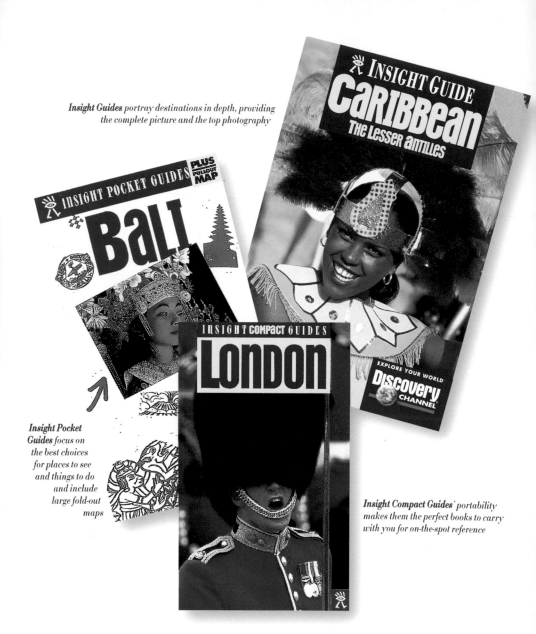

Insight Guides portray destinations in depth, providing the complete picture and the top photography

Insight Pocket Guides focus on the best choices for places to see and things to do and include large fold-out maps

Insight Compact Guides' portability makes them the perfect books to carry with you for on-the-spot reference

Three types of guide for all types of travel

INSIGHT GUIDES Different people need different kinds of information. Some want *background information* to help them prepare for the trip. Others seek *personal recommendations* from someone who knows the destination well. And others look for *compactly presented data* for on-the-spot reference. With three carefully designed series, Insight Guides offer readers the perfect choice. Insight Guides will turn your visit into an experience.

The world's largest collection of visual travel guides

CONTENTS

Getting Acquainted

Area 386,958 sq km (150,000 sq miles).
Location Norway stretches from Pysen Rock, south of Odden (latitude 57°57'33" to Knivskjelodden (71°11'8"). The westernmost point is Steinsøy by Utvær (4°30'12" E) and the easternmost point is Hornøy in Vardø (31°10'10" N).
Topography Norway is mountainous, with elevations ranging to around 2,500 metres (8,500 ft).
Capital Oslo, on the southeast coast at the head of Oslofjord.
Population 4.4 million in 1997. At about 11 people per sq km (29 per sq mile), Norway has the second lowest population density after Iceland.
Oslo is home to around 450,000 people – over 10 percent of the national total. Other major cities' estimated populations: Bergen 225,000, Stavanger 106,000, Trondheim 145,000. The north is very sparsely populated.
Language Norwegian, of which there are two variations: *bokmål* and *nynorsk*. The Sami population (Lapps) in North Norway speak Lappish. English is widely understood in the sizeable towns.
Religion Around 94 percent are Evangelical Lutheran Church of Norway. The church is supported by the state, and the clergy is nominated by the king, but complete religious freedom is guaranteed. Other churches, mostly Protestant and Roman Catholic, represent about 4 percent of the population.
Time zone Central European Time, 1 hour ahead of Greenwich Mean Time, 6 hours ahead of Eastern Standard Time. The clock is set forward an hour to summer time at the end of March, and back an hour at the end of September.
Currency Norwegian krone (NOK), divided into 100 ore.
Weights and measures Metric. Distances are given in kilometres (km) but Norwegians often refer to a *mil* which is 10 km (thus 10 mil = 100 km). When talking about land area you will often hear the word *mål*. This old measure of 984.34 m^2 has been rounded up to 1,000 m^2 (or 1 decare).
Electricity 220 volts AC, 50 cycles. Plugs have two small round pins, so you may need an adapter for appliances you bring with you.
International dialling code +47. To ring out dial 00 and then the international number.

Topography

Norway is a narrow country 2,600 km (1,600 miles) long, shaped like a tadpole swimming south. At points along the tail it narrows down to as little as 6 km (4 miles). Most of the country's 21,465-km (13,330-mile) long continental coastline lies along the North Sea. Norway has common borders with Sweden (1,620 km/1,005 miles), Finland (720 km/450 miles) and, in the north, Russia (196 km/122 miles). It also has sovereignty over a few islands within the Arctic Circle, the largest being Svalbard (or Spitsbergen).

The south is hilly and partially forested. The most fertile food-growing region is the southern quarter of the country. Although indented with fjords all around its coast, the west coast area from Stavanger to Bergen and Bergen to Trondheim contains the most-visited fjords.

The Glomma is the longest river in Norway. With its source in South Trøndelag and outflow into the Oslo fjord, the river and its tributaries drain about one eighth (41,500 sq km/25, 770 sq miles) of the country. Rivers flowing southwest along the steep western slope are generally short and have numerous rapids and falls. Those flowing southeast along the gentle eastern slope are generally longer.

Norway has thousands of glacial lakes, the largest of which is Lake Mjøsa in the southeast.

Climate

Oslo is one of the warmest locations in Norway during winter; in January the average 24-hour high is -2°C (28°F) and the low is -7°C (19°F). Up north it's a different story, however, with sub-zero temperatures reigning for months and a good number of roads shut over winter due to long-term snow.

Night Skies

● **Midnight Sun** In some parts of Norway the sun does not sink below the horizon for several weeks in the summer. The best time to see the so-called "Midnight Sun" is mid-May to late July. Longyearbyen has the longest period of Midnight Suns, from about 20 April to 20 August.

● **Aurora borealis** The Northern Lights, or Aurora borealis, are most likely to occur from November to February. You need to go north of the Arctic Circle, which cuts Norway just south of Bodø on the Nordland coast. There is, unfortunately, no guarantee they will occur every year.

Glaciers

One of the highlights of Norway is seeing the glaciers, but every year tourists die because they are not careful. Glaciers are in motion, so crevasses several metres wide and 30–40 metres (33–43 yards) deep occur, often covered with snow. Never climb or venture under a glacier without a guide.

Glacier Information Centres at the following places show films and exhibitions about the glaciers, and offer tours: Oppstryn (tel: 57 87 72 00) Fjærland (tel: 57 69 32 88) and Jostedalen (tel: 57 68 32 50).

February and March are the best skiing months. March and April and sometimes even early May are the wet spring months when skies are grey and roads are buckled due to thaws and refreezes; during this time the daily high temperature slowly lifts from about 4°C (39°F) to 16°C (61°F).

Come summertime and the season of the midnight sun, Oslo enjoys daily average temperatures in the low to mid-20°C (70°F), while the sunlight-bathed north has a perfect hiking temperature, hovering around or just below 20°C (68°F). October is the time for autumn rains as temperatures dip below 10°C (50°F), then continue their slide towards zero. The first snow can be expected any time from mid-October to early December, depending on the location.

May and September are very popular with visitors. Transport, hotels and museums are often crowded in these two months. The Easter ski break is a time of mass exodus from schools and jobs to the slopes and trails. Otherwise, Norwegians mainly holiday in July (fellesferie, when factories shut down) or August.

Government

Norway's national assembly, the Storting, is the mainstay of its political system. There are 157 members who sit in two chambers (Odelsting and Lagting); elections occur every four years. There are 19 major local government sub-divisions (counties or fylke), all of which are divided into smaller municipalities (kommune). The government is headed by a prime minister who leads the majority party or a coalition of parties in the Storting. The Norwegian monarch fulfils a symbolic role as the country's Head of State.

Across the political spectrum from left to right are the Red Electoral Alliance (RV), the Socialist Left Party (SV), the Labour Party (A), the Centre Party (SP), the Liberal Party (V), the Christian Democratic Party (Kr.F), the Conservative Party (H) and the Progress Party (Fr.P). Norway's constitution dates from 17 May 1814; a painting of its signing hangs in the Storting chamber. Previously, Norwegians were subject to Danish rule for many centuries, and then entered a union with Sweden which lasted from 1814 until 1905.

National Day is celebrated across the nation on the constitution's anniversary, 17 May, with parades, music and dance.

Economy

Norway has been a member of NATO and the OECD since 1949, and is a founder member of the UN. The nation spends more money per capita on foreign aid than any other country. It is also a member of the Council of Europe and the EEA (the country turned down European Union membership in referenda in 1972 and 1995).

With Denmark, Sweden, Iceland, Finland, the Faroe Islands and Greenland, Norway is also a member of the Nordic Council (founded in 1952). The Council has 87 members, meets once a year in full session and has a permanent secretariat in Copenhagen.

Its most successful agreement is granting freedom for all Nordic citizens to travel without passports within the Nordic region (Norden) and work without a work permit. The 1955 social security convention also guarantees them the welfare benefits, from unemployment to health care, of the country in which they are working. Discussions on a customs union have not had similar success. Sweden and Finland's accession to the EU has complicated matters and the EU is currently trying to renegotiate its position vis-à-vis the Schengen Agreement post-Amsterdam.

As well as funding a mass of technical, educational and arts initiatives, Norway has introduced Nordunet, a communications network for education, with regular educational exchanges; information networks for medical data; facilities for the handicapped, and public

Costs

Norway has a name for being expensive, and certainly this is true in many respects: a cup of coffee in a café can be exorbitant and even the smallest of items like toiletries can cost double the amount they are elsewhere in Europe. The cost of alcohol is enough to make even heavy drinkers think twice about another bottle of wine. But you can get good discount cards on accommodation (page 19) and public transport (page 13), plus Norway offers tourists Tax-Free Shopping (page29).

administration; and environmental programmes, including a Nordic convention on world environment. Individual subjects are based in different centres, such as Helsinki's studies on environmental monitoring, and Oslo's Nordic Industrial Council, which co-ordinates industrial collaborations.

Norway's economy has boomed due to North Sea oil. Other long-established industries include timber, pulp and paper, hydro-electric power, gas, shipping and some mining. Fish and agricultural products have long been staples of the Norwegian economy. The revenue from ocean fisheries has now been surpassed by fish farming, particularly salmon. Commercial whaling is carried out on a modest scale (roughly 600 minke whales a year) against the wishes of the International Whaling Commission (IWC). Newer industry revolves around computers and business services. Tourism is a continually increasing source of capital, too. Some of Norway's most successful ventures include Statoil, Norsk Hydro, Kværner, Aker RGI and Royal Caribbean Cruise Lines.

The People

Norwegians are great hand shakers. Whenever strangers meet, there is always a handshake accompanied by an exchange of full names. When meeting casual acquaintances, you usually shake hands as you arrive and leave.

Norwegians are pleasantly polite. Whenever you are served something you will hear the phrase *Vær så god*, which basically means "You are welcome" and "It is a pleasure to serve you" rolled into one. The only equivalent to "please" in Norwegian is *vennligst*, which is formal and not frequently used. Nor do they say *takk* (thank you) as frequently as English-speaking people.

The only thing remotely unruly in Norwegian manners occurs in the busy streets of Oslo. People jostle each other with impunity: don't be offended if you don't get an apology after someone bumps into you – as long as it's gentle. Of more concern, especially if you are driving, are the mad darts and leaps people take into and across streets, without regard for traffic lights.

Coffee is the national narcotic and served whenever people meet – you may end up awash with the stuff if you're doing the rounds in a day. But the real difficulty is coping with the mounds of pastry often served with the coffee; if you must refuse, do so politely, especially if you are turning down home-made pastries!

Note: if you're in Norway for a long time, Norwegian society is very closely tied to family and long-term friends from school days. Many do not feel inclined to go much further to extend their relationships to outsiders. Consequently, establishing friendships, even within a neighbourhood, could take time.

Doing Business

Norwegians have all the state-of-the-art props when it comes to doing business. Don't be caught out without a firm handshake, a good-looking business card and, if possible, a laptop and mobile phone (fax an added bonus).

Visiting a Norwegian Home

Norwegians usually eat dinner around 4 or 5pm, but dinner parties generally start later, at around 7.30pm. An invitation for any other time of the day usually means coffee and cake (if in doubt call the host and make certain). Let's say you've been invited to dinner and you want to make a good impression. Norway is not a 'drop-in' society so you can expect the food to be well-planned and of high quality. You could do far worse than taking note of the following protocol:

1 Rule number one is that Norwegians are very punctual and expect others to be. Guests usually arrive exactly on time, sometimes even early. Make sure you dress correctly for the occasion (again, if in doubt ask the host in advance).

2 When entering a room, shake hands with everybody present, unless a large function makes that impossible. Introduce yourself to those you have not met before; give a friendly greeting to those you do know, but still shake hands.

3 If it's your first visit to someone's home it is customary to take a small gift along (usually flowers, a plant or chocolates).

4 Dinner parties in Norwegian homes follow a fixed pattern and include short speeches even on family occasions. After tapping his glass, the host will always give a welcome speech and then propose a *skål*. It would be discourteous to touch the wine *before* this initial toast (but expect a liberal helping of *skåls*!).

5 Second helpings (*annen servering*) are so much the rule in Norwegian homes that the host will specifically point out if the dish is only to be passed round once. The secret is not to take too much the first time!

6 Every meal in Norway is concluded with a *takk for maten* (thank you for the food) and, if it's dinner, a general *skål*.

Like all Scandinavians, Norwegians take their summer holiday very seriously as a time for retreating to a fjord or mountain hytte (usually a timber cabin). From mid-June to the end of July/first week in August, offices and factories empty, and it is almost impossible to get an appointment or do any business. May, with its holidays, can also be a difficult time.

Nothing about doing business should take you too much by surprise here. People take work seriously, but also know how to maintain a pleasantly relaxed business atmosphere. Norwegians dress for business much as they do elsewhere; although in summer dress codes are relaxed slightly.

Norwegians, in common with other Scandinavians, are rarely duplicitous. They may well mention the bad points of something first, to get them out of the way; then it's on to the sell. In other words, you won't be drowned in a sea of hype, and the honesty's a little hard to get used to. Ultimately you'll appreciate not having to figure out the pitfalls for yourself.

If you are looking up someone's number in a phone book, you'll find his or her profession listed next to the name; not only is this a matter of professional pride, but a real help in a country with a limited number of surnames.

So much for generalisations; there will always be exceptions. The only really important things to remember are that liquid lunches are unusual, and the work day ends at 3.30 or 4pm.

Business Hours

Office hours in Norway are 9am–4pm. or 8am–4pm; lunch is taken early, usually 11.30am–12.30pm, or 12–2pm for a restaurant lunch or lunch meeting, which are business-like affairs.

Public Holidays

- **1 January** New Year's Day
- Palm Sunday *
- Maundy Thursday *
- Good Friday *
- Easter Sunday *
- Easter Monday *
(making a five-day Thursday to Monday holiday block)
- **1 May** Labour Day
- **17 May** National Independence Day
- Ascension Day *
- Whitsun *
- Whit Monday *
- **25 December** Christmas Day
- **26 December** Boxing Day

* Moveable holidays

Most Norwegian consulates and embassies have commercial attachés. Three organisations in Oslo deal with tourism, business and trade:

The Norwegian Trade Council
(Norges Eksportråd)
Drammensv. 40, 0243 Oslo
Tel: 22 92 63 00
Fax: 22 92 64 00
E-mail: oslo@ntc.no
Website: http://www.ntc.no

The Norwegian Tourist Board
(Nortra)
Drammensv. 40,
Pb, 2893 Solli, 0230 Oslo
Tel: 22 92 52 00
Fax: 22 56 05 05
E-mail: norway@nortra.no
Website: http://www.nortra.no

Oslo Promotion A/S
Grev Wedels plass 4 0151 Oslo
Tel: 23 10 62 00
Fax: 23 10 62 01
E-mail: pr@oslopro.no
Website: http://www.oslopro.no

ODIN, the central web-server for the Norwegian Government, Office of the Prime Minister and the ministries, can be found at: http://odin.dep.no/html/english/

Planning the Trip

Passports and Visas

A valid passport is all that is necessary for citizens of most countries to enter Norway. Visas are not required. If you enter from another Nordic country (Denmark, Finland, Iceland, or Sweden), you won't get a new entry stamp. Tourists are generally limited to a three-month visit; it is possible to stay longer, but you must apply for a visa after the initial three months (Scandinavian passport holders are exempt from this requirement) or if you plan to work in Norway.

Health and Insurance

The are no major health hazards in Norway. A degree of common sense is required when travelling in remote areas, especially during the winter. When hiking/skiing in the mountains always let someone know of your travel intentions, and use guides wherever possible. No vaccinations are necessary to enter Norway and the tap water is (generally) good.

Treatment Norway has reciprocal treatment agreements with the UK and many other European countries; your own National Insurance should cover you to receive free treatment at public hospitals (you will have to pay towards medicine, however). EU members should obtain the relevant documentation to entitle them to this (for British citizens a form E111 from post offices). People from countries without such agreements, and those without an E111, will have to pay a small fee. If you are concerned whether you need extra cover, check in your own country before you go.

Money matters

The Norwegian krone (NOK) is divided into 100 øre. Notes come in denominations of NOK 50, 100, 200, 500 and 1,000 (you may occasionally see higher) and coins are 50 øre and NOK 1, 5, 10 and 20.

You can change currency at post offices, the Oslo S train station, international airports, some hotels and commercial banks. It is always useful to carry a certain amount of cash with you in case of emergency (around NOK 500 should suffice).

Public telephones take either phone-cards (purchased from kiosks) or coins (NOK 10 to be on the safe side). Road toll stations are sometimes unmanned and require coins to be inserted (usually NOK 10) to lift the barrier.

Customs

The following can be brought into Norway by visitors:
● **Money** Notes and coins (Norwegian and foreign) up to NOK 25,000 or equivalent. If you intend to import more, you must fill in a form (available at all entry and exit points) for the Customs Office.
● **Alcohol** 1 litre wine (up to 22 percent proof) and 1 litre of spirits (up to 60 percent proof) or 2 litres wine if no spirits. 2 litres beer. On top of the tax-free quota you may bring in 4 litres wine or liquor against payment of duty.
Note: you must be 20 years or over to import spirits and 18 or over for wine and beer.
● **Tobacco** European residents over the age of 18 may bring 200 cigarettes or 250 g of

Credit Cards/Traveller's Cheques

Use of credit cards is widespread in Norway, with Eurocard, Visa, American Express and Diner's Club the most common. Few petrol stations will take them, however, so make sure you have a fair amount of cash with you. Check with your own credit card company about acceptability and other services.

Traveller's cheques are accepted and should be purchased before travelling to Norway. Eurocheques can be cashed in banks up to the equivalent of NOK 1,500. In most banks you can also get cash on a Visa card, up to a limit of NOK 2,500 a week.

What to Bring/Wear

You're in for a pleasant surprise if travelling to Norway in summer. As it is protected by the Gulf Stream it can get even warmer than some of its southern neighbours. In the south, temperatures in the

other tobacco goods.
● **Sweets** 1 kg duty-free chocolate and sweets.
● **Meat** Up to 3 kg of meat products can be imported from an EEA member country as long as the product is stamped with the country of origin.
● **Sundries** Other goods (excluding articles for personal use) may be brought in duty-free up to a value of NOK 1,200.
● **Prohibited goods** Narcotics, medicines (except for personal use), poisons, firearms, ammunition and explosives. Note: the mild narcotic leaf khat is illegal in Norway.
● **Agricultural produce** This comes under strict surveillance. If it concerns you, get specific details beforehand.

Animals

Some animals must be quarantined upon arrival in Norway, but if your pet comes from an EU country there is no official quarantine. Nor is there a requirement, as there used to be, to keep pets under "house arrest" for a month. Vets' fees are astronomical compared to the UK so pet insurance is essential.

upper 20°C (80°F) are not unusual. The average temperature for the country as a whole in July, including the far north, is about 16°C (60°F), 22°C (71°F) in Oslo.

Pack the clothes you would normally wear in northern Europe, including jumpers and a raincoat, and take some strong walking shoes. The mountains can be chilly, so bring some warmer garments. You are not usually required to dress formally for dinner at Norwegian resort hotels. Spring and autumn are rainy (an umbrella is always useful), and nights can be brisk.

In winter bring very warm clothing and dress in layers (cotton against the skin and then wool). Woollen mittens or gloves and hats (covering the ears) are strongly advised (and face cover, if you are skiing). In the far north, temperatures drop to below -20°C (-68°F). In January, the average daytime temperature in Oslo is -2°C (-35°F) and -7°C (-44°F) at night.

A first-aid kit is recommended for those who plan to make any trips to remoter parts. And be sure to include potions for preventing and treating mosquito bites, as from mid-summer into early autumn biting insects are rife, especially in Lapland.

Tourist Information

There are 350 local tourist offices around Norway, as well as 18 regional tourist offices.

General information
The Norway Information Centre, Vestbaneplassen 1 (between the Oslo City Hall and Aker Brygge), 0250 Oslo
Tel: 820 60 100 (in Norway) or +47 22 83 00 50 (from abroad)
Fax: +47 22 83 81 50.

Regional information
Regional tourist offices are experts in the county they cover. They are not open to personal callers, but will supply advice and information in writing or over the phone.

Oslo/Oslofjord
Oslo Promotion A/S
Vestbaneplassen 1
N-0250 Oslo
Tel: 820 60 100 (when in Norway),
Tel: +47 22 83 00 50 (from abroad). Fax: 22 83 81 50
Website: http://www.oslopro.no
Akershus Tourist Board
Schweigaardsgt. 4
N-0185 Oslo
Tel: 22 05 58 75
Fax: 22 05 58 99
Destinasjon Vestfold AS
St. Olavsgt. 4
N-3110 Tnsberg
Tel: 33 44 36 60
Fax: 33 44 34 47

East Norway
Olympia Utvikling
Troll Park A/S
P.O.Box 373
N-2601 Lillehammer
Tel: 61 28 99 00
Fax: 61 26 92 50
Hedmark Tourist Board
Grnnegt. 11
N-2300 Hamar
Tel: 62 52 90 06
Fax: 62 52 21 49
Oppland Tourist Board
Kirkegt. 76
N-2600 Lillehammer
Tel: 61 28 91 86
Fax: 61 28 94 98
Fjell og Fjord Ferie
DBC-senteret

N-3550 Gol
Tel: 32 07 45 44
Fax: 32 07 55 09
Website: http://www.tellus.no/fjellogfjord/fff-e.htm
Buskerud Adventure
Dronninggt. 15
N-3019 Drammen
Tel: 32 89 00 90
Fax: 32 83 47 51
E-mail: opplevel@online.no

South Norway
Syd Norge A/S
P.O.Box 91, N-4601
Kristiansand
Tel: 38 07 10 08
Fax: 38 07 11 01
http://www.sydnorge.no
Telemark Travel
P.O.Box 2813 Kjørbekk
N-3702 Skien
Tel: 35 53 03 00
Fax: 35 52 70 07
Website: destination.telemark@nano.no
Aust-Agder Tourist Board
Fylkeshuset
N-4800 Arendal
c/o Info-Sr, N-4993 Sundebru

Info from Home

AUSTRALIA
The embassy deals with tourist information.
17 Hunter Street, Yarralumia,
Canberra ACT 2600.
Tel: 062 733444
UK
Norwegian Tourist Board
Charles House, 5 Lower Regent Street, London
SW1Y 4LR
Tel: 00 44 20 7839 6255
Fax: 00 44 20 7839 6014
E-mail: greatbritain@nortra.no
Website: http://www.norway.org.uk/travel/
USA/CANADA
Norwegian Tourist Board
655 Third Avenue, Suite 1810, New York 10017
Tel: 00 1 212 885 9700
Fax: 00 1 212 885 9710
E-mail: usa@nortra.no
Web: http://www.norway.org

Tel: 37 15 85 60
Fax: 37 15 85 65

Fjord Norway
Fjord Norway
P.O.Box 4108 Dreggen
N-5023 Bergen
Tel: 55 31 93 00
Fax: 55 32 60 20
http://www.fjordnorway.no
Rogaland Tourist Board
P.O. Box 798
N 4001 Stavanger
Tel: 51 51 66 00
Fax: 51 51 68 85
Hordaland/Bergen Board
Slottsgt. 1
N-5003 Bergen
Tel: 55 31 66 00
Fax: 55 31 52 08
Sogn/Fjordane Tourist Board
P.O.Box 299
N-5801 Sogndal
Tel: 57 67 23 00
Fax: 57 67 28 06
Møre/Romsdal Tourist Board
P.O.Box 467
N-6501 Kristiansund N
Tel: 71 67 39 77
Fax: 71 67 00 70

Central Norway
Central Norway Travel
(Sør/Nord-Trøndelag)
P.O.Box 65
N-7001 Trondheim
Tel: 73 92 93 94
Fax: 73 52 04 30

North Norway
Top of Europe Norway
P.O.Box 771
N-9001 Troms
Tel: 77 61 05 80
Fax: 77 61 05 79
http://www.tellus.no/finnmark/
Nordland Reiseliv
P.O.Box 434
N-8001 Bod
Tel: 75 52 44 06
Fax: 75 52 83 28
http://www.nordlandreiseliv.no
E-mail: Ntravel@sn.no
Finnmark Travel Association
P.O.Box 1223
N-9501 Alta
Tel: 78 43 54 44
Fax: 78 43 55 59
E-mail: finnoppl@barentsnett.no

Getting There

BY AIR

Scandinavia's flagship carrier, SAS, runs a wide range of flights between Oslo Gardermoen Airport (open October 1998) and other world capitals (usually involving a feeder service to and from one of the main European hubs), with many direct services to and from Bergen, Oslo, Stavanger, Tromsø and Trondheim. SAS also operates a direct service from New York–Newark.

SAS and the Norwegian airline Braathens are joined by other major international airlines – including British Airways, Lufthansa, Air France, KLM, Swissair and Sabena – in connecting Oslo and other cities with daily flights to Europe.

Approximate flying times to Oslo are: London 2 hours, Frankfurt 1 hour 50 minutes, Paris 2 hours, Budapest 3 hours 35 minutes, and Warsaw 3 hours 25 minutes.
From the UK SAS offers four daily non-stop flights from Heathrow to Oslo and two to Stavanger. During the summer

months there is a twice-weekly non-stop service from Heathrow to Tromsø in northern Norway, and daily (except Saturday) non-stop flights from Manchester to Oslo. Three times daily flights go from Aberdeen to Stavanger.

Braathens operates daily flights from Stansted to Oslo and Stavanger/Bergen and six days a week from Newcastle Airport to Oslo and Stavanger.

British Airways operates up to four flights a day from London to Oslo (out of both Heathrow and Gatwick).

Air UK operates scheduled flights Monday to Friday from Aberdeen, Humberside and Teeside to Bergen. In addition, services operate between Aberdeen and Stavanger.

British Midland operates from several UK airports via London Heathrow to Oslo and Bergen.

Ryanair offers a cut-price service from Stansted to Torp near Sandefjord.

There are also charter flights to various airports in Norway (check with your local travel agent for details).

More foreign airlines are likely to start direct services to Oslo as the new Oslo Gardermoen

Airport will have unlimited slots. One rumour is that Braathens' partner, Northwest Airlines, will start flights to the US, Oslo's first foreign intercontinental operator since Delta pulled out in the early 1990s.

All airports are serviced by buses and taxis and the new Oslo Gardermoen Airport has a high-speed rail link to Oslo S (central railway station), the Nationalteatret station and stations through to Asker.

SAS Scandinavian Airline Services
In the UK
Star Alliance Office
7–8 Conduit Street,
London W1R OAY
Reservations from the UK
Tel: 0845-60 727 727
In North America
(Toll-free: 1-800 221 2350)
c/o United Airlines
437 Madison Ave (enter on 50th St), NY.

Braathens/KLM
Newcastle International Airport
Woolsington
Newcastle upon Tyne
NE13 8BZ
Tel: 0870 5074074 (UK only)

Specialist Tour Operators

● **Activity holidays**
Inntravel, Hovingham, York YO62 4JZ. Tel: 01653 628811.
Scantours, 47 Whitcomb Street, London WC2H 7DH. Tel: 020 7839 2927.
● **Arctic voyages/dog-sledging/whale watching**
Arctic Experience & Discover the World, 29 Nork Way, Banstead, Surrey SM7 1PB. Tel: 01737 218800.
Arcturus Expeditions, P.O. Box 850, Gartocharn, Alexandria G83 8RL. Tel: 01389 830204.
Scandinavian Travel Service, 2 Berghem Mews, Blythe Road, London W14 0HN. Tel: 020 7559 6666.

● **Christmas holidays**
Page & Moy, 136–140 London Road, Leicester LE2 1EN. Tel: 0116-250 7676.
● **Norway specialists**
Norsc Holidays, 1 The Lawns, Charmouth DT6 6LR. Tel: 01297 560033.
Taber Holidays, 30A Bingley Road, Saltaire, Shipley, Bradford BD1 2SX. Tel: 01274 594642.
● **Salmon fishing**
Flying Ghillies, P.O. Box 1, Morpeth NE61 6YX. Tel: 01670 737400.
● **Skiing/Walking**
Waymark Holidays, 44 Windsor Road, Slough SL1 2EJ. Tel: 01753 516477.

Mountain & Wildlife Ventures, Brow Foot, High Wray, Ambleside LA22 0JE. Tel: 015394 33285.
● **Tailormade holidays**
Specialised Tours, Copthorne Business Centre, Church Road, Crawley RH10 3RA. Tel: 01342 712785.
● **Tours**
Explore Worldwide, 1 Frederick Street, Aldershot GU11 1LQ. Tel: 01252 319448.
ScanMeridian, 28b Hampstead High Street, London NW3 1QA. Tel: 020 7431 5322.
Great Rail Journeys, Saviour House, 9 St Saviourgate, York YO24 1GX. Tel: 01904 679969.

British Airways

Speedbird House
PO Box 10
Heathrow Airport
Hounslow TW6 2JA
Tel: 0345 222111
Web: www.british-airways.co.uk

British Airways' office in Oslo

British Airways
Karl Johansgt. 16B
0105 Oslo
Tel: 22 82 20 00
Fax: 22 82 20 49
Opening hours Mon–Fri 9am–4pm

Air UK/KLM

Stansted House
Stansted Airport
Essex CM24 1AE
Reservations: 0870 5074074

British Midland Airways

Donnington Hall
Castle Donnington
Derby DE74 2SB
Reservations: 0870 6070555
Web: www.britishmidland.co.uk

BY SEA

Fjord Line operates the only direct year-round service from the UK to Norway with sailings from Newcastle to Stavanger, Haugesund and Bergen. Fjord Line's brochure offers a wide selection of holiday ideas for the winter and summer, ranging from chalets to resorts and motoring breaks in first-class hotels. For further details on fares, schedules and Fjord Line's inclusive holiday brochure, contact:

Fjord Line

Norway House
International Ferry Terminal
Royal Quays
North Shields
Tyne & Wear
NE29 6EE
Tel: 0191-296 1313

Color Line also operate services to Oslo out of Kiel, Germany and Hirtshals and Frederikshavn in northern Denmark, and from Hirtshals to Kristiansand and Moss.

From Denmark and Sweden

There are regular services among the Scandinavian countries. One of the main operators is DFDS Seaways, which sail from Newcastle and Harwich to, among other places, Gothenburg in Sweden. Their address in the UK is:

DFDS Seaways

Scandinavia House, Parkeston Quay, Harwich
Essex, CO12 4QG
Tel: 01255 243243
Fax: 01255 244475
Web: www.scansea.com/UK

BY RAIL

Numerous rail services link Norway with the rest of Scandinavia and Europe. From the Continent, express trains operate to Copenhagen, where inter-Scandinavian trains connect to Oslo. There are train connections in Oslo to other cities in Norway. First and second-class coaches are available on these express trains, plus sleeper coaches on all of the overnight expresses.

The Norwegian State Railway (NSB) is part of the Interail, Eurailpass and Eurail Youthpass system, which offers various discount tickets (including to students).

Trains from Stockholm and Copenhagen to Oslo usually run twice a day. You can also get to northern Norway from Stockholm, with Trondheim and Narvik the principal destinations, again usually twice daily (the line in Norway terminates at Bodø). In addition, there are several daily Copenhagen and Gothenberg connections.

International arrivals and departures are at Sentralstasjon (Oslo-S). Gardermobanen. The high-speed rail link from/to Oslo Gardermoen Airport has a terminal at Oslo S, and trains

Fjord Tours

● **Fjord Line**
International Ferry Terminal,
Royal Quays, North Shields
NE29 6EE.
Tel: 0191-296 1313
● **Huxley Holidays**
Greaves Lane East,
Threapwood, Malpas SY14
7AT. Tel: 01948 770661
● **Taber Holidays**
30A Bingley Road, Saltaire,
Shipley, BD18 4RS
Tel: 01274 594642
● **Scandinavian Travel
Service** (also offers cruises)
2 Berghem Mews, Blythe
Road, London W14 0HN
Tel: 020 7559 6666

also run from/to Asker via Nationalteatret station.

NSB provides train information and also operates as a travel bureau across Norway:

Norwegian State Railways

NSB Reisesenter
P.O.Box 673, N-5001
Bergen/Norway
Tel: +47 55 96 60 52
Fax: +47 55 32 72 70

BY ROAD

Most major shipping lines to Norway allow passengers to bring cars. But coming by car increases sea travel costs, and petrol is expensive in Norway.

Two Oslo-based organisations can help with queries concerning driving:

Norges Automobil Forbund

(NAF or Norwegian Automobile Association)
Storgt 2, 0105 Oslo
Tel: 22 34 14 00
Fax: 22 33 13 73

Kongelig Norsk Automobilklub

(KNA or Royal Norwegian Automobile Club)
Drammensv. 20C P.O. Box 2425
Solli, 0201 Oslo
Tel: 22 56 19 00

Practical Tips

Security and Crime

The streets of Oslo are relatively safe compared with the bigger cities of Europe and North America. The tabloids report an abundance of muggings, stabbings and other crimes of violence, as they do everywhere.

But crime against tourists is rare. If a foreign car is broken into, it's because the criminal has learnt that it's usually a good target. Again, common sense comes into play here; park safely and hide valuables out of sight.

The same applies when out on the town. Simply stick with the happy crowds and avoid the sleazy joints; if your taste is sleazy then you can probably handle yourself anyway. Norwegian cities late at night are usually full of young people, many of them drunk: this is mainly because of the lengthy opening hours and a lack of drinking culture (a Norwegian often drinks to get drunk). Most bars have good bouncers, so alert them if you're having trouble. Police patrols are supplemented by private-sector security personnel and *Nattravene* (Night Ravens, a Guardian Angel-type patrol). Out in the street, you're more likely to meet verbal harassment from drunks than bodily harm; often you'll just be asked for a cigarette or coins.

Worse than the drunks is the threat from drug abusers. Simply give them and the areas they frequent a wide berth (these are usually the cheaper bars and cafés around central railway stations and certain other areas). There is no strict rule here; a no-go area today could be tomorrow's in place.

Medical Services

Doctors and hospitals
The standard of health provision in Norway is very high, and even in remote areas you should have no problem getting medical help. Just about all doctors and nurses speak good English, and if they don't they'll soon find someone who does.

In medical emergencies EU members will receive free treatment at state hospitals (*see page 5 for reciprocal arrangements*), but have to pay towards the non-hospital costs and for prescriptions.

If you are ill, ask your hotel, tourist office or a pharmacy for the address of an English-speaking GP. Private doctors are listed in the directory under *Leger* (doctors). A visit will cost NOK 100-200. Make sure you keep receipts if you have medical insurance.

Pharmacies
For minor problems, head for a pharmacy, or *Apotek* (*for opening hours see above*). Most larger cities have all-night pharmacies (*see below*). In other cities enquire at your hotel; or try the emergency number in the phone book under *Legevakt* or *Lækjarvakt* (doctor on duty). Where there is a rota of 24-hour pharmacies in a city, a list will usually be posted on the door of them all.

Dentists
Emergency dental treatment in Oslo (for the times outside regular dentists' office hours) is available from:
Oslo Kommunale Tannlegevakt, Tøyen Senter, Kolstadgata 18, (near Tøyen T-bane station).
Tel: 22 67 30 00
Open every day 7am–10pm, Sun and public holidays 11am–2pm.

Blood donors
If you are interested in giving blood voluntarily, contact:
Norges Røde Kors Blodsenter
St. Olavs gate 28
P.O. Box 6892
St. Olavs plass
Tel. 22 20 29 39

Night Pharmacies

● **Oslo**
Jernbanetorvets Apotek, across from central train station, Jernbanetorget 4B
Tel: 22 41 24 82,
Fax: 22 33 69 2
Open 24 hours a day
● **Bergen**
Apotek Nordstjernen, Bus Station
Tel: 55 31 68 84
Open Monday to Saturday 8am-midnight, Sunday 9.30am-midnight
● **Stavanger**
Loeveapoteket. Olav V's gt. 11.
Tel: 51520607
Open daily until 11pm, Christmas, New Year, Easter and Whitsun 9am-8pm
● **Trondheim**
St Olav Vakt-apotek, Kjøpmannsgate 65
Tel: 73 52 66 66
Open 8am-midnight Monday to Saturday, Sunday 10am-midnight)

Media

Newspapers Most larger kiosks (like the Narvesen chain found at railway stations, airports and so on) and some bookshops sell English-language newspapers.Deichmanske Bibliotek, the main public library, is at Henrik Ibsen's Gate 1 in Oslo; you'll find a selection of international papers and periodicals in its reading rooms.

Bookshops There are several bookshops in Oslo with English-

Opening Hours

● **Shops** Monday to Friday
9am–5pm, Thursdays until
8pm, Saturday from 9am until
1, 2 or even 3pm
● **Shopping centres** Until 8 or
9pm on weekdays, 6pm on
Saturday
● **Banks** 8.30am–3pm,
weekdays only
● **Pharmacies** Monday to
Friday 9am–5pm, Saturday
mornings and on a rota basis
in larger cities

language sections, including;
Erik Qvist at Drammensveien
16, tel: 22 54 26 00 and Tanum
Karl Johan at Karl Johansgate
37/41, tel: 22 41 11 00.

Radio English broadcasts on
short wave can be picked up if
atmospheric conditions are
favourable. Best results can
usually be heard on short wave
frequency 9410.
During the winter months BBC
radios 1, 2, 3 and 4 can
sometimes be received on AM
but reception is often distorted.
Radio 5 can be picked up on
909 and 693 medium wave
(best reception in the evening).
On Sundays Radio Norway (93
FM) broadcasts the news from
Norway in English in *Norway
This Week*, a 30-minute
programme at 5pm. For local
frequencies of the BBC
World Service ask at a tourist
office.

Television Norway has three
main television stations: NRK
(Norsk Rikskringkasting), TV2
and TVNorge (TVN). Cable TV is
common here and allows you to
pick up a variety of channels
including Swedish TV1 and TV2,
Discovery, MTV, French TV5,
Eurosport, TV3 and so on,
depending on the distributor).
Most hotels have pay channels
in addition to the above. English
films on Norwegian television
are sub-titled, not dubbed.

Postal Services

The central post office in Oslo,
at Dronningensgate 15 (the
entrance is on the corner of
Prinsensgate), is open
Monday–Friday 8am–8pm and
Saturday 9am–3pm. Other post
offices are open weekdays
8am–4pm, Saturday 8am–1pm,
though there may be half-hour or
hour variations.
Letters and postcards are the
same price for the UK and
Europe, slightly more for North
America, air mail. Post takes
2–3 days to Europe and 7–10
days to the USA.

Telecommunications

Calls abroad can be made from
hotels – with a surcharge – or
from phone booths or the main
telegraph office at Kongensgate
21 (entrance Prinsensgate),
Oslo. You can also send faxes
and telegrams from this office.
Norwegian pay-phones take
1, 5 and often 20 kroner pieces;
the minimum charge is NOK 2.
Phonecards, which can be used
in the green phone booths, can
be bought in Narvesen kiosks
and at post offices. Credit cards
(Visa, American Express, Diners,
Eurocard and Mastercard) are
accepted in approximately
3,000 card phones.
When calling from Norway to
foreign countries always dial 00
first. Cheapest calling times are
outside business hours:
5pm–8am.
Telephone directories have a
page of instructions in English
in the index. When looking up
names, remember the vowels
æ, ø, and å come at the end of
the alphabet, in that order.

Religious Services

The Lutheran church is
Norway's state church, with
around 94 percent of the
population registered as
Lutherans. Oslo has many
Lutheran places of worship,

including one American Lutheran
church (Fritzners g. 15, tel: 22
44 35 84, fax: 22 44 30 15)
There is also a Quaker
Friends Society, Swedish
church, German Evangelical
church, Anglican/Episcopalian
church, a synagogue and a
mosque. Services are held in
English at the American
Lutheran church and the
Anglican/Episcopalian church
(St Edmund's, Møllergate 30,
tel: 22 69 22 14).
Minority religious groups are
Pentecostalists, Baptists,
Seventh Day Adventists,
Evangelical Lutherans,
Methodists, Catholics, Jews (the
synagogue is at Bergstein 13,
near St. Hanshaugen, tel: 22 67
23 83) and Moslems. The Oslo
Cathedral (Protestant),
(Domkirke at Storgate, tel: 22
41 27 93) puts on concerts for
tourists at 8pm every
Wednesday). For up-to-date
information, consult the daily
press, or latest *Oslo Guide*.

Tipping

Tipping is easy. Hotels include a
service charge and tipping is
generally not expected.
Restaurants usually have the
service charge included, in
which case it's your choice to
add anything (5–10 percent is
customary). The same applies
to taxi drivers. Table service in
bars (particularly outdoor tables)

Useful Numbers

● **Fire** 110*
● **Police** 112*
● **Ambulance** 113*
● **Medical problems**
For emergency medical
treatment in Oslo (*legevakt*)
ring 22 11 70 70.
● **Internal directory enquiries**
180
● **International directory
enquiries** 181

* No coin required

Embassies in Oslo

Canada
Wergelandsvn 7
Tel: 22 99 53 00

UK
Thomas Heftyesgate 8
Tel: 23 13 27 00

United States
Drammensveien 18
Tel: 22 44 85 50

requires tipping. With hairdressers a tip isn't quite as customary, but again 5–10 percent would be appropriate – and appreciated. Cloakrooms usually have a fixed fee of about NOK 5–10; if not, leave a few krone for the attendant.

Disabled Travellers

The directory for the disabled is no longer available from tourist information, but visitors in need of guidance could contact the Norwegian Association for the Disabled, P.O. Box 9217, Grønland, N-0134 Oslo, tel: 22 17 02 55, fax: 22 17 61 77.

Hotel listings in accommodation guides have symbols designating disabled access and toilets. In the *Oslo Guide* under Outdoor Activities you'll find some listings that specially mention capacity for disabled visitors, such as the Bogstad ski area, Nordmarka.

It is becoming more usual for hotels to adapt their furnishings to the needs of people with physical disabilities. These hotels are indicated in *Accommodation in Norway*. The Norwegian State Railways (NSB) have carriages specially furnished for the disabled and the new Coastal Express ships have elevators and cabins for disabled people. The Euro Booking Service AS, at Rådhusgt 17, N-0158 Oslo, offers brochures on coach tours around Norway especially for

wheelchair users. They also provide hotel bookings and hire cars, tel: 22 00 77 20, fax: 22 33 38 44. Guidebooks for Nordland county (North Norway) can be ordered free of charge from Nordland Reiseliv.

Travelling with Kids

Norway is a welcoming and safe place for children; this is one reason why you will see them out on their own here at a young age. Children can usually travel and stay in hotels for less than the adult tariffs.

Family attractions include:

IN AND AROUND OSLO

International Children's Art Museum (exhibits and workshops), Lille Frøensveien 4, tel. 22 46 85 73 (open all year, entrance fee).
Horseriding, minigolf and Minizoo Ekeberg near Ekeberghallen, tel: 22 68 26 69.
Puppet Theatre Frognerveien 67, tel: 22 42 11 88 (open May–Sept).
Tusen Fryd Amusement Park Ås, Østfold. Open Jun–Aug (May and Sept weekends only). Transport by bus 541 from Oslo-S or Rådhuset, tel: 64 94 63 63. Main attractions are: roller-coaster with loop and corkscrew, Spaceshot, flume ride, carousel, magic carpet,

climbing wall and so on. Height restrictions apply on certain rides. An entrance ticket plus day pass to all the different activities costs: NOK 75 for children taller than 140 cm, NOK 145 for those less than 140 cm, plus NOK 25 for high season.
VikingLandet (adjacent to Tusenfryd, open June–Sept), tel: 64 94 63 63. Live like a Viking for a day. VikingLandet gives you an authentic picture of the Viking Age. Experience the buildings, the market place, smithy, farm animals and fields. Not to be missed, Plus Toktet, a Viking Voyage deep in a mountain cave. Entrance costs NOK 70 for children, NOK 90 for adults. Combination tickets are available with Tusen Fryd, but you need two days to do the lot.

AROUND NORWAY

The Troll Family Park near Lillehammer, tel: 61 27 72 22. Main attractions are: The World's Largest Troll, Fairy Tale Cave, Supervideograph, The Photo Adventure, Energy Centre (exhibition centre for oil and gas), Wax Museum and Experience Centre for Ice Cream. Outdoor entertainment twice daily throughout the summer season. Prices: children NOK 130, adults NOK 150. Children under 3 free.

It's a Dog's Life

All dogs are required by law to wear a name tag showing the telephone number of the owner (these are available from pet shops for around NOK 25). Dogs must be kept on a leash between 15 April and 15 August while in forests and fields to protect the environment and the local wildlife.

During winter, special notices will be posted to inform you of

whether or not dogs have to be placed on leads.

Note that it is illegal for a dog to foul a public place – you are expected to pick up the mess using a plastic bag and to deposit this in a litter bin. Failure to do so may result in a fine. Dogs are not allowed in restaurants; shops and other public buildings usually show a sign if dogs are not welcome.

Kongeparken near Stavanger, tel: 51 61 71 11. More than 40 attractions, including life-sized model of The Giant Gulliver (85 x 7.5 m), riding tracks, bob track, farm, car track, Wild West City, birds and fun fair. Prices: NOK 30 per person. A 10-ride activity card costs NOK 100.

Telemark Sommarland Bø in Telemark, tel: 35 95 16 99. Norway's biggest water park with various wet and dry attractions, including many waterslides and Stuka, a 26-meter high water chute; Flow Rider, the world's biggest surf wave, and a floating river. Plus live entertainment, pony rides, Wild West City and children's playground. Prices including all activities: children NOK 125, adults NOK 150.

Kristiansand Dyrepark tel: 38 04 97 00. Norway's largest wildlife park and most-visited tourist attraction. The park has a wide range of other attractions: amusement park, water park, show and entertainment park, leisure park and Cardamomaby – a tiny village from a well-known children's book by the Norwegian author Thorbjørn Egner. Prices for one day passes: children NOK 150, adults NOK 175.

Youth Information in Oslo provides information on all subjects for young people: Address: Møllergata 3, Oslo, tel: 22 41 51 32. http://www.unginfo.oslo.no Opening hours: Mon–Fri 11am–5pm, closed weekends.

Getting Around

Public Transport

Within Norway there is an excellent network of domestic transport services, a necessity in a country so large and often impassable by land. You may have to use more than one means (for example, train and bus or plane and bus) but if you're determined to travel beyond Oslo you'll find these services indispensable.

Although covering great distances can be expensive, Norway offers transport bargains through special tourist cards like the Fjord Pass, the Bonus Pass (all Scandinavia), plus some of the pan-European programmes like InterRail and Eurail. Within larger cities, tourist passes cover urban transport and many museums.

FROM THE AIRPORT

Oslo will have a new airport with effect from October 1998: the Oslo Gardermoen Airport. This replaces the old Fornebu Airport, with which some of you may be familiar.

Gardermoen is roughly 50 km (30 miles) north of Oslo, and will be served by motorway (buses, taxis and private vehicles) and a new high-speed rail link. This will run to and from a special terminal at the Oslo S (central railway station) and further to Asker via the Nationalteatret station. Soon after Oslo S these specially designed trains enter a tunnel and do not emerge until just

before Lillestrøm (some 16 km/10 miles later). The aim is to provide a quick and efficient service so that around 52 percent of passengers will use public service transport to get to and from the airport. There are also plans to provide a helicopter shuttle service to Oslo.

If you arrive from London Stansted at Torp (which is being marketed as Oslo's second airport but which is, in fact, at Sandefjord almost 2 hours down the west side of the fjord), buses and trains will take up to 2½ hours depending on traffic conditions).

All other major city airports are serviced by buses and taxis.

BY AIR

Considering its size, Norway is exceptionally well served by domestic airlines, with about 50 airports and airfields scattered throughout the country.

The three domestic airlines are SAS, Braathens and Widerøe, and each has discount travel. SAS offers a Visit Scandinavia Pass, Braathens a summer Visit Norway Pass (discount rate flight coupons) and Widerøe the Summer Pass.

A fourth low-cost, no-frills airline, Color Air (same principal owner as the shipping company) will commence operations by the opening of the new Oslo Gardermoen Airport in 1998. Initially the airline plans to operate to Ålesund, Trondheim, Bergen and Stavanger.

SAS Scandinavian Airlines System
Bookings tel: 810 03 300
Info tel: 67 59 67 19
Main office tel: 67 59 60 50

Smoking

It is illegal to smoke in all public places, including on public transport. Restaurants must have a non-smoking area walled off from smokers.

Braathens
Oksenøyveien 3, 1330 Oslo
tel. 67 59 70 00
fax. 67 59 13 09
Wideroe's Flyveselskap ASA
Vollsv. 6, Pb 131, 1324 Lysaker
Bookings tel: 67 11 14 60
fax: 67 11 14 56
Info tel: 67 11 14 70
Main office tel: 67 11 60 00
fax: 67 11 61 95

BY RAIL

Rail services are far more comprehensive in the south than in the north, and tend to fan out from Oslo, so you will have to supplement your trip with ferries and buses, unless you are travelling strictly in the south or to the major towns. The Oslo-Bergen line is hailed as one of the world's most spectacular for its scenery.

Oslo S (Oslo Sentralstasjon) is Norway's busiest railway station, located in central Oslo at the eastern end of Karl Johansgate on Jernbanetorget. Long-distance, express and local suburban trains arrive and depart here. It is also the terminal for the Oslo Gardermoen Airport high-speed rail link (some trains continue on under the city to Asker via Nationalteatret station). The end of the line in Norway is at Bodø, but the most northerly railway station is at Narvik, which is reached through Sweden by train or by bus from Fauske. Most of NSB's lines run through tourist country, presenting continuous panoramas of unspoiled scenic beauty.

Most trains are modern and efficient, but the older rolling stock has a touch of nostalgic luxury. New inter-city express (ICE) trains offer one class only. There is a wide range of special offers that can make your holiday reasonable. The Norway Railpass offers one or two weeks of unlimited rail travel in Norway, 1st or 2nd class, or three travel days in a period of one month. The Scanrail Pass offers unlimited travel all over Scandinavia, as well as discounts on certain ferries, buses and hotel chains

If you plan to take special fast trains, you must book ahead. Ticket sales are from the main hall of the train station (tickets for ordinary trains may also be bought on board).

For information about timetables, ticket prices, bookings, seat reservations and so on, tel: 815 00 888 + 1 for operator, or fax: 22 36 64 58.

Trafikanten (see Tickets and Info) also helps with transport and booking queries.

BY BUS/COACH

Where the rail network stops, the bus goes further: you can get to practically anywhere you want by bus. Usually it is not necessary to book in advance, but pay the driver on boarding. NOR-WAY Bussekspress (bus pass) guarantees a seat for all passengers. On sale only outside Norway through the company's agents, the pass is valid all year round and offers two categories for travel on the national network:
(i) unlimited travel within seven consecutive days or
(ii) unlimited travel within a 14-day period. Children from 0 to 4 years travel free, 4 to16 years pay 75 percent of the adult price.

NOR-WAY Bussekspress AS
Karl Johans gt. 2, N-0154 Oslo
tel: 23 00 24 40
fax: 23 00 24 49

BY WATER TRANSPORT
Ferries
Norway is a country where you are never very far from the sea. Ferries are an invaluable means of transport that allow short cuts across fjords to eliminate many road miles. In Oslo, ferries to the fjord islands leave from the quay near Aker Brygge.

Ferries (such as the Horten-Moss ferry across Oslofjord between Vestfold and Østfoldare) are crucial to commuters in busy areas. Almost all town marinas have places for guest boats, with mooring fees running from NOK 30 per night.
Long-distance Boats
Hurtigruten, the Norwegian Coastal Express service, is a vital means of water transport

---

Norway in a Nutshell

One of the most pleasurable ways of seeing Norway is to take a **Norway in a Nutshell** journey. These use a variety of public transport and take you through some of the country's most beautiful scenery.

The difference in altitude on the Flåm railway between Myrdal and Flåm is 865 metres (946 ft); the line a masterpiece of engineering. When you have made the descent you are at the head of one of the longest fjords in the world, Sognefjorden, and on the brink of another scenic high.

The trips can be made in either direction and from any of the stations between Oslo and Bergen.

Norway in a Nutshell round trip: train from Oslo to Myrdal/Flåm, boat to Gudvangen, bus to Voss, train to Oslo.

Norway in a Nutshell one way: train from Oslo to Myrdal/Flåm, boat to Gudvangen, bus to Voss, train to Bergen.

Tickets are sold at the railway station in Oslo and Bergen or from travel agencies. A special price is available for children and senior citizens (67 or over).

for Norwegians, but also a superb way for visitors to see Norway's dramatic coast. In summer, boats leave daily, travelling between Bergen and Kirkenes in 11 days and putting in at 35 ports.

Travel agents can give details, and sell special Coastal Passes to 16–26-year-olds. The steamers take cars, and should be booked well in advance. Either contact your local travel agent or:

Troms Fylkes Dampskibsselskap AS
Bookings tel: 77 64 82 00
fax: 77 64 81 80,
E-mail: booking@tfds.no
Ofotens og Vesteraalens Dampskibsselskab ASA
Narvik tel: 76 96 76 00
fax: 76 96 76 01
Bookings tel: 76 96 76 96
fax: 76 96 76 11
E-mail: booking@ovds.no
http://www.hurtigruten.com

Travel Cards

The Oslo Card (*Osloskortet* – issued for one, two and three days, with half price for children) is your ticket to unlimited public transport (including city ferries) and free entry to many museums. If you want a card for travel only, there are all kinds of passes including a Minikort (four rides at a discount) and Maxikort (14 rides at a discount), plus passes appropriate for longer stays.

The Oslo Card may be purchased at the Central Railway Station (Oslo S), Trafikanten (see Travel and Info), as well as all Narvesen kiosks and hotels, campsites and tourist offices.

Other cities offer similar tourist travel cards: for example, the Bergen Card (24-hour and 48-hour passes from tourist information offices, the railway station, hotels, campsites and the Hurtigrute terminal) and the Bergen Package (all details in the *Official Bergen Guide*

Tickets and info

For tickets, routes, times and all other queries about public transport, Trafikanten in Oslo offers an information and booking service. Its office is at:

● Oslo S Station, at the bottom of the glass tower at the front of the station
Tel: 22 41 70 30.
Open weekdays 7am–11pm, weekends 8am–11pm.

produced by the Bergen Tourist Board).

BUSES AND TRAMS

Oslo's bus and tram system is comprehensive and runs on schedule; there are detailed timetables at every stop. Single fares are NOK 18; with an Oslo Card you travel anywhere for free. Trafikanten can suggest bus or tram routes to get you where you're going. There are night buses on some routes and very early morning buses (starting at 4am) so that public transport is available virtually around the clock. Bergen and Trondheim also have tram systems.

UNDERGROUND

Oslo's underground is called the T-bane and is very simple to use. There are basically eight lines, four from the east and four from the west that converge under the centre of Oslo. You can catch any train to any of the far-flung suburbs from any of the stations between Tøyen and Majorstuen. Station entrances are marked with "T". Trafikanten has route maps. The most scenic route must be T-bane 1 up to Frognerseteren.

TAXIS

Taxis are widely available, even in many suburban and rural areas, so you need never risk

getting caught for drunken driving (for which penalties are severe).

No matter where you are in Oslo telephone 815 44 815 and you will be transferred to the nearest taxi rank. Taxis can also be booked for up to four people on tel: 22 38 80 90, and mini-buses on tel: 22 38 80 70. Otherwise, you can take a taxi from one of the many taxi ranks scattered around the city.

In Oslo taxis are more expensive at night or if ordered by phone. At night there are two things to watch out for: when everyone leaves the bars and restaurants late, long queues build up at taxi ranks. This can be extremely uncomfortable in the winter if you are not dressed correctly. The problem has given rise to a second difficulty: "pirate" taxis. These either cruise up out of the blue or a "dummy" (usually a foreigner) comes and asks you if you want a taxi without queuing. This guide recommends against using pirate taxis, but if you want to take the risk agree a price beforehand.

Private Transport

BY CAR

Norway's roads are extremely good, particularly in view of the treacherous weather conditions encountered in winter. Be prepared for tunnels, though, as some routes have long lengths of road underground .

EU driving licences are valid in Norway, but drivers from other countries must carry an International Driving Licence.

You drive on the right, and traffic regulations are strictly enforced (for guidelines see page 15).

Winter driving With Norway's winters, you should never assume all roads are passable. Small roads in the north are often closed so the authorities can put all manpower into keeping main roads safe, and

Rules of the Road

It is essential for visitors to Norway to be aware of Norwegian driving regulations, some of which vary significantly from those in the UK and on the Continent. Here are a few tips to help you drive safely, but for further guidance it's worth getting a copy of *Velkommen på norske veier* (Welcome to Norwegian Roads), which includes an English section and is available at tourist offices.

• **Speed Limits** The maximum speed limit is usually 80 kph, though 90 kph is permitted on some roads (mainly dual carriageways). The limit is reduced to 50 kph in built-up areas, and even as low as 30 kph on certain residential roads. On-the-spot fines are given for drivers found speeding (this may be as much as NOK 100 per km over the limit). Some roads have automatic cameras, others radar traps.

• **Giving Way** This is very confusing to the visitor. Roads marked at intervals by yellow diamond signs indicate that you have priority. On all other roads you are required to give way to traffic entering from the right. This is further confused by the fact that some roads have a series of white triangles painted across them at junctions, which mean stop and give way, though as you can imagine these easily become obliterated by snow and ice in the winter!

On roundabouts priority is, from the left. Note that roundabouts are a relatively recent innovation in Norway and Norwegian drivers are not always adept at following the code here. Always give way to trams, buses and taxis. Many roads have a lane (usually the one to the right) for buses and taxis only.

• **Drinking and driving** You are strongly advised not to drink at all if you anticipate driving within at least 8 hours. The current permissible limit is 0.02 per ml, and penalties are severe (21 days' imprisonment, a high fine and loss of licence are automatic).

• **Documentation and equipment** You must always have the following with you in your car: driving licence, car registration documents, European accident statement form, insurance policy and a reflective warning triangle. A snow shovel and tow rope are also useful in winter. For regularly updated information, the AA runs a very good fact line for just a small charge on tel: 0836 401877.

• **Lights** It is obligatory to drive with dipped headlights on during the daytime, even on the brightest summer day. This rule applies to all vehicles, including motorcycles and mopeds. We recommend you carry spare bulbs. Do not forget that right-hand drive cars require black adhesive triangles (often supplied by ferry companies), or clip-on beam deflectors, so you don't dazzle oncoming drivers.

• **Seat belts** must be worn, both front and back (again, there are on-the-spot fines for failing to comply).

• **Tyres** It is obligatory to use winter tyres from October to April. These are either tyres with studs (*piggdekk*) or specially designed tyres for use in ice and snow. Studded tyres are preferred but these may soon be prohibited in urban areas for environmental reasons. Every car bought into Norway has to have two sets of tyres!

manpower into keeping main roads safe, and even the E6 highway from Oslo to Trondheim has been known to close occasionally. If you intend to travel on minor roads, seek a local's advice and go prepared for anything.

Breakdown and accidents

The AA and RAC are affiliated to the AIT (Alliance Internationale de Tourisme), so members receive free assistance (with journey planning as well as backup in case of breakdown or accident) from Norway's NAF (Norges Automobilforbund) . More comprehensive repairs can be carried out at NAF contracted garages (for which you will have to pay). NAF also patrol Norway's main roads and mountain passes from 16 June to 14 August. They have emergency phones along the mountain passes.

NAF, Storgt. 2. N-0155 Oslo
tel: 22 34 14 00
fax: 22 33 13 73
24-hour emergency service (for members of RIT clubs) tel: 22 34 16 00, fax: 22 42 88 30.

If you are involved in an accident where there are no injuries, telephone either Falken Redningskorps A/S on 800 30 050/22 95 00 00 or Viking Redningstjeneste A/S 800 32 900/22 08 60 00. These offices cover all of Norway and provide a 24-hour service (800 is a freephone number).

It is not necessary to call the police for minor accidents, but drivers must exchange names and addresses; leaving the scene without doing so is a crime. Only call the police (on 112) or an ambulance (on 113) if it's a real emergency.

Tolls

Several roads have tolls to pay for construction work and you have to pay to enter some of the larger cities. Changes to the numbering of some toll roads, for example the E39, E134 and E136, are taking place.

Caravanning

For information contact:
The Norsk Caravan Club,
Solheimveien 18, N-1473
Skårer
tel: 67 97 49 20
fax: 67 90 13 13

Car hire

Hiring a car in Norway can be expensive, but may be worthwhile if shared between several people. Otherwise, watch for special weekend and summer special prices.

Avis Bilutleie/Liva Bil AS
PO Box 154, N-1361 Billingstad (near Oslo),
tel: 66 77 11 11
fax: 66 77 11 22
Oslo reservations, tel: 22 83 48 00, fax: 22 83 18 24
Bergen reservations, tel: 55 32 01 30
Trondheim reservations, tel: 73 52 69 15, fax: 73 52 64 66

Europcar/Interrent
PO Box 7041 Homansbyen,
N-0306 Oslo
tel: 22 60 70 22
fax: 22 60 82 44

Hertz Bilutleie
PO Box 331, N-1324
Lysaker/Oslo
tel: 67 16 80 00
fax: 67 16 81 00.
Oslo reservations, tel: 67 12 55 55, fax: 67 58 02 22
Bergen reservations,
tel: 55 96 40 70
Trondheim reservations,
tel: 73 50 35 00.

Road Information

Vegmeldingssentralen (The Road User Information Centre) is an office of the *Statens Vegvesen* (Public Roads Administration). Its main function is to monitor and provide information about roads and road conditions. You may also get information about distances and ferry timetables. Open 24 hours all year, tel: 22 65 40 40.

Toll Roads

ROAD/Toll area/Price (in NOK)
E6 Trondheim–Stjørdal 30
E6 Leirfjorden, Nordland 40
E10 Nappstraumen Tunnel, Nordland 65
E18 Oslo–Drammen 15
E18/16 Oslo–Hønefoss 12
E18 Larvik–Porsgrunn, Telemark 15
E39 Nordhordalands Bridge, Hordaland 45
E39 Rennafast, Rogaland 80
E39 Kristiansund, Møre og Romsdal 55
5 Nastdals Tunnel, Sogn og Fjordane 35
5 Fjærland–Sogndal, Sogn og Fjordane 120
E134 Akrafjorden, Hordaland 40
17 Helgelands Bridge, Nordland 66
36 Skien–Porsgrunn, Telemark 15
64 Atlanterhavsvn, Møre og Romsdal 40
64 Skålavn, Møre og Romsdal 40
108 Hvaler Tunnel, Østfold 50
457 Flekkerøy Tunnel, Vest Agder 75
562 Askøy Bridge, Hordaland 100
658 Ålesund-Ellingsoy-Glske-Møre og Romsdal 50
714 Hitra mainland, SørTrøndelag 60
726 Hitra-Fjellværøy, SørTrøndelag 50
755 Skarnsund Bridge 55
863 Kvalsund Bridge, Troms 66
Oslo Toll Road 12
Bergen Toll Road 5
Trondheim Toll Road 11

Toll prices are for a private car (with trailer of maximum weight 3,500 kg). They are subject to change without notice, so Norwegians tend to keep a stash of change handy in the car.

CYCLING

A lot of people cycle in Norway (particularly in Oslo), and do so safely as there is so little traffic on many minor roads. But you must still go with caution as, though there are a few cycle routes, it is not an integrated system. Cyclists are not allowed to go through the larger tunnels, for example (because of car fumes). Out in the countryside you'll find surfaced cycle paths.

Cycling is an excellent way of exploring outside Oslo because bicycles are allowed on most trains and buses (even rural services) for a small charge.

There are even special cycle trains laid on during the summer. The *Oslo Guide*, under Outdoor Activities, gives detailed suggestions for a *Nordmarka* (Oslo's forest land) route, and tourist offices have details of mountain cycle tours.

Information The Syklistens Landsforening (Cycling Association) can help planning tours and cycling holidays. Cycling Association, Storg. 23C Pb. 8883 Youngstorget, 0028 Oslo
tel: 22 47 30 30
fax: 22 47 30 31
E-mail slf-bike@online.no

Cycle rental Bikes can be hired from hotels, campsites, local tourist offices or sports shops, as well as small cycle hire shops. In Oslo Vestbanen AS rents out anything from rollerblades to motorcycles to electric cars (bikes are included somewhere here!) for the day or longer periods.
Vestbanen AS, Vestbaneplassen 2 (near Aker Brygge)
tel: 23 11 51 00
fax: 23 11 50 70

Mountain bike rental Off-road and mountain bikes are for hire from White Water AS, which deals in extreme sports gear. White Water AS, Cort Adelers g 27, Oslo
tel: 22 55 11 07
fax: 22 55 11 48.

On Foot

There is nowhere in Norway you can't go happily on foot; it is a nation of devout walkers, and walking is still probably one of the most popular outdoor activity at weekends.

The law of access to the natural environment, known as everyman's right, allows you to walk wherever you want in the wilderness areas such as seashore, forests, mountains and in other non-cultivated regions. This should be done with consideration. Use paths and roads when you go for walks in agricultural and populated areas.

It is preferable to make use of campsites if you are staying overnight outdoors. If you pitch a tent in the wilderness, it should be situated at least 150 metres (160 yards) from the nearest house or hut. Open fires are prohibited from 15 April to 15 September.

Detailed maps are available from Norway's Touring Association. Anyone can join the association; simply write for an application to the address below (family membership is available). Membership gives you rights to use the association's huts. If you subscribe at a slightly higher rate, you'll get the magazine and yearbook. The map and guidebook selection is excellent; survey maps of all Norway are sold; sketch maps are free.

The Norwegian Tourist Board publishes a handbook, *Mountain Hiking in Norway,* which gives suggested itineraries for mountain walks

Hitching

Hitching is not as common here as it is elsewhere in Europe; this is not to say it is impossible. You'll have the best chance on busier south and west coast roads. Using a sign is recommended.

Walking in the National Parks

The Ministry of Environment has set up 21 National Parks to ensure the protection of the distinctive characteristics of the country's various regions. They are:

Børgefjell 1,007 km², on the border between Nord-Trøndelag and Nordland.

Dovrefjell 256 km², central Norway, comprising a chain of valleys.

Femundsmarka 390 km², between Hedmark and SørTrøndelag.

Gressåmoen 182 km², in Nord-Trøndelag.

Gutulia 19 km² directly south of Femundsmarka, bordering with Sweden.

Hardangervidda 3,422 km², covering parts of the regions Hordaland,

Telemark and **Buskerud**, in southern central Norway.

Jostedalsbreen 1,230 km², situated between the Sognefjord and the Nordfjord, is the largest glacier in mainland Europe, being 80 km long.

Jotunheimen 1,145 km², extends over parts of Oppland and Sogn and Fjordane.

Ormtjernkampen 9 km², just northwest of Lillehammer, in the county of Oppland.

Rago, 167 km², approximately 25 km north of Fauske in Nordland.

Reisa 803 km², in Nordreisa in Troms, about 60 km from the Finnmark region.

Rondane 580 km², just south of Dovrefjell Park, in the region of Oppland.

Saltfjellet – Svartisen 2,105 km² in the county of Nordland.

Stabbursdalen 98 km², south of Porsanger peninsula in Finnmark.

Øvre Anarjåkka 1,399 km², in the south of Finnmark.

Øvre Dividal 743 km², in the region of Troms, bordering on to Sweden.

Øvre Pasvik 67 km², the easternmost corner of Norway in Finnmark, bordering on to Finland and Russia.

Ånderdalen 69 km², on the island of Senja in Troms.

Svalbard North-west Spitsbergen National Park, 3,560 km², covers the north-western corner of Spitsbergen. Large colonies of sea birds, reindeer and walrus are found here as well as areas of cultural and historical interest.

Forland National Park 640 km², a long, thin island with flat beaches, high mountain peaks and small glaciers. Due to the warming effect of the Gulf Stream, this is the northernmost nesting place of some bird species.

South-Spitsbergen National Park 5,300 km², covers the southern parts of Spitsbergen. 65 percent of the park consists of glaciers or permanent snow and ice.

More information

To learn more about the parks, contact the relevant regional tourist board in Norway, or ask for a leaflet from the Ministry of Environment at:

The Ministry of Environment Information Centre, Myntgt. 2, N-0030 Oslo, tel: 22 24 57 87, fax: 22 24 27 56.

and details of chalets and where to stay (£12 plus P&P, from Nortrabooks Scandinavia Connection, 26 Woodsford Square, London W14 8DP). If you read Norwegian, there is a very good guide for long tours in the Oslo area called *40*

Trivelege Turer i Oslo og Omegn.
Touring Association (Den Norske Turistforening), Storgate 3, Pb. 7 Sentrum, 0101 Oslo, Closed weekends. tel: 22 82 28 0 fax: 22 82 28 01

Where to Stay

Norwegian hotels are notoriously expensive, but, in common with the rest of Scandinavia, they slash their rates during the outdoor summer holiday period when business decreases. This makes the summer holidays (May to September) seem attractive when compared with standard rates. Weekends are also usually cheaper. Normal weekday rates outside summer are geared towards business

Booking from Home

Canada
En Route Holidays
Toronto, Ontario
Tel: 905-882-9655

UK
Color Line
Int. Ferry Terminal
North Shields
Tel: 0191-296-1313
Scottish Choice Itineraries
Aberdeen.
Tel: 01224 821193

USA
Kontiki Travel
NY.
Tel: 718 748 7400
Five Stars of Scandinavia
Gig Harbor, WA.
Tel: 206 857 4852
Passage Tours of Scandinavia
Fort Lauderdale, Florida
Tel: 954 776 7070
Jason Travel
Scandinavian Dept, San Francisco
Tel: 415 957 9102

occupants, which partially explains why they're so high.

When it comes to places to stay, Norway has something to suit every pocket and every requirement. The range covers hotels from the luxurious to the comfortable, to more modest guesthouses, campsites, cosy self-catering chalets, and youth and family hostels. Facilities and service are of international standard. A lot of hotels provide luxury attractions like fitness centres, secretarial services, and newer Norwegian hotels are very business conference-oriented.

British-style bed and breakfast is developing in Norway, and country or farm holidays offer an opportunity to experience day–to-day farm life at close quarters.

Full pension terms are available to guests staying at the same establishment for at least 3–5 days. Reductions for children are 75 percent for under 3s and 50 percent for 3–12-year-olds, providing the child occupies an extra bed in the parents' room. Guesthouses (*pensjonat*) offer lower rates but are generally good.

There is no central Norwegian hotel booking service, so you have to go through travel agents and tour operators to find rooms, or book direct (as practically everyone speaks English this is very easy).

The *Accommodation in Norway* brochure, available from Norwegian embassies and consulates, is a useful tool. You may also order the brochure from the Norwegian Tourist Board (NORTRA) in Oslo.

Another practical guide, the *NRI Guide*, is prepared by Norsk Reiseinformasjon AS (NRI). This free book provides details of around 1,000 establishments, ferry timetables, domestic car ferries in Norway and the Coastal Express Steamer. It is available from tourist offices or contact:

Norsk Reiseinformasjon AS, Tollbugt. 32, N-0157 Oslo
tel: 22 47 73 40
fax: 22 47 73 69

Over the page is a sampling of hotels in Norway's main cities, and from page 23 details of other accommodation.

Hotel Chains

The major hotel chains are all well represented in the five main congress towns of Oslo, Stavanger, Bergen, Trondheim and Tromsø:

Best Western Hotels Norway,
Cort Adelers g 16, N-0254 Oslo
Tel: 22 55 09 10
Fax: 22 55 61 23
Free booking number: 800 11 624
Choice Hotels AS
Olv V's g 6 Pb. 1936 Vika
0125 Oslo
Tel: 22 40 13 00
Fax: 22 40 13 10
First Hotels
Tel: 800 104 10 (in Norway);
+46 8 692 44 50 (internation)
E-mail: first.res@firsthotels.se
http;//www.firsthotels.com
Radisson SAS International Hotels
P.O. Box 185, N-1324 Lysaker
Tel: 67 12 02 20
Fax: 67 12 00 11
Rica Hotel og Restaurantkjede
ASA, Løkketangen 10, Bærum
Tel: 67 80 72 00
Fax: 67 80 72 50
Scandic Hotels A/S
Sjølyst pl 5, P.O. Box. 173
Skøyen 0212 Oslo
Tel: 23 15 50 00
Fax: 23 15 50 49

Booking in Oslo

In Oslo, the Tourist Information at the Information Centre and at Central Station will book accommodation for those arriving in person. It is open every day 8am–11pm and deals with all grades of accommodation from private rooms in houses to pensions and hotels in the Oslo area.

Discounts

As well as the Fjord Pass (*see below*), most of the major hotel chains offer discount cards:

Best Western Euro Guestcheque, valid from 1 January to 31 December in 43 Best Western Hotels in Norway (and 800 throughout Europe). Rates US$ 95–175 for a double room, single room US$ 95. Breakfast and bath/shower included.
Best Western Hotels Norway,
P.O. Box 2773 Solli
N-0204 Oslo
Tel: 22 55 09 10
Fax: 22 55 61 23
Norlandia Summer Pass, valid from mid-June to mid-August in 19 hotels. Prices NOK 245–395. Every fifth night free. Norlandia Hotellene,
P.O. Box 6615 St Olav's Place,
0129 Oslo
Tel: 22 20 03 90
Fax: 22 20 90 23
Rica Hotellferie Pass, valid from around mid-June to mid-August in 50 hotels. Price for the pass NOK 75. Discounts on hotel accommodation and every fifth night free.
Rica Hotel and Restaurant Chain, P.O. Box 453,
1301 Sandvika/Oslo
Tel: 67 82 70 00
Fax: 67 82 70 50
Radisson SAS Hotel Worldwide/ Family Magic Pass offers summer prices from mid-May to September. Every fifth night free. Book through travel agents or directly at hotels.
Scandic Holiday Card costs NOK

Price Categories

Price categories are indicated by dollar signs and are per night for two people in a double room with breakfast
$$$ More than NOK 1,700
$$ NOK 1,100–1,700
$ Less than NOK 1,100

The Fjord Pass

If you are travelling around Norway in summer, The Fjord Pass is well worth buying because it gives you a 20 percent discount on all categories of accommodation.
Valid at 236 hotels, guest houses, apartments and holiday cottages throughout Norway in summer, it is the only Norwegian discount card to be accepted by members of several hotel chains.
Fjord Pass rates for hotels range from NOK 195 to NOK 470 per person per night in a double room, with breakfast included. One Fjord Pass costs NOK 75 and is valid

100 and is valid during summer and weekends all year. Scandic Hotels AS, P.O. Box 2458 Solli, N-0202 Oslo
Tel: 22 44 99 09
Fax: 22 44 83 23
Nordic Hotelpass offers 50 percent reduction during summer at 52 Choice Hotels in Norway, including 11 designated as "children's" hotels (plus around 250 other hotels in Scandinavia and Europe).
Choice Hotels International,
Olav V's Gate, P.O. Box 1936
0125 Oslo
Tel: 22 40 13 00
Fax: 22 40 13 10
E-mail: post@choice.no
http://www.choicehotels.no

Hotels

The hotels are listed geographically starting with the most expensive to the least. There is also a seperate box on the opposite page for budget hotel accommodation.

OSLO

Grand
Karl Johansgate 31, N-0159
Tel: 22 42 93 90
Fax: 22 42 12 25
Opposite the Stortinget, one

for two adults and children under the age of 15. You can book in advance or on a day-to-day basis. You can reserve a room either through the booking office in Bergen or by contacting the hotel direct.
The Fjord Pass is available from travel agents or tourist information offices, as well as hotels and the Mix kiosk chain. Otherwise, contact:
Fjord Tours A/S
P.O. Box 1752 Nordnes
N-5024 Bergen
tel: 55 32 65 50
fax: 55 31 20 60
E-mail:
vibecke@reiselivsutvikling.no

suite is reserved for the winner of the Nobel Peace Prize in December, and official government receptions are held in the rococo banqueting hall. Spacious contemporary-style decor in the bedrooms. **$$$**
Radisson SAS Scandinavia Hotel
Holbergsgate 30, N-0166
Tel: 22 11 30 00
Fax: 22 11 30 17
Luxurious, like all SAS hotels, this one also has very fine restaurants and a rooftop bar. Buses to and from airport. **$$$**
Bristol
Kristian VII's Gate 7, N-0164
Tel: 22 82 60 00
Fax: 22 82 06 01
Superb Moorish-style lobby and close to the city's main shopping street. Rooms are decorated with antiques. Patronised by the wealthy. **$$**
Continental
Stortingsgaten 24–26, N-0161
Tel: 22 82 40 40
Fax: 22 42 96 89
Established 1909 and still run by the family of the founders, the place where Norwegian guests of state are accommodated. **$$**
Clarion Royal Christiania Hotel
Biskop Gunnerus' Gate 3, N-0106
Tel: 23 10 80 90

Fax: 23 10 80 80
Recently restored luxuriantly;
magnificent atrium, spacious
rooms, wonderful service and
breakfasts and convenient
location near Oslo S station. **$$**
First Hotel Millennium,
Tollbugaten 25, P.O. Box 289
N-0106
Tel: 23 00 30 00
Fax: 23 00 30 30
One of two new hotels built in
Oslo by the Swedish First Hotel
group. This was built in an
existing city centre building with
the help of leading Norwegian
architects Platou. **$$**

Gabelshus Hotel
Gabelsgt 16, N-0272
Tel: 22 55 22 60
Fax: 22 44 27 30
A pleasant ivy-clad hotel with
excellent service and a good
traditional kitchen. **$$**
Holmenkollen Park Hotel Rica
Kongveien 26, N-0390
Tel: 22 92 20 00
Fax: 22 14 61 92
Set high in the leafy
Holmenkollen district, this grand
old-style, wooden building looks
right out over Norway's most
famous ski jump; a modern
annexe was added in the

1980s. Excellent facilities. **$$**
Noble House Hotel & Suites
Kongensgt 5, N-0153
Tel: 23 10 72 11
Fax: 23 10 72 10
A member of the World Hotels
(First Class Collection) group,
this newly built hotel in the heart
of old "Christiania" won the "Prix
Européen de la Reconstruction"
for its design. **$$**
Radisson SAS Plaza Hotel
Sonja Henies pl 3, N-0134
Tel: 22 93 87 95
Fax: 22 17 73 00
This is the tall glass structure
between Oslo S and Oslo

Budget Hotel Accommodation ($)

Ålesund
Atlantica Hotel
R. Rønnesbergsgt. 4
Tel: 70 12 91 00

Bardufoss
Bardufosstun
Ole Reistads vei 4
N-9200 Bardufoss
Tel: 77 83 46 00

Bergen
Hotel Hordaheimen
C Sundtsgate 18
5004 Bergen
Tel: 55 23 23 20

Bodø
Bodø Hotel
Prof Schyttesgt 5
P.O. Box 1055
N-8001 Bodø
Tel: 75 52 69 00
Midnattsol B & B
Storgt. 65
Tel: 75 52 19 26

Drangedal
Gautefall Hotel & App
Gautefallheia
N-3750 Drangedal
Tel: 35 99 97 77

Geilo
Solli Sportell
Skurdalsvegen 25
N-3580 Geilo
Tel: 32 09 11 11

Ustedalen Høyfjellshotel
N-3581 Geilo
Tel: 32 09 01 11

Geiranger
Hotel Utsikten Bellevue
P.O. Box 19
N-6216 Geiranger
Tel: 70 26 30 03

Honningsvåg
Hotel Havly
Storgt 12
N-9751 Honningsvåg
Tel: 78 47 29 66

Leirfjord
Petter Dass Hotel
N-8890 Leirfjord
Tel: 75 04 92 99

Lillehammer
Mølla Hotel
Elvegaten 12
N-2600 Lillehammer
Tel: 61 26 92 94

Molde
Hotel Nobel
Amtm Kroghsgt. 5
N-6400 Molde
Tel: 71 25 15 55

Mosjøen
Sandvik Gjestegård
Mjåvatn
N-8650 Mosjøen
Tel: 75 18 78 11

Moss
Mitt Hotel
Rådhusgt. 3
N-1500 Moss
Tel: 69 25 77 77

Oslo
Hotel IMI
Staffeldtsgate 4
N-0166 Oslo
Tel: 22 20 53 30
WestSide Hotel
Eilert Sundts gt. 43
N-0355 Oslo
Tel: 22 56 87 70

Sognefjord
Sognefjord Hotel
P.O. Box 144
N0-5840 Hermansverk
Tel: 57 65 34 44

Stord
Grand Hotel
N-5401 Stord
Tel: 53 41 02 33

Svolvær
Hotel Havly
N-8301 Svolvær
Tel: 76 07 03 44

Spektrum, with external panorama lift and roof-top pool. Popular among rock stars playing at the Oslo Spektrum, to which it is connected by a covered walkway. **$$**

Ritz Hotel
Frederik Stangs gate 3, N-0272
Tel: 22 44 39 60
Fax: 22 44 67 13
Close to the foreign embassies. **$$**

Golden Tulip Rainbow Hotel Stefan
Rosenkrantz' gate 1, N-0159
Tel: 22 42 92 50
Fax: 22 33 70 22
One of a chain of hotels scattered throughout Norway. Its location couldn't be more central and the buffet lunches are great. **$**

Norrøna Hotell
Grensen 19, N-0159
Tel : 22 42 64 00
Fax: 22 33 25 65
Completely renovated 3-star hotel but with century-old atmosphere intact. Central. **$**

Norum
Bygøy Alle 53, N-0265
Tel: 22 44 79 90
Fax 22 44 92 39
Beautiful old building just west of the centre; quiet, with cosy bistro. **$**

OSLO AREA

Clarion Oslo Airport Hotel
N-2060 Gardermoen
Tel: 63 94 94 94
The first of many chain hotels to be built around the new airport development. **$$**

Quality Airport Hotel
N-2050 Jessheim
Tel: 63 97 30 11
Another established hotel perfectly situated for the new Oslo Gardermoen Airport. **$$**

Gardermoen Gjestegård
2060 Gardermoen
Tel: 63 97 85 30
A small family-run hotel with bar and restaurant. **$**

Rica Hotel Oslofjord
Sandviksvn 184, 1330 Sandvika
Tel: 67 54 57 00
Fax: 67 54 27 33
Set in a handsome fjord town 15 km (9 miles) from central Oslo (shuttle buses and public transport available). Great views over fjord and islands. **$**

Scandic Hotel Høvik/Oslo
Drammensvn 507,
N–1322 Høvik
Tel: 67 12 17 40
Fax: 67 53 52 83
Attractive hotel with good dining and bar facilities; 6 km (4 miles) from Oslo centre. **$**

Price Categories

Price categories are indicated by dollar signs and are per night for two people in a double room with breakfast
$$$ More than NOK 1,700
$$ NOK 1,100–1,700
$ Less than NOK 1,100

BERGEN

Clarion Admiral
C. Sundtsgate 9–13
Tel: 55 23 64 00
Part of the Choice chain and one of Bergen's finest. The hotel's restaurant has superb views and cuisine. **$$**

Radisson SAS Hotel Norge
Ole Bulls Plass
Tel: 55 57 30 00
One of Bergen's best-loved hotels and meeting places, right in the centre, with 350 rooms and suites of highest standard. Four restaurants including gourmet Grillen. Winter garden, swimming pool. **$$**

Radisson SAS Royal Hotel
Bryggen
Tel: 55 54 30 00
Fax: 55 32 48 08
The influence on the hotel's architecture of the classic Norwegian building style makes this an unusually handsome hotel. High-grade facilities. **$$**

Rainbow Hotel Rosenkrantz
Rosenkrantz 7
Tel: 55 31 50 00
Fax: 55 31 14 76
Comfortable, early-20th-century hotel in street behind Bryggen (the wharf) in heart of old town; 129 rooms, well-modernised in light, airy colours. Restaurant and piano bar. Hotel nightclub entrance next door. **$$**

Victoria Hotel
Kong Oscarsgate 29
Tel: 55 31 50 30
Fax: 55 32 81 78
Once a staging-post inn, this now has 43 comfortable, modern rooms with own facilities. Full of character and an admirable art collection. Family-run hotel in the Best Western group. Fully licensed lobby bar. Central. **$$**

Fagerheim Pension
Kalvedalsveien 49A
Tel: 55 31 01 72
A friendly pension with a good central location. **$**

Hotel Park Pension
Harald Hårfagresgt 35
Tel: 55 32 09 60
Fax: 55 54 44 44
You can choose between rooms with or without their own facilities. **$**

Strand Hotel
Strandkaien 2B
Tel: 55 31 08 15
Fax: 55 31 00 17
Superb harbour views make for a pleasant stay. Family-run hotel with a cosy breakfast room and dinner served in the restaurant Lido. New bar facilities, Femte Etage. **$**

STAVANGER

City Gjestehuset
Lagårdsvn 47
N-4010
Tel: 51 52 04 37
Typical guesthouse with basic facilities. **$**

Radisson SAS Royal Hotel
Løkkeveien 26
Tel: 51 56 70 00

The hotel has SAS's usual complement of excellent services. **$$**

Scandic Hotel
Eiganesvn 181
P.O. Box 570 Madla
N-4040 Hafrsfjord
Tel: 23 15 50 00
Fax: 23 15 50 01
One of the quality Scandic hotels ideal for conferences. The Scandic chain has a "green" policy and includes "environmental rooms" that are constructed from 97 percent recyclable material. **$$**

Commandør Hotell
Valberggt 9, N-4006
Tel: 51 89 53 00
Fax: 51 89 53 01
Home comforts in a cosy milieu. Licensed for wine and beer only. **$**

Havly Hotel
Valberggt 1, N-4006
Tel: 51 89 67 00
Fax: 51 89 50 25
Modest with well-appointed rooms. Pets allowed. **$**

"The Little House"
Hostess: Grethe Aasvestad
Vaisenhusgt 40,
N-4012 Stavanger
Tel: 51 89 40 89
The Little House was built in 1869 and still retains the century-old atmosphere, with its home-from-home rooms (each with bath and access to kitchen). Central for restaurants and shops. **$**

TRONDHEIM

Radisson SAS Royal Garden Hotel
Kjøpmannsgt 73
Tel: 73 52 11 00
Well-appointed rooms plus more: solarium, indoor pool, gymnasium, sauna and several good restaurants. Runs an airport bus. **$$**

Grand Olav Hotel
Olavskvartalet
Tel: 73 53 53 10
Fax: 73 53 57 20
Top-class hotel situated in the heart of historic Trondheim.

Close to shops, bars and restaurants. Runs an airport bus. **$$**

Ambassadeur
Elvegate 18
Tel: 73 52 70 50
Not only is this one of Trondheim's most reasonably priced hotels, it also has a roof terrace. **$**

Elgeseter "Bed & Breakfast"
Tormodsgate 3
Tel: 73 94 25 40
Fax: 73 93 18 73
Convenient location 10 minutes' walk from the centre. **$**

Prinsen
Kongensgate 30
Tel: 73 53 06 50
A wealth of facilities here includes the fine Coq D'Or restaurant, a bistro, bar, grill room, wine tavern and beer garden. **$**

TROMSØ

Rica Ishavshotel Tromsø
Fr. Langesgt. 2
Tel: 77 66 64 00
Fax: 77 66 64 44
First-rate luxury hotel close to the centre, specialising in conferences and comfort. **$$$**

Grand Nordic
Storgt 44
Tel: 77 68 55 00
Fax: 77 68 25 00
Close to the centre, 4 km (2½ miles) from the airport. Full conference facilities and well-appointed rooms. **$$**

Saga Tromsø
Richard Withs plass 2
Tel: 77 68 11 80

City Packages

The Oslo Package and Bergen Package include hotel accommodation (with breakfast) and respectively the Oslo/Bergen Card. This is a great discount offer and is available through travel agencies, tourist information and main railway stations.

Fax: 77 68 23 80
Small conference hotel with relaxing atmosphere. **$$**

Scandic Tromsø
Heiloveien 23
Tel: 77 67 34 00
Fax: 77 67 67 40
Modest conference hotel located in Tromsø suburb close to the airport. Well-appointed rooms. Outside pool. **$$**

With Home Hotel
Sjøgata 35–37, N-9000
Tel: 77 68 70 00
Fax: 77 68 96 16
A new first-class hotel with a difference. Situated by the waterfront in Tromsø's dock district, it offers a beautiful view to the Tromsø bridge and the famous Arctic Cathedral. The hotel itself is something of a museum with a maritime atmosphere. **$$**

Chalets (hytter)

There are abundant holiday hytter (cabins or chalets) available for rent. These come in various sizes, but usually house four to six people. If you want to spend just one night in a chalet and then move on, you can stay in one on a campsite without booking ahead. You can obtain a comprehensive brochure with details about holiday chalets (including price list) from:
Den Norske Hytteformidling,
Kierschowsgate 7,
P.O. Box 3404 Bjølsen,
N-0406 Oslo
Tel: 22 35 67 10
Fax: 22 71 94 13

Fishermen's cabins (rorbuer)

In the Lofoten islands in northern Norway, you can rent a traditional former fisherman's cabin, called a "rorbu". The fishermen used to come to Lofoten from other parts of the coast for the winter cod fishing season from January to April, and would make these cabins their temporary homes for the duration.

Most of them have been modernised, and a number of them have their own shower and toilet.
Contact: Destinasjon Lofoten, P.O. Box 210, N-8301 Svolvær
Tel: 76 07 30 00
Fax: 76 07 30 01

Camping

Norway has more than 1,000 campsites. The sites are classified by 1–5 stars, depending on the standard and facilities available. Normally the fixed charge per plot is NOK 80–150, with additional charges per person.

With the Norwegian camping card (*Norsk Campingkort*) you receive faster checking-in service along with special discount deals. The card (priced NOK 75) is available from participating campsites. Many campsites have cabins that may be booked in advance. Some are small and basic, but others are large and well equipped with a sitting room, 1/2 bedrooms, kitchen, shower and toilet. Prices range from NOK 200 to NOK 600.

For more information about camping in Norway, write to: Norwegian Camping Guide, Essendropsgt. 6, N-0305 Oslo.

B&Bs

British-style bed and breakfasts are beginning to catch on in Norway, and they are all of a high standard. You can book at local tourist offices or at Oslo's central railway station. Or look out for signs for *Rom* or *Husrom* outside houses as you drive along. In larger towns rooms are around NOK 170 for a single and NOK 300 for a double per night.

A B&B guidebook, *Rom i Norge*, with listings throughout Norway is available from bookshops in Norway or from: Norsc Holidays, 1 The Lawns, Charmouth, Dorset, DT6 6LR.

Tel: 01297 560033
Fax: 01297 560833
Alternatively, it can be bought by mail order on credit cards by ringing tel: +47 22 27 85 09.

Youth and Family Hostels

There are approximately 100 youth hostels in Norway, all with a relatively high standard of accommodation. They are divided into three categories, indicated by a corresponding number of stars.

A night's accommodation costs between NOK 75 and NOK 175, breakfast NOK 60–70 for members of the YHA. Further information can be obtained by contacting Hostelling International Norway, or your local YHA office.

Reserving space during the high season is a must, as hostel accommodation is the cheapest way to travel and everyone knows it.

Hostelling International Norway, Dronningens gate 26, N-0154 Oslo.
Tel: 23 13 93 00
Fax: 23 13 93 50
E-mail: hostels@sn.no

Where to Eat

What to Eat

Norwegians eat hearty breakfasts, but light lunches; the size of the evening meal (*middag*) depends on the day of the week and the occasion. With the abundant supply of seafood and what can be gleaned from forest and field, the Norwegian diet is in the main healthy and appetising, and is becoming more so as Norwegians get more diet-conscious – although advertisements for non-greasy, non-fat, non-sugar products are on the increase.

The hunting season (early autumn) throws up some irresistible temptations: pheasant, grouse, fresh elk and reindeer steaks served with peppercorns and rich wild mushroom sauces. It is also a good time of year to make the most of seafood (usually available in months with an R in them).

Outside main meals, there are many coffee breaks. Inevitably pastries will be served too if you are in someone's home or having an informal meeting. The dish may be laden with *bolle* (raisin buns) and *vienerbrød* (lighter pastries laced with fruit or nuts) and

Price Guide

The symbols at the end of each entry give an indication of prices, based on a typical three-course evening meal per head, excluding wine.
$ Less than NOK 120
$$ NOK 120-27
$$$ More than NOK 270

anything else the baker can conjure up.

Frokost (breakfast) is more or less a variation of the lunch *Kaldtbord*, a spread including breads (try *grovbrød*) and *flatbrød* (oblongs of crisp cracker), sausages, cheeses (try the piquant *Gudbrandalsost*, a delicious burnt goats' milk cheese with a dark golden colour), eggs, herrings, cereal, *gravlax* (marinated salmon), cereals, and coffee and tea. The lunch version has hot dishes, such as sliced roast meats, meatballs or fish. *Øllebrød* (beef marinated in beer and served inside pitta bread with salad) makes a hearty, inexpensive lunch; an open-faced shrimp or ham sandwich is another staple.

Dinner in a city restaurant these days can be anything you wish. In someone's home you might eat mutton stew or a fish ragout. Boiled potatoes with dill or parsley usually accompany a hot main course. When dining in more remote places, the menus will invariably be limited by availability. *Smørbrød* is a snack (called *aftens* when eaten late at night), usually of rye crackers with butter, cheese and salami or ham.

For dessert, ice cream is a favourite, as is apple pie. In summer there are all kinds of puddings based on the fresh berries that grow so profusely in the Norwegian woods.

Where to Eat

There has been a significant increase in the variety of what's on offer if you eat out. Pizza is very popular and the cynic would describe it as the Norwegian national dish, and Asian and oriental food is becoming so (note: Indian restaurants tend to tone down the spices to suit uncultured Norwegian taste, so you have to tell the waiter to beef it up a bit). Continental European cuisine has always played a role too in Norwegian

food (such as Viennese and French-style dishes). But pride in the native cuisine is growing apace with this competition from foreign foods.

At lunchtime many restaurants offer special fixed-price menus. More casual meals can be had from more informal establishments, which come under a range of names such as *stovas*, *kaffistovas*, *kros*, *bistros*, *kafés*, *kafeterias*, and *gjæstgiveris* and may sell beer and wine as well as coffee and soft drinks. For an even more casual meal buy a hot dog (*pølser*) or a waffle from a kiosk; these stay open late to catch the traffic going to and from bars and nightclubs. And yes, there is McDonald's.

Evening dining yields up some wonderful surprises in terms of choice, some unpleasant ones in terms of cost. Any large city should give the best cross-section of what you can get throughout the country. The following is merely a tiny selection of what is on offer.

Restaurants

OSLO

Chinese
Dinner
Stortingsg. 22
Tel: 22 42 68 90
No punches spared Szechuan. **$$**
Mr Hong
Storlingsg. 8
Tel: 22 42 20 08
Chinese, Mongolian and Japanese, three restaurants, 1,000 flavours. **$$**
Deijing Palace
Torgg. 18.
Tel: 22 20 79 04
Best *dimsum* in town. **$**

Greek
Zorbas
Torgg. 32
Tel: 22 29 78 56 **$$**
Dionysus Taverna
Calmeyersgate 11
Tel: 22 60 78 64 **$**

Indian
Peacock
Toyengate 26
Grønland
Tel: 22 68 93 75
First Indian to open in Oslo. Genuine tandoori oven. **$$**
Natraj
Bygdøy Allee 9
Tel: 22 44 75 33
Excellent food. Good portions. **$$**
Mother India
Pilestredet 63 B
Tel: 22 60 81 04
Near Bislett Stadium. Indian atmosphere. Great food. **$**

Italian
Mama Rosa
Øvre Slottsgate 12
Tel: 22 42 01 30
Popular downtown restaurant with real pizza oven. **$$**
La Tavola
Skoveien 1–3
Tel: 22 55 26 76
Cosy place with good selection of wines. **$**
Peppe's Pizza Pub
Kjøpmannsgate 25
Tel: 73 50 73 73 **$$**

Japanese
Fuji
Munkedamsveien 100
Skillebekk
Tel: 22 43 11 80
If you like sushi... **$$$**
Sushi Nam Kang
Torgg. 24
Tel: 22 20 19 40 **$$**

Mexican
Quatro Amigos
Stortingsgate 16
Tel: 22 43 48 00
Friendly service, hot food. **$$**
Bedrock Steakhouse
Aker Brygge Stranden 3
Tel: 22 83 06 48
Mexican chilli, beer and tequila. **$$**
Mucho Mas Cafe
Thv. Meyersgate 36
Tel: 22 37 16 09 **$**

Western

Annen Etage
Hotel Continental
"Grand Hotel" style, setting and food. **$$$**

Bagatelle
Bygdøy alle 3
Tel: 22 44 63 97
The best restaurant in Scandinavia with 2 stars in the 1998 Guide Michelin.
Chef/owner Eyvind Hellstrøm uses nothing but the best Norwegian raw materials. **$$$**

Blom
Karl Johansgate 37–41
Tel: 22 42 73 00
Expensive – the place to impress someone. A large selection of savoury classic Norwegian dishes, such as reindeer meat served in pastry with port. **$$$**

Brasseriet
Radisson SAS Hotel
Holbergsgate 30
Tel: 22 11 30 00
Continental menu interspersed with Norwegian seafood specialities. Fish and meats served with delicious sauces. **$$$**

Feinschmekker
Balchensgate 5
Tel: 22 44 17 77
Expensive but culinary value for money. **$$$**

Price Guide

The symbols at the end of each entry give an indication of prices, based on a typical three-course evening meal per head, excluding wine.

$	Less than NOK 120
$$	NOK 120-27
$$$	More than NOK 270

Markveien Mat og Vinhus
Torvbakkgate 12
(entrance Markveien 57)
Tel: 22 37 22 97
No fixed menu because the owners pick what looks best at the market each day; fresh salads, excellent game steaks in season. Arty decor. **$$$**

Gamle Raadhus
Nedre Slottsgate 1
Tel: 22 42 01 07
Old-style restaurant in 17th-century building serving hearty Norwegian specialities plus surprises like catfish. **$$**

Grand Café
Karl Johansgate 31
Tel: 22 42 93 90
A virtual shrine to Ibsen, who spent many hours here. Choose anything from pastry and coffee to elk stew and whalemeat platter; salad bar. **$$**

Hos Thea
Gabelsgate 11
Tel: 22 44 68 74
Good kitchen. Modest prices. **$$**

Hotel Bondeheimen/Kaffistova
Rosenkrantzgate 8
Tel: 22 42 95 30
This restaurant, owned by the Farmers' Association, is known for enticing Norwegian fare served cafeteria style; portions are generous. **$$**

Hotel Stefan
Rosenkrantzgate 1
Tel: 22 42 92 50
Justifiably famous buffet lunch selection. **$$**

Kafé Celsius
Rådhusgate 19
Tel: 22 42 45 39
Lunch and dinner, or coffee/snacks/wine and beer. Wild mushroom pie, pasta, salads and seafood soups. **$$**

Kastanjen
Bygdøy Alle 18
Tel: 22 43 44 67
Bistro serving spicy Norwegian-influenced food. **$$**

Stortorvets Gjæstgiveri
Grensen 1
Tel: 22 42 88 63
In the warm atmosphere of this authentic Christiania inn, you can eat traditional food to the accompaniment of live jazz. **$$**

Drinking Notes

No one talks about a trip to Norway without complaining of the high cost of alcohol.

Stronger beer costs about NOK 40 for a half litre (which is about 15 percent larger than the British pint); *lettøl* (low-alcohol beer) is about NOK 30. And from here it gets worse. A single glass of wine costs about NOK 30; average wines start at about NOK 150 for a bottle on a restaurant menu. Spirit prices are through the roof. (So it's small wonder that home brews are common in Norway.)

For those who can afford the prices, serving hours are long;

in Oslo you can drink spirits until midnight and wine or beer until 3am. Outside Oslo it's unpredictable; the Christian Democratic Party (Kr.F), a member of the ruling coalition, is virulently anti-alcohol and holds sway in many west-coast areas, rendering some counties virtually dry.

But some hotels, and consequently their restaurants, are the exception to the area they are in: in Oslo, for example, there are some no-alcohol hotel/restaurants and in the "dry" counties it is always possible to find a hotel/restaurant that serves

some form of alcohol.

The *Vinmonopolet* (state off-licences/liquor stores) in cities are open weekdays 9am–5pm and Saturday 9am–2pm; but closed on election days, holidays and the preceding day.

Most Norwegians drink beer – although *akevitt*, derived from potato and caraway seeds, is a favourite for anyone doing some serious drinking. Akevitt can be savoured on its own (sipped neat in small glasses preferably at room temperature), or served cold with beer as an accompaniment to salty, spicy or pungent dishes.

Theatercafeen
Hotel Continental
Stortingsgate 24
Tel: 22 82 40 50
Famous Viennese-style café. **$$**
Peppes Pizza
A chain with numerous branches
specialising in pan-fried pizzas.
The first of its kind to grace
Norway's doorstep. Meals are
cheaper on Mondays. **$**
Vegeta Vertshus
Munkedamsveien 3B
Tel: 22 83 40 20
Vegetarian heaven; this place
even got a New York Times
write-up. Self-service lets you
taste the variety. **$**

BERGEN

Exclusive
Bellevue
Bellevuebakken 9
Tel: 55 31 02 40
The fjord view from this
restaurant in a 17th-century
building is superb. Serves
Norwegian and Continental
cuisine. Takes groups only. **$$$**
Emily
Hotel Clarion Admiral
C Sundtsgt 9–13
Tel: 55 23 65 00
Style, style and style. **$$$**
Fiskekrogen
Fish Market
Tel: 55 55 96 60
What they can't do with fish is
not worth writing about. **$$$**

BERGENSIAN

Bryggen Tracteursted
Bryggen 6
Tel: 55 31 40 46
Your selection from the fish
market will be prepared to your
specifications by the cook; in
old Hanseatic district. **$$**
Fløien Folkerestaurant
Top of Fløien funicular
Tel: 55 32 18 75
Good, reasonably priced food
with intoxicating view. Work up
an appetite by walking there! **$$**

Holbergstuen
Torvalmenning 6
Tel: 55 31 80 15
Another restaurant that will cook
fresh fish from the market to
your specifications; lively. **$$**
Wesselstuen
Engen 14
Tel: 55 90 08 20
Fish and stews are served here
to a loyal local crowd. **$$**

TRONDHEIM

Gourmet
Bryggen
Øvre Bakklandet 66
Tel: 73 53 40 55 **$$$**

Fish & seafood
Havfruen
Kjøpmannsgt. 7
Tel: 73 53 26 26 **$$**
Hos Magnus
Kjøpmannsgt. 63
Tel: 73 52 41 10 **$$**

Steakhouses
Abelone Mat & Vinkjeller
Dronningens gt. 15
Tel: 73 53 24 70 **$$**
Big Horn Steakhouse
Munkegt. 14
Ravnkloa
Tel: 73 50 94 90 **$$**

Traditional
Grenaderen
Kongsgårdsgt. 1e
Tel: 73 51 66 80 **$$**
Vertshuset Tavern
Sverresborg
Tel: 73 52 09 32 **$$**

Pizza
Zia Teresa Pizzeria Trattoria
Vår Frue Strete
Tel: 7352 64 22 **$$**

Culture

Music and Opera

In summer the arts take to the
outdoors in Norway, and
classical music and opera are
no exception. For Oslo dates,
pick up the *What's On in Oslo*
guide. The very active Oslo
Philharmonic, founded by Edvard
Grieg, is conducted by Mariss
Jansons, with frequent visits by
acclaimed guest conductors
and soloists.

At Holmenkollen in summer,
orchestral and operatic
performances are given from a
floating stage on the lake.

Each September, a "drive-in"
opera performance is held at
Youngstorvet (Young's Market
Square), outside the Opera
House in the open air.

Akershus Fortress and the
Henie Onstad Art Centre
(Høvikodden) are two other fine
settings for summer concerts.

Whether the performers are
Norwegian or foreign, the
season winter or summer,
Norway has a rich and varied
musical and operatic life
(consult area guide for festivals
schedule; some English and
American newspapers do a
pan-European list of festivals at
the start of each summer). This

Bergen Festival

Bergen's International
Festival in late May offers
music, drama, ballet, opera,
jazz and folk arts.
    For further details contact
the tourist office or:
Tel: 55 31 21 70
Fax: 55 31 55 31

may be your chance to listen to some of the conductors and performers you'd previously only experienced on Deutsche Gramophone album jackets, or a first chance to see Grieg performed by Norwegian musicians.

Theatre and Dance

Theatre is booming in Norway, with small, contemporary theatres springing up everywhere; but performances are in Norwegian. The exception is September's Gløgerne Kommer festival of performing arts, when international dramatists take to the stage.

Dance is also coming into its own here and is now a significant part of the Gløgerne Kommer. Classical ballet is performed at the Oslo Opera House. Traditional folk dances can be seen in many towns on National Day (17 May), or at Oslo's Konserthus every Monday and Thursday at 9pm in July and August, when the Bondeungdomslaget folk dance group performs.

Cinema

The Norwegians love films, a fact attested to by the vast number of cinemas; Oslo has around 40 screens including the latest Panasonic IMAX Theatre at Aker Brygge. First-run and repertory films are always shown in the original language, with Norwegian subtitles. Kiosks, newspapers, and local city guides have listings. Booking by telephone is possible and recommended for Sundays, the traditional movie night.

Festivals and Cultural Events

January
● Tromsø: Northern Lights Festival. Classical and contemporary music.
Tel: 77 68 90 70

February
● Kristiansund Opera Festival. Opera, ballet and concerts.
Tel: 71 58 99 60
● Lillehammer Winter Arts Festival.
Tel: 61 27 97 00
● Narvik: Winter Festival, with music, dance, ceremonies and carnivals, including steam engine trips on the region's famous Ofoten railway.
Tel: 76 94 77 39

May
● Ål: Norwegian Folk Music Week, with bands playing the oldest folk music, is held in the small village of Ål in the eastern valley of Hallingdal.
Tel: 32 08 10 60
● International Church Music Festival. Choirs, orchestras, dance, soloists and folk music.
Tel: 38 02 13 11

June
● Sarpsborg: Gleng Music Festival, with folk, rock, blues, jazz and classical music.
Tel: 69 15 68 00
● Harstad: Festival of North Norway. Nine days of concerts, theatre, dance, art and film by amateurs and professionals. Plus the special Children's Festival for the young.
Tel: 77 06 65 99
● Honningsvag: North Cape Festival.
● St Hans midsummer night celebrations all over Norway.
● Sandvika/Oslo: Kalvoya Festival with outdoor rock concerts by international and Norwegian musicians.

June/July
● Vestfold International Festival, with music, theatre, dance and art throughout the entire county.
Tel: 33 30 88 50

July
● Førde Folk Music Festival. Music and dance from all over the world, incuding Norway's best folk musicians.
Tel: 57 72 19 40
● Molde International Jazz Festival, one of the oldest in Europe, established in 1961. Exhibitions, plays, festivals and street music as well as jazz, including many free concerts.
Tel: 71 21 60 00
● Stiklestad/Verdal: the St Olav Play (historical play about the christening of Norway and the death of St Olav in the battle of Stiklestad in 1030).

● National Folk Dance and Music Festival. Competitions and performances, hosted by a different town each year.
Tel: 22 42 45 92

July/August
● Vinstra/Gala: Peer Gynt Festival. Outdoor concert and various musical and cultural events, including outdoor performances of Peer Gynt.

August
● Oslo Jazz Festival: six days of jazz from worldwide artists.
Tel: 22 42 91 20
● Oslo: Ibsen Festival celebrating the author's work and life.
Tel: 22 00 14 00
● Elverum Music Festival: Concerts and art exhibitions.
Tel: 62 41 69 15
● Vadsø: Varanger Festival. Jazz concerts, parades and jazz cruises on the coastal steamer.
Tel: 78 95 38 51
● Bø: Telemark International Folk Festival. Folk music from Norwegian and world artists.
Tel: 35 95 19 19

October
● Agder: International Puppet Theatre Festival, staged in odd-numbered years, with puppet shows throughout the county.
Tel: 38 12 28 88

Nightlife

Oslo, once considered a big yawn at night, is now vying with Stockholm and Copenhagen to be Scandinavia's nightlife capital. Loads of new bars, pubs and clubs have come on to the scene, but many can't recoup their investments quickly enough and go out of business (some also regularly go out of business because they have made a quick killing!). So check locally for up-to-date venue listings. All the major cities have both official and unofficial nightlife guides.

In Bergen, Stavanger, Trondheim and Tromsø nightlife exists to a much lesser extent. But you can guarantee that most large hotels have nightclubs and bars. In small towns, you may be out of luck altogether – unless you have a locally compatible video recorder, for video clubs have infiltrated, and probably forever changed, rural Norway.

Famed non-classical musicians (rock, folk, and jazz groups) often include Oslo on European tours; some even start their tours here. Oslo Spektrum and sports stadiums such as the Valle Hovin have seen Luciano Pavarotti and Michael Jackson perform.

There are only two things you need to be warned about before a night out: the high cost of drinking, and age restrictions: some clubs have minimum ages as high as 26 (although 21 and 23 are more common).

Constitution Day

15 May is Norway's Constitution Day. To celebrate the signing of the constitution in 1814, streets throughout the country are filled with brass-band music, colourful children's processions and flag-waving crowds.

Shopping

What to Buy

Popular souvenirs from Norway include knitted jumpers, cardigans, gloves and mittens, pewter, silver jewellery and cutlery, hand-painted wooden objects (like bowls with rose designs), trolls and fjord horses carved out of wood, goat and reindeer skin, enamel jewellery, woven wall-designs, furs, handicrafts, glassware and pottery – to name just a few (see *Tax-free Shopping* for how to reclaim VAT on souvenirs).

The major department stores are Glasmagasin and Steen & Strøm, both of which will have a good selection of most of these items. However, if you want speciality stores in Oslo, there is a Where to Shop guide, as well as a detailed "Shopping" section in the Oslo Guide. Karl Johansgate, Grensen, and Bogstadveien are all major shopping streets. With the exception of Oslo, most Norwegian towns are so compact that your best bet is to window shop and go into the places that look most appealing.

Anyone interested in buying Norwegian art will have ample prospects – from south to north, Norway abounds in galleries. Get a local recommendation.

If you are food shopping, fruit and vegetable prices vary considerably throughout the year. Look out for *Lavpris* (low-price) shops offering discounts. Bear in mind that most bottles (whether plastic or glass) have a returnable deposit of NOK 1.

Tax-free Shopping

The Norwegian Tax-Free Shopping scheme covers around 2,600 stores.

For purchases over NOK 300, the store issues you with a tax-free slip for the amount of VAT paid. When you leave Norway, a refund of 11-18 percent (depending on the sale price) will be refunded (in your local currency) on presentation of the goods, the tax-free slip and your passport, on condition that the item has not been used while in Norway.

Norway Tax-Free Shopping has its own representatives at a total of 70 refund places, including all airports, on board all international ferries and at the main border crossings. Check opening times, however, as they are not open 24 hours, and make sure there is a refund desk if you are using a small border crossing. Customs officials cannot refund VAT. Look out for the Norway Tax-Free Shopping representative, or leaflets at participating stores.

Enquiries to Norway Tax-Free Shopping AS. Tel: 67 14 99 01.

Shopping Hours

● **Weekdays**
Generally 9am–5pm, with late Thursday opening for many stores until 7pm.
Stores may close earlier in summer, especially Fridays.
● **Saturday**
Approximately 9am–2 pm.
● **Shopping centres** such as Aker Brygge, Palléet and Oslo City in Oslo, Galleriet in Bergen and City Syd in Trondheim are open later, until 8pm some nights.
● **Kiosks** tend not to close until 10pm or even 11pm and are usually open all weekend.
● **Supermarkets** Most stay open until 8pm.
● **Petrol stations** are usually open until 11pm.

Sport

Participant Sports

If Norwegians can contrive a sport as an excuse to be outdoors, they'll do it. That's why there are such great facilities here; all Norwegians love sport. (For a full listing of the range of sports and sports facilities in the Oslo region, see the Outdoor Activities pages of the *Oslo Guide*.) There is a Forest Safari programme, where for a half or whole day you can partake in a range of activities in the Marka (Oslo's forest) in between which you are carted around by Land Rover – visit the main tourist information office for details.

Boating

Foreign visitors are always welcome in boating circles, and there are hundreds of sailing and boating clubs and associations throughout Norway. The national organisation for recreational and competitive motor-boating is: Det Kongelige Norske Båt-Forbund (The Royal Norwegian Boat Association)
P.O. Box 170 Sentrum,
0102 Oslo
Tel: 22 33 96 00
Fax: 22 33 96 10

The most popular volumes of the six-volume *Den Norske Los* (Norwegian Pilot), the meticulously detailed manual of all navigable waters, is now available with Norwegian and English texts. Volume 3 covers the southwest coast from south of Stavanger to north of Bergen; Volume 2 the Oslo Fjord and the south coast.

But without your own boat, sailing of any sort can be expensive, and the closest you may get is a small catamaran or even a windsurfer. In Oslo you can hire equipment from:
Seasport Oslo AS, Dronning Mauds g 1/3
Tel: 22 83 79 28
Fax: 22 83 92 95
White Water AS, Cort Adelers g 27
Tel: 22 55 11 07
Fax: 22 55 11 48

Canoeing

Numerous rivers and lakes in Norway offer canoeing and kayaking. Some of the best are: the Femund area, Østfold, Aust and Vest Agder, Telemark and suburban Oslo. Contact the local tourist office for details.

Cycling

For details see *Getting Around*, *page 17*.

Fishing

With a coastline of 21,465 km (13,330 miles), as well as countless fjords, lakes and rivers, Norway is a fisherman's paradise. In summer there are many boat cruises, and in some fjord towns groups can charter boats for fishing or pleasure.

The fishing is excellent in Norway, whether you're at sea or on a fjord, lake or river; enquire locally about short-term permits. To fish sea char, salmon, sea trout or inland fish, you must be over 16 and pay a fee (NOK 90 per annum, or NOK 45 for a week). See the tourist board's *Angling in Norway* for full details.

Golf

This popular sport is catching on in Norway and many landowners, be they farmers or municipal authorities, are turning over land to developing golf links.

Norwegian golf courses are by and large difficult and challenging. Ninety-nine percent of them require either a Green Card or a handicap under 20. Green fees are in line with European golf courses at NOK 150–250 for weekdays and NOK 250–350 at weekends. Some 9-hole courses offer day fees.

In the Oslo region professional competitions are held at Bogstad, Larvik, Borre and Vestfold golf clubs, but by far the most beautifully situated is the Tyrifjord golf links. For further information and club details, contact:
The Norwegian Golf Federation
Hauger Skolevei 1, 1351 Rud
Tel: 67 15 46 00
Fax: 67 13 86 40

Hiking

One of the country's favourite pastimes, hiking can be done anywhere and combines

Winter Norway

Norway is often dubbed the "Cradle of Skiing". What we today know as a sport is the way Norwegians used to get around, and Norway is said to be responsible for the invention of ski waxing and the laminated ski.

But skiing is just one of Norway's winter attractions. There are snowmobile trips to the North Cape, reindeer safaris and dog-sled races over the plane of Finnmarksvidda.

You can go on horse-drawn sleigh rides, or try your hand at ice fishing, snow boarding or ice skating. Several companies offer winter train journeys along the spectacular coast

For details of tour operators who specialise in winter holidays in Norway, see *Specialist Tour Operators* on page 354. Or contact the Norwegian tourist board, which has a list of holiday agents offering packages.

Glacier Hiking

Not for the lily-livered, glacier hiking is an exhilarating and exciting experience – which should only be attempted with an experienced local guide.

Several Norwegian tour companies offer guided glacier walks (*breer*), most particularly in the following areas:

Fjord Norway: Hardangerjøkulen, Folgefonna, Buarbre,

Bondhusbre, Smørstabbre, Fannaråkbre and Nigardsbre. **Oppland:** Styggebre. **Norland Reiseliv:** Svartisen and Engenbreen.

Alternatively, you could contact one of the **Glacier Information Centres in** western Norway at Oppstryn (tel: 57 87 72 00), Fjærland (tel: 57 69 32 88) and Josterdalen (tel: 57 68 32 50).

pleasurably with other activities such as berry-gathering or a swim in a lake. The country's expansive mountain ranges and high plains make ideal walking terrain. The most popular areas include the Jotunheim mountain range; the Rondane and Dovrefjell mountains; the Hardangervidda plateau in the Trollheimen district; and the Finnmarksvidda plain. Mountain cabins are open from the end of June until mid-September, plus Easter.

The Norwegian Mountain Touring Association (DNT) runs about 300 guided hikes of varying difficulty during the summer, and glacier walks in winter. It also has a wealth of information on hiking and maps for all Norway and can recommend cabin-to-cabin hiking holidays. Foreigners can write requesting membership, which gives you certain free publications and hut access. Den Norske Turistforening (The Norwegian Mountain Touring Association) Storgate 3, P.O. Box 7 Sentrum, 0101 Oslo Tel: 22 82 28 00 Fax: 22 82 28 01

Skiing

Along with hiking, this is the primary participant sport in Norway. Even in the summer Norwegians take to the slopes (as a rule from June to September), and the sight of

people swooping down the slopes in bikinis and trunks is something to behold.

The main ski resorts are at Lillehammer, Trysil, Geilo, Hemsedal, Norefjell (the nearest to Oslo) and Voss, but there are many more; all tourist offices can advise on local ski facilities for cross country and slalom. For the latest ski conditions in winter, in the UK you can call the Norwegian Tourist Board's Ski Hotline: 0171-321 0666.

Swimming

Beaches along the coast and inland reach 20°C, and even in the north it can be warm enough to swim. Nude beaches are to be found in Oslo, Moss, Halden, Drammen, Tønsberg, Larvik and Molde.

Most larger hotels have pools and there are numerous leisure centres throughout Norway.

Watersports

There are several possibilities for waterskiing and windsurfing along the coast, as well as on Norway's numerous lakes.

White water rafting is available on the following rivers: Sjoaelva in Oppland, Trysilelva in Hedmark and Driva in Sør-Trøndelag.

The Norwegian coast offers very good conditions for diving. There are several diving centres along the west coast, particularly in the counties of Møre and Romsdal.

Spectator Sports

Skiing is the primary spectator sport in Norway for annual competitions, such as the Hol menkolen Ski Festival and Bislet Games. Check local guides. There are several horse trotting and race tracks in Norway. Other popular spectator sports include marathon running, football, ice hockey and boat races. Again, check Oslo or local area guide or tourist office for details.

Sporting Events

February
● Alta: Finnmark Race, Europe's longest dog sled race.

March
● Lillehammer: World Cup downhill skiing competition, and famous cross-country ski race from Lela to Lillehammer.
● Oslo: Cross-country and ski jumping competition.
● Beitostølen: Ridderuka sports for the disabled.

May
● Oslo: Holmenkollstaffetten street relay race from Bislet stadium to the Holmenkillen and back again.

June
● Trondheim: Den Store Styrkeprøven, Test of Strength, 560 km cycle race from Trondheim to Oslo.

July
● Tromsø: Midnight Sun Marathon.
● Oslo's Mobil Bislet Games: international athletics.

August
● Risør: Wooden Boat Festival.
● Ålesund: underwater photography championship.

September
● Oslo Marathon.

Language

There are two variations of the Norwegian language: *bokmål* and *nynorsk*. Both belong to the western group of the Scandinavian branch of the Germanic languages, one of the subfamilies of the Indo-European languages. The Sami population (Lapps) in North Norway speak Lappish. English is widely understood in the sizeable towns.

Useful Words and Phrases

Yes	*Ja*
No	*Nei*
Good morning	*God morgen*
Good afternoon	*God eftermiddag*
Good evening	*God kveld*
Today	*I dag*
Tomorrow	*I morgen*
Yesterday	*I går*
Hello	*Hei*
How do you do?	*Goddag?*
Goodbye	*Adjø/Har det bra*
Thank you	*Takk*
How much is this?	*Hvaor mye koster det?*
It costs	*Det koster...*
How do I get to...?	*Hvordan kommer jeg til...?*
Where is...?	*Hvor er...?*
Right	*Høyre*

To the right	*Til høyre*
Left	*Venstre*
To the left	*Til venstre*
Straight on	*Rett frem*
Phrase book	*Parlør*
Dictionary	*Ordbok*
Money	*Penger*
Can I order please?	*Kan jeg få bestille?*
Could I have the bill please?	*Kan jeg få regningen?*
Could I have the key please?	*Kan jeg få nøkkelen?*
What time is it?	*Hvor mye er klokken?*
It is (the time is...)	*Det er... (Klokken er...)*
Could I have your name please?	*Hva er navnet?*
My name is	*Mitt navn er...*
Do you have English newspapers?	*Har du engelske aviser?*
Do you speak English?	*Snakker du engelsk?*
I only speak English	*Jeg snakker bare engelsk*
May I help you?	*Kan jeg hjelpe deg?*
I do not understand	*Jeg forstår ikke*
I do not know	*Jeg vet ikke*
It has disappeared	*Den har forsvunnet*
Chemist	*Apotek*
Hospital	*Sykehus*
Doctor	*Lege*
Police station	*Politistasjion*
Parking	*Parkering*
Department store	*Hus/ Stormagasin*
Toilet	*Toalett/WC*
Gentlemen	*Herrer*
Ladies	*Damer*

Vacant	*Ledig*
Engaged	*Opptatt*
Entrance	*Inngang*
Exit	*Utgang*
No entry	*Ingen adgang*
Open	*Åpent*
Closed	*Stengt*
Push	*Skyv*
Pull	*Trekk*
No smoking	*Røyking forbudt*
Breakfast	*Frokost*
Lunch	*Lunsj*
Dinner	*Middag*
Eat	*Spise*
Drink	*Drikke*
Cheers!	*Skål!*
Aircraft	*Flymaskin*
Bus/coach	*Buss*
Car	*Bil*
Train	*Tog*
To rent	*Leie*
Free	*Ledig*
Room to rent	*Rum til leie*
Chalet	*Hytte*
Grocery store (in countryside)	*Landhandel*
Shop	*Butikk*
Food	*Mat/kost*
To buy	*Kjøpe*
Sauna	*Badstue*
Liquor store/ off-licence	*Vinmonopol*
Clothes	*Klær*
Overcoat	*Frakk*
Jacket	*Jakke*
Suit	*Dress*
Shoes	*Sko*
Skirt	*Skjørt*
Blouse	*Bluse*
Jersey	*Genser*
Wash	*Vaske*
Launderette	*Vaskeriautomat*
Dry cleaning	*Renseri*
Stain	*Flekk*

Numbers

0	*null*	11	*elleve*	22	*tjue-to*
1	*en*	12	*tolv*	30	*tretti*
2	*to*	13	*tretten*	40	*førti*
3	*tre*	14	*fjorten*	50	*femti*
4	*fire*	15	*femten*	60	*seksti*
5	*fem*	16	*seksten*	70	*sytti*
6	*seks*	17	*sytten*	80	*åtti*
7	*syv or sju*	18	*atten*	90	*nitti*
8	*åtte*	19	*nitten*	100	*hündre*
9	*ni*	20	*tjue*	200	*to hundre*
10	*ti*	21	*tjue-en*	1,000	*tusen*

Further Reading

Tourist Publications

Some useful publications available from the Norwegian Tourist Board include:

Accommodation in Norway, ***Norwegian Camping Guide*** and ***Tourist Timetables in Norway.*** These booklets are issued free by the Norwegian Tourist Board or from the nearest Norwegian embassy or consulate.

Road Map of Norway A 1:1 million map covering the entire country on one sheet, this is particularly suitable for tourists because of its easy-to-follow legend. First and foremost it shows all trunk roads, as well as secondary roads of special interest to travellers. The reverse side suggests motoring tours, and there are town maps of Oslo, Bergen, Trondheim, Stavanger, Kristiansand and Tromsø. New edition 1998. Price: NOK 38 +p&p.

Motoring in Norway Λ soft-cover book with colour illustrations and sketch maps. The 1997 edition has 180 pages with new road numbers, describing the most attractive routes in Norway, road conditions, sights and scenery. Symbols indicate accommodation, catering and service stations. Price: NOK 130 + p&p.

Adventure Roads in Norway Where is the best scenery? A selection of fascinating routes chosen by some of Norway's foremost travel experts. The routes and places of interest are marked on maps and the book is illustrated with beautiful colour photographs. Price: NOK 248 + p&p.

2,500 miles on the Coastal Steamer A description of the popular coastal voyage from Bergen to Kirkenes in Arctic Norway and back. Illustrated by attractive colour photos and explanatory maps. Price: NOK 50 + p&p.

Mountain Hiking in Norway Λ soft-cover book with colour illustrations and sketch maps, which describes Norway's mountain regions and suggests itineraries. It also has details about chalets and other accommodation in the mountains. Price: NOK 120 + p&p.

Angling in Norway A 160-page illustrated guide with soft cover. Covers salmon, sea trout and fresh water fishing, as well as updated information on the latest fishing regulations and conservation measures. Price: NOK 130 + p&p.

Cruising in Norwegian Waters With soft cover and colour illustrations, this 120-page book gives accounts of harbours along Norway's coastline and fjords. Price: NOK 42 + p&p.

Orders for any of these books should be sent to: Nortrabooks, P.O. Box 2893 Solli, N-0230 Oslo, Norway, E mail: nortra@online.no.

Rutebok for Norge is a complete list of ferry, train, bus and plane timetables for Norway, together with details of thousands of hotels, guesthouses and other accommodation. Price: NOK 210 + p&p. Order from: Norsk Reiseinformasjon AS, Tollbugt 32, 0157 Oslo, Norway. Tel: 22 47 73 40 Fax: 22 47 73 69

Other Insight Guides

Europe is comprehensively covered by the 400 books in Apa Publications' three series of guidebooks which embrace the world. **Insight Guides**, providing the reader with a full cultural background and top-quality photography. Titles which highlight destinations in this part of Europe include: *Finland*, *Denmark* and *Iceland*.

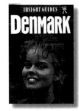

Apa Publications also publish **Insight Pocket Guides**, written by local hosts and containing tailor-made itineraries to help users get the most out of a city or region during a short stay. Each title comes complete with a detailed pull-out map that can be used independently from the guide. Scandinaviah destinations in the series include *Oslo & Bergen*, and *Denmark*.

To complete all the needs of travellers, Apa has introduced another series, **Insight Compact Guides**, in essence mini encylo-pedias which give you the facts about a destination in a very digestible form, supported by maps and colour photographs. Titles in the series include *Finland* and *Denmark*.

ART & PHOTO CREDITS

Picture Spreads

Cartographic Editor Zoë Goodwin
Production Stuart Everitt
Design Consultants
Carlotta Junger, Graham Mitchener
Picture Research
Hilary Genin, Victoria Peel

Index

Numbers in italics refer to
photographs

The World of Insight Guides

400 books in three complementary series cover every major destination in every continent.

Insight Guides

Alaska
Alsace
Amazon Wildlife
American Southwest
Amsterdam
Argentina
Atlanta
Athens
Australia
Austria
Bahamas
Bali
Baltic States
Bangkok
Barbados
Barcelona
Bay of Naples
Beijing
Belgium
Belize
Berlin
Bermuda
Boston
Brazil
Brittany
Brussels
Budapest
Buenos Aires
Burgundy
Burma (Myanmar)
Cairo
Calcutta
California
Canada
Caribbean
Catalonia
Channel Islands
Chicago
Chile
China
Cologne
Continental Europe
Corsica
Costa Rica
Crete
Crossing America
Cuba
Cyprus
Czech & Slovak Republics
Delhi, Jaipur, Agra
Denmark
Dresden
Dublin
Düsseldorf
East African Wildlife
East Asia
Eastern Europe
Ecuador
Edinburgh
Egypt
Finland
Florence
Florida
France
Frankfurt
French Riviera
Gambia & Senegal
Germany
Glasgow

Gran Canaria
Great Barrier Reef
Great Britain
Greece
Greek Islands
Hamburg
Hawaii
Hong Kong
Hungary
Iceland
India
India's Western Himalaya
Indian Wildlife
Indonesia
Ireland
Israel
Istanbul
Italy
Jamaica
Japan
Java
Jerusalem
Jordan
Kathmandu
Kenya
Korea
Lisbon
Loire Valley
London
Los Angeles
Madeira
Madrid
Malaysia
Mallorca & Ibiza
Malta
Marine Life in the South
  China Sea
Melbourne
Mexico
Mexico City
Miami
Montreal
Morocco
Moscow
Munich
Namibia
Native America
Nepal
Netherlands
New England
New Orleans
New York City
New York State
New Zealand
Nile
Normandy
Northern California
Northern Spain
Norway
Oman & the UAE
Oxford
Old South
Pacific Northwest
Pakistan
Paris
Peru
Philadelphia
Philippines
Poland
Portugal
Prague

Provence
Puerto Rico
Rajasthan
Rhine
Rio de Janeiro
Rockies
Rome
Russia
St Petersburg
San Francisco
Sardinia
Scotland
Seattle
Sicily
Singapore
South Africa
South America
South Asia
South India
South Tyrol
Southeast Asia
Southeast Asia Wildlife
Southern California
Southern Spain
Spain
Sri Lanka
Sweden
Switzerland
Sydney
Taiwan
Tenerife
Texas
Thailand
Tokyo
Trinidad & Tobago
Tunisia
Turkey
Turkish Coast
Tuscany
Umbria
US National Parks East
US National Parks West
Vancouver
Venezuela
Venice
Vienna
Vietnam
Wales
Washington DC
Waterways of Europe
Wild West
Yemen

Insight Pocket Guides

Aegean Islands★
Algarve★
Alsace
Amsterdam★
Athens★
Atlanta★
Bahamas★
Baja Peninsula★
Bali★
Bali Bird Walks
Bangkok★
Barbados★
Barcelona★
Bavaria★
Beijing★
Berlin★

Bermuda★
Bhutan★
Boston★
British Columbia★
Brittany★
Brussels★
Budapest &
  Surroundings★
Canton★
Chiang Mai★
Chicago★
Corsica★
Costa Blanca★
Costa Brava★
Costa del Sol/Marbella★
Costa Rica★
Crete★
Denmark★
Fiji★
Florence★
Florida★
Florida Keys★
French Riviera★
Gran Canaria★
Hawaii★
Hong Kong★
Hungary
Ibiza★
Ireland★
Ireland's Southwest★
Israel★
Istanbul★
Jakarta★
Jamaica★
Kathmandu Bikes &
  Hikes★
Kenya★
Kuala Lumpur★
Lisbon★
Loire Valley★
London★
Macau★
Madrid★
Malacca★
Maldives★
Mallorca★
Malta★
Mexico City★
Miami★
Milan★
Montreal★
Morocco★
Moscow
Munich★
Nepal★
New Delhi
New Orleans★
New York City★
New Zealand★
Northern California★
Oslo/Bergen★
Paris★
Penang★
Phuket★
Prague★
Provence★
Puerto Rico★
Quebec★
Rhodes★
Rome★
Sabah★

St Petersburg★
San Francisco★
Sardinia
Scotland★
Seville★
Seychelles★
Sicily★
Sikkim
Singapore★
Southeast England
Southern California★
Southern Spain★
Sri Lanka★
Sydney★
Tenerife★
Thailand★
Tibet★
Toronto★
Tunisia★
Turkish Coast★
Tuscany★
Venice★
Vienna★
Vietnam★
Yogyakarta
Yucatan Peninsula★

★ = Insight Pocket Guides
with Pull out Maps

Insight Compact Guides

Algarve
Amsterdam
Bahamas
Bali
Bangkok
Barbados
Barcelona
Beijing
Belgium
Berlin
Brittany
Brussels
Budapest
Burgundy
Copenhagen
Costa Brava
Costa Rica
Crete
Cyprus
Czech Republic
Denmark
Dominican Republic
Dublin
Egypt
Finland
Florence
Gran Canaria
Greece
Holland
Hong Kong
Ireland
Israel
Italian Lakes
Italian Riviera
Jamaica
Jerusalem
Lisbon
Madeira
Mallorca
Malta

Milan
Moscow
Munich
Normandy
Norway
Paris
Poland
Portugal
Prague
Provence
Rhodes
Rome
St Petersburg
Salzburg
Singapore
Switzerland
Sydney
Tenerife
Thailand
Turkey
Turkish Coast
Tuscany
UK regional titles:
Bath & Surroundings
Cambridge & East
  Anglia
Cornwall
Cotswolds
Devon & Exmoor
Edinburgh
Lake District
London
New Forest
North York Moors
Northumbria
Oxford
Peak District
Scotland
Scottish Highlands
Shakespeare Country
Snowdonia
South Downs
York
Yorkshire Dales
USA regional titles:
Boston
Cape Cod
Chicago
Florida
Florida Keys
Hawaii: Maui
Hawaii: Oahu
Las Vegas
Los Angeles
Martha's Vineyard &
  Nantucket
New York
San Francisco
Washington D.C.
Venice
Vienna
West of Ireland